University of Northumbria at Newcastle

BRITISH INDUSTRIES
IN THE TWENTIETH CENTURY

General editor: Derek H. Aldcroft

THE BRITISH MOTOR INDUSTRY

James Foreman-Peck,
Sue Bowden and
Alan McKinlay

Manchester
University Press
Manchester and New York

distributed exclusively in the USA
and Canada by St. Martin's Press

Copyright © James Foreman-Peck, Sue Bowden and Alan McKinlay 1995

Published by Manchester University Press
Oxford Road, Manchester M13 9NR, UK
and Room 400, 175 Fifth Avenue,
New York, NY 10010, USA

Distributed exclusively in the USA and Canada
by St. Martin's Press, Inc.,
175 Fifth Avenue, New York, NY 10010, USA

British Library Cataloguing-in-Publication Data

A catalogue record for this book is available from the British Library

Library of Congress Cataloging-in-Publication Data
Foreman-Peck, James.
    The British motor industry / [James Foreman-Peck, Sue Bowden, and
Alan McKinlay].
        p.   cm. —— (British industries in the twentieth century)
    ISBN 0–7190–2612–1
    1. Automobile industry and trade——Great Britain——History.
I. Bowden, Sue. II. McKinlay, Alan. 1957– . III. Title.
IV. Series.
HD9710.G72F67   1995
338.4'76292'0941——dc20   94–33151

ISBN 0 7190 2612 1 *hardback*

Phototypeset in Linotron Times
by Northern Phototypesetting Co. Ltd, Bolton
Printed in Great Britain
by Bookcraft Ltd, Midsomer Norton

CONTENTS

LIST OF FIGURES

LIST OF TABLES

PREFACE
AND ACKNOWLEDGEMENTS

This book is one of a series on twentieth century British industries. The objective is to contribute to an understanding of the remarkable slide of the British economy in the world over the last generation. During the 1950s, the motor industry was Britain's single largest manufacturing sector and exporter. Twenty years later the sole British-owned car mass producer was nationalised to save it from bankruptcy, and two of the three multinationals were also contracting and unprofitable. This spectacular decline prompted a number of recent books on an industry which has anyway always attracted the attention of car lovers. Why then another book? Those which provide an economic analysis are now out of date. Most recent studies have been polemical, merely descriptive, concerned with particular firms or with single factors deemed responsible for the industry's problems, such as government policy or labour relations. The objective of the present work is to provide a fairly succinct, primarily economic, analysis of key issues and opinions in the literature on the industry. Because each author has already researched some aspect of the industry's history, we have not felt inhibited in including some original material as well. We take the story back to the beginnings of the motor car because we want to appraise the judgement of a number of recent writers that the seeds of the collapse of the 1970s were planted many years earlier.

Some of the work for the book was supported by financial assistance from the Nuffield Trust and from the Research Initiative Fund at Leeds University; we would like to thank the Nuffield Trustees and John Chartres and the funding committee at Leeds for their support. The librarians and archivists at the London School of Economics, at the Library and Record Centre of the Manchester Museum of Science and Industry, at the Brotherton Library, Leeds University and the London Business School all generously gave time and expertise. The Finance Houses Association, and Joanna Edwards in particular, gave us unlimited access to their archives and much valuable advice.

We should also like to thank the following. Michael Day, Noel Simons, David Simpson, Tony Thompson, Geoffrey Whalen and Peter Wickens all spent time giving us the benefit of their experience of the industry. Steve Broadberry, Nick Crafts, Bob Millward, Neil Rollings, Malcolm Sawyer,

Nick Tiratsoo and Jim Tomlinson provided helpful insights (not necessarily consensual) on the postwar years. Andrew Coutts and Peter Moizier commented on the financial aspects of industry performance. We are particularly indebted to Paul Turner for useful comments and support throughout and for allowing us to draw on both his published and unpublished works. John Armstrong, Derek Aldcroft, Tom Donelly, Bill Latey, Ray Loveridge and Jonathan Story, all very generously commented on one or more chapter drafts. Our reader, Steven Tolliday, made numerous suggestions on an entire earlier manuscript.

Without in any way implicating them in remaining shortcomings, we are particularly grateful to them all for the improvements to which they have contributed.

ABBREVIATIONS

ACAS	Advisory Conciliation and Arbitration Service
AEU	Amalgamated Engineering Union
AJ	After Japan
ASE	Amalgamated Society of Engineers
BAe	British Aerospace
GATT	General Agreement on Tariffs and Trade
IRC	Industrial Reorganisation Corporation
JIT	Just-in-time
MTA	Motor Traders Association
NEB	National Enterprise Board
DEDC	National Economic Development Council
NUGMW	National Union of General and Municipal Workers
NUVB	National Union of Vehicle Builders
PSA	Peugeot
SMMT	Society of Motor Manufacturers and Traders
TGWU	Transport and General Workers Union
UAW	United Automobile Workers
VER	Voluntary Export Restraint
WU	Workers' Union

Note on text

It should be noted that figures in tables, etc. include Northern Ireland.

THE RISE AND DECLINE OF AN INDUSTRY

National industries, such as motor vehicle production, grow under specific conditions. They include technological possibilities opened up by the growth of practical knowledge and an effective demand for the fruits of that technology. In the case of the motor industry, the internal combustion engine was the key innovation, followed by a host of others. These two prerequisites are not sufficient for a new industry because in any national economy during a given period the natural or acquired endowments of human and natural resources may be unavailable. In Britain a workforce skilled in nineteenth century engineering techniques and especially in bicycle manu-facture, together with abundant capital, ensured the three neces-sary conditions were satisfied for motor vehicles.

Industrial decline may be precipitated by the appearance of sub-stitutes (either similar products manufactured elsewhere or competitor goods), market saturation or other environmental changes, such as pollution or congestion. Supply side changes influence the vulnerability of an industry to substitutes, but a failure to transform industrial organisation in an expanding world market can be equally decisive. Motor industry production technology is distinguished by substantial economies of scale, so that as vehicles are standardised and demand expands, there is room for fewer and fewer firms and products in the market. Either the less successful businesses leave the industry or they are merged with the better performers. If they are not adequately integrated then they merely drag down the healthier enterprises that take them over. Acquired advantages, such as a labour force trained in skills appropriate for technology geared to small batch production, may not be suitable for equipment efficient at higher output rates. In that case what was formerly a resource becomes a brake upon development or even upon survival.

In an atomised industry like that of Edwardian motor vehicles, individuals (as entrepreneurs, engineers, workers or managers), through firms, take advantage of economic and technological opportunities but they rarely decisively shape industry development. Even in the 1920s, if there had been no William Morris, Lord Nuffield, then some other entrepreneur may well have taken his place. Later, when a few firms dominated the industry, their 'culture' or 'strategies' may have been more vital, for by then there were far fewer opportunities for their replacement. In the absence of Alec Issigonis small cars would still have been popular in Britain of the 1960s, but perhaps not as small as the Mini. With no Michael Edwardes the 'down sizing' of what is now Rover may well have pursued a different course at the beginning of the 1980s, but would still have occurred. If Nissan had not judged Britain a useful export platform for the EC, the chances are that another Japanese car maker would have seized the opportunity to get under the Common External Tariff earlier than they did. Less apparent is what could have happened had the pool of entrepreneurs, managers and engineers been wider, but the ready opportunity for entry by other nationals suggests there was little more that could be attained from this source, until the Japanese arrived in the 1980s.

National demand conditions and demand crises were originally more formative influences. The affluence, occupations and distribution of income of inhabitants, road surfaces, average distances travelled, running costs, all determine the character and strength of demand for motor vehicles. Two world wars changed the timing of industry evolution, and two oil crises altered the path. By determining the nature and weight of vehicle taxation, the protection of the industry from foreign competition or the opening up of the market to the EC, the attitude to foreign subsidiaries, and by nationalising or subsidising national firms, state policy too was influential.

But it is the organisation of production that has attracted most attention. Increasing import penetration during the 1960s, in motor vehicles as much as any product, showed Britain to be poor at manufacturing. For many of the Edwardian years as well, the majority of motor vehicles sold in Britain were imported, but exports then were also typically high. Labour relations were hardly a problem during the rapid expansion between the wars but, with full employment during and after the Second World War, the spread of trade union membership in the industry and increasing plant size, they became more controversial. Whereas there was little reason to suppose that the best British production methods were not adequate to conditions between 1919 and 1939, during the 1950s and 1960s there was. British motor industry management did not transform its businesses to cope with rising international competition, and the penalty was paid in the much more difficult conditions of the 1970s. Just as Ford US earlier recruited from General Motors (US), Ford UK management personnel were regularly hired by British Leyland from the 1960s but proved unable to remedy the shortcomings arising from its vast collection of unintegrated plants and products. Bankrupt British Leyland was nationalised and Chrysler UK, that had acquired the Rootes group plants, was bailed out by the British government, before independent production and design facilities were effectively shut down by the new French owners. Though Ford UK fared much better during the 1980s, by the beginning of the 1990s, together with the other American multinational, General Motors (Vauxhall), it also had radically reduced the scale of British production.

Why the industry declined so rapidly and what, if anything, might have remedied the ailments remain controversial. Many of British Leyland's products by the 1970s were clearly uncompetitive. Inadequate planning, product research and development and market research were at least proximate causes. In turn lack of investment funds was blamed, but they were not forthcoming because low profits reflected low productivity. Stoppages dogged the industry and were only limited by management concessions which perpetuated inefficient work practices. British workers never readily accepted 'Fordist' practices whereby machinery and management determined the pace of work but British management failed to find a competitive alternative. That was also broadly true of two other mass producers, Rootes/Chrysler and Vauxhall. A simpler internal structure and more formal planning allowed Ford UK to profit, along with imports, at British Leyland's expense during the 1970s and 1980s. But Ford also was ultimately unable to find a formula that accommodated motor industry production technology to the British environment. That was left to the Japanese, whose influence filtered in to Rover during the 1980s through partnership with Honda, and in Nissan's Sunderland subsidiary.

The rise and decline of the British motor industry is approached as follows. Chapter 1 describes the first stage of the product and industry cycle, when products were unstandardised and manufacturers were searching for vehicles and technologies that best met the needs of the British market. Just as they were succeeding in doing so, development was stopped by the First World War. Phase two of the cycle described in Chapter 2, took place in a much more nationalistic environment where the opportunities for a global industry were increasingly restricted. Scale economies in production became far more important and the number of businesses in the industry declined markedly. Vehicles adapted to the needs of the British market dominated sales at home but failed to find much of a market abroad. The British industry soon grew to the second largest in the world. Chapter 3 assesses the contribution of domestic demand and government policy to the distinctive and relatively successful performance of the interwar industry. The Second World War marked a break in the industry's history. The stronger pressure of demand, and the wartime accommodation with trade unions, transformed the environment in which the industry worked.

Chapter 4 outlines the radical changes in the industry's fortunes over the thirty years from the end of the war, from boom when the continental European and Japanese industries were still recovering from the aftermath of the war, to slump as foreign competition eliminated British sales at home and abroad. It discusses the production technology that determined the possibilities open for the organisation of work, the efficient size of plant and the degree of specialisation of the firm, as well as the cost of production. Chapters 5 to 7 consider how other factors interacted with the motor industry's distinctive technology between 1945 and 1978. A dynamic perspective is adopted in Chapter 5 with the focus on the stream of new products essential for the long term survival of a motor business. Research and development, marketing, finance for investment and sales, the nature and extent of competition, and relations with retailers are all addressed. Industrial relations were the public face of the industry in the 1960s and 1970s. Chapter 6 examines the social and cultural influences bearing upon relations between management and workforce, and upon the pace, effectiveness and flexibility of work. Chapter 7 pursues for the period 1945–78 the theme developed for the interwar years in Chapter 3. Demand and government policy have been strong candidates for explaining the decline of the motor industry in these years. Such matters as 'stop-go', in particular as applied to hire purchase controls, regional policy, nationalisation and government inspired mergers, are appraised.

In the third phase of the cycle, the world cars of the 1980s spread development costs over a large number of markets for multinationals. Such companies could also choose in which markets to concentrate production and to locate product development facilities. None of these were options for BL/Rover, which lacked a substantial overseas presence. Chapter 8 considers the transformation of the British motor industry under the influence of the Japanese successes, the reduction of British production by the American multinationals, the retrenchment of Rover and the arrival of Nissan.

CHAPTER ONE

LATE DELIVERY AND RETARDED DEVELOPMENT: VICTORIAN ORIGINS AND EDWARDIAN GROWTH

Mid nineteenth century Britain was widely regarded as the world's foremost industrial power and certainly the richest county in Europe. British achievements in engineering were particularly prominent. It is no surprise therefore that during the 1890s the British bicycle industry was in the forefront of innovation and expansion. More puzzling was Britain's laggardly interest in the related, and potentially far more important motor car industry, emerging in the same decade. The essential advances in motor vehicle design were made in France, Germany and Austria, not in Britain, and France, not Britain, dominated the European motor industry before 1914.

Explanations offered for this backwardness include a desire on the continent to find, through the internal combustion engine, an alternative source of energy to coal. A second reason proposed is that the British Highways and Locomotives (Amendment) Act of 1878 (and earlier acts of 1861 and 1865), constraining road vehicles to a maximum of 4 mph, impeded British inventiveness. Once this restrictive legislation had been repealed in 1896, H. J. Lawson's attempt to gain a patent monopoly over the industry may have slowed development. Possibly the concentration of population and a dense rail and tramway network reduced the demand for 'horseless carriages' in Britain relative to other advanced countries.[1]

Yet another account turns on the attitudes of the British workers to the private motor car and the other services a mature economy could afford.[2] Had workers' attitudes been less moulded by the hierarchical society in which they lived, the demand for cars would have been more buoyant and the Edwardian British economy would have entered the 'age of high mass consumption' propelled by the motor and associated industries. Others have argued that the small impact on the economy of the British industry, in comparison with the French and the American motor producers, can be traced to failings on the supply side of the market. The absence of commercial acumen in the industry's entrepreneurs before 1914 allegedly led to a passion for technical perfection and individuality for its own sake, preventing the tradition-bound firms following the American lead in mass production.[3] An alternative hypothesis is that resistance from the workforce prevented the introduction of American systems of manufacture that would have widened the market.[4] Distinguishing among these alternatives is one of the first tasks facing an industry historian. Explanations for the industry's adoption of the internal combustion engine and other technologies are equally central. Whether the motor car was to be electric- or petrol-powered was very much in the balance in the early days. Steam also was an important competitor, especially for commercial vehicles. At the turn of the century, electricity would have been preferable if only the range which the batteries would support could have been increased a little more and had charging facilities been more widely available. Since neither condition was satisfied, petrol slowly won out. A suggestion of considerable interest is that the success of the petrol engine was more due to chance and institutions than to technological, engineering and physical facts, for, as it was, steam road vehicles remained in production well into the 1930s.[5]

The motor industry grew from already established road transport suppliers. Manufacture of horse-drawn carriages provided the tradition, skills and labour for the more expensive motor vehicles. Workers in this segment were extremely skilled and a large premium was placed upon high quality materials, workmanship and durability. The best coaches received as many as 20 or 30 coats of paint. Steel springs for such carriages provided the suspension for early motor cars. The biggest of these manufacturers attained a considerable volume of output. Thomas Tilling, a company of omnibus and cab proprietors and builders, made 1,600 vehicles in 1899.[6]

Experience with bicycles was valuable for design of brakes,

drives, tyres, gears and, to some extent, of steering, but other components such as clutches had to be developed from scratch. The concomitant evolution of the motorbicycle was another source of learning. Some firms could grow up as mere assemblers of components manufactured by others. Such vertical disintegration could allow utilisation of both scale economies and product variety. But, in fact, during this early stage of the product cycle, variety was largely a response to uncertainty about product potential, and quality control of components ordained the emergence of larger companies which were vertically integrated.

In this chapter we first briefly examine the rise of the bicycle industry, because of the technological and demand side relatedness with the later motor industry, because many motor manufacturers emerged from cycle companies, and because Britain was prominent in the first industry but not the second. For each of these reasons, the experience with cycles will throw light upon motor industry development.

Section 2 discusses entry to and exit from the infant motor industry and the resulting firm size distribution. The emergence of a standardised vehicle and the stages of the production process forms the subject matter of Section 3. Supply and demand interacted in the British motor vehicle market to generate patterns which have often been attributed primarily to the wrong side of the market. Section 4 describes the distinctive characteristics of British demand, its luxury nature and dependence on imports in the early years, followed by a shift towards more practical uses before the outbreak of the First World War. Whether the industry was retarded by insufficient availability of capital and the contribution of retail agents is considered in Section 5, and the effect of Britain's allegedly turbulent labour relations on the comparatively slow development of motor production is analysed in Section 6. Government policy shaped industry demand and supply by the taxation of vehicles and by the provision of roads and motoring regulations. Section 7 recounts these influences before 1914.

1.1 The bicycle industry as
an incubator for motor vehicles

From bicycle manufacture came the machine-tool development and skilled labour essential to the production of motor cars. Although the bicycle industry began in Paris during the 1860s, from the late 1870s French bicycle output never exceeded the British. When Darracq wanted to enter bicycle manufacture in 1891 he hired an English bicycle engineer. Early problems with horses show that British superiority in the bicycle industry, at least until the early 1890s, owed much to the strength of national demand for short-distance transport stemming from the relatively high population density. Fears that the demand for horses was about to outrun supply led to the appointment in 1873 of a Select Committee to investigate the matter. The bicycle was to some extent a substitute for horses in response to the great pressure of demand. On the supply side, unlike the other new industries of the time, the bicycle industry did not have greater scientific requirements than the old. Unlike chemicals and electrical engineering, the bicycle industry did not need management and labour that had passed through formal further and higher education (in which Britain was weak), to provide the new technical knowledge. Rather, as in the old industries, bicycle makers could learn their trade from the production experience itself.[7]

Industry entrants both originated in other sectors and started from scratch. British Small Arms (BSA) entered the bicycle industry originally in 1879 because the company had shut for a year in the absence of demand by the government for their main product, firearms. Their bicycle was not very successful nor was it as lucrative as the new orders for weapons that were eventually placed. The firm that was eventually to dominate the British industry in its later name of Raleigh began rapid growth in 1877 when bought by a businessman from Hong Kong 'with only a few months to live', who had taken up cycling for his health. By 1896 the Nottinghamshire firm owned the largest cycle works in Britain, covering 7.5 acres, employing 850 people, and with an annual production of about 30,000 cycles. The industry's turning point came in the mid 1880s with the safety bicycle. The limit to the growth of the industry as a whole in the early part of that decade was that the main bicycle in use, the Ordinary or 'Penny-farthing', was too cumbersome for all but the young and active. J. K. Starley, the founder of the Rover company, removed this constraint when he manufactured and marketed the Rover safety bicycle in 1885. Starley himself was not modest about his contribution; he suggested that three-quarters of the cycling ten years later was due to his invention. His basic idea was to change the shape of the cycle so that all the essentials such as the crankshaft, pedals, seat and handles could be made easily adjustable, in contrast to the Ordinary cycle. Although several people at different times had independently invented the various elements of the safety bicycle of the 1890s, none had combined them all in one machine before Starley. By 1891, 11,500 were employed in the cycle industry, 35 per cent of them in Coventry. Six years later, the figure had more than quadrupled.

Starley's contribution to bicycle design spread rapidly and eroded Rover's initial competitive advantage. H. O. Duncan (author of the early motor history *The World on Wheels*) was awarded an agency for the Rover, in Montpellier in the south of France towards the end of 1885. The Rover was the first type of rear-driven chain 'bicyclette' imported into France, but the manufacturers could not supply Duncan's orders quickly enough or in quantities. While touring, Duncan showed his Rover cycle in 1886 to Gauthier, who three weeks later completed a similar machine, the first French-made safety bicycle, at his workshop in St Etienne.

In north Germany Schwinn quickly put Starley's idea to use and there made some of the first German safety bicycles for Kleyer, eventually to become Adler. Moving to Chicago in 1891, Schwinn, four years later, set up the firm that was to become one of the largest in the American industry. Like many cycle manufacturers Schwinn began experimenting with power-driven vehicles, making an electrically powered car in 1896 and four more vehicles subsequently, the last in 1905.

1.2 Motor industry structure: entry and exit

In contrast to Schwinn, Humber, a major British bicycle producer, went beyond experiments and moved into car manufacture early and prominently. Tom Humber invented and built the first diamond frame cycle, and in 1890 constructed the first sprung forks. The 5 hp

Humberette of 1900 began Humber's early and rapid growth as a motor vehicle producer.

From 1893 BSA used its shell-making equipment for the manufacture of cycle parts and allowed many small firms of assemblers and repairers to earn a profitable living. One such firm, William Morris of Oxford, entered car manufacture late, in 1913, and became the largest British motor vehicle manufacturer of the interwar years.

Diversification into motorcycles was an alternative to motor cars. Triumph began as a small cycle export business in London in 1885, moving to Coventry to manufacture bicycles four years later. The first Triumph motorcycle was produced in 1902. By 1907 sales exeeded 1,000 and continued to increase very rapidly despite the slump the following year. Rover's refusal to diversify immediately like Humber into cars, or like Triumph into motorcycles, in an attempt to return profits to the levels of 1896 and 1897 is, at first sight, surprising in view of Starley's interest in motor vehicles. He had built and tested an electrically powered three-wheel vehicle in 1888, while in 1896, the year of the repeal of the so-called 'Red Flag' legislation, his public statements implied he had decided on the petrol engine as the motive power for road vehicles, in whose future he had great confidence. Three years later the company sent a three-wheeled powered vehicle to the Royal Automobile Club Show in Richmond. Yet in 1901, at the same time as the Board was asking the shareholders for permission to spend more money on motor vehicle development, Starley was advocating caution in entering the new industry. Going back on his earlier views he claimed the appropriate motive power was still uncertain, as a result of which this line of business would cause fluctuations in dividends (which as a major shareholder he did not want). In similar circumstances, similar views were advanced by Lord Rendel in his criticism of Armstrong Whitworth's unsuccessful move into motor vehicles.[8]

The only available proxies for output, the trade statistics, imply that Starley was right about the uncertainties of the motor car trade because both car exports and imports were more unstable than bicycle imports and exports. Their growth was, however, much stronger as Table 1.1 shows. Humber, Hillman, Sunbeam, Rover, Singer, Star, were all major motor manufacturers that entered from the cycle industry. Morris and Dennis previously ran cycle shops. Rolls-Royce, Daimler, and Austin entered motor manufacture without any history. The experience of their entrepreneurs was gained in Austin's case with Wolseley and in agricultural machinery and railways; Royce also acquired his engineering knowledge in railways, and Daimler in 1901 imported Percy Martin, an American, as works manager. Possibly there is some slight indication that the cycle makers took more easily to a democratic product in this period, though Austin ultimately (in 1922) designed and manufactured one of the most successful 'baby cars', the Austin Seven.

Table 1.1: The growth and instability of the British trade in bicycles and motor cars, 1897–1914

	Instability index I^a	Average growth rate (% p.a.)
Bicycle exports	2.17	6.6
Motor car exports	2.69	19.8
Bicycle imports	4.42	Not significant
Motor car imports	5.37	2.9

Note: $^a I = \dfrac{100}{\log y} \sqrt{\dfrac{\sum\limits^{N} (\log y - \log \hat{y})^2}{N-2}}$ where y is the OLS

trend value estimated from $\hat{y} = ae^{bt}$ and N is the number of observations.

Sources: J. Foreman-Peck, 'Diversification and Growth of the Firm: The Rover Company to 1914', Business History, Vol. 25, No. 2, July 1983, pp. 179–92; 'Exit, Voice and Loyalty as Responses to Decline: The Rover Company in the Inter-War Years', Business History, Vol. 23, No. 42, 1982, pp. 865–81.

In 1897, half a dozen companies were delivering vehicles built in Britain, with several more about to begin production.[9] Over the next decade industry entry was rapid, until the depression of 1907/8. This slump was particularly hard on those companies that had entered in the previous six years. Longer-established companies weathered the slump better and those established during the slack period of demand were more closely adjusted to the new conditions (the stronger demand for more modest vehicles). Table 1.2 shows that firms entering the industry between 1901 and 1905 had only a one-in-ten chance of surviving until 1914, whereas firms founded earlier, and so exposed to risk for longer, had a one-in-three chance. Industry structure was highly atomised as Table 1.3 shows, by 1913 dominated by Ford (assuming these vehicles, assembled from American-made components in Old Trafford in Manchester, were counted in the total). Even though designed for other market conditions than Britain's, volume production in North America brought costs down so far as to make the 22.4 hp Model T Ford an extremely competitive product. At £125–£135, the Model T was perhaps one-third of the price of the average car sold in the British market. Although they were much larger employers, the biggest British manufacturers in 1913 – Humber, Sunbeam, Daimler and Rover – nowhere approached Ford's volume of vehicles.

With the rise of Ford, the changing pattern of locational advantage within the United States foreshadowed a similar pattern in the rest of the world; the centre of gravity moved from the East Coast, high income, population centres to the Mid-West where a standardised product could be distributed more easily to the less fashion-conscious buyers on the farms. In Europe in general, and in Britain in particular, there was no such high income mass market and for the moment, there was no locational shift of production.

1.3 Technology: the product

The motor car technology that eventually was to dominate the industry had not been fully decided even by 1905. Three power sources were still in the competition: steam, petrol and electricity. Each had advantages and drawbacks. How these were established and the process by which the internal combustion engine eventually emerged as the dominant power source varied between countries, primarily because of their different legislative environments. But technological selection does seem eventually to have worked reasonably well, given the market demand for reliability and range.

Table 1.2: Probability of exit of British motor firms by entry period before 1914

	Probability of exit				
Entry date	Pre-1900	1901–5	1906–10	1911–14	Total probability of survival by 1914
Pre-1900	0.10	0.30	0.20	0.05	0.35
1901–5	0	0.27	0.51	0.13	0.10
1906–10	0	0	0.26	0.24	0.49
1911–14	0	0	0	0.28	0.72

Source: Calculated from S. B. Saul, 'The Motor Industry in Britain to 1914', *Business History*, December 1962, p. 23.

An advantage of the steam car over the internal combustion engine powered vehicle was that no gears were required, except where very heavy loads were carried. Britain imported considerable numbers from the United States in the early years of the industry,

Table 1.3: British motor vehicle output by firms, 1906 and 1913

Firm	1906	1913
Albion	221	554
Argyll	800	622
Armstrong-Whitworth	–	80
Arrol Johnston	–	1,150
Austin	123	1,500
Belsize	–	1,000
Clement-Talbot	–	500
Crossley	–	650
Daimler	–	1,000
Dennis	–	500
Ford (assembly)	–	7,310
Hillman	–	63
Humber	1,000	2,500
Iris	–	50
Jowett	–	12
Lanchester	–	200
Maudslay	–	50
Morris	–	303
Napier	299	743
Riley	–	15
Rolls	–	650
Rover	690	1,600
Singer	–	1,350
Standard	–	750
Star	–	1,000
Sunbeam	151	1,700
Swift	–	850
Vauxhall	15	388
Wolseley	450	3,000

Note: These 1913 numbers total 31,080. Total industry output was 34,000 in that year according to the SMMT.
Source: Saul (1962) and various.

but few of them were capable of driving more than 25 miles before more water and fuel was needed. In addition, they needed considerable time before they could move off from a cold start. Britain's own development of the steam motor vehicle was not helped by legislation and pricing. Yet at first these were probably justified from society's viewpoint. Sir Goldsworth Gurney travelled from London to Bath in his steam carriage in 1828 and a regular steam carriage service between Gloucester and Cheltenham was inaugurated soon after. But these vehicles were extremely heavy, causing more wear and tear on road surfaces than horse-drawn traffic, and they attracted commensurately heavy charges. Subsequent concern with public safety during the 1860s and 1870s so restricted the use of motor vehicles on the public road that the incentive to invent in Britain was markedly reduced until the repeal of the 'Red Flag Act' in 1896. Although when agitation against the 1878 Highways and Locomotives Act arose, the legislation was quickly repealed, the Act may well have constrained innovation while in force. An entrepreneur is not inclined to consider supplying a new market restricted by legislation unless that market has been clearly identified. By that time, entrepreneurs in other countries will have achieved a lead.[10]

The internal combustion engine eventually adopted for the motor car originated with Dr Nicolaus A. Otto's four-stroke gas engine of 1876. Otto developed his engine from a working model built by the Belgian Jean-Etienne Lenoir in 1859. Gottlieb Daimler, born in Württemberg in 1834, worked for Sir Joseph Whitworth in England and then co-operated with Otto near Cologne in the production of the gas engine, becoming director of the factory. In 1882, he retired to work on engines and later the motor car. Independently of Daimler, Benz in 1885 produced a petrol-engined tricycle.

In keeping with the trans-European background of the engine, the French, rather than the Germans who had undertaken much of the early development work, took up the petrol-engined motor car most enthusiastically. In 1889, Panhard and Levassor acquired Daimler's French and Belgian rights, constructing their first car in 1891. The French had long been interested in finding alternative energy sources to coal. In Britain the early motor vehicle substitutes were likely to be in the congested towns; the elecric tram and the horse-drawn cab. In the absence of restrictive legislation it is not clear why Britain, a highly urbanized, industrial society, should have been backward. If a general entrepreneurial failure was at the root, we would not have expected to see such a dynamic British cycle industry.

Despite the success of the electric tram, the electric road vehicle carrying its own power source was a latecomer to the competition. Experiments were made in 1887 but not until a decade later was a really practical electrical road vehicle entered for a race in France. The batteries needed recharging every 16 miles but such vehicles were clean and quiet. In 1901, a 2.5 ton Krieger travelled 190 miles without recharging but the general problem remain the great weight of the batteries and the time consumed in their recharging.[11]

The terms of the competition between power sources were established largely in France. Efficient product designs were selected in Europe primarily by French, and later British, road races and endurance trials. The French motoring lead was acknowledged by the international supremacy of the Automobile Club de France. The first race from Paris to Rouen in 1894 was won by a De Dion steam tractor, but in the more ambitious second 750-mile trial from Paris to Bordeaux, a 4hp Panhard triumphed. Pneumatic tyres also made the first appearance in long distance motoring in this race. In this way, air-cooling was eventually defeated by water, belt-transmission was eliminated along with solid tyres and tiller steering. Manufacturers were encouraged to enter their latest and best products in such events because a win was immensely valuable publicity for their cars. The excellent French infrastructure of straight inter-city roads may have strengthened the French willingness to innovate cars relative to the British.[12] In 1897, the Automobile Club of Great Britain and Ireland was founded and introduced a series of annual reliability trials.

Motor technology was then subject to a process very much like Darwinian natural selection. The long gestation period of the petrol engine and the nature of the selection process suggests final success was due not to chance but to technological potential. An indication of the 'genetic variation' from which the market was allowed to select is that as late as 1912, cars appeared at the annual Motor Show advertised as capable of running on gin, brandy or whisky, and on 'liquid air'. By this date though, when mass production had begun in the United States, dominant product characteristics had been decided. They were chosen *before* economies of scale conferred a cost advantage on the internal combustion engine, contrary to the 'technological lock-in' argument. In any case, as Table 1.4 shows, the economy that embraced mass production of internal combustion engine powered cars was the one in which the strongest interest in steam vehicles was shown. Because steam cars were able to use many components – stronger alloy steels, more reliable electrical equipment – whose costs were cut by mass production of internal combustion cars, they were able to extend their competitive lives.

It was not merely Darwinian, but also Lamarckian technological evolution that promoted the internal combustion engine. De Dion turned from steam to petrol in 1895 despite winning the Paris–Rouen race with steam the previous year. The White Brothers of Cleveland, Ohio, began to leave steam for petrol in 1909 even though they had made 1,500 steam cars in 1906. Steam cars were undoubtedly fast, as Leon Serpollet showed in 1902 and the Stanley brothers in 1906 demonstrated with their world land speed records. But what was needed was a combination of reliability and convenience that were better revealed by endurance, than by speed, trials.[13]

Britain fixed on the internal combustion engine, rather than steam or electricity, earlier than the United States, partly because of the French example and partly because patent restrictions on the development of the internal combustion engine were removed earlier in Britain than in the United States. Table 1.4 shows that just under 3 per cent of all British models manufactured before 1962 were steam powered but in the United States the proportion was more than double. In France the electric car proportion was similar to Britain's, nowhere near American levels, which was exceeded by Germany. Internal combustion engines developed more precociously in Europe; the De Dion–Bouton engine of 1895 was as much an advance as Daimler's invention a decade earlier.[14]

Table 1.4: Power sources by car model produced as a proportion of the total to 1962

	Steam (%)	Electric (%)	Petrol (%)	Other (%)	Total
United States	7.0	5.6	86.9	0.5	2,431
Britain	2.9	2.8	93.7	0.6	1,001
France	1.5	2.8	94.5	1.2	976
Germany	0.2	6.9	91.3	1.5	393

Source: Calculated from G. R. Doyle, The World's Automobiles 1862–1962, revised by G. N. Georgano, London: Temple Press Books, 1963.

At the turn of the century European petrol-driven cars were regarded as greatly superior to American products, at least by Europeans (high tariffs kept down their imports into the United States). The largest European manufacturer, Benz, claimed to have made a cumulative total of 2,500 by 1900, whereas Olds made 400 cars from mid 1899 through to 1900. Benz admitted to a manufacturing capacity of three cars a day. The Selden patent monopoly, where Selden claimed to hold the master patents, was a constraint upon United States development of the internal combustion engine. Selden's patent, apparently covering all internal combustion-engined road vehicles, was issued in 1895 and assigned to the Electric Vehicle Company in 1899. Every motor vehicle produced in the United States was then required to pay 1.25 per cent of the price to the patent holders. Ford was distinguished by his stand against the monopoly, eventually winning in the Supreme Court in 1911, one year before the expiry of the patent.[15]

Harry Lawson attempted an analogous monopoly in Britain for all petrol-driven cars but was successfully challenged earlier. Lawson formed the British Motor Syndicate in 1895 with the intention of acquiring the original German Daimler and other major patents. The Syndicate then expected to be able to exploit its position by charging substantial royalties like Selden. The Daimler Motor Company was established the following year as a subsidiary of the Syndicate and maintained a dominant position in the pre-1914 industry (from 1909 helped by one of the most creative British motor engineers, Frederick Lanchester). A court decision of 1901 put paid to Lawson's monopolistic aspirations before the United States was freed from Selden's, giving British engineers a stronger reason to favour the internal combustion engine than Americans. Technical progress was making the patents obsolete in any case, but in Britain and the United States such a monopoly, even for a few years at such a crucial stage, was almost certain to retard development. Herbert Austin abandoned development of the first Wolseley he built because it so closely resembled a model the patent for which was held by Lawson's Syndicate.[16]

The emergence of the motor vehicle illustrates a principle of technological development; in the freer economic environment innovation will be stronger. As soon as state virtual prohibitions were abolished in 1896, Lawson's own profit-oriented restrictions were introduced. The beneficiaries were the French manufacturers, whose demonstration effects were stronger in Britain than in the United States.

The manufacturing process

Manufacturing techniques were closely tied to the stage the product had reached in its life cycle. Whatever the stage though, the basic processes of motor manufacturing were involved: casting, machining, pressing and assembling. A good number of the components used in motor vehicles required all of these processes, although some would be undertaken by component suppliers rather than by the vehicle manufacturer. The 1907 Census showed about 40 per cent of the industry's output value was bought from outside the industry but there was substantial vertical specialisation within the industry as well. Some companies were primarily assemblers, perhaps buying engines from Daimler or carburettors from White and Poppe, magnetos from Bosch, radiators from the Motor Radiator Manufacturing Company, pressed steel wheels from Joseph Sankey or chassis from Rubery Owen. In 1913, Morris, a new entrant, was operating in this way but most of the established larger companies believed their reputation and security of supply depended upon a high degree of vertical integration.

As early as 1906 the Argyll Motor Company (then the largest in the industry) well understood the way in which techniques of production could change with the scale of operations. With a volume of 400 cars per annum, the company was hoping to lower its price, believing their car was now suitable for a larger output. Three stages of production corresponded to successively greater rates of production. The first was the production of the one-off blue print car, the second involved the use of jigs for the tools to make the parts of small batches of the car, while the third stage required the use of special tools for each car part. Special tools made production far cheaper, but they could only be employed when there was no further necessity for alteration of the product. This stage corresponded to the 'flow production' for which the motor industry has become famous. Subsequent developments involved only the further specialisation of these ideas.[17]

Cost reductions, expected and actual, from flow production methods were very substantial. In 1906, replacement of jigs and ordinary tools by special tools for each component were expected to reduce unit wage costs by 75 per cent and these outlays amounted to about half of variable costs. Success, however, required a stable demand for the product, which Argyll failed to find; the slump of 1907 bankrupted the company.

No British manufacturer before 1914 had proceeded far in the direction of flow production because they had not found a suitable product. Even Morris's pre-1914 method of construction at Cowley was not such as to encourage confidence in the firm's later ability to adjust to flow production. The lay-out of the factory was limited by the three storeys over which production had to be distributed. Machining and drilling was done on the ground floor, then the chassis and parts were lifted to the middle floor for assembly. Chassis were laid out in a row. First the engines were fitted and then the axles, wheels and other components followed. In this batch production, the chassis were stationary and workers moved along the line performing their special tasks. By the time a worker had finished with the last chassis of a batch, he was ready to begin again at the other end of the row. On the top floor the car bodies were fitted, any essential touching up took place, and completed vehicles were stored.[18]

Austin's works of the same period consisted of small shops each producing components or carrying out assembly with the chassis and body departments quite separate. The parts would be assembled in the chassis erecting shop, tested with a temporary body, and then fitted with the final body elsewhere and tested again. Chassis were erected in groups, as was the case with Daimler, where there were gangs of 20 or more under a charge-hand. Subdivided into groups of 3 or 4, they were given the frame and the necessary components and each individual was required to be competent at fitting any part.

At Sunbeam, the most advanced manufacturer before 1914, the erecting shop consisted of many small gangs, each responsible for one job only. The frame was delivered at one end and as soon as the first job was done, it was hoisted upon a girder tramway suspended from the roof beam and taken a step further. Because the shop was intended to be a true assembly bay, an effort was made to eliminate fitting and a systematic progression of components during assembly was attempted.

Despite the absence of a high-income mass market, British (and other European) manufacturers were as anxious to extend motoring as businessmen in North America. The evidence comes from the motorcycle, the cycle car and and the light car. Each was a way of bringing down prices in an environment where the scope for volume production was limited. The cycle car originated in Paris in 1909 with the Bedelia, a two-seater air-cooled engine model. Morgan and GN cycle cars began production in Britain in 1911. By the following year, at least 60 British manufacturers were engaged in making cycle cars. They were defined as small motor cars of narrow wheel gauge, but light in construction, selling at a lower price and costing less to operate than the usual motor car, with a possible speed of 30–40 mph. These cars might have three or four wheels, a track of 36–40 inches and 2–4 seats. The cycle car had to be less than 1100 cc engine capacity and 784 lb weight; above these limits a reverse gear was needed. It was thought that at least 350,000 in Britain could afford them. *Motor* magazine claimed that their output was well over 20,000, with home manufacturers supplying two-thirds of home demand. The cycle car boom may well have been encouraged by the rising price of petrol which began 1910 at 1/0d a gallon rising to 1/7d a gallon by 1912, far above American prices.

The cycle car was essentially a crossbreed of a motorcycle with a car, with all the discomfort that combination implied. The more successful species was the light car, or 'voiturette', a category that had been identified by the French motoring magazine *L'Auto* in 1905 inaugurating a special race for them. In 1908, the category was extended to include four-cylinder engines, as well as those with one and two cylinders. From this event, Bugatti designed a model which, when sold to Peugeot, propelled that company to the top of the French car-makers league in 1913. Light cars soon crossed the Channel. Singer's 1912 Ten and the Morris Oxford of 1913 were to set the trend for the new era of the British motor industry. Comparatively good roads and the horsepower tax favoured such cars in Britain, in contrast to the United States.[19]

In developing new models, scarce design engineers were essential to success.[20] The French may have possessed an advantage in this respect in their recognition of the role of advanced technology science and engineering, backed up by an infrastructure of elite education in engineering.[21] British 'theoreticians' such as F. R. Simms acted as itinerant consultants.[22] That was probably not the formula for sustained corporate success. Rover's recovery in 1912/13 may be traced to the hiring of the design engineer Owen Clegg, formerly of Wolseley, from September 1910. He remained for only 18 months before resigning to take a position with Darracq, but within a year of becoming works manager with Rover, he had finished and satisfactorily tested a new 12 hp four-cylinder car. During the boom of 1913, this car generated Rover's restored prosperity, taking sales over the previous peak of 1907 and allowing the payment of 40 per cent dividends.[23]

Rover management strategy favoured concentration of production, for the Board turned down the managing director's proposal for a 100 guinea cycle car in February 1913. They judged a new product unnecessary in view of the satisfactory state of their current and prospective car and motorcycle trades. The previous year they had divested the company of an old product by selling the unprofitable cycle business for cash. The success of the 12 hp car in 1912/13 encouraged the Board to make this model in two chassis only. With this programme, the output for the financial year of 1914 rose by one-fifth to almost 2,000 cars before the outbreak of war, and another 40 per cent dividend was paid. Increased output had been obtained not only by specialisation but also by the expenditure of £7,000–£10,000 on new machinery in 1912, including electric drive from Siemens for the machine shop. Machinery alone does not explain the success, however, because the automatic machinery installed in 1909 had reduced unit wage costs of 30 per cent within a year, yet proved insufficient to restore profits. Then the programme had been spread over many models; it comprised a 6 hp car in various forms, an 8 hp in various forms, a 12 hp in the 8 hp chassis, a new 15 hp model with four-cylinder engine and a new 26 hp car to replace the old 20 hp car. When the right model was found, specialisation did occur, although it may be doubted whether progress was rapid enough. K. Richardson suggests the growth of the industry just before the war was a response to the challenge of the Model T assembled at Old Trafford, Manchester from 1911. In the case of Rover, the most that can be said is that the immediate prewar expansion was based upon a strategy that Ford had showed could be successful.

The excessive variety of products of Edwardian motor firms stemmed from unsuccessful diversification, such as Rover's after 1908. In turn this may be explained by the vagaries of the market and the shortage of talented designers like Clegg. The Rover Company's willingness to specialise, once the right product had been found, removes some of the responsibility for excessive product variety, and thus for the failure to take advantage of economies of scale, from the management. However the intervention of the war prevents a fully informed judgement of their response. The remarkable constancy of the trend growth rate of the firm (Table

1.5) before and after the move into motor vehicles suggests that expansion costs ultimately constrained growth, rather than problems with the saleability of particular models and products (which account for some of the deviation from trend). Rover sales on trend grew more slowly than the market. If management could have coped with a faster rate of efficient expansion before or after 1903, growth would have been faster. Even when the management had a successful model like Clegg's 12 hp it is likely that they would have been unable to expand production rapidly enough to take full advantage of it.

Table 1.5: The growth and instability of the Rover Company's sales revenues, 1890–1914

Period	Instability index	Average growth rate (% p.a.)
1890–1914	1.86	10.2
1890–1903	1.93	12.6
1904–1914	1.52	12.1

Notes: As for Table 1.1, p. 12.
Sources: J. Foreman-Peck, 'Diversification and Growth of the Firm: The Rover Company to 1914', *Business History*, Vol. 25, No. 2, July 1983, pp. 179–92; 'Exit, Voice and Loyalty as Responses to Decline: The Rover Company in the Inter-War Years', *Business History*, Vol. 23, No. 42, 1982, pp. 865–81.

The jump in sales revenue between 1912 and 1913 (37.8 per cent) becomes less noteworthy when it is realised that the value of British motor vehicle production also rose by more than one-fifth at the same time. Although between these years Rover's share of production increased, for Rover to have maintained this performance, in the absence of the First World War, when other manufacturers such as Morris would have produced competitive models in volume, the company would have had to have shown an interest in production organisation unprecedented in its history. Rover's interwar experience (Chapter 2) supports the view that 1913 and 1914 would have been the company's high point even if hostilities had not broken out. For the industry matters were different. The war came on the verge of a new era.

1.4 British demand for motor vehicles

For most of the period before 1914, the first phase of the industry, the British demand for cars was dominated by wealthy and leisured buyers. The public would defer purchases when summer weather was poor enough to spoil the pleasure of motoring. Luxury trades, such as guns and jewellery supplied close substitutes for cars. They complained of a decline in demand when car sales rose. At the peak of the first motor car boom in 1907, buyers continued to prefer higher quality foreign, usually French, cars; the price per horsepower of British manufactured vehicles was lower than that of imports. But in recognition of the improving design and thorough workmanship of English-made bodies, buyers were increasingly inclined to buy only foreign chassis, and fully equip them in England.[24]

With the onset of the slump, customers still in the market were no longer obliged to wait. Cars were delivered by business hungry manufacturers almost immediately orders were received. Soon unsold car stocks could only be reduced by radical price cuts, especially since during the slump customers were looking for cheaper vehicles anyway. A change in the pattern of business depressed sales further. Buyers no longer bought a new car every year partly because of the greater durability and reliability of the product. Fashion continued to influence buyers throughout the depressed years after 1907, as the annual variations in car colours showed. In 1909 green or crimson lake predominated, the following year's colour was blue and in 1911, when an upturn was underway, light tones, such as slate, were in favour.

Greater commercial use followed on increasing reliability. Demands for taxis, doctors' cars and buses all grew in the Edwardian period. Between 1907 and 1909 Wolseley sold 500 taxis and by 1912 motor buses had completely replaced horse-drawn omnibuses in London. Doctors became a sufficiently powerful car-using group to lobby successfully for a reduction of one-half in their horsepower and petrol taxes. Taxis also gained a 50 per cent reduction in their petrol tax payments.

Like the domestic product, imported cars were generally cheaper in the slump after 1907. American cars were however overcoming their reputation for shoddiness and the higher average price in these years showed that British car owners were choosing a higher grade. But France still remained the most favoured source for British buyers.[25] Exactly how the market was split between imported and home produced vehicles is not immediately obvious for the early years of the industry. Some inferences must be drawn from a number of series. Motor industry production differs from total home demand by sales of imports and exports of home products:

$$\text{Production} = \text{Home Sales} + \text{Exports} - \text{Imports}$$

But the vertically separated structure of the early Edwardian industry, the tendency to buy components from other manufacturers for further processing, before selling to yet other producers, introduces additional complications. Many of the components for British vehicles were made abroad and, as the industry became more competitive in assembled vehicles, imported components increased to satisfy expanding domestic demand.

Putting together a number of estimates, 1906 car business was perhaps as much as double that of 1905. On average about 30 per cent of a 'British' car was manufactured abroad. British manufacturers sold roughly the same value as imported complete cars in 1906, about £4.5 million each. Perhaps another £2.5 million was accounted for by the receipts of agents and of the many small builders who bought foreign components and assembled them. The total value of British motor trade was, then, about £7 million but the British component of this was probably around £5 million. The boom continued until 1907, when fairly reliable production data become available. The Census of Production records £9.8 million of complete cars produced and another £1.6 million of bodies and chassis, but a net output of cars, cycles and aircraft of about £5.9 million, less than 1 per cent of Census trades' net output.

Registration figures provide an indication of the stock of motor vehicles in use in any year. Annual sales of motor vehicles in Britain added to this stock and scrapping or laying-up reduced it. Ambiguities in trade statistics and uncertainties about when owners took their vehicles permanently or temporarily off the road restrict the inferences that can be drawn from these figures about demand. In 1907 sales to the home market on the basis of the production series, ignoring imports and exports 'not for sale', amounted to 14,200, while the increase in registrations of private and commercial vehicles was only 300 less.[26] The calculation behind the bottom row of Table 1.6 is shown for 1907:

Apparent home sales, 1907
Home sales = Production + Imports − Exports = New registrations
(14,200?)   (11,700)   (4,800[a])   (2,300[a])   (13,900)
+ Scrapping + Laying-up
  (300[a])

Note: [a] Estimated.

Combining the evidence from the two Censuses of Production, Table 1.6 suggests that imports were taking a large share of the market and that there was a tendency for the value of motor imports to rise more slowly than the value of gross British production of car chassis and bodies. More definite is the change in the composition of imports from 1911 onwards as cars from the United States took an increasing share. Yet even by 1913 the Americans were still so occupied with the massive expansion of their home market (American factory sales of passenger cars were 43,000 in 1907 and 460,000 in 1913) that imports from France into Britain were still greater than those from the United States. Not until the First World War did the United States finally dominate world trade in motor vehicles.

1.5 Finance and retailing

Like the cycle industry, the motor industry experienced little difficulty raising capital from the market. Those car firms that went public generally found their new issues were over-subscribed. In this, as in many other respects, it contrasted markedly with the American motor industry. The yield of the shares of 16 motor companies before 1914 averaged 17.5 per cent, well above the British norm. Only one of the sample (Argyll) failed, two merged (Sunbeam and Deasy) and one, Rolls-Royce, was the target of a takeover bid. Returns were probably low before 1905, but were then very substantial until the collapse of 1907. Recovery came in 1909. Small firms outperformed large in the sample, either because niche markets were more profitable, or because they were

Table 1.6: British motor trade, production and market widening, 1905–1913

	1905 ('000)	1906 ('000)	1907 ('000)	1908 ('000)	1909 ('000)	1910 ('000)	1911 ('000)	1912 ('000)	1913 ('000)
Increase in registration of private motor cars on previous year[a]	7.4	7.3	9.3	8.5	7.2	5.1	18.9	16.2	17.5
Increase in registration of commercial vehicles[a]	7.5	5.3	4.6	6.3	5.6	16.2	18.7	14.3	14.7
British motor vehicle production (inc. chassis)[a]	n.a.	n.a.	11.7[b]	10.5	11.0	14.0	19.0	23.2	34.0
Retained imports (inc. chassis)[c]	5.6	5.8	4.8	6.5	7.7	9.9	11.9	13.2	13.0
Imports not for sale[c]	n.a.	n.a.	n.a.	2.2	2.6	1.5	1.8	2.1	2.6
Exports (inc. chassis)[c]	1.1	1.4	2.3	2.4	2.8	4.1	5.3	6.5	8.8
Exports not for sale[c]	n.a.	n.a.	n.a.	1.0	1.1	1.3	1.4	1.6	1.6
Apparent home sales[d]	n.a.	n.a.	14.2	15.8 or 14.6	17.4 or 16.0	20.0 or 19.8	26.0 or 25.6	30.4 or 29.9	39.2 or 38.2

Sources: [a] SMMT, *The Motor Industry of Great Britain*, selected years.
[b] Census of Production, 1907.
[c] British Parliamentary Papers.
[d] Calculated from production and trade data.

(incorrectly) judged to be risker than large enterprises. A similar result is obtained from considering the ratio of profits to net assets in balance sheets.[27]

The bulk of capital expansion was provided from external sources. Between 1905 and 1914, 91 per cent of the increase in net worth of the sample came from capital markets and 70 per cent of profits were paid out as dividends. Both these percentages were higher than for a sample of eight American firms before 1926. In the absence of taxation and with full information and perfect markets, whether profits are paid out as dividends and external funds sought for investment, or whether profits are retained for investment, should make no difference to the growth of the firm. In practice, the availability of external financing could have reduced growth rates if wealth owners had higher rates of time preference, were more impatient, than owner/managers who wanted to 'build an empire'.[28]

It is possible to point to companies like Fred Hopper's that failed to raise external funds for expansion, but that does not indicate that capital market provision was inadequate.[29] What matters is that start-up firms were inevitably going to be disadvantaged in attracting capital because they lacked a track record. Similar considerations apply to capital market issues for longer established firms that had entered the new industry. American motor industry reliance on ploughed-back profits demonstrates this theme. In the Midlands, local capital, less 'blind', contributed to cycle and motor industry growth. Arguably the excesses of company promoters such as Harry Lawson and Terah Hooley made externally financed firms in London less viable by burdening them with the obligations to pay excessive dividends from their earnings. High dividends 'signalled' high profits to a poorly informed capital market. Financial reconstruction was common, but considerable damage could be done before that nettle was grasped.

Once model production moved into batch mode, manufacturers appointed agents to deal with retailing. Any one agent typically dealt in the cars of a number of companies. Percival Perry, who sold Ford cars in England from 1904, was one of the more enterprising retailers, and was to be a major influence on the industry in the interwar years. In 1911, the driving of a Model T Ford up Ben Nevis boosted sales enormously. With such publicity stunts he was, of course, treading a path that was well worn; racing and endurance trials had long proved themselves effective forms of advertising.

The considerable size of early manufacturers such a Daimler, Humber and Rover meant that, in selling, they were not at the mercy of retailers but the motor car was an expensive durable that needed finance for its purchase, an after sales repair service and extensive advertising. Building 'speculatively' necessitated tying up capital in finished stock, and even the largest firms were anxious to avoid that level of commitment when they needed working capital to finance work in progress. The solution widely adopted in Edwardian times was to require the buyer to put up one-third of the final price when the chassis was laid down. Ostensibly this allowed the customer the right to dictate his personal specifications but actually the motive was risk-sharing. After the slump of 1907 and the switch towards lower-priced vehicles, bespoke production became more common and motor companies scrambling for business resorted to hire purchase. Other selling techniques included the production of monthly company magazines to maintain the loyalty of repeat buyers.

With hard times and increasing competition, salesmen were tempted to cut retail prices. To prevent such behaviour the manufacturers formed the Motor Traders Association (MTA) in 1910 as a branch of the Society of Motor Manufacturers and Traders. By 1911, the MTA had established a 'stop list' of price-cutting agents with whom no Association members were to trade. The Association also standardised a 15 per cent agent's discount on the manufacturer's retail price.[30]

1.6 Industrial relations

The industry was forward in organising the retail trade but in industrial relations comparable progress was not apparent. The motor industry attempted little modification of arrangements inherited from engineering. That inertia is one possible explanation for the British industry's low productivity compared with American motor vehicle production. Lewchuk contends that British labour ensured that businesses were unable and unwilling to install American machinery and methods.[31] British managers believed their workers were too 'individualistic' and insufficiently malleable to acquiesce in American-style direct control. They preferred to rely on incentive contracts and minimal management. Under the

'British system', piece rates and effort bonuses did the driving in the engineering industry.

Engineering management turned to piece rates from the 1880s. By 1913, they had become the norm; 84 per cent of fitters and turners in Coventry were paid by the piece. Perhaps half of the doubling of labour productivity in the decade after 1903, Lewchuk believes, was due to the adoption of such incentive payments. These controls were no panacea however, for foremen were liable to threaten and bully men into greater effort to enhance their own payment, and the setting of rates was fertile soil for disputes.[32]

In the American system machinery determined the pace of work and therefore employees' supply of effort. Machine technology increasingly removed skilled workers from the central position in production. Management thereby acquired more power to organise and pace work, so long as the labour force conceded the transfer. British firms before 1914 adopted modern grinding and milling machinery, an essential characteristic of the 'American system'. But the Amalgamated Society of Engineers (ASE) managed to gain operating rights for the new technology, such as Potter and Johnson lathes, at the quality end of the market; at Belsize in Manchester, Leyland in Lancashire and Argyll near Glasgow, some employers took machines out of production rather than pay the union skilled rate. However the ASE certainly did not gain control everywhere. They were excluded from Humber's Beeston factory after 1906 and generally non-union, semi-skilled workers came to dominate the industry. The Workers' Union aimed to recruit both semi-skilled and unskilled in Coventry from 1906 and, supported by successful strikes at Humber and Daimler, raised the Coventry labourer's rate by 10–20%, narrowing the wage lead of ASE members.[33]

Technical progress also increased the expense of machinery, which could leave management vulnerable if workers chose to contest management authority, as they did in Britain according to Lewchuk. Unionised labour could win concessions from firms or deter investment by the threat of strike action. In an international economy, where Britain had to compete with non-union foreign labour, failure to resolve a conflict between management and labour lost world market share for the export industries and encouraged imports. Lewchuk maintains this failure stemmed from a 'social crisis' which reached a peak in the mid 1890s. Possibly the dispute culminating in the engineering lock-out of 1897–8 discouraged engineering firms from entering the infant motor industry.

In fact the so-called 'British system' was not confined to Britain, as Lewchuk's argument implies. It was determined by the nature and strength of demand and by the type of labour available. The American motor industry did not eschew managerial delegation of the type favoured by the British. As Ford grew bigger, 'paternalism' had given way to an 'internal contract' system, whereby foremen were responsible for hiring, firing and payment of their men. By 1913, this managerial strategy provoked so much labour unrest and turnover that Ford were forced to establish central employment and payments departments. Piece rates were introduced at the same time as American machinery in the German Siemens company in the 1880s. If piece rates were a response to a social crisis, then apparently Germany, that paragon of late Victorian economic growth, must have been similarly traumatised.

Time rates and continuous flow production would have been wholly inappropriate for British or German manufacturers before the First World War because their domestic markets could not have absorbed the volume necessary to make the system viable. Export markets could not provide an additional source of demand to create American-length production runs and production styles because in many traditionally British-dominated areas, such as Argentina, Canada and Australia, where incomes were high enough to support considerable car populations, American products were more appropriate. Elsewhere the British had to compete with the French who held a first mover advantage.

Rather than the British choice of technology and payments system limiting the size of the market by holding up car prices, it is more likely that causation ran instead from market size to technology and thence to piece rates. The small British market restricted the extent to which specialised machinery and moving assembly lines could be used and costs brought down by volume production.

1.7 Taxation, road finance and motor vehicle demand

If labour resistance was not the key to the British motor industry's sluggish start, then did the state contribute? The home demand for the motor industry's products was crucially dependent upon the availability, quality and pricing of roads. And the Victorian state, at the local government level, bore the responsibility for them, on the grounds that rate-payers were principal beneficiaries of horse-drawn traffic. A horse tax had been imposed in 1784 but was repealed 90 years later. George Goschen (Chancellor of the Exchequer 1887–92) failed in his attempt to make road users pay for the upkeep of the roads through taxation in 1888. Hence in 1902–3 rate and tax payers were paying out £7.5 million in effect as a subsidy to road users. The private costs of road use were lowered below their social costs so encouraging more resources than ideal to be devoted to road transport, and less resources to other activities.

As motor traffic increased, so too did wear and tear on the roads. By 1906, when the Royal Commission on Motor Cars reported, better road surfaces and more money from new sources to pay for them were matter or urgency. German 'Kleinpflaster' road was the most economical means of obtaining a strong, smooth and dustless surface for roads to carry light and heavy motor traffic, while tarring on ordinary metalled roads in the French fashion was suitable for ordinary country traffic. Costs of the improved road surfaces are presented in Table 1.7

Table 1.7: Cost of improving Britain's roads to take motor traffic, 1906

Country	Class of road	Cost of construction or renewal per mile £	Yearly expense of upkeep £	Life in years	Total present value outlay per mile at 4% p.a.	Annual cost per mile £
France	Tarred (matalled)	1,900	89	Unlimited	4,125	164.90
Germany	Kleinpflaster- (old foundation)	2,529	44	27½	4,931	197.14

Source: Royal Commission on Motor Cars 1906.

The annual cost of improving the 27,000 miles of main road to the level appropriate for motor traffic would have been approximately between £4.45 million and £5.32 million at 1906 prices. This calculation excludes any extraordinary expenditure necessitated by motor traffic on the 95,000 miles of road controlled by the Rural District Councils. The Road Board, set up under the 1909 Finance Act, was partly responsible for such expenditures, but the Board's outlays never reached anything like that level. By March 1916, out of a revenue of £7.24 million it had spend only £3.41 million. Although the Board received the petrol duty of 3d a gallon and licence fees, the rate-payers were still obliged to finance the major portion of road expenditures. Total expenditure by Local Authorities in Britain on maintenance, improvement and cleansing of roads and bridges, including loan charges, but excluding expenditures out of loans, amounted to £17.89 milion in 1910–11.[34]

Taken with expenditure by the central authority, it is clear that road expenditures far exceeded motor taxation; there was a net subsidy to motor vehicle use. Certainly, motor vehicles were not the only road users, but the increase in road expenditure would seem to be due to the use of motor vehicles. A certain amount of expenditure, that on by-roads, provided benefits to the railway system, as feeder routes, but this will have been included in the 1902–3 figure. Between that year and 1910–11, prices rose about 13 per cent. This implies that without motor vehicles, road expenditure in 1910–11 would only be £8.5 million.

The net subsidy to vehicle use in 1910–11, and therefore to the demand for motor vehicles, was around £9.4 million. But this subsidy was gained by users of imported as well as domestically made vehicles. It was not solely a subsidy to the domestic industry. All competing foreign motor industries received tariff protection which allowed home producers a larger market to utilise scale economies. By contrast, British government policy expanded domestic demand without correspondingly encouraging supply. A balance of trade deficit in motor vehicles was the result.[35]

1.8 Conclusion

The evidence points to industry development, initially constrained by legislation and patents, subsequently accelerating as manufacturers accumulated experience which the French had already gained. The size of the American market by then conferred a great advantage on Ford whose product increasingly dominated British sales by 1913, thanks partly to the Old Trafford assembly plant established in 1911. As to whether the choice of the internal combustion engine was arbitrary, for Ford's primarily farm market, electric vehicles lacked the performance and charging facilities. The other alternative technology, steam, was embodied in traction engines that were too heavy and expensive for wider use, although steam commercial vehicles lived on into the 1930s.

Did British entrepreneurs fail? On the above account, as a group they were largely victims of circumstances and history at this stage. The cycle car boom illustrates the speed with which they could respond to a market opportunity and the very different nature of demand which they had to satisfy compared to the American producers. A more equal distribution of British income may have changed that demand somewhat but may also have reduced it. Labour resistance was not the reason that British firms did not thoroughly adopt American technology. By deskilling jobs, the technology adopted allowed access to non-traditional, non-union labour which was generally pliable. Though domestic production was constrained by the effects of early legislation, foreign competition and by first mover advantage, state policy encouraged demand by its tax policy and thus contributed to the substantial volume of imports.

War broke out just as the British industry was ready to leave the first stage of the motor car 'product cycle'.[36] As for the earlier bicycle and the later radio set, this initial phase was marked by a wide variety of product specifications supplying a specialised and limited market at relatively high cost. In the first stage, experience was accumulated as to the best ways of catering to British preferences for various qualities at acceptable costs. The American industry, led by Ford, left this era around 1910 and the British were about to follow in 1914.

CHAPTER TWO

COMING OF AGE: INDUSTRIAL STRUCTURE AND PERFORMANCE BETWEEN THE WORLD WARS

Together with the postwar boom and slump of 1919–21, the First World War lost the British motor industry another five years of development. The period was immensely profitable but companies were encouraged to grow in ways that were unsustainable in a stable economy at peace. Only in the 1920s did Britain pass into the second stage of the motor vehicle product life cycle, ten years or more behind the United States. In this phase, the car became standardised, new locational patterns of production emerged and economies of scale began to dominate product characteristics. Although still far behind the American industry, between the world wars the motor industry overcame its pre-war inferiority to the French industry and vastly exceeded French annual output. Moreover by 1938, an unpropitious year for world trade, 20 per cent of British motor industry output was exported, compared with only 10 per cent of production sold abroad by France.

Despite attaining the status of second largest motor industry in the world from an unpropitious start, the interwar industry has been subjected to a barrage of criticism, both then and now. Allegations have included the claim that the particular development path chosen (small vehicles with economical 'low power' engines by comparison with American types) must have been inefficient. Later critics responding to the decline of British manufacturing capacity in the 1970s and 1980s, looked back to the earlier years to find the roots of uncompetitiveness, and judged the interwar industry by the deficiencies of a later period. Companies supposedly did not develop professional management organisations, productivity was therefore low and models were proliferated unnecessarily. Labour conditions were poor and when war broke out again, the motor industry's products failed to perform adequately, or so it was alleged.

The present and following chapters systematically examine these claims. Section 1 shows how after an extraordinary spate of new firms entering in the industry in the boom of 1919–20, competition and depression steadily winnowed out the less efficient producers while the industry expanded rapidly. Though survivors needed to supply reliable and popular models, concentration upon one, in imitation of Ford, was demonstrably inappropriate. Attempting to cover the full range of market preferences, even successful British manufacturers increased their model variety in the 1930s. Whether that reflected managerial or entrepreneurial failure is considered in Section 2. The technology that gave rise to the central feature of the interwar industry, economies of scale, is examined in Section 3. Scale economies also encourage the growth of large component suppliers. The difficulty this vertical disintegration created is described in Section 4. 'Downstream', manufacturers tried to extend their control over retailers to enhance aftersales service, a process discussed in Section 5. Section 6 examines the upshot for employees of motor companies.

2.1 Evolution of industry structure, 1914–1939

Had there been no First World War, British motor industry development would have been a good deal less troubled as well as considerably faster. Hostilities did, however, give the motor vehicle a chance to demonstrate its worth. The armies of Europe's young industrial giant, Imperial Germany, were stopped at the Battle of the Marne, partly by the flexibility of the new motor vehicle. Taxis, buses and lorries ferried British and French troops rapidly to the front for the decisive battle. Thereafter warfare on the Western Front became mainly static but motor vehicles continued to contribute behind the lines. The Indian Army used 1,300 AEC London buses, complete with advertisements, as transports in France. Napier and Rolls-Royce gained orders for armoured cars, and other manufacturers prospered from the military demand for commercial vehicles. For the industry as a whole, the war stifled the boom of 1913 and light car makers, such as Austin and Morris, who were to lead the rapid advance of the motor industry in the 1920s and 1930s, were at first particularly hard hit by the decline in civilian orders. Eventually Austin and Morris were recognised as efficient mass producers of a variety of munitions. From that experience they may have learned something of organisation for later high volume car production, but the other side of the coin was very considerable disruption to production and marketing, shortly after the end of the war driving Austin into the hands of his creditors.[1]

Motor vehicle technology, if not the motor industry, promised to break the stalemate of trench warfare with the introduction of the tank by the British. Prototypes first emerged from the Royal Navy because of an initial lack of army interest. And though a light tank was soon made in France by Renault, the British motor industry was not called upon to make a contribution to the British weapon. However, Harry Ricardo, later to sell path-breaking internal combustion engine innovations, gained considerable experience in engine design and in fuel combustion from his work in the development of the tank. Frank Woollard, later a British exponent of flow production in the motor industry, was responsible for the production of tank gearboxes.

What made immediate postwar conditions particularly difficult was the strength of the Lloyd George demobilisation boom of 1919–20; an expansionary monetary policy boosted demand, ensuring that returning soldiers would find jobs and not turn to Bolshevism. Prices rose and production bottlenecks abounded as output failed to match the growth of spending. Industrial unrest, in particular the moulders' strike, and shortages of steel, caused acute problems for motor manufacturers.[2] These difficulties temporarily dammed the flood of new entrants to the industry, so that numbers did not peak until the depression year of 1922. Without the boom, resources would not have been so dissipated in an excessive number of small firms at this relatively late stage in the industry's evolution. Most of them, and many established firms, were squeezed out by the slump following the downturn in the summer of 1920, and by intense competition in the following two decades. One of the largest manufacturers before 1914, Napier, recognised the changes in the market towards small, cheap, volume-produced cars, and tried to bow out gracefully. 'I do not think it is so much a question of our giving up the motor car trade as it will be the motor car trade giving us up'[3] Napier told his senior management, when they tried to resist his policy of concentrating on aircraft. As figure 2.1 shows, by the later 1920s the number of car manufacturers was half that of the beginning of the decade. Car output grew strongly, permanently overtaking the French for the rest of their interwar period after the end of the 1920s (Table 2.1). Market shares changed radically as well. Ford fell from complete market dominance with the Model T in 1920 to the status of a minor competitor by the end of the decade, while Morris's and Austin's fortunes soared. During the 1930s British output remained well ahead of accelerating German motor vehicle production, comfortably holding the British motor industry in the position of second largest in the world.

Figure 2.1 Car manufacturing, number of British firms, 1920–1938

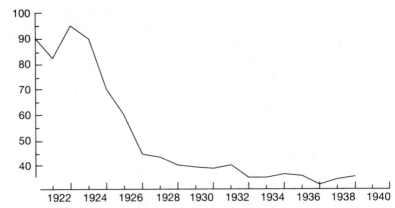

Source: Derived from data from SMMT, *The British Motor Industry*, selected years.

Table 2.1: *International motor vehicle production, 1929 and 1936 ('000)*

	Britain	France	Germany	Italy	United States	Canada
1929 total	241	254	96	60	5,358	262
Passenger cars	182	191	74	n.a.	4,587	203
Lorries, buses	59	63	22	n.a.	771	59
1936 total	481	203	298	48	4,454	162
Passenger cars	367	180	240	36	3,676	131
Lorries, buses	114	23	58	12	778	31

Source: League of Nations, *Annual Statistics*, Geneva.

William Morris's leadership of the industry may be traced to his policy during the slump of 1921 and 1922, when stocks were accumulating and the market stagnating. Recognising that any contribution to his overhead costs was worth having, he slashed prices in February and again in November. In 1922 he reduced the Morris Cowley two seater to £225, £70 below full average cost, and his sales responded. He then cut his outlays by improved production methods and bulk buying, so that profits also began to rise quickly.[4] Morris's price cut has been heralded as the origins of his success, but there was much more to it than that. He had fine products and careful production techniques, which other companies lacked. Bean cut prices at the same time as Morris, on the same principle, but that did not save the company.[5]

Austin standardised production on his 20 hp model in an attempt to replicate Ford's strategy, instead driving himself to the edge of bankruptcy. Eventually he restored his fortunes with a much smaller car, the 'Seven'. Weighing 7 cwt, the car could reach 50 mph and achieve 50 miles to the gallon. Originally priced at £225, by 1930 the Seven was selling for £125.

Morris and Austin achieved a joint share of about 60 per cent of British motor production by 1929, while Ford held less than 5 per cent. Ford's operations in Britain declined from when Sir Percival Perry was sacked as managing director in 1920, until he was reappointed in 1928. Perry felt he had an advantage being a native of the British Isles. He wrote in 1929 'It is certainly true that all Americans sent over here never wanted to stay permanently, and are always looking forward to the time they will return home.'[6] American management's desire to keep their stays short did not allow them to become familiar with British cultural differences, which could be a handicap when trying to improve efficiency. The principal difficulty faced by American motor companies in the British market of the 1920s though was their unsuitable products.[7]

American companies sold their domestic vehicles in Europe, merely reducing transport costs and avoiding import tariffs by exporting cars 'completely knocked down' for assembly in European plants. A Dodge market analysis of 1927 pointed out the weight of taxation and high expenditure on petrol incurred in Europe by Dodge's principal American model. The most marketable car in Europe that would also sell in the United States, the report concluded, was a high quality six cylinder with a high m.p.g. Ford introduced a small cylinder bore version of their American Model A in 1928 to succeed the Model T, but sales were disastrously low. About the same time General Motors was considering the introduction of a small bore Chevrolet into England but Ford's experience convinced them otherwise. What success General Motors achieved in the British market of the 1920s was with their Bedford commercial vehicle range rather than their cars.

If big American firms could not compete during the 1920s, small firms like Clyno were likely to be squeezed out of the industry completely. Under Frank Smith, Clyno managed to sell 11,000 of their 10.8 hp car in 1926, yet two years later, the business was in liquidation. An unsuccessful new model followed by abandonment by their dealers, Rootes, finished them. Other firms managed to survive despite falling market shares. How they did so and where they failed to compete, elucidates the evolution of the industry, as well as casting light on the achievements of Morris and Austin.

Rover, whose name in the early 1990s represented the surviving indigenous motor manufacturing capacity, bought the Tyseley Works, Birmingham in 1919 for the manufacture of the 8 hp twin cylinder air-cooled Rover, which proved immensely popular. At first this small car sold in volumes comparable with Morris's (Table 2.2) and Austin chose this model for the prototype of the 'Seven'. Only in 1923 did Rover fall back. Frustrated by the lack of divi-

Table 2.2: Model sales and production: Rover, Austin and Morris, 1920–1927

| | Rover sales | | | Austin | Morris |
| | Light cars | Heavy cars | Number produced | Number produced | |
	8,9 & 10 hp	12 & 14 hp	Total	7 hp	11.9 & 14.6 hp
1920	–	1,389	1,389	–	1,932
1921	3,021	1,409	4,430	–	3,076
1922	4,907	1,384	6,291	178	6,956
1923	3,734	1,459	5,193	2,409	20,048
1924	5,202	1,590	6,792	4,800	32,918
1925	5,319	555	5,694	8,024	55,582
1926	4,845	588	5,433	13,174	48,330
1927	4,119	341	4,460	21,671	61,632

Source: Rover Company Records; R. Church, Herbert Austin: The British Motor Car Industry to 1941, London: Europa, 1979, p. 84, P. W. S. Andrews and E. Brunner, The Life of Lord Nuffield, Oxford: Basil Blackwell, 1954, pp. 112, 185, J. Foreman-Peck, 'Exit, Voice and Loyalty as Responses to Decline; The Rover Company in the Inter-War Years', Business History, Vol. 23, No. 2, July 1981, pp. 191–207.

dends, shareholders demanded committees of inspection at company annual general meetings in 1925 and 1926, despite the 1923 appointment of a shareholder director. A resolution on the matter was only just defeated in 1927.[8]

The two major problems faced by the Rover company were that they were not sensitive enough to emerging competition and they were incapable of reorgainising for efficient production in the volume required by the market. While their small car's market was threatened by Austin in 1923, their 12 hp's sales were endangered by Morris (Table 2.2). Yet in May 1923, the new management, J. K. Starley jnr. and the works manager Mark Wild, wanted to keep this part of the production range unchanged (except for improvement to the 8 hp), and to introduce a large six-cylinder car.[9] Only after the balance sheet had been made up and a loss recorded for the financial year was a new programme proposed in November to match the competition of Austin and Morris.

Had the company been able to rival Austin or Morris in efficiency, it would have expanded the production of its light car and reduced its price, even when experiencing difficulties with the 14 hp model. But the layout of the Tyseley works was unsatisfactory; departments had been added where space was available, regardless of whether the positions were ideal for internal works transportation and the progress of parts.

At the end of 1923, the first important step in producing new models had been taken, with the appointment of P. A. Poppe as consulting engineer for the new cars. Through the firm White and Poppe, Poppe had supplied Morris with carburettors and engines. The record of that relationship was not promising in all respects for the new appointment. His new car, the 14/45, was on the road in September 1924 but deliveries could not begin until February the following year. The speed of introduction of this model was no greater than that of the successful Austin Seven, and therefore did not justify the failure to deal adequately with the valve gear noise, which by July 1925 had caused orders to fall off and led to the accumulation of over half a million pounds in stock at the end of the financial year. To emphasise the point, the experience was virtually repeated in 1927 with the new six cylinder. By August, the criticism of agents and others forced Rover to stop deliveries.

Even when design problems were overcome, prices of the cars remained too high to sell in the forecasted quantities in 1926, and in the following year, production problems prevented the fulfilment of the sanctioned output. An obvious possible solution, the separation of the functions of chief designer and works manager, both held by Poppe, was suggested by one of the new directors in August 1927, but was effectively blocked by the other new director. Starley's proposed remedy was to delegate supervision of these matters while he concentrated on selling, but Rover's falling market share and lack of profits showed that was no solution. Starley was ousted from the business his father founded and a new managing director took over in 1929. As the world depression broke, that proved a poor year to embark upon expansion, and Rover sank further into debt.

The 1930s

Those British car firms which came to dominate the market by the end of the 1920s tended to increase the variety of the products that they placed on the rapidly widening market of the 1930s. Austin's activities did not seem well coordinated although the company was adept at producing permutations on its five basic models. Austin made eight engines, five chassis types, six wheelbase lengths and 51 models. Morris also proliferated his models in attempts to find a best-seller. In 1934, Nuffield operations showed such a lack of conformity that no body had two models in common and only one engine did so. Seven side-valve Morris's and one ohc model, three ohc MGs, four ohc Wolseleys and four small six-cylindered sports cars were produced. But in that year the right formula was found; the new Morris Eight sold 47,000 in ten months and 100,000 in under two years.

Singer pursued a similar policy, but unlike Morris, the company did not eventually find a really large market. In 1932, this now comparatively small firm offered six models – two pushrod ohv, two ohc, and two side-valve engined, as well as a sports car, inevitably with dire financial consequences. Standard, by contrast, was growing rapidly under J. P. Black, formerly of Hillman's. Standard produced a successful 9 hp model in 1928 which almost competed on price with Austin and Morris. By 1934, the firm's sales exceeded 20,000.[10]

Specialist cars still offered niche markets where scale economies were less fundamental, since advantage could be taken of the component industry and the opportunity to buy from other manufacturers. Jaguar cars originated in a Blackpool motorcycle sidecar building firm in 1922 founded by William Lyons. Lyons moved to Coventry in 1928, making special bodies for the Austin Seven and other cars. Two years later he designed his own chassis that would take a Standard engine. For his first Jaguar, Lyons persuaded Standard to carry the cost of the new cylinder head he had designed. Unleashed in 1935, the Jaguar achieved over 5,000 sales in the year war broke out.

Ford's Detroit model Y of 1932 was the first successful American attempt at producing a European car. It revived Ford's fortunes in Britain, despite the disastrously expensive move to the new Dagenham factory. General Motors was slower to follow in Britain because their investment in Opel was much greater than in Vauxhall. When General Motors eventually recognised the necessity to produce a special product for the British market, with the successful Vauxhall 'Light Six' of 1934, the resemblance to the corresponding German Opel was close. This was also true of the first Vauxhall small car of 1938, the 10/4, a scaled-down American sedan. Opel products consistently incorporated technical advances before Vauxhall, throughout the 1930s, which in view of its greater size, accounting for 36 per cent of the German output when acquired by General Motors in 1928, is not surprising.

American owned firms did not invariably achieve greater profitability and market share than the indigenous competition, contrary to expectations if American management teams or company techniques were superior. But by 1938, the resurgence of American interest and the entry of former retailers, Rootes, had reduced industry concentration. Table 2.3 shows Morris and Austin's share of production by volume was markedly reduced and matched by the combined outputs of the Americans and Rootes together with Singer. Table 2.3 also reveals a similar concentration in commercial vehicles but it conceals the difference between the heavy vehicles and those produced by the 'Big Six'.

The 'Big Six' concentrated on commercial vehicles which principally required only fitting different bodies on to motor car chassis. For such products they could utilise their scale economies, but because they could not do so for heavy commercial vehicles, a niche was left for small producers. Most successful by 1938 was Leyland, despite an inauspicious start to the decade. Leyland originated as the Lancashire Steam Motor Company, based near Preston, and was financially severely compromised by refurbishing army surplus lorries bought at excessive prices when all prices were falling in 1921. The son of the founder, Henry Spurrier II, was displaced and retrenchment began. Production of the exotic Leyland 'Straight Eight' was abandoned and the modest two-stroke Trojan instead generated cash for the company. Henry Spurrier III as managing

Table 2.3: Distribution of British motor vehicle production by manufacturer, 1938

	Cars and taxis	Commercial vehicles
'Big Six'		
Nuffield[a]	26.6	26.5
Ford	17.8	20.0
Austin	17.0	4.2
Vauxhall	10.1	24.6
Rootes[b]	9.6	5.5
Standard	9.0	–
Specialist cars		
Rover	3.2	–
Singer	2.6	–
BSA (+ Daimler and Lanchester	1.2	–
Jaguar	1.1	–
Armstong-Siddeley	0.6	–
Jowett	0.4	–
Rolls-Royce and Bentley	0.3	–
Alvis	0.3	–
Other	0.3	–
Heavy vehicle builders		
Leyland	–	4.1
ACV (AEC)	–	2.1
Albion	–	2.3
Dennis	–	1.5
Other	–	8.2

Notes: [a] = Morris, MG, Wolseley, Riley.
　　　　[b] = Hillman, Sunbeam–Talbot
Source: Political and Economic Planning, *Motor Vehicles: A Report on the Industry*, London, 1950.

director demonstrated that the tradition of family management still had considerable vitality. Production of buses and trucks rose steadily through the 1930s, earning net profits of over £0.6 million in 1937. Of Leyland's vehicles 20 per cent were sold abroad in 1939.[11]

Leyland's rival, the Associated Equipment Company (AEC), was founded to supply the London bus market through a series of exclusive agreements with the London General Omnibus. Buses were sold to other firms through an exclusive agency arrangement with Daimler. The cosy environment was disturbed when, in 1926, the company moved from Walthamstow to Southall, where twelve component assembly lines fed into the main L shaped chassis assembly. With workers on time rates and a group bonus, average labour costs per chassis fell by about 30 per cent by mid 1927. Lord Ashfield of AEC, proposed to Leyland in 1929 a grand design for rationalising the entire commercial vehicle industry. But this, and other merger proposals later, fell through, leaving an atomistic market structure. Compared with car manufacture, heavy commercial vehicles were only small employers; in total they provided only 18,000 jobs in 1938. The industry fortunes largely turned on entrepreneurship and organisation in car manufacture.[12]

2.2 Entrepreneurship and management

Criticisms have been aimed particularly at Austin and Morris, at the prevalence of the family firm in British industry in general, including the motor industry, and at the alleged widespread British failure to develop professional management organisations. Neither Morris nor Austin can be accused of clinging to family firms for neither entrepreneurs had sons to succeed them; Morris was childless and Austin's only son was killed on the Western Front in 1915. In any case during Austin's postwar financial difficulties, the company creditors appointed senior professional managers. Turner presents 'the sins of the Founding Fathers', as not sustaining the achievement that captured 60 per cent of the market by 1929.[13] Both Morris and Austin companies in the 1930s, Turner maintains, were one man operations, which had outgrown their founders. They lacked 'management in depth and organisations geared to growth'. Morris made frequent lengthy trips abroad from the later 1920s and when in the country his working days were short. Yet he was furious if important decisions were taken without him. The claim that Morris and Austin did not employ professional managers is belied by the powerful figure of Leonard Lord, first at Morris and then from 1938 at Austin. Englebach, Woollard, and Perry-Keene as well, were managers/engineers of stature in the Austin and Morris companies between the wars. The problem was more likely in some prevalent attitudes; Morris refused to employ graduates and Lord did not believe in training apprentices.

Did founder vested interests inhibit desirable change? Morris refused to merge with Austin in 1924 but during the early 1930s, when Morris's managerial grip slackened, that was probably an advantage for the industry as a whole, for he would have assumed control of the merged business and retarded a larger section of the industry. Looking across Europe, Church concluded there was no reason to distinguish between the performance of family and professionally managed motor firms.[14] That does not exactly address the alleged failure to adopt American management organisation, if the European environment did not offer the full range of firm types, including professionally managed firms. But because British motor entrepreneurs Austin and Morris were able to compete successfully with the Americans, at least in the home market (unlike firms in the shipbuilding, railway equipment and non-electrical machinery industries), there is little reason to convict them of Turner's charges for the interwar years.

By contrast with Morris and Austin's success, Ford's insistence on the Dagenham location for the new factory in the 1920s ensured excess capacity and low profits through the 1930s in this American company. General Motors bought the Vauxhall company in 1925 to get under the tariff. This exemplar of American managerial hierarchy did then achieve the highest rate of return among British larger firms in the 1930s. Yet it did so with British management, backed by American resources, and remained relatively small. Vauxhall shifted to direct control of the workforce, away from piece rates, in the slump. Operations were given a time in which the job was to be completed. By such methods, General Motors raised weekly output by almost four times. Charles Bartlett became managing director in 1930, practising enlightened paternalism. Vauxhall ran its own trade school, high wages were paid through the group bonus system, attempts were made to alleviated instability of employment, and profit-sharing was introduced in 1935 (as it was by Morris and Standard).

Rather than pointing to organisational limitations of the British companies, the revival of Ford and General Motors in Britain during the 1930s more plausibly suggests that limited British organisation was a reflection of British market size, which was further constrained by presence of the American multinationals. Their enormous financial power allowed them to sustain mistakes, such as Ford's Dagenham marsh site, that would have finished smaller,

British firms, and to finance new product development with overheads paid for from the enormous American sales. American management styles were not particularly successful in the British market and British managers, like Perry-Keene at Austin, were hostile to American authoritarian 'herd' methods, which they judged unacceptable to the workforce. Austin and Perry-Keene favoured incentive payment to create the right spirit in the workers. Frank Woollard was a believer in machine pacing and in low volume production lines, introducing machine systems on the frontiers of technology at Morris. The 'British system of mass production', with a relatively limited management function, worked well for the industry during the interwar years. Trade unions were weak and the persistence of high unemployment made labour self-regulation difficult.[15]

2.3 Technical progress

The product
An important function of both entrepreneurs and management was product innovation and enhancement. Throughout the interwar years motor firms raised vehicle performance by metallurgical development and improved component designs. New steel alloys and aluminium replaced cast-iron in engines; they reduced engine weight per horsepower and aluminium pistons could move twice as fast as old ones. Ricardo's turbulent head combustion chamber increased the power output of the side-valve engine until higher octane petrol became available in the mid 1930s and allowed the use of overhead valves. Engine output rose by 20 per cent during the 1930s so that smaller, more economical engines could be fitted to generate the same power. A rotating cam shaft opened and shut the valves, allowing the petrol and air mixture to be sucked into the combustion chamber more quickly. Air-cooling (for instance of the Rover Eight in the earlier 1920s) could no longer compete with water-cooling, nor, despite their simplicity and small number of moving parts, did two-stroke engines attain any popularity, except with the Leyland Trojan, first made in 1922.

Higher standards of comfort and reliability were necessary if the motor vehicle was to become a mass consumer product, an end to which electricity contributed substantially. The magneto was replaced by the more durable coil (except for heavy commerical vehicles) and improved electrical equipment allowed effective lighting at last. Until around 1924, oil lamps were used for side and rear lights. Electrical starters were normal by 1925 and electrical windscreen wipers later made all-weather driving less hazardous. Synchromesh gears, which automatically matched the speeds of engaged gears, were generally adopted by 1935.

Most cars in 1919 were fitted with open touring bodies of wood (later of fabric) but by 1938, when the car was a utility vehicle from which all-weather performance was expected, the vast majority were closed saloons, sometimes with sunshine roofs. Angular bodies of the 1920s gave way to sleeker and lower forms, generally made from pressed steel that improved road holding. Independent front wheel suspension, pneumatic tyres as standard and brakes on all four wheels allowed higher speeds with less danger for those inside and outside the vehicle.

The cumulative impact of these component innovations and improvements (and the system of motor taxation discussed later) was seen in new products. During the 1920s the light car emerged as the dominant British motor species, virtually eliminating the cycle car, as well as the large engine capacity Fords, from popular motoring. By 1924 the light car had become standardised with a front-mounted in line four-cylinder side-valve water-cooled engine of up to 1500 cc, a plate clutch, integral three-speed and reverse gearbox and a final shaft drive to the rear axle. Most successful of the sub-species of ultra-light cars was Herbert Austin's 1922 Austin Seven. In the final, supercharged version, a maximum power output of 80 bhp was produced, more than ten times that of the original.

Morris's answer, the 847 cc Minor with an overhead camshaft, came out in 1928. Soon Morris reverted to the more robust side-valve engine for his £100 1930 model. Morris's earlier staple model, the Cowley, was continuously produced from 1919 to 1933 with a 1.5 litre four-cylinder water-cooled engine covering 25 miles to the gallon. Excellent servicing facilities and a robust design underwrote the model's popularity.

In the heavy commercial vehicle sector, the more flexible trolley bus began to replace the tram and the solid-tyred open charabanc of 1919 gave way to the pneumatic-tyred closed coach. Steam power survived for heavy commercial vehicles into the 1930s, but the introduction of taxation by unladen weight in 1920 penalised the heavier steam lorries. The fuel-efficient diesel engine quickly came into use, proving more popular in Britain during the 1930s than in the United States, where fuel costs were lower. AEC diesel engines using the Ricardo Comet combustion chamber began to power London buses. Rudolf Diesel had patented a 'compression ignition' engine in 1892 and 1893, which proved remarkably economical in the use of fuel. However until Diesel's death in 1913 all engines made under his licences were effectively restricted to run at a very low speed. Hence they were large and heavy in relation to their power output. Not until 1922, in Germany, was a diesel engine built light enough for use in road vehicles.[16]

The process

Choice of the right models was central to production strategy. Only then could prices be cut, as output expanded, and competitors eliminated who were unable to utilise scale economies. Costs were reduced by the use of special tools for each car part instead of jigs holding general purpose tools, as in the early stages of the industry's development. More typical of the process changes of the interwar years were three distinct ways in which larger sales volume allowed cost reduction from the application of more specialised machinery; improved factory layout for the continuous flow of components, balancing flows so that all special machine tools were continually employed, and the introduction of three-shift systems, so that capital charges for the tools could be spread over the greatest number of vehicles.

The new machinery brought with it much greater management problems than the old by making profits much more sensitive to short-run variations in output; the higher proportion of fixed to total costs drove up unit costs rapidly as production fell, while the length of life over which the special machines could be depreciated could be as low as two years because of obsolescence, compared with ten years for ordinary machines. By buying a large proportion of the value of the vehicle from component suppliers, the problem of paying fixed capital charges when demand declined, could be reduced. Small manufacturers who failed to realise this principle, such as Scout Motors of Salisbury, which even made its own nuts and bolts, were eliminated in the 1920–1 slump or in the intense competition that followed.

At Austin's, costs were controlled by a preliminary figure for each part being decided by the works, and then the accounting section would compare this number with a target figure based on overall vehicle cost. The planning department, engineering department and the accounting section next re-examined the specification and production technique, sometimes producing special machines to bring the cost down to target. To facilitate cost control and to save clerical labour before 1930, Austin spent £50,000 on analysing and computing machinery and received the money back in twelve months. A system of operation cards was introduced to follow each part – which amounted to 20 million pieces a week, since each car had 6,800 pieces. Buff cards gave details of the operation when work went through, red cards indicated when work was faulty.[17]

Examples of the change in average fixed costs, and the decline in overall unit costs for various processes as a result of the change in technique, between the pre 1914 period and 1930, are shown in Table 2.4. Cost reductions were mainly by saving labour because of the introduction of more specialised machinery allowed by greater output volumes.

Increased sensitivity to capacity utilisation, consequent upon higher fixed costs, is brought out by Table 2.4. Profits could still be made at only 36 per cent capacity utilisation with the old technique, but with the new, losses were incurred at 75 per cent utilisation. The

Figure 2.2 Austin short run cost curves, 1914 and 1930

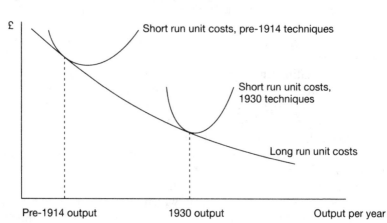

Source: Derived from data from A. Perry-Keene, 'The Incidence of On-Costs', *Journal of Production Engineers*, Vol. 40, 1931.

diagrammatic representation of this data (Fig 2.2) shows the two short-run cost curves tangent to the same long-run declining unit cost curve, but the 1930 curve has a steeper gradient than the pre-1914 curve. At the level of the three processes examined above, similar short run cost behaviour can be observed (Table 2.5). The turning and boring process with the largest proportion of fixed costs at normal capacity working, shows the greatest rise in unit costs as capacity utilisation falls.

Table 2.4: Austin's short run costs and profits, 1914 and 1930 (£'000)

	% of target	Money value of output	Materials cost	Labour cost	Fixed charges	Total cost	% profit
Pre-1914	120	780	312	211	140	663	15.0
technique	100	650	260	175	122	557	14.4
	75	488	201	132	97	430	12.0
	50	325	137	88	73	298	12.0
	36	234	98	63	61	222	4.2
1930	120	1,200	588		420	1,008	16
technique	100	1,000	490		400	890	11
	75	750	384		380	764	−1.87
	50	500	263		356	619	−23.87

Source: A. Perry-Keene, 'The Incidence of On-Costs', *Journal of Production Engineers*, Vol. 40, 1931.

Table 2.5: Austin's short run costs for selected processes, 1930 (pence)

% of target output		Sheet metal working	Turning and boring	Gear cutting
120	Labour	4.50	4.30	11.10
	Oncost	9.50	13.70	22.42
	Unit cost	14.00	18.00	34.00
75	Labour	4.50	4.30	11.10
	Oncost	15.23	22.00	35.87
	Unit cost	20.00	26.00	47.00
50	Labour	4.50	4.30	11.10
	Oncost	22.34	33.00	53.80
	Unit cost	27.00	37.00	65.00

Source: A. Perry-Keene, 'The Incidence of On-Costs', *Journal of Production Engineers*, Vol. 40, 1931.

Shift working was one possible way in which the greater overheads of large scale production could be spread. F. G. Woollard remarked that in working a 24-hour day on three shifts at the Morris Coventry engine factory, the savings on overheads were consumed in overtime. He concluded there were no advantages from increasing the intensity of utilisation of capital.[18] The optimum or long run production technique did not require three-shift working nor were short run costs (with given capacity) reduced by a 24-hour day.

Long run costs

Contemporary estimates of long run cost reductions through output expansion tended to be pessimistic. In the 1920s the SMMT maintained that if volume were doubled, unit costs would fall by 20 per cent. For an output above 40,000 per annum, the internal cost reductions that might be obtained they believed were negligible. This judgement was based on the assumption of similar, and not more, specialised machinery and organisation however, a limitation which may also have applied to the Board of Trade's assessment of Morris's engine plant. The Board of Trade claimed that the Morris engine factory, although entirely British, was second to none in the United States and produced 200 engines a day, in 1924. Above that level, the Board of Trade stated there were no economies to be gained from increasing output. Morris notes his unit costs had fallen by 30 per cent as weekly output rose from 300 to 500 cars, by 66.6 per cent in the same year. Woollard's figures for productivity increases achieved when weekly output rose were spectacular for all inputs, as Table 2.6 shows.

Table 2.6: Inputs and weekly rate of output at Morris's engine factory, 1924

	100 engines	1200 engines
Men per engine	4	1.83
Space per engine	53 sq yds	15.6 sq yds
Machines per engine	2.1	0.64
Horse power per engine	3.5	1.27

Source: F. G. Woollard, 'Plant Depreciation and Replacement Problems', *Proceedings of the Institution of Automobile Engineers*, February 1925.

In practice the distinction between a reduction of unit costs because of a greater output volume and cost reductions that could be attained with no rise in prouction, was often hard to make. For the British industry electrical power and improved, especially American, machine tools, clearly did boost productivity independently of the scale of output, even if full advantage could not be taken of them. Before the First World War, forests of belting had been a familiar sight in almost every machine shop, but improved electricity supply allowed their replacement by more flexible, individual motor drive. Specially tipped tools permitted Leyland to increase its car chassis output from 50 to 80 a week in the early 1930s, without increasing the numbers employed.

In his Coventry engine factory Morris used a great deal of American specialized machinery during 1927, and generally the British industry imported large quantities of American stamping and pressing machinery and lathes. But the lack of demand for cars in Britain meant that Morris had been obliged to disassemble cylinder block and fly-wheel machinery and make it less automatic in performance. The Sunbeam plant, with a capacity of a mere 45 cars a week in 1924, used multiple spindle Ingersoll machines for milling larger aluminium components such as crank cases and gear boxes. These machines were so efficient that the cutting time tended to be less than the time taken for placing the components in position, suggesting a disjunction between the organisation of production as a whole, based on small output, and a technology developed for a much larger output rate.

The Rhode Motor Company, with a 30-car a week capacity, developed a simple form of moving track line for chassis assembly, largely constructed of timber baulks. A series of work-holding tables with the various unit-locating devices was arranged so that all parts were located at a convenient height for the operators. Once the wheels were on, the whole assembly was lowered onto the track. It seems unlikely that this assembly technique, borrowed from the high volume producers, was commercially necessary at Rhode's output rates, and more likely, side-by-side assembly, as practised by Sunbeam, would have been just as satisfactory, if not more so.

At Morris's Oxford works, buildings were so well laid out that the assembly progressed almost in a straight line from building to building, rather than in circles as in the United States.[19] By and large however, visiting Americans in the 1920s judged that European factories lagged those in the United States by seven to ten years. The US Trade Commissioner in Britain concluded, in 1928, that 'mass production' had not been extensively developed; relatively few firms manufactured cars in large quantities. Not until 1934 did Morris operate moving final assembly lines with overhead rails for the delivery of parts at Oxford.[20] If 'batch' rather than continuous production was the norm in British private car manufacture during the 1920s, this was even more true of heavy commercial vehicles. Demand for coaches, large lorries and buses was far smaller than for cars and so production methods were more customised.

Radical changes in product or process technology were unlikely to be achieved by the collective research efforts of the industry, despite state support. The motor industry was the first branch of engineering to form a research association when the Department of Scientific and Industrial Research made a grant to the British Motor and Allied Manufacturers Research Association, registered in 1919. Initial subscriptions came from Vauxhall, Albion, Standard, Rover, Wolseley, Commer Cars and Straker Squires; Morris, Austin and Ford are conspicuous by their absence. By the end of the decade, the Department had ceased giving a grant because manufacturers did not match the state money. The Institution of Automobile Engineers took over the common research fund at the beginning of the 1930s and managed to obtain increased subscriptions, while the SMMT undertook to bear the costs of standardisation. Nevertheless, in 1935–6 the income from the industry of the motor research association was well below that of the research organisation of the cotton, the electrical, or the non-ferrous metal industries, both in absolute terms and per thousand employees.[21]

Companies may have been uninterested in collective action because research was being undertaken by the individual firms, because copying foreign technology was cheaper, or because of 'short-termism'. Certainly motor businesses spent money on development, but not on research. Lucas, the component manufacturer, established a developmental engineering department before 1914 arising from Harry and Joseph Lucas's attempts to invent a new starter. Lucas's Testing and Development Department was opened in 1927 to monitor and 'reverse engineer' product improvements among foreign counterparts. Morris Motors did not employ university graduates, and did not undertake any fundamental research, but the company did operate an Experimental Department. The Department's projects included, towards the end of the 1930s, a two year study of bearing life. The findings allowed an engine to run continuously for 300 hours without damage, whereas 50 hours' continuous operation would have damaged the engine previously. The power output of the 8 hp Morris Minor was increased by two-thirds as a result of the Department's work. Pressed Steel, a business with four American directors using new American technology, from their inception were interested in graduates for experimental and control work.

Before the First World War the major British makers of oil and gas engines were licensees of mainly German firms, who carried out a great deal of long term research and development. British management believed it was cheaper to buy designs and know how from abroad. Lawrence Pomeroy at Vauxhall was unusual in developing his theoretical analysis of the relation between piston size and piston speed and of the dynamics of valve operation. For production technology the second possibility, that copying the Americans was cheaper, was plausible. The high dividend pay-out ratios described below are also consistent with the third option, that investing in uncertain research and development projects took a low priority.

A commercial business, without monopoly power, cannot afford to be interested in technical novelty for its own sake. It has an incentive to 'free-ride' as far as possible on other people's basic research. The problem is that such free-riding by all businesses means there is inadequate investment in research. The patent system, which Harry Ricardo's company used, is intended to allow succesful research to be rewarded. Research into engine design did prove profitable for Ricardo, who opened his research business in 1917. Vauxhall and Tilling Stevens entered into consulting agreements. Ricardo's high turbulence cylinder head raised the efficiency of side-valve engines by 20 per cent and brought in substantial royalties.

In a world market the patent system was by no means perfect. Ricardo's research was less profitable than it might have been because of the refusal of the US Patent Office to recognise the high turbulence head, so long as a British citizen was trying to patent it. Moreover American manufacturers encouraged even British licensees to challenge the validity of the patent so that imported American cars would not be liable to a royalty levy. Matters came to a head with an action against Humber-Hillman in 1933. Harry Ricardo won the case at a cost of £20,000, of which he was only allowed one-third in the damages awarded, and a year of his time. Ironically by 1934 the octane number of commercial petrol had been so far improved that high compression ratios, only possible with overhead valves, could be used. The side-valve engine, even with the turbulent head, was eclipsed. Merely because Ricardo's business survived it would be rash to assume that the optimum volume of research was undertaken by the British industry. The fragmented structure discouraged industrial research, by holding down the size of the business and thus limiting the private returns, while patent protection for the specialised researcher was uncertain.[22]

2.4 Component makers and industry suppliers

In the supply of components, rather low volumes of vehicle output could be compensated for by vertical separation. As the market for motor vehicles extended, more producers were able to specialise in the production of particular components. By employing these mass-produced parts, assemblers could supply model variety without excessively high costs. About 60 per cent of the production cost of a car in 1938 was bought-out components. One indication of the relative success of the strategy is obtained from British and American productivity comparisons of 1935–7. In assembly American operatives produced five times as much as the British. But in components, the difference was similar to the British national manufacturing average, at one half the American level.[23] By specialisation and vertical separation the British industry had overcome some of the disadvantages of a smaller market. Vertical separation was not without disadvantages though. Manufacturers were vulnerable to unnecessarily high prices from suppliers, and perhaps also the reverse was true. If the scale of output in relation to costs permitted, integration was preferred, as when Morris bought SU Carburettors in 1926.

Among the largest component manufacturers was the Birmingham company, Lucas, which entered the industry in 1902. The outbreak of the First World War exposed British dependence upon German magnetos. Lucas acquired Bosch's British assets and so gained a strong market position which it reinforced by buying competitors or reaching agreements with them. As a Morris supplier, their motor industry sales of electrical equipment soared in the first half of the 1920s. By acquiring competitors C. A. Vandervell and Rotax in 1926, Lucas became suppliers to the other high-volume British car producer, Austin. An agreement with the German company Bosch five years later excluded them from direct access to the British market but allowed Lucas to use Bosch technical know-how through the joint ownership by the two firms of CAV. At the same time, the American company Autolite was paid to stay out of Britain and induced to supply Lucas with expertise. Lucas acquired all the shares in CAV in 1937.[24] Lucas's dominance was thus achieved or permitted by quasi-political action, as much as by internal efficiency. The full benefits to the industry from this vertically separated industrial structure were therefore unlikely to have been forthcoming.

The tyremakers Dunlop also grew rapidly with the motor industry. Originally they had supplied the cycle industry with a product based on the 1888 patent of a Belfast vet, John Boyd Dunlop. During the First World War, the company developed a new textile which, when coated with rubber, would make a pneumatic tyre capable of carrying heavy loads and thus suitable for motor vehicles. They were less able to exclude foreign competition than Lucas and when tariff protection was extended to tyres in 1926, Goodyear and Firestone from the United States, Michelin from France and Pirelli from Italy established British plants.[25] These new entrants suggest that production economies of scale in tyres were exhausted at lower proportions of industry demand than in more complex electrical equipment.

Replacement of wood and fabric bodies by pressed steel required very substantial capital investment in new plant. If that could be shared among motor manufacturers, they could limit the cost disadvantage from small annual output volumes. As a result of visiting the United States in 1925 to study all-steel body-pressing techniques, Morris formed in 1926 a joint company, Pressed Steel, to utilise the American Budd know-how. A 99-year contract with Edward G. Budd Manufacturing Company of Philadelphia conferred an exclusive licence for the necessary patents. Until 1929, Morris was Pressed Steel's only customer, but from 1930 he severed connections and other manufacturers felt able to become buyers. Utilisation of scale economies pulled industry organisation towards vertical separation. The desire for security of supply or market, together with the interest of both body makers and car manufacturers in avoiding being exploited once they had committed themselves to a relationship, impelled the industry towards vertical integration. The compromise was in the form of the contractual relationship between the businesses. Rover was obliged to buy the dies for pressing Rover bodies at Pressed Steel during the 1930s. That reduced Pressed Steel's commitment to Rover, and to the extent that Rover could recover their dies, Rover was free to take their business elsewhere if contract terms became adverse.[26]

In the supply of safety glass, a similar nervousness about sharing components with competitors was apparent as with steel bodies. There was always the possibility that a rival company could monopolise the upstream activity and impose a cost disadvantage on other component users. Triplex, working a French patent of 1909, began operations in Britain just before the First World War. Austin's decision in 1927 to fit Triplex safety glass windscreens allowed the company to build another factory. Morris, concerned about the special terms Austin had negotiated with Triplex, acquired a controlling shareholding in the company and took his first batch of safety glass at a price so low that Triplex made a loss. During the 1930s, Morris began selling his Triplex shares, persuaded by experience that his glass supplies were secure and his purchase prices reasonable.[27] Triplex, for its part, was made aware of the need to be sensitive to all its large customers, who could exercise various forms of countervailing power.

Not all motor industry suppliers were exclusively devoted to motor manufacturing and therefore were as vulnerable to pressure as Triplex. Steel companies regarded the industry as rather marginal to their concerns but steel was vital to car makers, who watched steel prices carefully. Austin even threatened to set up his own steel company when he believed he was being expoited by the steel cartel. Steel prices paid by Ford UK were 50–70 per cent higher than those of the parent company at Dearborn. Part of the price differential may have been due to the price rings, the SMMT suggested 15 per cent. Having allowed for this there still remained a substantial divergence between American and British input prices (not only in steel but in glass and imitation leather as well).

To gain some idea of the importance of material prices in the overall price of a car, the SMMT supposed that they could be reduced by 15 per cent. Then, assuming the weight of a typical car to be one ton and the cost of production 14.3 pence per lb, the total cost of the car would be £133 and the retail price £200. If 65 per cent of the factory value were available at a 15 per cent lower cost factory cost would reduce by about £13 and retail price by £20, an extremely significant amount in the popular car range.

Because of government encouragement to the formation of the steel cartel, at the end of the 1930s the Board of Trade investigated the allegation that high steel prices were adversely affecting the British motor industry. Attention was given both to the efficiency of the steel industry and its effects on the motor industry. The conclusion that emerged broadly confirmed the SMMT's case about steel prices and their effects on car prices.[28] But the motor industry's concerns were not adequately addressed by the time war broke out. Physical shortages of steel rather than high prices dominated the following decade.

2.5 Retailing and corporate finance

Motor industry 'downstream' relations were generally more favourable to the manufacturers because dealers tended to be so much smaller. Repair and maintenance became more closely linked with retailing through after sales service and was a major source of employment. Manufacturers aimed both to expand the number of outlets selling their vehicles and to increase their control over them. Their products' reputation depended upon adequate repair and maintenance facilities, while the margins available to finace these activities required that dealers should not cut prices unilaterally. Why, then, did manufacturers not integrate forward and take full ownership of retailers? The answer seems to be that they could achieve the same result at a lower cost through annual dealers' agreements. These specified the retail prices to be charged, the trade discounts allowed, the dealer's territory and the spares and services which should be available. The British Motor Trade Association (dominated by manufacturers) was concerned with the administration and enforcement of these price policies (through a 'stop list'). It was particularly anxious to control the allowances on traded-in cars – potentially an easy way of avoiding their retail price maintenance. By 1938, the annual turnover of the second-hand market reached around 700,000 per annum, twice the volume of new sales.

Exclusive dealerships were unusual at the beginning of the inter-war period. The very individual nature of each vehicle type prevented much direct competition between them and therefore reduced the scope for dealer opportunism. Ford, in 1919, decided the time had come to modernise retailing practice. In August, 1,000 Ford agents were dismissed and replaced by exclusive dealers. Over the next two years Ford allowed dealers to compete anywhere in Britain, inevitably driving down prices. Retailers felt they were required to take stock that could not be sold or on which they would make losses. Their dissatisfaction, as they turned to competitor vehicles, contributed to Ford's declining market share.[29]

Another indication that dealers were not always pawns in the hands of manufacturers was the history of the Rootes brother, who ran the largest motor agents business in Britain during the 1920s. They acquired the coach-builders, Thrupp and Maberley, and in 1929 bought the Coventry companies Humber and Hillman, becoming one of the 'Big Six' of the 1930s.

Overseas, British motor sales offices failed to transform themselves into lasting production bases, in contrast to the American companies, but like the French. Morris at first hired overseas distributors but they were not directly controlled by Morris Motors. In order to increase French sales Morris formed the Société des Automobiles Morris in Paris in 1924, the same year that he established an export department at Cowley. He went on to buy Leon Bollée at Le Mans also in 1924, but he withdrew in 1931 during the world depression. Morris's more successful Australian sales branch was founded in 1927. The much smaller Rover company failed in its ill-timed attempt to establish production in New Zealand in 1931. Austin seemed to have found a more workable formula when he licensed production of the Austin Seven in France, Germany, Japan and the United States. In this way Austin's product passed under foreign tariff barriers but did not require control and supervision by Austin management. As long as the fee was adequate and the quality of the product was not allowed to deteriorate, and so besmirch the Austin reputation, the arrangement was satisfactory to licensor and licensee, for Austin was only selling the right to a product. Unlike Ford and General Motors, Austin's modest success did not depend upon continually evolving unique knowledge of production tehniques that was virtually impossible to license.

As important to most producers as maintaining the goodwill of customers and dealers was satisfying shareholders, for that determined the availability of new, external sources of finance. Ability to keep shareholders happy depended on profitability and dividend

policy. Consistent with increased competition for a more standardised product, the rate of return on motor industry equity was
lower between 1921 and 1938 than between 1905 and 1914, slightly
less than the British average and far below that for American
motors (which had earned enormous profits in the first half of the
1920s). Ford UK recorded a low rate of return of less than 10 per
cent during the 1930s, Vauxhall appeared to be singularly profitable
among the larger companies, with returns above 20 per cent, and
Austin, Morris, Humber and Standard lay between the two
American companies. External financing became less important
between 1919 and 1932, possibly because it was less necessary in the
more concentrated industry, with bigger firms that were perceived
as better risks by the capital market.

Determined to avoid drawing on the capital market and so losing
absolute control, Morris before 1930 retained about 90 per cent of
after-tax profits. But Austin, already in the hands of his bankers,
paid out 65.1 per cent between 1922 and 1939 and Rover paid 59 per
cent during the early 1920s. Morris's policy changed after 1930.
Between that year and 1951 his retention ratio averaged only 34 per
cent.[30] The abandoned Morris super tax case, in which Morris was
charged with evading tax by retaining profits, underlined the
favourable tax treatment of retentions rather than dividends. That
implied ploughed-back profits were a cheaper form of investment
funds than could be obtained from the capital market. Financial
decisions that favoured low retention ratios were likely to constrain
growth and investment, other things being equal.

2.6 Industrial relations

Rapid expansion of motor industry production, even though linked
with substantial advances in labour productivity, required a growing
labour force. However employment was unstable because of the
seasonal demand for cars that transmitted instability. Probably lack
of job security was exacerbated by the 'linked spell' rule for receipt
of unemployment benefit. Employers must have been tempted to
lay off workers for a few days each week when demand was slack, as
a way of cutting wages, knowing those laid off could draw unemployment benefit and would therefore be unlikely immediately to
take another job. Car worker George Mason, was sent home

on 21 days out of the 47 he worked between 20 February and 14 July 1933. He signed on at the Labour Exchange 28 times during those 21 weeks, at Cowley. Pressed Steel employees sometimes worked three days, on a schedule of 300 chassis for instance, and when that was finished then spent three days on the dole, signing on for Thursday, Friday and Saturday.

A corollary of the strong growth in the motor output was high wages. Average earnings of skilled and unskilled workers reached £4 a week in 1927 and exceeded that in the mid 1930s at a time when a middle class income was about £250 per annum. In marked contrast to the Ford style, these high wages were not earned from time rates and a pace of work set by the production line. Piece rates or group bonuses remained the norm in British firms and eventually Ford was forced to modify its British strategy. Some years after wage cuts in 1932, Ford brought in pension schemes, paid holidays and rising wages in part, no doubt, to forestall union activity, to which the company remained implacably opposed. Standard and Morris introduced profit-sharing schemes.[31]

High wages were not earned easily though. Harry Wardley joined the American managed Pressed Steel at the age of fifteen in 1936. On his first day he earned 25 per cent more than he received for one week's work at his former job at the Univesity Press. The day was spent in the chassis shop, carring red hot rivets from the furnace with tongs to the chassis, paid on piece rates. Stripped to the waist because of the heat, his eyelashes and eyebrows were burned off and his hair singed. The smoke and noise beggared description. Ford workers of the 1920s were subject to other hazards as well. New employees were visited by the company welfare man to check that their home life conformed with Mr Ford's ideals. No less radical in the British environment was Ford's 1926 cutback of the working week form 48 hours to 40 without cutting wages. Productivity rose substantially.

Unionisation naturally proved difficult under these circumstances and there was little infringement of motor manufacturers' rights to manage. Union strategies compounded union difficulties. The Workers' Union, so influential in Coventry just before the First World War, lost 90 per cent of its membership in the 1920s because of the postwar slump and financial mismanagement. The Amalgamated Engineering Union (AEU), defeated in a lock-out in 1922, insisted on fining members who returned to work early and so lost 80 per cent of them between 1920 and 1925. Unlike the AEU, the National Union of Vehicle Builders (NUVB), formed in 1919, did not oppose piecework, but it did, like the AEU, restrict itself to craftsmen. Until the depression and changes in technology and demand, it proved quite successful, becoming the largest union in Coventry in the late 1920s.

Some 65–70 per cent of workers were semi-skilled or unskilled by 1937. Steel bodies and spray painting reduced skilled employment. The large-scale car makers virtually abandoned apprenticeships as a form of training. The Transport and General Workers' Union (TGWU) entering the industry in 1929, and taking over the remaining Workers' Union membership, was especially appropriate for such a workforce. Nominally, it pursued a more open membership strategy than the AEU or NUVB, but its conservatism rendered it rather uninfluential. As a consequence, even as late as 1936, the light car industry remained almost completely free of trade unions. The average motor car worker believed in individualism and the survival of the fittest, a contemporary remarked. Trade unionists, who would have held different views, were not allowed to work for the largest firm, Morris, because the firm had been blacklisted by the union. In any case, Morris held such a strong position that in 1935 he could tell the Labour Exchanges not to send him any more men for South Wales because these formed the majority of the strike committees. Fewer than 10 per cent of semi-skilled and unskilled workers were unionised before 1940 and trade unions lacked authority in their dealings with management. By the end of the 1930s the AEU and NUVB, which had traditionally restricted themselves to skilled craftsmen, were trying to improve their bargaining power by extending membership beyond the machine and body shops, and were coming into competition with the TGWU.

Ford, Vauxhall, Morris at Cowley, Briggs Bodies, Kelsey Hayes Wheel Company were all outside the Engineering Employers' Federation and all refused to recognise trade unions. Other, more unionised, motor firms were not wholly free of sizeable stoppages. Austin suffered two big strikes over wage reductions in 1929, one of them involving 11,000 men and Pressed Steel experienced six, averaging 6,000 striker days, between 1934 and 1938.[32]

Of all the local labour markets in the interwar years, Oxford's was most transformed by the industry, with 30 per cent of Oxford workers being found in the motor vehicle industry alone, by 1939. Many of these industrial employees were drawn from local agriculture in the 1920s. Surprisingly, such labour was more prone to join unions than town workers. Nonetheless, unionisation in the Oxford motor industry remained weak until after the upturn of he economy in the 1930s. By contrast the long-established Oxford printers showed a higher union density than the national average throughout the period.

Workers migrating from outside the Oxford area created an industrial problem for Pressed Steel during the 1930s, although wages and working conditions also contributed to difficult relations. The TGWU could not persuade its stewards to follow the disputes procedure and, allowing the chief stewards access to top management, in 1937, failed to reduce disputes. Pressed Steel, rather than Morris with its fringe benefits and profit-sharing scheme of 1936, was the harbinger of the industry after 1945.[33]

Differential labour resistance might possibly explain the interwar success of Oxford motor industry compared with that of Coventry. Before 1914, much of the motor industry was located in Coventry, yet between the world wars, none of the major products were made there. The longer established labour tradition of Coventry may have reduced the control of work organisation and pace within the discretion of management, thereby raising costs and constraining expansion. Coventry experienced a greater militancy among car workers than elsewhere during the General Strike, whereas Morris's two factories at Oxford continued working. They were typical of the volume producer's plants between the wars where the management's 'right to manage' was disputed only rarely. Management and entrepreneurship were therefore less constrained than after 1945. However, no less plausible explanations are to be found in overcrowding of traditional sites and the inability to expand from them sufficiently for the needs of volume production. The de-skilling of work due to the introduction of new (often American) machinery also reduced the reliance of manufacturers on traditional centres of labour expertise.

2.7 Conclusion

The principal achievement of the motor industry was that, on the basis largely of domestic technology and skills, by the outbreak of the Second World War, the motor vehicle had permeated British society. The low horsepower, fuel efficient car brought motoring to two million private owners or more. Commercial motor vehicles on the road rose from 6,200 to over half a million between 1919 and 1939.

At the beginning of the interwar years, before this process had gathered momentum, a large number of small enterprises competed with a dominant assembler, Ford. Scale economies and Ford's management failure ensured that by 1929 two domestic manufacturers dominated the light motor vehicle market. World conditions and the policy of Ford and General Motors, helped by the entry of a retailer, Rootes, transformed the dominant duopoly into a much more atomised structure, a decade later. Moreover, the American companies possessed the financial resources to survive despite mistakes, unlike the smaller British firms which inevitably experienced periods of bad luck or poor management. The lower market shares of the leading British companies limited their ability to utilise special machinery and cut costs through volume production. Specialisation by component makers, such as Lucas, went some way to offset the handicap of a smaller market, but was a mixed blessing. Manufacturers' fears of exploitation (particularly Morris's) by suppliers, including Triplex and Pressed Steel, on whom they were dependent, made inter-company relations highly sensitive. Relations with retailers could also be badly handled, as Ford amply demonstrated in the early 1920s.

There were periods in the 1930s of managerial weakness at Morris and Austin, although not so long-lasting as at Fords in the previous decade. One consequence was the production of a large number of models and inadequate standardisation. But the professionally managed American companies did not by any means dominate the British firms, although they gained a hold on the market in the 1930s. Therefore, the differential of average competence between the two groups cannot have been great, and model variety was more a reflection of market demand characteristics than supply side failures. The failure of motor vehicles, as a new industry, to make more of an impact upon interwar employment and unemployment must be seen in this light. What role there was for state industrial policy, as against macro-economic policy, to expand the industry further, is considered in the next chapter.

Employment did grow and wages were high, forestalling unionisation. Where wages were lower and conditions poorer, at Pressed Steel, labour militancy took hold. But in most plants, workers more closely approximated the American ideal than did management. At the same time, paternalism persisted. Austin, Morris and other industry leaders took pride in recognising their longest serving employees on the factory floor.

CHAPTER THREE

FORMATIVE INFLUENCES: CONSUMER DEMAND AND GOVERNMENT POLICY, 1920–1945

Both government policy and more fundamental traits of the British economy shaped the growth of the motor industry between the world wars. Low productivity and incomes throughout the economy constrained demand relative to that faced by American manufacturers. On the other hand, compared with continental Europe, the 1930s were rather prosperous in Britain and the home demand for motor vehicles was accordingly buoyant. Motor vehicle taxation and road expenditures were no less decisive in moulding the industry. The horsepower tax, the petrol tax and the import tariff not only depressed spending but diverted it. Road quality and safety legislation could similarly channel product demand, as well as influencing the benefits society gained from this by now extraordinarily pervasive industry. Like most other concerns of society, warfare was transformed by the motor vehicle. The motor industry played a central, and controversial, role in supplying the armed forces between 1939 and 1945. In that mode also, demand was critical. State intervention during the war years, and afterwards, continued to shape the industry.

Section 1 describes the peculiarities of interwar demand; Section 2 discusses the impact of the horsepower tax; Section 3 considers the role of the protective tariff; and Section 4 assesses official industry rationalisation attempts. In Section 5 a simple measure of the importance of the industry to the economy in the mid 1930s is offered; Section 6 looks at the contribution of government policy to the industry through road expenditures and road safety measures and the seventh section reappraises the military contribution of the industry.

3.1 Determinants of demand

Demand for the industry's products originated from two distinct sources, businesses and households. At the beginning of the 1920s, the two types of customer wants were sometimes met by the one vehicle, the Model T Ford, as in the United States, but petrol prices, taxation and road conditions were increasingly unfavourable to this development, as was the different social structure of Britain. By the end of the 1930s, one estimate of business purchases was 25 per cent of the total demand; another was as high as 40 per cent.[1] Shorter distances and lower incomes in the British market also meant that the motorcycle was a close substitute for a private car. Well-developed financial institutions encouraged the spread of the motor vehicle by rapidly diffusing hire purchase agreements. As the car became more durable and utilitarian, a stock accumulated that was traded in the second-hand market. This market increased the liquidity of new cars and so encouraged demand, although the industry was prone to focus on the substitute that the second-hand vehicle provided for the new.

During the war, demand was restricted by moral suasion, taxation and rationing of petrol, while the supply of vehicles to the civilian economy was gradually virtually eliminated. The end of the war released pent-up demand. By 1919, there was a 'famine for cars' in which price ceased to be a consideration. As the postwar boom began, supply restrictions on the British industry allowed imports to become the main source of satisfying home demand. During 1920, 24,000 cars came into the country, while 46,000 Model T Fords were sold.[2]

Had petrol maintained the same relation to other prices as in 1898, the 1920 cost of a gallon would have been under two shillings instead of 3s 8½d. This inflation was blamed on foreign oil magnates. It was a sign of the intensity of the concern and the radical spirit of the age that the industry's journal, the *Motor Trader*, could suggest that nationalisation of oil was a possible means of bringing down the prices. Despite high petrol prices, demand for cars far exceeded supply; in some parts of the country there were seven to eight months' waiting times for deliveries, with the consequence that second-hand prices were often above the manufacturers' quoted new price.[3]

The demand for cars collapsed as rapidly as it had expanded. By June 1920, there was talk of demand returning to normal and by November, of how to beat the slump. In his budget speech of 1920, the Chancellor announced that a new horsepower tax would be introduced to replace the old tax based on a lower rate and the wartime petrol tax would be abolished. By 1922, the industry was claiming that this horsepower tax had killed the second-hand market for any cars over 10 hp and that it was having a disastrous effect on new vehicle sales. Nevertheless, car sales rose between 1921 and 1922 although they probably fell between 1920 and 1921.[4]

The term motor car subsequently developed the connotation of private motor car, but in this period it applied both to private and commercial motor vehicles. Thus, the official trade statistics distinguished between touring motor cars and commercial motor car. When, in 1926, the question of whether to extend tariff protection to commercial vehicles was raised, the two categories could only be distinguished by the use to which they were put.[5] The versatility of the Ford Model T played a large part in this intermingling of categories; a commercial vehicle body could be lifted off on Saturday evening and replaced by a touring body ready for the Sunday drive to church.[6] Advertisements were carried in a motoring journal for chassis lengthening kits to add to the carrying capacity of the Model T.

The majority of vehicles, however, served a single purpose and therefore the release of an estimated 60,000 army surplus trucks on to the second-hand markets, by 1924, exercised a depressing effect primarily on those manufacturers specialising in heavy commercial vehicles.[7] The silver lining was that commercial vehicles beame so widely used that practically every large industrial firm in Britain owned a fleet of lorries. A further boost to the market came from the War Office which gave a subsidy to 30 and 15 cwt lorries fulfilling its specifications. Road hauliers competed very strongly with the railways for freight business, while in passenger services there were around 30,000 buses operating and 60,000 taxis by 1927. Sales fell with the decline in national income 1929–31, but by less than 10 per cent in each year. It was the persistence of the decline for two years that made the depression severe. Even so, 1931 new private car purchases were only 13 per cent below 1929 levels.

Assistance for small car producers came from the demand of former motorcyclists. Registration of motorcycles in 1929 reached their highest level for the interwar period, despite a rise in income of 15 per cent in the 1930s compared to 5 per cent in the 1920s.

Car prices continued to fall between 1929 and 1933 by about one-third – largely as a result of the sales of the baby cars – while motorcycle prices fell by only one-ninth. Compulsory third-party insurance, introduced in 1930, was a blow to motorcycle sales. Way back in 1924, a comparison of the light car and the motorcycle and side-car had shown that an 11.9 hp car valued at £325 cost 2.29 pence per mile while a 4 hp motorcycle and side-car value £135 cost 1.36 pence per mile. Even then, the falling costs and the greater convenience of the light car were expected soon to bite into the side-car market and eliminate it. But, like the car, the motorcycle remained beyond the working man's income or aspiration in the 1930s, by and large, as their sales bear witness. Instead, the middle-class motorcyclist of the 1920s now travelled by car.[8]

Heavy motor vehicle sales were not encouraged by the spate of Road Traffic Acts. Entry was restricted into the bus industry in 1930 so new bus sales were ultimately constrained, though they were boosted immediately before the Act by the belief that existing operators would have their routes confirmed. The 1933 Act restricted entry to road haulage with a licensing system, increased commercial vehicle taxation and speed enforcement. Truck registrations declined after 1934. Restrictions of one part of the transport system stimulated development in another; the net effect was probably to encourage the growth of private ownership and operation of transport – to reduce the division of labour. While expenditure on passenger transport, and the division between road and rail, showed little change between 1931 and 1934, bicycle and car use increased.

After 1933, prices stopped falling as the boom got under way. Annual private car sales more than doubled between 1932 and 1937, but by 1936, it was clear that the boom was losing its strength. This was the period of the proliferation of models by the remaining manufacturers. The SMMT, in admittedly special pleading, suggested a 15 per cent price cut might double small car sales. For individual manufacturers, the issue was how competitors would react to a price cut. But if the SMMT's estimate of the price elasticity was correct, even a matched price reduction would radically expand sales and create possibilities for lowering unit costs. A car could cost nearly as much as a semi-detached house in a provincial town (£300–£500). But annual running costs (including taxation and insurance) could be as important for extending the market as price. By the end of the 1930s for a small, 8 hp car, they amounted to well over one-third of the purchase price when new. The cut in the horsepower tax in 1935, and lower petrol prices therefore both contributed to widening the market.

Regional demand was not as concentrated in London and the South East as many interwar accounts of depressed 'Outer Britain' might be taken to imply, though the distinction between regions where income was generated and where it was spent, is apparent (Table 3.1). The combined total of new goods vehicles registered in Yorkshire and Lancashire in the year ending September 1936 exceeded those registered in London and Middlesex. The south was more dominant in new private car registrations, but London alone accounted for less than Lancashire and Yorkshire combined.

Table 3.1: British motor vehicle registrations, 1936 (selected counties)

| | Registrations year and September (%) | |
	New English goods vehicles	Private cars
London	14.6	17.5
Middlesex	5.1	6.2
Lancashire	11.3	9.7
Yorkshire	10.0	8.9
Warwickshire	4.9	6.7

Source: SMMT, The Motor Industry of Great Britain, 1936.

Hire purchase

Perhaps 50–60 per cent of all new car sales were made by instalment purchases at the end of the 1920s. In London and some other large cities, 60–65 per cent of all passenger cars were sold in this way (the American figure for 1929 was variously estimated between 44 per cent and 75 per cent). The Morris company financed its own sales, as did some of the big London dealers, but most of the business was handled by half a dozen finance companies in London. The American influence was apparent in this sector. Continental

Guaranty of America established a British subsidiary in 1919, the United Dominions Trust, to extend the success of American schemes to Britain. The usual terms were 25 per cent down with 12–18 monthly payments, or even spread over two years (which was long by American standards, where 12 months was the norm in the mid 1920s, rising to 18 months by the mid 1930s). Credit was easy and moral hazard low in comparison with more fluid American society. In 1927 two large dealers in London agreed to delivery cars on the payment of the first of 12 monthly instalments, 5 per cent being added for credit accommodation, or if a 10 per cent cash deposit was paid the balance, plus 7.5 per cent, could be paid in equal instalments for 18 months. If payment in full was completed before the end of the specified period, the whole of the interest chargeable on the remaining instalments could be repaid to the purchaser.

During the later 1930s, sales on hire purchase had become even more widespread than in the 1920s. Perhaps 65–70 per cent of all cars, except the most expensive, were bought on hire purchase and 70–80 per cent of the motorcycles. A high proportion of these were bought for trade purposes. The annual value of new motor vehicle hire purchase was about £30 million, and in second-hand vehicles where turnover was in the region of £20 million, hire purchase contracts were worth perhaps £15 million. So, about £45 million of the £120 million of annual hire purchase contracts were for motor vehicles. Motor business was more reliable than other types with only about 1.5 per cent of turnover written off.[9]

Export demand

These efforts to extend the home market were more successful than attempts to stimulate foreign sales during the 1920s. Foreign demand for British motor vehicles accounted for about one-third of British production before the First World War, largely from countries without motor manufacturing industries themselves. The industrialised countries took care to ensure that prohibitive tariff rates excluded British vehicles. Even the American industry felt sufficiently insecure to retain a 45 per cent tariff. After 1914, while the European industrialised nations spent their economic strength destructively, the United States spread its influence into foreign markets for motor vehicles previously dominated by Britain and France, and the American motor industry's production grew at an astonishing rate, with unit costs falling accordingly. The process had begun before the war and would have continued without it, but European hostilities undoubtedly accelerated American influence in third country markets, especially for motor vehicles. Much less important as an explanation for the immediate postwar lower British exports, was the shift in the terms of trade against the primary producers who constituted these third country markets.

Despite the disruption of international trade with tariffs, quotas and prohibitions during the 1930s, British motor vehicle exports reached new peaks, because of the greater suitability of the distinctive small car to the changed economic environment. Imports collapsed, yielding a strong positive motor industry balance of trade (Figure 3.1). The Ottawa Agreement of 1932, establishing for the first time mutual Commonwealth trade preferences, may have helped, since the principal British motor markets were Australia and New Zealand. But if Commonwealth preference had been a sufficient condition for export success, British motor vehicles would have made some progress in Canada, which they did not. In 1936, 80 per cent of motor vehicles' exports by volume went to Empire countries. Ten years earlier the percentage had been 90 per cent. If ability to sell outside the Empire, even in a world dogged by unemployment and divided into trade blocs, is the criterion of competitiveness, then that of the British industry was improving.[10] Export demand, though, could hardly be expected to compare in magnitude with spending by domestic buyers.

3.2 The impact of the horsepower tax

The industry naturally designed models primarily for the closer and more secure home market, where the weight of taxation, among other influences, required vehicles less suitable for the regions of recent European settlement such as Australia and the mid United States. The other side of the coin was that the horsepower tax protected the British market from American competition by encouraging the development of long-stroke engines which paid less tax than comparable American engines of similar capacities, but approximately equal bore and stroke. The long-stroke engine had been developed and was widely used in Europe before 1914. Then, however, cars with larger engines were also made. By 1926 the same bore/stroke ratios were used but large engines were rare because of the weight rather than the form of taxation. This reduced sales volume, raised price and excluded British cars, because of their small size, from import and export markets.[11]

Figure 3.1 British motor vehicle imports and home production, 1922–1938

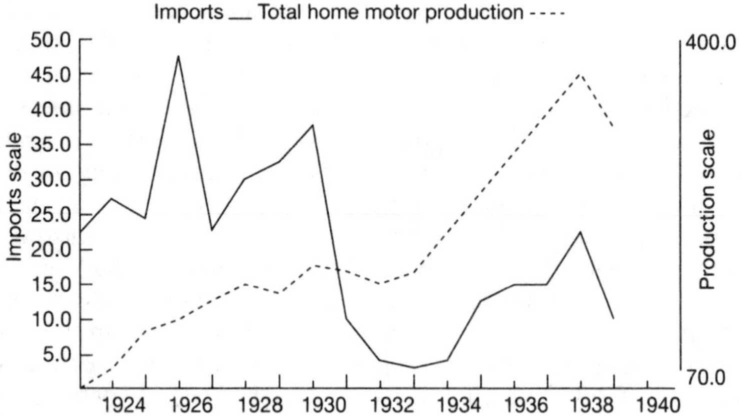

Source: Derived from data from SMMT, *The Motor Industry of Great Britain*, selected years.

The discriminatory effect of the 1920 horsepower tax is the extent to which the demand for British cars would have contracted if the tax were abolished and replaced by an alternative tax that depressed equally the demands for imported and home-produced vehicles. Such a tax would have made little difference to the size of the toral demand but would have altered the shares of the market. The fall in British produced sales, as imported car sales rose, would be an indication of the distortion introduced by the horsepower tax.

One particular change in the tax rate offers a useful opportunity to isolate the importance of the tax in encouraging the demand for British, rather than American, cars. In the budget of 17 April 1934, the tax was reduced from £1 per hp to 15s per hp. The stated intention was to encourage home production so the greater utilisation of scale economies would permit the expansion of exports. The new duty rates came into force on 1 January 1935. Immediately after the announcement of the forthcoming tax change, imports of private cars from the United States rose substantially.

The number of cars brought into the country during the first three months of 1935 after the tax change, was 347 per cent higher than in the first three months of 1934. A similar proportionate increase is found by comparing the numbers imported in the last three months of 1934 with the last three months of 1933, 327 per cent. These increases cannot have been a response to changes in the relative prices of American and British cars, for they hardly changed. Nor are exchange rate movements 1934–5 likely to have much encouraged imports. The average dollar-sterling rate rose between 1933 and 1934 and fell only 1 per cent in the following year. It therefore seems reasonable to ascribe most of the increase in imports 1934–5 either to the same forces as were increasing the demand for home produced cars, such as increased consumer spending, or to the change in tax regulations.

Registration of new cars between 1933 and 1934 rose 23.8 per cent and between 1934 and 1935, 21.9 per cent. Some of this increase will have been due to greater sales of large British cars as a result of the tax change, and some due to increased imports. Therefore, the rise in new registrations is a slight over-estimate of the expansion of demand for small British cars. Sales could be expected to rise after the tax change had been announced, but before it came into force, because the tax payment was an annual obligation. Users in 1934 would benefit from the 1935 reductions, either through a higher resale car price or through lower future running costs.

The conclusion is that if the rise in consumer income and other factors increasing the total demand for cars acted on British cars and imported cars equally, imports would have risen little more than 22 per cent if the tax regulations had not changed, whereas in fact they rose 347 per cent. The 25 per cent tax reduction was responsible for a 300 per cent increase in American imports relative to home produced car sales. This in turn might suggest, by extrapolating the relationship, that the complete removal of the tax may have led to a 1200 per cent increase in the ratio of imports to home-produced cars in total, or a 900 per cent increase on the 1935 ratio.

Because of the extremely close connections between the United States and Canadian motor industries, it is appropriate to consider their joint British imports in 1935 as being responsive to horsepower tax changes, although monthly car import figures are not available for Canadian cars only. American and Canadian 1935 imports amounted to 4 per cent of 1935 home-produced cars sold on the home market. The inference appears to be that the complete removal of the horsepower tax may have raised this ratio to (4 per cent × 900 per cent =) 36 per cent. This rough and ready conclusion, that without the horsepower tax the ratio of North American cars sold to the home product would have exceeded one-third, is almost certainly an overstatement, for it neglects the stock adjustment effect of demand. The short run, flow, response to a change is greater than the long run. But even dividing the first approximation to the protective effect of the tax by say four to allow for stock adjustment suggests the impact was not negligible, especially when combined the lower unit costs that a greater output permitted. On top of that there was also the protection afforded by the tariff.

3.3 Tariff protection

Soon after the outbreak of war, British motor-industry production was severely curtailed while demand was not, with the result that imports of touring cars alone more than doubled between the first and the second years of the war. In 1915 the McKenna Duties, including a 33.3 per cent *ad valorem* tariff on motor cars and parts imported into Britain were imposed in order to save shipping space.

Before the war had ended, British motor manufacturers were agreed on the necessity for a tariff to protect them from American competition for at least five years after hostilities ceased. The McKenna Duties were duly maintained but with the different justification that they were a tax on a luxury to provide much-needed revenue. Why a luxury tax should discriminate between home produced and imported luxuries was never satisfactorily explained. Commercial vehicle producers also asked for protection. This, the President of the Board of Trade denied them for, he said, they were already excessively protected because of the position of international trade in their industry. In the case of private cars, the minister claimed there was an additional protection of 54.6 per cent arising from freight and packing charges, insurance, and depreciation of the exchange rate, bringing the total 'effective' protection to 88 per cent, while in the case of commercial vehicles these factors gave a protection equivalent to 45 per cent duty.[12]

During the early 1920s, under protection, the industry appeared to make up the ground lost during the war very rapidly. By 1924, vehicle and complete chassis output was 155,800 per annum compared with 25,200 in 1912, and Morris, making vehicles designed specifically for the British market surpassed British Ford sales for the first time in that year with 22 per cent of industry production. The same year also saw the repeal of the McKenna Duties by the first minority Labour government. The government argued that the motor industry's proper response to American competition was to develop the cheap car, the production of which may have been discouraged by the tariff. Imports doubled, and home produced sales to the domestic market virtually stagnated. The Labour government was defeated in the election of November 1924 and the duties were reimposed the following year. Accusations of poor performance encouraged by protection of a stronger and more substantial nature than those of the Labour government, appeared as a minority view in the Balfour Committee's 1929 Report, where statistical evidence of an unsatisfactory export achievement was presented. Just before Britain adopted a general protectionist policy in 1931, a committee of economists under the chairmanship of Sir William Beveridge, in their case against the abandonment of free trade, chose the motor industry as an example of the inefficiencies fostered by tariffs. They claimed that there were too many separate manufacturers making an excessive variety of models, precluding any of the advantages of large-scale operations.[13]

If protection reduced the efficiency of the British motor industry between 1913 and 1920, there would be some indication in its export market performance relative to the French. The expansion of British exports compares favourably with the French, suggesting prices were being driven down with the growth of the industry to the greatest extent that might be expected. Despite the decline of the franc against sterling from 54.6 to 75.6 between 1922 and 1923, the number of British motor vehicles exported grew by the same 75 per cent as the French. Similar figures are found for 1923 and 1924; British export volume doubled compared to a 53 per cent increase in French exports, while the franc further depreciated against sterling. The motor exports of both countries were being driven out of many markets which did not grant preferential access by the American industry. Argentina, in 1913, was the fifth most important buyer of French motor vehicles, yet by 1926 only 886 were imported, falling to 70 in 1928, when imports from the United States reached 5,202. British exports to Argentina were falling similarly. In 1913, Argentina had also been the fifth most important buyer by value of the small British exports of complete motor cars, taking 304. By, 1926 only 62 British touring and commercial vehicles were sold and in 1928, 196, together with 22 tractors.

Such evidence is consistent with the hypothesis that there was no tariff-induced decline in the efficiency of the British motor industry relative to the French. It follows that tariff protection, by widening home producers' markets and allowing them to utilise scale economies, must have been beneficial. However, a caveat must be attached. In Britain, American multinational companies attenuated the expansion of domestic production during the 1930s when they adopted models suitable for European conditions, in marked contrast to other motor industries. Elsewhere, Ford and General Motors were either effectively excluded (France, Italy, Japan) or acquired the largest producer (Germany).[14]

3.4 State-sponsored rationalisation

Competition brought a long term decline in the number of firms in the industry, and thus concentrated production, allowing cost reduction. In the 1930 depression, the Labour government felt that this concentration was proceeding neither quickly enough nor in the most rational manner, at least in the heavy motor vehicle section of the industry. It believed government-encouraged 'rationalisation' would have particularly beneficial effects in export markets, a matter of great immediate concern because of the problems with sterling.

There had been a number of earlier attempts to encourage exports by the collective action of manufacturers. An arrangement between Daimler, Armstrong Siddeley, Austin and Wolseley had failed, in 1919, becaue of personal differences. In 1926, through the efforts of Lord Ashfield, Daimler and AEC established a joint seling company but it lasted only two years, again because of 'differences'. Tilling Stevens Motors Ltd had made approaches to

AEC, Guy Motors, Leylands and Thornycroft, without success. Tilling Stevens concentrated on only one type of vehicle, a 32–40 seat passenger bus of which the company made 30 per cent of the total production of the type, of about 2,000. In spite of success in the home market, as a small company it could not sell abroad because it could not afford the expense of an overseas representative with only one model. An agent would prefer to be able to offer a range of vehicles and it could not amalgamate with competitors making different version of the same bus. So, although one model was the right policy for the home market, more had to be considered for exports. One solution would be co-operation at home by mutual agreement to restrict the range offered and produce the model for which the firm was best suited. Tilling Stevens thought it would only require a little 'pressure' to secure a combination of effort in the heavy motor vehicle trade. The 'pressure' suggested by Tilling Stevens was the favouring of the combination in contracts with the government, the railways, bus operating companies and the municipalities. However, the government appeared either to lack the will or the time to apply such pressure.[15]

Guy Motors judged that some reorganisation was inevitable, and merging was propitious in 1930 since there were fewer orders. But there was not much advantage to be had from a co-operative marketing organisation because of the problems of selling competing products and maintaining a stock of many spare parts.

Eventually, from discussions with the Department of Overseas Trade emerged the suggestion that Lord Ashfield of AEC would be the most suitable person to take a lead in the re-organisation. Ashfield wrote back to say that he was not willing to take the formal steps of convening the manufacturers and did not believe this was the best way to proceed. But he 'recognized the importance of exports'. Nothing, therefore, emerged from the government's proposals. Market forces and private institutions were left to determine the number and size of the firms in the industry during the 1930s, and even in the late 1940s, despite further consideration of rationalisation, this time brought about by nationalisation (Chapter 4).

3.5 Impact of the Industry

Though perceived as unnecessarily fragmented, interwar motor vehicles was recognised as a technologically advanced and rapidly growing new industry. Yet closer examination shows it lacked some of the characteristics generally associated with hi-tech sectors. Surprisingly the capital–labour ratio in motor vehicles and net output per employee were not high compared with other manufacturing industries. Nevertheless, motor manufactruring's linkages backwards to oil refining, rubber manufacture and electric batteries, virtually gave birth to a whole family of enterprises. In this respect motor vehicles was the most dynamic of the new industries, such as electrical generation, artificial fibres and domestic electrical appliances, that some have associated with the revitalisation of industrial structure in the 1930s.

To measure their importance, suppose output of all these new industries did not rise after 1930. How much lower then would employment have been across the economy in 1935? According to an input–output model, direct employment would have fallen by 170,000 and total employment would have been cut by more than half a million. When the focus is restricted to manufacturing industry, the most powerful linkages of the motor industry and other 'new' industries were to the old export staples such as, cotton, coal and steel. But motors also linked forward strongly with services. The SMMT estimated that in 1936, whereas some 300,000 worked in manufacture and repair (of cycles and aircraft as well), 'conservatively' 1.27 million earned their livelihood from the manufacture, sale, operation and repair of motor vehicles (compared with a workforce of around 22 million). This substantial figure would have been raised further had employment in the manufacture of materials consumed by the industry been included.[16]

These, perhaps upwards biased, numbers suggest motor transport was coming to dominate interwar activity, almost to the extent that railways had towered over the Edwardian economy. Table 3.2 estimates the work done by the sector. The private car use figures were probably optimistic, whereas closely monitored coach and bus (hackneys over eight seats) passenger miles were reasonably accurate. Road passenger miles carried commercially may well have exceeded those generated by private traffic therefore. But private traffic was much more important to the manufacturing industry. A 'social saving' estimate of motor vehicles in 1935, how much worse off the British economy would have been in that year had the same volume of freight and traffic been carried by traditional alternative means, depends on how much more would have been paid for each ton- or passenger-mile without motor vehicles. The debate on the social savings of railways has shown the problems of assessing what rates would have been charged under the hypothetical alternative transport system, and these cannot be addressed here. Merely as markers, to hint at the plausibility of more or less than one penny a mile reductions, it may be noted that a third class return railway fare for six miles in 1934 worked out at three pence a mile and coal, on 25 mile rail haul, might be charged two pence a mile. For every penny that motor transport cut ton/mile freight rates over horse transport and rail, the social savings of motor vehicles increased by roughly 0.5 per cent of gross national product in 1935 ([6 billion/240]/4.5 billion). For every penny that comparable passenger miles were reduced, social saving rose by 3.5 per cent of gross national product ([42.7 billion/240]/4.5 billion). Railway rates had not fallen substantially since the Edwardian era but other prices and wages had risen. On balance, it seems unlikely that more detailed social savings measures would conclude that the interwar motor industry quite matched the impact of late Victorian railways, even though its weight was considerable.[17]

Table 3.2: Motor vehicle use in Britain, 1935

	Number in use	Est. average mileage	Est. average load		Ton/passenger miles (billions)
Private cars	1,505,019	8,000	2	passengers	24
Hackneys up to 8 seats	40,746	16,000	2	passengers	1.3
Hackneys over 8 seats	46,637	33,100	11.3	passengers	17.4
Goods vehicles	442,187	16,000	17	cwt	6

Source: SMMT, The Motor Industry of Great Britain, 1935.

Without the motor vehicle, railways would have been more prosperous and horse-drawn traffic more pervasive. The pattern of household and job location would have been different too. The 'ribbon developments' of the 1930s housing boom would have been absent and business agglomerations like those along the Great West Road coming out of London would have pressed closer to railway lines.

What gains the motor vehicle conferred on the economy were extremely controversial at the time. The greater cheapness of the road haulier, so the railway interest argued, stemmed from not being required to supply the track. If road transport were correctly costed, taking into account the public resources consumed and the damage to the environment and to life and limb, they maintained the motor vehicle would be far less competitive. By implication, the demand for the motor industry's products would also have been considerably reduced.

3.6 Road expenditures and road safety

These were matters of political controversy because the state provided 'road services' and decided on the charges to be levied for them. The volume and quality of road services supplied strongly influenced British vehicle design; ground clearance, suspension, gearing, engine power, general robustness, all responded to the high quality of British road surfaces compared with those in North America or other regions of recent European settlement. With less road expenditure, road transport would have been less competitive with rail and British motor manufacturers obliged to make stronger, more expensive, products.

Expenditure on the roads ceased during the war. The Treasury appropriated the receipts of the Road Improvement Fund, established under the 1909 Act, leaving road conditions to deteriorate until 1918. The Treasury gave a special grant, in December 1918, towards the reconstruction of roads and bridges. Rising unemployment in autumn 1920 prompted the government to create a special fund for the construction of new arterial roads as well as for the improvement of existing roads. But the receipts from the horsepower and petrol taxes flowed into the Road Fund faster than they could be spent on roads. The Chancellor of the Exchequer, Winston Churchill, therefore diverted some of the Fund for general purpose, and the Treasury set its face against earmarked taxes in the future.

Railway lobbying that gave rise to road traffic regulation gained force from the widespread belief that payment for the roads was unfair. According to the Royal Commission on Transport, the total annual cost of the highways in Britain was £60 million, of which the ratepayer paid two-thirds and the motorist one-third. However, another one-third of the annual cost was paid by users of private cars and cyclists into the Treasury. That ratepayers were obliged to pay so much for the roads reflected the traditional absence of user charges, rather than a fair or efficient distribution of road costs. During the early 1930s, when employment would have benefited from the greater net spending, petrol tax was raised, and the Labour government's road programme was ended, so that road user taxation began to exceed road spending. What was almost certainly a subsidy to road users, which must have raised the demand for motor vehicles, became much less apparent.[18]

The second major public effect on the demand slide, the road accidents resulting from motor vehicle use, were far greater than those caused earlier by railways and horse transport. In 1934, the peak road casualty year before the war, 7,343 people were killed and 231,603 injured. During the 1920s motor vehicle casualties rose faster than the number of vehicles in use, which themselves increased rapidly. The 20 mph speed limit was neither observed nor enforced and so the Road Traffic Act of 1930 abolished it. The Act also licensed bus operators, nominally at least, to eliminate the setting of bus timetables that required excessive speed. Compulsory third party insurance was introduced and insurance companies were required to pay up to £25 to the voluntary hospitals treating accident victims.

Neither the rising trend in road accidents nor the medical costs of treatment were adequately addressed by the 1930 Act.[19] Cyclists killed on the road and the number of private cars registered rose respectively by over 70 per cent (1930–4) and by over 20 per cent (1931–4). Some, but not all, of higher cyclists casualties must be attributable to the abolition of the motor vehicle speed limit. Some must have been due to more cycling.

In 1934 a new Traffic Act therefore introduced a 30 mph limit from March 1935, driving tests for new drivers and small fixed compulsory payment by motorists for medical costs of accident victims regardless of fault. Road deaths began to fall from a peak which was not exceeded until the 1960s. Fatal accidents declined by 15 per cent the following year despite a normal increase in vehicle registrations. The joint effect of the 1930 and 1934 Acts was probably to reduce fatal road accidents by about one-fifth. Nevertheless, deaths soon stablised around 6,500 per annum, a substantial cost of motor vehicles, much greater than incurred from railway operations at their peak, and certainly far more than in most years after 1945. A deliberately understated estimate of accident costs in 1938 was 1.3 per cent of national income.[20] Had society chosen to invest more in safety, the toll could have been reduced earlier. Countries without motor industries, in particular the Scandinavians, were much quicker to introduce effective legislation, most probably because of the lack of industry lobbies. But in the later 1930s British attention was more often turning to defence against foreign, rather than domestic, killers.

3.7 The motor industry at war

When European hostilities broke out again in 1939, the motor vehicle and the aeroplane transformed warfare. Instead of attrition by masses of artillery and infantry, characteristic of the years between 1914 and 1918, success in the Second World War turned on capital-intensive high technology equipment. National industrial capacity, in which the motor industry was a keystone, supplied these essential materials. The 1936 Defence White Paper recognised this new world and enlisted seven motor companies in the 'shadow factory' scheme to make aircraft and components, especially engines.[21] The shadow factories, owned by the government but which the companies were paid to operate, and later, government military contracts, proved to be a Trojan horse for the motor industry's labour relations.

As the motor industry became almost entirely devoted to war production, and car output dwindled, employers were required to recognise terms and conditions agreed between district employers and unions, regardless of whether they recognised unions themselves. Under the Essential Work Order management's ability to hire and fire was limited. Vauxhall established a district negotiating agreement with the AEU and NUVB in 1942. Even Ford signed its first collective agreement, after strikes, at arms length through the Trades Union Congress (TUC) in 1944. The agreement with unions on a Joint Negotiating Committee gave stewards and local officials no role. Shop representatives, at Ford's insistence, did not represent any union. The TUC did not like Communist influence among the stewards and so was happy to cut them out. That meant ultimately that unions lacked direct control over the workforce. In consequence, unlike the American industry union, the UAW, they could not enforce agreements.[22] Under the Coventry toolroom agreement, skilled men were to receive the average of skilled production workers in the district. In the face of rising unskilled pay, the agreement was intended to mollify skilled toolroom workers. It turned out to be a recipe for wage inflation and did little for industrial relations harmony. Days lost through industrial disputes did not fall during the war.[23]

Despite disputes and heavy bombing, the second particularly damaging in Coventry, the motor industry produced almost three-quarters of a million service trucks and cars, 80 per cent heavy lorries. In addition motor manufacturers assembled about 30 per cent of tracked vehicle production. Almost all tracked carriers were made by the industry and all armoured cars. The industry also manufactured 18,000 aircraft and 230,000 aero engines. This record was insufficient to protect the industry's long term reputation though. The (Indian) army had expressed dissatisfaction with Morris products before the war, but Corelli Barnett's influential *Audit of War* has dominated recent opinion. Barnett deployed great rhetorical skill to show that the British motor industry, before and after the Second World War was incompetent. The war demonstrated the deep-seated incapacity of the industry.[24]

> With few exceptions . . . British tanks until late in the war were mechanical abortions that foreshadowed the disastrous car models launched into world markets by the British automobile industry in the post war era . . . the mechanical failings of British tanks were largely the fault of commercial firms incompetent at design, development and manufacture.

Barnett goes on to assert that Nuffield Mechanization (Morris's subsidiary) between 1936 and 1937 was responsible for the botched and overhasty piecemeal development of the cruiser tank. Centaur and Cavalier designs failed to get as far as production, and the Covenanter never fought. The Nuffield turret in the Churchill tank, the responsibility of Vauxhall, suffered from a lack of organisation and planning. 'Technically backward native firms like Morris' made military vehicles that were 'quiet as a pneumatic hammer' and prone to disintegrate at speeds above 45 mph. The motor industry failed to produce a jeep equivalent or a jerrican.

As a technique of persuasion, this piling of example upon example is effective, but for those who aspire to a more objective or scientific understanding of British industrial evolution, it is far from satisfactory. There is little doubt that British military motor products of the Second World War were generally undistinguished. The most successful tracked vehicle developed during the rearmament period was the Bren-gun carrier. The Crusader tanks were revealed as undergunned in North Africa in 1941. Moreover, developed from a campaign in Europe, they were designed on the assumption they would not be far from replacement and repair facilities, which were just not available in the desert. In 1940/1 of the first 1,200 Churchill tanks, nearly 1,000 had to be reworked. Armoured car and scout car development, by AEC, Humber and Daimler, was not spectacular. Not until 1942 did collaboration between Leyland and Rolls-Royce provide a tank engine that generated adequate power, and that suffered from a drawback that the fuel was liable to ignite the tanks into 'tommy-cookers' if hit.

So much for the facts. The explanation is not generalised incompetence in the motor industry, however. It is primarily that the defence of the British Empire was overstretched for the resources that the state was prepared to make available. As a consequence, army re-equipment in the 1930s was dilatory, parsimonious and vacillating. It was confused by the belief that the principal demands on the army would be colonial campaigns. Consequently weapons specifications were pulled in different directions. The long tank design gap after 1918, when interest in the vehicles by the War Office was dropped, was exacerbated by three factors; first the death in a plane crash of Vickers' tank designer Sir John Cardan in 1935; second by the General Staff being unable to agree on the tactical employment of tanks and so failing to issue specifications for armour, armament or performance in 1936 after rearmament had begun; and third, by the War Office's unwillingness to make money available for engine development. Yet another contributor to less than outstanding active service performance of British tanks was that tank transporters were assigned a low priority by the War Office. German desert war successes were made possible by tank transporter and repair units.

Germany relied on commercial design sources which was effective and German private armament firms were more numerous and better equiped. War Office uncertainty or ignorance over specifications transmitted confused signals to British manufacturers. Morris was obliged to use his initiative to compensate for the initial product specification errors of the War Office. On the cruiser tank, official collaborators demanded 10 inch pitch tracks; Nuffield prepared 1.5 inch pitches for when the specified tracks were found unsatisfactory, as he knew they would be. All British tank designers faced the problem that very little development work had been done on tank engines, unlike aircraft. There was no engine available to provide the 350 bhp needed for the Cruiser tank. Nuffield staff remembered the Liberty engine from the First World War and reconstructed a set of drawings from which they developed a modified engine (popular because it was cheap). Vauxhall's work with the Churchill tank is generally rated a success; faulty products in the first batches were caused by the extreme pressure to provide Britain with some tanks to repel the expected invasion, at a time when she possessed virtually none, coupled with lack of experience of tank mass production.

Further evidence that the demand and procurement for tanks and other military vehicles was the root of the problem is improved British motor industry performance after the war. It is true that during the war the industry did not innovate amphibious transport, like the American DUKW or the German Schwimmkübel, nor did they hit upon such a durable all purpose vehicle as the jeep. On the other hand, under the stimulus of the postwar export drive and steel rationing, the best selling Land Rover was designed and manufactured in record time. Moreover, if Britain's late resumption of tank design and manufacture in 1935 handicapped development under war conditions, by the end of hostilities the Vickers Centurion tank began a production run that lasted until the 1960s and proved a major export success as well.[25]

3.8 Conclusion

Small cars and a wide variety of models reflected a predominantly middle class private demand, even without the intervention of government policy. State policy profoundly influenced the industry's development, though in general it was not intended to do so. Taxation discriminated against North American cars, encouraging the domestic industry and the development of special American

CHAPTER FOUR

INDUSTRY STRUCTURE AND SCALE ECONOMIES, 1945–1978

During the 1950s and 1960s motor vehicle production was the foremost British manufacturing industry. Economies of scale dictated that fewer producers with larger plants were making more and more vehicles at lower unit costs. As prosperity increased, motor vehicle ownership spread down the social pyramid, pervading all aspects of everyday life. At the same time, the British economy grew at rates not seen before or since, and manufacturing employed the largest ever proportion of the workforce. Compared with other European countries, performance was mediocre but in these decades the continental economies still generated lower real incomes per head than did Britain.

The rapidity of the rise of the motor industry was later more than matched by a precipitate decline. Relative to other national motor producers from the mid 1960s, and absolutely from 1974, this remarkable contraction has prompted a so far inconclusive search for explanations. One reason for the indecisive nature of the debate about the decline of the motor industry is the nature of the explanations. A common approach is to list all plausible 'factors' – management, industrial relations, under-investment, and, sometimes implicitly, attribute a causal role to each. Here description can masquerade as explanation. Another, more ambitious line is to pick one explanation and show how a selection of evidence is consistent with it. A drawback is that another author may well conduct a similar exercise for a different explanation.

More conclusive approaches to the motor industry's history must recognise that correlation or association does not necessarily imply causation. Not every characteristic of the industry inevitably contributed to the decline. Some aspects of the industry may have been symptoms, others may have been immaterial to long run performance. Small plants, unable to take full advantage of technical economies of scale, may have reflected the greater disruptive impact of industrial disputes in larger units. In that case small plants would be a symptom rather than a cause of lack of competitiveness. High dividend pay-outs may not have caused low investment. Low investment may have been a response to, for example, poor returns on capital which in turn may have followed from under-capacity working as a result of government policy or industrial relations. Alternatively, low returns on capital perhaps stemmed from inadequate investment or failure to rationalise production. An inability to market sufficient successful new models may originate with too little investment in development or research or with an inability to identify market niches. Or poor planning and design and research capabilities may have produced poor models, low sales revenues, profits and investment.

Management can perform a transcendental role in explanations of industrial performance. Management is always responsible in one sense, but an objective assessment must ask whether any body of management, however trained or motivated, including a higher or lower proportion of university graduates, could have been expected to address the particular challenges of the industry. Should the Mini have been sold at a higher price? Was the shift from piece rates to measured day work a mistake? Management is paid to find the right answers to such questions. But suppose the right answer made or would have made little difference? In all cases the ideal is to find a critical test that discriminates between the hypotheses.

Government policies impinging on the industry, on location, taxation, exchange rates, mergers, tariffs and ultimately subsidisation and nationalisation, have all been strongly criticised, sometimes from opposed positions. Some policies were clearly responses to the industry's difficulties, others may have been largely irrelevant. Even when causality is established, it still remains to identify relative and absolute quantitative significance. Almost certainly government use of hire purchase controls was harmful to the industry, but much less certain is that a policy of complete stability of hire purchase terms would have solved a good proportion of the industry's problems.

What is acceptable as an explanation for an industry's performance may depend in part upon what alternatives are considered feasible or desirable. Thus two analysts might agree that the industry would have benefited from more intense competition in the later 1950s, but they might fall out over whether Britain's failure to sign the Treaty of Rome was the explanation for the industry's less than satisfactory performance from the 1960s. That could be because they are at odds over whether Britain would have been allowed to sign, or should have done so, on other grounds. Another might contend that certain attitudes, such as worker dissatisfaction with monotonous, repetitive employment, and industry characteristics, such as a fragmented trade union structure, are inevitable concomitants of early industrialisation and these make large-scale motor vehicle production uncompetitive. In this instance, if demonstrated, the explanation for the decline of the British motor industry is early British industrialisation, a conclusion not especially helpful for those concerned with industrial policy.

To begin untangling these possibilities, this chapter first outlines the chronology of the rise of the industry to the second largest exporter in the world in the mid 1950s, to declining absolute productivity and output through the 1970s (Section 1). Then we set the scene for the analysis with an account of postwar reconstruction during the later 1940s (Section 2). During the postwar years, the motor industry became one of the most highly concentrated industries in the British economy, but also one in which American multinationals came to play an ever increasing role. Section 3 traces the structural evolution of the industry and shows how increased concentration followed from internal growth and merger. Section 4 considers the motivations behind the merger movements of the postwar years and the reasons for their perceived failures. Structural industrial policy was influenced by the belief that 'big was beautiful' – as it apparently was in the United States. Justifying that attitude were views about economies of scale which are therefore considered in Section 5. In short, Chapter 4 attempts to assess how structure and scale influenced the industry.

Chapters 5, 6 and 7 address different aspects of the industry's history between 1945 and 1978. Management should ensure the designing and marketing of a range and quality of models that maintains the competitiveness of their business. Management styles, successes and failures are therefore analysed in Chapter 5. The chapter considers in what sense the industry, or sections of it, were handicapped by poor product development and failure to identify market niches, by under-investment, and by lack of access to EC markets in the years of rapid growth.

Although large-scale production could lower unit costs, it did not necessarily do so. Company organisation and industrial relations broadly defined, needed to adjust to the greater volumes. The industry became a by-word for poor labour relations at a time when Britain's industrial decline was symbolised by the state of motor vehicle manufacture. What truth there is in this opinion forms the subject of Chapter 6. Much of the environment which management was obliged to take as given was influenced by government policy. How that impinged upon the industry between 1945 and 1978 is addressed in Chapter 7.

4.1 The performance of the British motor vehicle industry

The domestic and international economic environment of the motor industry during the long boom after 1945 was wholly different from the interwar years. In the immediate aftermath of war, the balance of payments deficit and the global dollar shortage gave exports top priority.[1] The prospect of an eventual recovery in the home market added to the incentive to produce large volumes of motor vehicles.[2] Foreign demand and perhaps greater state intervention encouraged investment (though more erratically in Britain than in the rest of the industrial world). Unemployment in Britain virtually disappeared. Later, the liberalisation of international trade in a series of GATT (General Agreement on Tariffs and Trade) Rounds and the formation of the EEC in 1957 expanded opportunities for exports, imports and international production.

Judged by annual turnover at the end of the 1940s (estimated to be over £500 million) and by the volumes of raw material consumed, motor vehicles were among the five largest British industries.[3] Over the period 1948 and 1979 it was responsible for between 4.5 per cent and 6.8 per cent of the net output of manufacturing industry.[4] The motor industry's share of manufacturing output was greater at the end of the 1970s than at the beginning of the 1950s. In 1979 the industry was still responsible for 6.7 per cent of manufacturing output and never accounted for less than 5 per cent over the preceding 30 years.[5]

As a major exporter, the motor vehicle industry bolstered the balance of payments. In the 1950s and 1960s road vehicles and aircraft comprised the largest export sector, exceeded only by non-electrical machinery. The peak share of exports in 1960 was 16.9 per cent.[6] When motor industry exports were less buoyant, falling to 11.4 per cent in 1974 and 1977, there were adverse repercussions for the balance of payments.[7] Declining competitiveness that lost export markets also increased the British propensity to import motor vehicles. The positive balance of trade in cars of about one-quarter of a billion pounds in 1964, by 1979 had become a deficit of considerably more.[8] By then motor vehicles constituted 8.9 per cent of British imports.[9]

Motor industry jobs were equally strategic. In 1948 one and a half million people were employed directly and indirectly in the manufacture, selling, maintenance and operation of vehicles. The industry in the 1950s accounted directly for between 4.4 per cent and 4.8 per cent of manufacturing employment, 6 per cent in the 1960s and between 4.8 per cent and 5.2 per cent in the 1970s.[10] Nearly half a million were employed in the industry during the 1960s; only agriculture and mining exceeded this figure. The fortunes of the industry therefore were closely monitored at a time when low unemployment was a major policy objective and when the motor industry and strikes became almost synonymous.

In the industrialised world as a whole, the 1950s and 1960s have often been described as the decades of the motor vehicle. The motor vehicle producing nations all experienced marked surges in car output (Table 4.1). World production of automobiles which in 1946 amounted to 3 milion, by 1955 had grown to just under 11 million. Five years later, world production was 12.8 million; by 1973 it had more than doubled to 29.8 million.[11] A similar rate of increase was recorded for commercial vehicles (Table 4.2); from 5 million in 1946 to 10 million in 1955, 16 million in 1960 and 30 million in 1970.[12] Although Britain joined in this general pattern of growth, performance could hardly be described as spectacular.

Output of Britain's motor industry grew less strongly after 1955 than that of her European and Japanese competitors. The trend in car production in these nations was steady, the only exceptions being the slight falls in 1967 recorded by both France and Germany. No such smooth growth is apparent in the case of the British industry. Car production in West Germany, France and Italy between 1962 and 1973 expanded at an annual average rate of 7 per cent, 10.2 per cent and 9.4 per cent respectively. Britain, by contrast, only achieved rates of growth of 4.8 per cent between 1961 and

Table 4.1: International production of motor cars, 1945–1979 ('000s)

	Britain	France	Germany	Italy	Japan	United States
1945	17	2	1	2	n.a.	70
1946	219	30	10	11	n.a.	2,149
1947	287	66	10	23	0	3,558
1948	335	100	30	44	0	3,909
1949	412	188	104	65	1	5,120
1950	523	257	219	101	2	6,666
1951	476	320	277	119	4	5,338
1952	448	370	318	114	5	4,321
1953	595	371	388	144	9	6,117
1954	769	444	561	181	14	5,559
1955	898	562	762	231	20	7,920
1956	708	663	911	280	32	5,816
1957	861	738	1,040	319	47	6,113
1958	1,052	969	1,307	369	51	4,258
1959	1,190	1,128	1,503	471	79	5,591
1960	1,353	1,175	1,817	596	165	6,675
1961	1,004	1,064	1,904	694	250	5,543
1962	1,294	1,340	2,109	878	269	6,933
1963	1,608	1,521	2,414	1,105	408	7,638
1964	1,868	1,390	2,650	1,029	580	7,752
1965	1,722	1,423	2,734	1,104	696	9,306
1966	1,604	1,786	2,830	1,282	878	8,598
1967	1,552	1,777	2,296	1,439	1,376	7,437
1968	1,816	1,833	2,862	1,545	2,056	8,848
1969	1,717	2,169	3,313	1,477	2,611	8,224
1970	1,641	2,458	3,528	1,720	3,179	6,550
1971	1,742	2,694	3,697	1,701	3,718	8,584
1972	1,921	2,719	3,522	1,732	4,022	8,828
1973	1,747	2,867	3,650	1,823	4,471	9,668
1974	1,534	2,699	2,840	1,631	3,932	7,325
1975	1,268	2,546	2,908	1,349	4,568	6,717
1976	1,333	2,980	3,547	1,471	5,028	8,498
1977	1,328	3,092	3,791	1,440	5,431	9,214
1978	1,223	3,111	3,890	1,509	5,748	9,176
1979	1,070	3,220	3,933	1,481	6,176	8,434

Source: SMMT, The Motor Industry of Great Britain, 1992, Table 12, p. 50.

1973.[13] Her share of world car production consequently halved. In 1955 Britain was the second largest producer in the world. In 1956, British output was overtaken by the Germans, in 1961 by France and in 1968 by Japan. By 1973, Britain's share had fallen to 6 per cent and she had slipped to near bottom of the league, with an annual output only exceeding that of Sweden. British unit volumes reached 60 per cent, 47 per cent and 39 per cent of French, German and Japanese production respectively (Table 4.1).

Table 4.2: International production of commerical vehicles, 1945–1979 ('000s)

	Britain	France	Germany	Italy	Japan	United States
1945	122	33	6	8	n.a.	656
1946	146	66	14	18	15	941
1947	155	71	14	18	11	1,239
1948	173	98	31	16	20	1,376
1949	216	98	60	21	28	1,134
1950	261	100	87	27	30	1,337
1951	258	128	98	26	35	1,427
1952	242	129	111	25	34	1,218
1953	240	126	203	31	41	1,206
1954	269	156	119	36	56	1,042
1955	340	164	147	38	49	1,249
1956	297	164	165	36	79	1,104
1957	288	190	172	33	135	1,107
1958	313	159	188	34	138	877
1959	370	155	215	30	184	1,137
1960	458	194	238	49	316	1,194
1961	460	181	244	65	564	1,134
1962	425	196	247	69	722	1,240
1963	404	216	254	75	876	1,463
1964	465	226	259	61	1,123	1,540
1965	455	219	243	72	1,179	1,752
1966	439	239	221	82	1,409	1,731
1967	385	233	187	103	1,771	1,539
1968	409	243	245	119	2,030	1,972
1969	466	291	292	119	2,063	1,982
1970	458	292	314	135	2,110	1,773
1971	456	316	286	116	2,093	2,088
1972	408	298	294	107	2,272	2,483
1973	417	351	299	135	2,612	3,014
1974	403	376	260	142	2,620	2,747
1975	381	315	278	110	2,373	2,272
1976	372	423	321	119	2,814	3,000
1977	386	415	314	144	3,083	3,482
1978	385	397	296	148	3,293	3,716
1979	408	393	317	150	3,460	3,046

Source: SMMT, *The Motor Industry of Great Britain*, 1992, Table 12, p. 54.

A similar picture emerges for the commercial vehicles sector (Table 4.2) – a near doubling of output between 1952 and the early 1970s, the volatility of production throughout the period, and a decline in relative shares of world production from 1963. Although relative output was more impressive than that for motor cars, by the early 1960s Britain was a poor third in the world ranking, after the United States and Japan, and her share of world production more than halved between 1952 and 1973. The British proportion of world production averaged 11.2 per cent between 1952 and 1962; but between 1963 and 1973, the share fell from 8.9 per cent to less than 5 per cent. The situation became even more disturbing in the 1960s when Britain recorded absolute declines in production. At a time when world output of commercial vehicles more than doubled, production in Britain actually declined.[14]

Figures for relative trade performance tell a similar story. When viewed in international perspective, Britain's trade performance was dismal. British car export volumes were overtaken by Germany in 1956, by France in 1969 and by Japan in 1969. Moreover, the British industry's tendency to export a diminishing share of total production was not replicated in any of Britain's major competitors, in either the car or the commercial vehicle sectors.[15] After 1957 car imports surged and from 1973 the overall balance of trade in cars turned negative.[16] The rise in import penetration was not unique to motor vehicles among British industries in this period, but the motor vehicle trade balance deterioration was particularly acute. By 1975, the import penetration ratio had reached 26 per cent in the motor vehicle industry (as against 22.8 per cent for manufacturing industry in general); three years later penetration ratios were 35 per cent and 26 per cent respectively.[17] In other major producing nations, the overall trend was to export a growing percentage of output, while maintaining and even increasing shares of the home market.

For much of the 1950s and 1960s, optimists could dismiss this as catching up by competitor economies. But by the beginning of the 1970s that explanation would no longer do. Something was very clearly wrong with the industry.

4.2 Reconstruction and redirection

Relatively slow growth in the 1950s and 1960s might be blamed at first on the head start the British motor industry gained over its continental competitors at the end of hostilities. Over the war years and the aftermath British industrial structure and employment was transformed. Engineering (and government) expanded massively and retailing contracted. Government policy strained to bridge the balance of payments deficit, no longer cushioned by earnings from overseas investments (sold off during the war) or by Allied aid.

Commercial vehicle output in 1946 was 40 per cent above the 1938 level but car production, requiring far greater conversion to peacetime demand, attained only two-thirds of prewar output, well below planned production. The industry remained free of the strikes that racked its North American competitor. But the dollar shortage limited the industry's access to American or Canadian specialised machine tools. The chairman of Vauxhall had no doubts as to the ramifications of such policy:

> Left to ourselves we should now be installing new plant machinery and equipment costing very large sums of money . . . We are not at present able to take all these steps. Indeed, we are very much restricted as a consequence of the Government's investment policy.[18]

Other bottlenecks were in the supply of raw materials and, to a lesser extent, also of manpower. The fuel crisis of 1947 further curtailed production. Employment levels were up on prewar totals because of the introduction of the five day week and the increased employment of clerical staff. The home market was obliged to conscript ex-military lorries to the extent of one-quarter of new registrations of trucks two years after the end of hostilities. With such an excess demand, that complaints of inadequate quality control and after sales facilities began to filter back from overseas markets, is not surprising. Until the early 1950s, there were few alternative producers to whom customers without dollars could turn. Thereafter, with the recovery of formerly war-torn Europe's motor industry, British output was first rivalled and then surpassed.

In 1947 it was estimated that the industry needed to produce cars at an annual rate of 475,000 in order to meet the government's export target plus 160,000 cars for essential home requirements.

The targets were subsequently revised to 500,000 cars and 170,000 commercial vehicles.[19] Total output was too low (Table 4.3). Mass production was hampered by the low total output of the industry and by product differentiation, which allowed no one producer to achieve output volumes sufficient to reap economies of scale.

In 1947 the minimum efficient scale of production for a firm was an overall output of between 100,000 and 150,000 units a year.[20] Although this was to increase substantially in subsequent years, in 1947 the largest firm's (Morris) production was only 60,000 units.[21] None of the six major producers, who between them were responsible for 90 per cent of output in 1947, was achieving output volumes sufficient to realise scale economies (Table 4.4). There appeared to be too many producers and products. The Labour government believed therefore that rationalisation was needed. Fewer producers with larger plants were required. Reducing the number of producers without plant rationalisation would merely increase market power, without correspondingly cutting unit costs.

Table 4.3: Production of British motor vehicles: actual and target output, 1924, 1938, 1947 and 1948 ('000s)

	Private cars and taxis	Target output 1947	Goods and passenger service vehicles	Target output 1947
1924	116.6		30.0	
1938	342.4		105.2	
1947	287.0	475.0	155.7	170
1948	334.8		173.3	

Sources: Production: Political and Economic Planning, *Motor Vehicles; A Report on the Industry*, 1950, Table 2, p. 10; target volumes: Labour Party, Research Department, 'Report on the British Motor Industry: Possibilities of Future Development with Special Reference to the Advantages and Disadvantages of Public Ownership', May 1948, Labour Party Archive, National Museum of Labour History Manchester, para. 86, p. 27.

A further constraint on production was the obsolesence of plant and machinery in the immediate aftermath of war. Prewar buildings and equipment needed replacing and updating, in addition to capacity expansion. A survey of the investment shortfall after the war reported that at Singer 'there did not seem to be a single up-to-date machine tool in the place', very few of the specialist car firms were equipped with modern plant, and commercial vehicle firms such as Crossley and Maudsley worked 'with a good deal of semi-obsolete machinery'.[22] In 1943, of the 43 motor vehicle companies surveyed by the SMMT, 35 worked in buildings which were over 11 years old, and 10 had buildings which were over 16 years old. Although many of the firms did occupy some new buildings, they were not suited to mass production methods (many had been built during the war to produce aircraft or other war materials).[23] The same survey revealed that 24 of the 43 firms surveyed operated machinery which was over 11 years old.[24] A conservative estimate of the cost of investment in building and fixed plant and equipment needed to raise output to the 470,000 vehicles required for export and essential home market requirements for 1948 amounted to £15 million.[25]

Table 4.4: British motor vehicle production by firms, 1947 (estimated percentages by volume)

	Cars and taxis	Commercial vehicles
The 'Big Six'		
Nuffield	20.9	13.6
Ford	15.4	22.9
Austin	19.2	14.3
Vauxhall	11.2	20.3
Rootes	10.9	7.9
Standard	13.2	
Specialist car producers		
Rover	2.7	
Singer	2.1	
BSA[a]	0.6	
Jaguar	1.6	
Armstrong-Siddeley	0.8	
Rolls-Royce and Bentley	0.3	
Alvis	0.3	
Others	0.8	
Heavy vehicle builders		
Jowett		4.3
Leyland		2.2
AEC (ACU)		2.9
Albion		1.3
Dennis		0.9
Thornycroft		1.0
Scammell		0.7
Guy		2.4
Others		5.3

[a] Includes Daimler and Lanchester.
Sources: Political and Economic Planning, *Motor Vehicles: A Report on the Industry*, Political and Economic Planning, Engineering Reports II, January 1950, Table 14, p. 26.

Restructuring the industry was suggested when the postwar Labour government considered including motor vehicle production in the nationalisation programme. Nationalisation was the most radical reorganisation of British industry since the Industrial Revolution. In part it was motivated by a desire to improve performance by the rationalisation which the market had seemed incapable of implementing – privately arranged mergers between succesful companies had proved abortive on several occasions in the interwar years.[26]

In May 1948 the Research Department of the Labour Party issued a consultative document outlining the advantages and disadvantages of public ownership of the British motor vehicle industry.[27] Very quickly, in October of the same year, the Party's Sub-Committee on Industries for Nationalisation agreed that the motor industry was an unsuitable candidate.[28] Several arguments were to dissuade the Party and the government from taking the industry into full, or even partial, state ownership.[29] It was argued that the historical evidence suggested that the industry had been efficient in the past and, on that basis, it was hoped that it would prove as capable of dealing with the changed conditions of the 1940s and 1950s as it had been of dealing with the depressed conditions of the interwar years.[30] Equally persuasive was the performance of the American motor vehicle industry, viewed by many as the barometer of efficiency and low production costs, which was entirely privately owned and subject to hardly any control from the American administration.[31]

The eventual decision to leave the industry alone, however, was determined by the short term need for export earnings.[32] Johnman has shown how ultimately the country's short term balance of payments position assumed greater priority within the Board of Trade and the government than the 'luxury' of a long term strategy.[33] The motor vehicle industry, more than most, given its export potential, was drawn into this agenda. The premium on export earnings, moreover, gave industrialists bargaining power with the government. As Tiratsoo has shown, the motor industry, which had built up considerable influence within government during the war, actively lobbied members of parliament and civil servants in defence of its interests.[34] When in the framing of the 1947 Transport Acts, the industry was faced with the prospect of nationalisation of commercial vehicles, the SMMT backed by the

Federation of British Industries successfully lobbied the government to ensure strict limits on the power of the Transport Commission to manufacture chassis and bodies as well as major components.[35] The argument was that export volumes could not be achieved if industry were preoccupied with long term restructuring and rationalisation.[36] The longer term necessity to reorganise and rationalise the industry would, so it was maintained, disrupt exports.[37] While the motor manufacturers could meet export targets and thus contribute to the balance of payments, their bargaining position was assured. In the final analysis, the government's first concern had to be that the industry should operate in the interests of the balance of payments, rather than be restructured. This they intended to achieve by direct controls.[38] Talk of reform was played down and Stafford Cripps in particular pursued his determination to make cars the cutting edge of the export drive on which, he believed, 'everything depended'.[39]

The Labour Party was able to achieve its aims of integrating the motor vehicle industry into the planned economy without disturbing the industry's all important contribution to export earnings, by opting for indirect control of the industry. Industries had been regulated during the war mainly through the state allocation of manpower and raw materials. Restrictions, notably over access to raw materials, continued in force afterwards. This gave the government scope for control without, as they believed, jeopardising the export trade. The motor industry needed steel, fuel and other raw materials. In 1947 the industry consumed 8 per cent of the country's total deliveries of finished steel (over 20 per cent fewer tons than before the war).[40]

Allocation of these basic inputs to the industry was made dependent on the industry exporting a very high percentage of its products. Manufacturers were only allocated steel if they sold a large proportion of output overseas. In the *immediate* aftermath of the Second World War, motor vehicles were not originally included in the export quota policies of the government. The 'escape', however, was shortlived. During 1946 the agreed basis was a quota of 50 per cent for cars and 33.3 per cent for commercial vehicles.[41] At the beginning of 1947 the overseas quota was 46 per cent for cars and 30 per cent for commercial vehicles. By the last three months of that year quotas were raised respectively to 64 per cent and 37 per cent. The following year saw export allocations reach 70 per cent and 46 per cent.[42] Difficulties ensuring a supply of materials continued to dog the industry into the early 1950s, as rearmament with its demands on steel and other materials crowded out motor vehicle production.[43]

Dependence of scarce steel supplies on exports concentrated the minds of at least two motor manufacturers (the Wilkes brothers), as shown by their invention of the Land Rover. The Land Rover utilised an aluminium sheet body on a wooden frame because production in the early postwar years was hampered by shortages of materials, notably steel, and skilled labour. Rover needed the Land Rover as an export product so it could buy steel for its traditional British family saloons which would not sell abroad.

Restrictions on input availability and the priority assigned to exports therefore ensured the British motor industry entered the great postwar boom with outmoded plant and a rather atomised industrial structure for an industry with scale economies. Concentration among a few component suppliers, notably Lucas, together with specialisation by component suppliers, only partly offset the higher than necessary unit costs. The decision not to take the motor industry into full or partial public ownership may have constituted one 'missed opportunity' for rationalisation to increase plant size. Public ownership, however, did not constitute the only route to greater plant size and scale economies. Nor did government intervention constitute a recipe for success. The close involvement of the government in Standard after the war hardly constituted a success. But the problems, as Tiratsoo has shown, stemmed less from structural constraints than from commercial and marketing factors which lay at the feet of management.[44] The Labour Party's consultative document placed great faith in the ability of the industry to put its own house in order in the postwar years. Subsequent decades were to call into question the correctness of that view.

4.3 Industrial structure

The car producers

At first sight, Labour's trust in private ownership and the market for the motor industry was vindicated. If economies of scale mattered a great deal, the motor vehicle industry should have become one of the most highly concentrated industries in the British economy in the postwar decades, as it did[45] (Table 4.5). In the immediate

Table 4.5: Concentration ratios in the British motor vehicle industry, 1946–1978 (output based, percentages)

	CR3	CR5
1946	69.3	89.0
1950	72.1	92.2
1955	77.3	95.6
1960	77.5	96.6
1965	80.5	97.6
1968	86.0	95.6
1970	88.6	99.5
1975	92.0	99.9
1978	92.0	99.9

Notes: CR3 = 3 firm concentration ratio.
CR5 = 5 firm concentration ratio.
Sources: Estimated from D. G. Rhys, *The Motor Industry: An Economic Survey*, London: Butterworths, 1972, Table 9.2, p. 312; and D. G. Rhys, 'Motor Vehicles', in P. S. Johnson (eds.), *The Structure of British Industry*, London: Granada, 1980, Table 8.1, p. 180.

Table 4.6: Production by the 'Big Five' as a percentage of total British motor vehicle output, 1946–1978

	BMC	Standard	Ford	Rootes	Vauxhall	Others
1946	43.4	11.5	14.4	10.7	9.0	11.0
1950	39.4	11.1	19.2	13.5	9.0	7.8
1955	38.9	9.8	27.0	11.4	8.5	4.4
1960	39.5	11.2	26.8	10.0	9.1	3.4
1961	38.3	6.5	32.8	10.5	8.5	3.4
1964	38.5	6.5	28.0	11.7	12.6	2.7
1965	38.2	6.5	29.5	10.6	12.8	2.4
	BMH	Standard	Ford	Rootes	Vauxhall	Others
1966	39.0	7.6	29.0	10.7	10.7	4.2
	BLMC	Standard	Ford	Rootes	Vauxhall	Others
1968	45.1	7.6	30.5	10.4	13.5	4.4
1970	48.0	–	27.3	13.3	10.8	0.5
1975	48.0	–	26.0	18.0	8.0	0.1
1978	50.0	–	26.0	16.0	7.0	0.1

Note: Standard-Triumph became part of Leyland in 1961.
Sources: 1946–68: D. G. Rhys, *The Motor Industry: An Economic Survey*, London: Butterworths, 1972, Table 9.2, p. 312; 1970–1978: D. G. Rhys 'Motor Vehicles', in P. S. Johnson (ed.), *The Structure of British Industry*, London: Granada, 1980, Table 8.1, p. 180.

postwar period there were some 24 motor car producers. Between them, Austin, Morris, Rootes, Singer, Ford and Vauxhall accounted for 88 per cent of production. In 1970, there were only four major producers who together accounted for some 99.5 per cent of car production in Britain.[46] Eight years later three firms manufactured 92 per cent of output (Table 4.6).

Enhanced concentration was a characteristic of most vehicle producing nations in the 1960s and 1970s. In France, Renault, Citroën, Peugeot and Simca supplied between them 98 per cent of French passenger car output. In Germany, Volkswagen, Opel, Mercedes and Ford accounted for 87 per cent of German passenger car output. In Italy, Fiat and Alfa-Romeo held 85 per cent of Italian passenger car output. By 1973, the four largest producers accounted for 94 per cent of German, 99.6 per cent of French, 94 per cent of North American, 79.7 per cent of Japanese and 86 per cent of Spanish motor vehicle production.[47] What was different in Britain was that three of the four major motor vehicle producers were subsidiaries of American multinational enterprises.[48] Of the four only one, British Leyland Motor Corporation (BLMC), was British-owned. The others, Ford, Vauxhall and Chrysler were all subsidiaries of American multinationals. The remaining producers included small specialist firms such as Rolls-Royce, Lotus and Aston Martin.

The stronger presence of the multinationals, reflects in part the increased globalisation of the motor vehicle industry. What was unusual in the case of Britain was the extent of production and market share held by Ford and General Motors (Vauxhall) and, from 1964, Chrysler which acquired 30 per cent of voting shares and 50 per cent of non voting shares of Rootes (Table 4.6).[49] Among the other European nations with domestic motor vehicle production the American presence was less marked. In 1961 only 31 per cent of German passenger cars were made by Opel and Ford whilst the French and Italian motor vehicle industries were entirely independent of the North Americans.[50] In 1973 Ford and General Motors accounted for 33.6 per cent of German motor vehicle production (11.5 per cent and 22.1 per cent respectively). In France the American presence was effectively limited to Chrysler at this time who took only 16.4 per cent of national motor vehicle output. Elsewhere among the European domestic producers the percentage of national output accounted for by the 'Big Three' were 11.4 per cent in Spain (Chrysler, 11.4 per cent), 14.6 per cent in the Nether-lands (Ford having the entire 14.6 per cent) and Portugal 21.9 per cent (Ford 12.5 per cent and General Motors 9.4 per cent).[51] To some extent the relative fortunes of the multinationals in the domestic European markets was the result of government interven-tion to limit their presence. In France, for example, official permis-sion from the Ministry of Finance was required if foreign firms wished to purchase more than 20 per cent of the shares of a French firm. The Ministry used its power to block any takeover which it viewed harmful to French interests or contrary to the government's industrial strategy. In Germany it was the banks rather than the Government which resisted foreign takeovers, as in the 1960s when Daimler-Benz was under threat.[52] Similar resistance in the Italian industry excluded multinationals, most notably when Ford tried to take over Lancia in 1969. Whilst in the 1950s and 1960s institutional resistance to foreign takeovers and the use of tariffs probably did protect the domestic industry and secure its national market, restrictions on American multinationals within Britain's European competitors was only part of the story. The remainder was the home-grown problems of the domestic motor vehicle producers.

The period also witnessed the growing presence of European and Japanese producers, initially in the form of import penetration. This phenomenon was to become increasingly important in the 1980s and 1990s, reflecting the growth of the European and Japanese motor vehicle industries and the importance of the EEC trading bloc. By 1970, of the 1,076,865 new cars registered in Britain, 14.3 per cent were imported. Of new car registrations in 1970, 1,327 were Japanese, of which 1,311 were produced by Honda. The substantial presence of Japanese cars in Britain market dates from after 1972. By 1978, Japanese cars accounted for 10.96 per cent of new car registrations in Britain.[53]

The Japanese market share was, however, dwarfed by comparison with that of the European producers who by 1978 accounted for just under 33 per cent of new car registrations in Britain. Import penetration by the European producers dates from the early 1960s, at which time Volkswagen was the only major established importer. By the late 1960s, Renault and Fiat were exporting significant volumes of cars to the British market.[54] Italian registrations were dominated by Fiat.[55] The principal German import was Volkswagen which by 1978 held 4 per cent of British new car registrations.[56] Other German makes were BMW (0.7 per cent of new car registrations), Mercedes-Benz (0.4 per cent), and Opel (1.4 per cent).[57]

In the late 1970s European and Japanese producers took over and/or began production in Britain. The first such venture dates from 1978 when Peugeot-Citroën took over Chrysler UK, the second in 1980 when Nissan announced plans to build 200,000 cars in Britain from 1984. Finally, joint ventures were developed, such as British Leyland's attempts in 1979–80 to forge links with Honda, initially to assemble a middle car range under licence to be marketed in the EEC.[58]

The commercial vehicle producers

Concentration of production proceeded more slowly for commercial vehicles than cars. The commercial vehicle section of the motor industry in the immediate postwar period consisted of two distinct categories. The first, the mass producers who concentrated on the production of car-derived vans, medium sized vans and pick-ups. Since these were fairly standardised goods which were produced in large volumes, they were made by the mass producing car firms. In 1947, the mass producers accounted for 124,000 of the 155,000 commercial vehicles produced. The second group consisted of specialist producers, many of whom concentrated on light and medium weight ranges, and heavy vehicle builders who, in the early postwar period, accounted for about one-tenth of the total number of commercial vehicles produced, but much more than one-tenth of the value of commercial vehicle production.[59] The structure of the commercial vehicle industry in the postwar period was dominated by a breaking down of this distinction as the mass producers moved into the heavier commercial vehicle market and many, but by no means all, of the original specialists were either absorbed into the mass producers or left the industry. At the end of the 1970s there were still a number of prosperous independent specialist producers such as ERF, Foden and Dennis.

In 1947, there were five mass producers: Nuffield, Austin, Ford, Bedford, Rootes, who between them held 79 per cent of the market. Of the five mass producers, Ford and Bedford, dominated the market. Seven firms dominated the specialist and heavy vehicle market: Leyland, AEC, Albion, Dennis, Thornycroft, Scammell and Guy, who together held 11.4 per cent of production. It was, however, three firms, Leyland, AEC and Guy who dominated the specialist and heavy vehicle branch of the commercial vehicle industry (Table 4.4). Firms such as Guy, Seddon, Albion, Vulcan, Jensen, Dennis, Dodge and Thornycroft in the immediate postwar period concentrated on the production of light and medium weight vehicles. The heavy vehicle group consisted of Foden, ERF, Atkinson, Scammell, AEC and Leyland.

In the early 1950s the mass producers began to move up the weight scale to produce larger vehicles. First Rootes and then Bedford, Ford and BMC slowly encroached on the specialist producers' traditional markets. The original producers of light and medium vehicles thus faced increasing price competition from the mass producers and many were forced out of this industry either through bankruptcy or merger or adopted a policy of switching to the production of heavier vehicles. Two such casualties were Jenson and Vulcan. The former was absorbed by Rootes, whilst Jensen withdrew from the commercial vehicles and concentrated its activities in the car market. The remaining original light and medium weight specialists phased out production of their small vehicles from the early 1950s and moved into the heavier weight market. Only Dodge and Seddon of the medium weight builders achieved long term profitability, initially by concentrating on well-made medium heavy vehicles and ultimately by producing heavy vehicles.[60] The strategy however brought them into direct competition with the established heavy vehicle makers. By 1954, there were five principal firms operating in the mass production market, whilst the specialist market was dominated by Leyland and AEC.

The growth of Leyland is particularly important, not least for its eventual merger with BMC in 1968. Throughout the postwar period Leyland grew rapidly, largely as the result of acquisition. In 1947 it had been one of several specialist producers, specialising in this instance on bus and lorry production. Mergers with Albion in 1953 and Scammell in 1955 extended the company's interests beyond medium heavy to heavy trucks to include both light weight chassis and heavy duty specialist vehicles. In 1962 the company acquired Associated Commercial Vehicles (ACV).[61]

From the early 1950s the commercial vehicle sector was highly competitive, with each of the mass producers dominating one area of the commercial vehicle industry. Ford and BMC competed fiercely for the light and medium van market. In 1965 and 1966 Ford launched a new range of vans which met with immediate success. From 1967, BMC lost its ascendancy in the medium and pick-up market, although it retained its leading position in the light van sector. Similar fierce competition ranged in the medium weight truck market between Ford, BMC and Bedford. The introduction of Ford's new successful range of vans in 1965 and 1966, notably the 'Transit' which was introduced in 1965, displaced Bedford from its dominant position in this category.

From 1968 the commercial vehicle sector was dominated by the effects of BLMC's wider problems on its commercial vehicle activities. The 1968 merger of BMC with Leyland Motors brought together the mass production car and light and medium weight commercial vehicle interests of BMC and the truck, bus and luxury car concerns of Leyland Motors.[62] The truck and bus division, however, were to suffer from the subsequent concentration of managerial and financial resources at BLMC in the reconstruction of the car division's fortunes. Investment in plant expansion and modernisation and in the introduction of new products was sacrificed to expenditure in the less profitable car divisions. In 1969, BLMC accounted for 39.8 per cent of commercial vehicle production in Britain. The shares of Ford and Vauxhall (Bedford) were 29.5 per cent and 22.0 per cent respectively.

The 1970s witnessed a steady decline in commercial vehicle production and market share by BLMC. By 1972, when the company produced 140,000 commercial vehicles, its share had fallen to 34.3 per cent of British production. Ford in 1972 held 35 per cent and Bedford 22.3 per cent of the market. By 1977 BLMC's share of the market had fallen to 31.1 per cent of the 386,000 commercial vehicles produced in Britain. By the late 1970s, Ford had established leadership in most areas of the commercial vehicle market and held 38.3 per cent of British production. Bedford in 1977 held 23.8 per cent of British commercial vehicle production.

By 1978 commercial vehicle production had become largely concentrated in the hands of the mass producers. The 40 separate commercial vehicle producers of the immediate postwar period had been reduced to ten, of which Ford, Bedford (Vauxhall), BLMC and Chrysler accounted for 98 per cent of total production. Only in the heavy goods and highly specialised markets (for example fire engines and refuse collectors) did the small independent firm survive. In the period from 1945 to 1978 commercial vehicle production in Britain had seen its share of world production halve from 10 per cent to 4 per cent. From 1974, it was the French commercial vehicle industry which became Europe's largest commercial vehicle producer.[63]

The components manufacturers

Concentration of production impelled by scale economies was a characteristic of component manufacturing as well. The main change in the postwar period involved the integration of car body plants into the activities of the mass producers, now capable of demanding volumes at which minimum efficient scale could be attained. Vehicle producers wanted control over 'upstream' firms to guarantee security of supply, to avoid monopoly exploitation and, perhaps, to take advantage of technological complementarities. But they could only afford to do so when their scale of output was very large, for they had to be prepared to take the entire minimum cost production of the body plant, which itself needed massive throughputs.

In the early postwar years independent firms accounted for the large majority of production of car bodies.[64] The leading independent producers were Pressed Steel, Briggs Motor Bodies, Fisher and Ludlow and Mulliners. From the mid 1950s the mass producers, through a series of mergers, integrated body making into their production process. In 1953 Briggs Motor Bodies was acquired by Ford and BMC acquired Fisher and Ludlow.[65] In 1954 Mulliners retained independence but entered into a long term agreement to supply Standard with bodies. By the late 1960s no large scale independent body producer existed and each of the mass producers manufactured their own car bodies. When, in 1965, BMC took over Pressed Steel, the company became self sufficient in car body production. The merger with Leyland Motors in 1968, brought under the BLMC umbrella the body building capacity of Pressed Steel, Fisher and Ludlow, Morris Bodies, Nuffield Bodies and Mulliners.

No British firm made its own electrical equipment, as General Motors did in the United States, or its own glass, as did Ford in the United States. The extent of bought out components was also higher in the British motor vehicle industry than in its European competitors. In Japan, Germany, Italy and France only 25–40 per cent of the average factory value of a car was bought from outside suppliers;[66] manufacturers in these countries had dealt with the delayed growth of a components industry by making a large proportion of their own parts and components. In 1954 the bought out content of a typical volume produced car amounted to 75 per cent of the total cost.[67] In the 1960s BMC and Ford purchased over 70 per cent and 50 per cent respectively of the value of their vehicles from outside.[68] In 1967, BMC spent £320 million purchasing items from 4,000 outside suppliers.[69]

Although there was a large number of component manufacturers in the industry, many important items were produced by only a few firms and, in some areas, by one firm only. Two of the main areas of bought out components were electrical goods and tyres and wheels. Four firms dominated electrical supplies to the motor industry: Joseph Lucas, Chloride, S. Smith and Sons and Champion. Lucas produced almost a complete range of products but had a virtual monopoly in lamps, windscreen motors, dynamos and ignition coils, whereas Smith's had a virtual monopoly in heaters and electric instruments.[70] The tyre market was dominated by six manufacturers: Dunlop, Avon, Firestone, Goodyear, Pirelli and Michelin. Unlike most component suppliers, tyre manufacturers were not all British-owned. Firestone and Goodyear were American, Pirelli Italian and Michelin a French company. In 1971 Pirelli and Dunlop merged.

Rhys and Bhaskar have offered four explanations for the high proportion of bought-in parts and components: the reluctance of manufacturers to become involved in areas of technology with which they were unfamiliar; capital considerations involved in establishing component making plants insofar as manufacturers may not have or may not wish to tie up large amounts of capital in such ventures; economies of scale considerations in which many parts constituted too small a proportion of costs to be worth the trouble making; and the additional economies of scale argument that the optimum size of plant needed for the production of some components were of such magnitude that if all the economies of scale were to be reaped just one or two firms would be able to meet the needs of the entire industry.[71]

4.4 The merger movements

Reasons for mergers

In any industrial sector, the proximate cause of increased concentration may be either merger or rapid internally generated growth or both. In the motor vehicle industry, it was the British-owned producers who underwent several waves of merger activity (Table 4.7), while the American multinationals expanded by internal growth. When BLMC was formed in 1968, the company became the sole major domestic producer of cars.

Empirical work on merger activity in British industry has provided no single overriding explanation for why mergers took place. The desire for monopoly power and profit maximisation, for the realisation of scale economies, the impact of the business cycle, the implications of the economic environment (particularly at times of

Table 4.7: Mergers in the British motor vehicle industry, 1945–1978

1945	Standard and Triumph
1952	Austin and Nuffield (BMC)
1955	Rootes and Singer
1960	Jaguar and Daimler
1961	Leyland and Standard-Triumph
1966	BMC and Jaguar Group
	Leyland and Rover
1968	Leyland and BMH[a] (BLMC)
	Commercial vehicles
1951	Leyland acquire Albion Motors
1955	Leyland and Scammell Lorries
1963	Leyland and the bus manufacturers ACV
1967	Leyland and Rover, Alvis
	Aveling Barford
	Components
1953	BMC acquire Fisher and Ludlow
1953	Ford acquire Briggs Motor Bodies
1965	BMC acquire Pressed Steel

Note: [a] BMC changed its name to BMH in 1967.

uncertainty) and/or the intensification of international competition have all been canvassed.[72] The motor vehicle industry exemplifies both changing motivations over time and the absence of any single objective at any one point of time. Motor vehicle mergers came in waves and took the form of both vertical and horizontal integration.

The two 'big' horizontal mergers of the period were between Austin and Morris in 1952 and Leyland and BMH in 1968. Austin's and Morris's decision to form BMC in 1952 has been variously ascribed to the need to obtain marketing economies of scale, particularly in relation to export markets, to obtain scale economies, to co-ordinate research and development and to strengthen the constituent firms' grip on the market. Another way of looking at this however is to ask why the merger was delayed until 1952, given that these reasons had existed for a number of years. The impetus came less from the realisation of the potential benefits of merger or indeed from any defensive movement to compete with Ford, than from the removal of an obstacle. By 1952, Morris had settled the succession problem and was ready to retire. His departure removed a real impediment to the merger of the two companies.[73]

Other horizontal mergers also demonstrate a variety of motives – from the offensive move by Chrysler when it took over Rootes with the singular objective of gaining a foothold in Britain in particular and Europe in general, and Leyland's acquisition of five producers between 1951 and 1967, again ostensibly to meet American competition in worldwide markets, to the defensive merger of BMH and Jaguar in 1966 and that of BMH and Leyland in 1968. The latter, in particular, is illustrative not only of the mixture of motivations behind the merger movements –

> The combination of British Motor and Leyland provides a single strong British owned company which will be competitive with American, Continental and Japanese motor manufacturers in the markets of the world. The rate of investment and expansion by major competitors, particularly the American companies, is now so high that it was becoming increasingly difficult for British Motors and Leyland separately to sustain adequate growth. The merger provides the opportunity for rationalisation of products, economies of scale in production, the opportunity to combine overseas companies and marketing organisations into an immensely stronger force to promote the sale of British vehicles abroad.[74]

– but also of the activities of the then Labour government which was instrumental in the merger of BMH and Leyland in 1968 (see Chapter 7).

The vertical merger movements of the 1950s were inspired by the need to protect components and materials, especially car bodies.

Those of the 1960s were to improve production schedules and to reduce production costs by increasing efficiency and abolishing the value-added by independent component makers. Until the mid 1960s there was a tendency for motor manufacturers to try to secure control of their component suppliers by integrating component production into their industry. In 1965, for example, BMC absorbed Pressed Steel, which had been responsible for supplying two-fifths of the bodies required by the motor industry.[75] The rationale for this trend was twofold: to control costs of production 'by increasing efficiency and abolishing the value added by independent component makers' and to improve the planning of production schedules, both of which assumed increased importance with the advent of increased output facilitated by the introduction of mass production techniques.[76]

The failure of merger policy

Unfortunately the stated aims of the mergers were not achieved. While the British producer supplied a falling proportion of output (Table 4.6), culminating in rescue by the government, Ford and Vauxhall raised their production and market shares. At first sight the American companies' success suggests the superiority of growth by expansion of existing facilities over merger. But to conclude that Ford was successful *because* of internal growth whereas British Leyland declined *because* of mergers, ignores the interlinkages and feedbacks between market structure, conduct and performance. The problem was less the fact of merger than the failure to realise the potential benefits of merger. The merger movements of the 1950s and 1960s constituted another missed opportunity to rationalise adequately, and indeed may have been an attempt at avoiding more fundamental reforms.

Merger was not accompanied by any serious rationalisation programme. BMC failed to integrate adequately after the Austin–Morris merger in 1952 and the two companies continued to operate as separate competing entities.[77] After 1968 British Leyland presided more as a holding company over separate Austin and Morris empires as well as other distinct firms, until 1978.[78] One explanation for the failure was personality clashes dating back to the interwar antipathy of Morris and Austin, which continued into the postwar decades. Neither Morris nor Lord would cede personal con influenced a generation of managers in mutual

Undoubtedly, there was a feeling of mutual suspicion and distrust between individuals in the old Austin and Morris sections of BMC/ British Leyland which hampered integrated production and effective competition.[79] What is less explicable was the failure to realise the long term effects of this antagonism. Competition between independent firms may be desirable for efficiency but in a merged enterprise, co-operation requires a change of spirit which may be problematic without a radical change of personnel as well.

A second explanation, which also applies to the early postwar years, relates the failure to integrate to the immediate short run necessities of achieving high export volumes. The premium on the export drive and the pre-eminence of the British industry in the European arena distracted managers from taking a longer term view. The postwar export drive encouraged a policy of boosting output immediately at all costs. British manufacturers tended to concentrate on producing more and more vehicles to the detriment of either rationalising the structure of the industry or taking a longer term view of model development.[80] The demand for vehicles in a world eager for the products of the industry reinforced this view.

A third explanation turns on government supply side policy in the 1960s. The government's regional policies of the 1960s, which encouraged manufacturers to build new plants in depressed or deprived areas is seen by critics such as Dunnett to have added to the industry's fixed costs and to have been instrumental in the labour relations problems of the period.[81] Many of the strikes of the period can be traced to attempts to maintain differentials between different plants in different areas run by the same company and between different plants in different industries.[82] Plant expansion, unaccompanied by any rationalisation, led to duplication of effort and negated full realisation of economies of scale. As the Central Policy Review Staff found in 1975: 'there are too many manufacturers with too many models, too many plants and too much capacity'.[83]

A final argument is that the inability to rationalise was less the outcome of government regional policy than a failure on the part of management to carry out any rationalisation programme, which owed more to an attempt to contain labour relations problems than to the costs of complying with supply side policies. Two reasons are given for this perceived failure.

The first relates to the employment costs. As Johnman has

shown, the best plans of the Board of Trade for industrial restructuring after the war were dogged by widespread fear of unemployment. Not surprisingly, the fear was most vociferously voiced in the Midlands where industrialists reported that full employment was vital – not least since failure to achieve this aim could provoke serious disturbance.[84] It is hardly surprising then that the employment costs of plant rationalisation counted particularly heavily against public ownership in 1948. The Labour Party's consultative document warned against the employment costs of instigating a major rationalisation scheme. Closure of inefficient firms and plants would, it was claimed, create large scale unemployment in the industry – a spectre which the government was unwilling to raise:

> The closing of even one of the factories would not be very popular with the several thousand employees – in Luton, Dagenham or Oxford they could not easily be absorbed in other local industries – even if they were told that it was necessary in the national interest and for the economical operation of the major vehicle industry.[85]

The employment costs of reform were not limited to the immediate postwar years. Davis Smith has shown how full employment became part of an implicit contract between governments of both persuasions and the union movement to secure wage restraint.[86] The employment costs of rationalisation at a time when full employment was a major policy objective was to continue to constrain the industry in the 1950s and 1960s and were cited as a major factor in the failure to pursue a major rationalisation exercise after the Leyland/BMH merger in 1968:

> we still have a long way to go if we are to achieve all the economies and improvements in efficiency which the merger has made possible. We could have moved ahead more quickly with rationalisation measures but we have gone out of our way to avoid large scale redundancies.[87]

This would suggest that the industry's ability to reform and restructure not only the productive capacity of manufacturing, but also as Chapter 6 demonstrates, industrial relations was seriously impeded even before the war was over, and that this may have acted as a key constraint on the industry's long run competitive performance in the postwar years.[88]

The second explanation, favoured by Prais, focuses on management's decision to keep plant size small to reduce the cost of labour stoppages. His analysis of plant sizes in the motor vehicle industry in Britain, Germany and the United States between 1925 and 1973 demonstrated that the relative lag in the development of large vehicle plants largely occurred after 1961. Prior to that date, motor vehicle plants in Britain were similar in size to those in Germany and narrowed between Britain and America after the war mainly as a result of the increase in the size of British plants. The divergence of plant size after 1961 was traced to the merger waves of the 1950s and 1960s which did little to bring about the larger plant sizes typical of other countries:[89]

> in assembly, where leading plants abroad have about 40,000 employees, it is clear that a British plant of that size would have to expect an intolerable frequency of stoppages; and this, it must be inferred, is a major reason why British assembly plants have not grown to the typical size found in America and Germany.[90]

The conclusion was that the mass production of cars involving tens of thousands of workers in a single plant was not viable unless and until labour relations problems had been resolved.[91] The evidence thus suggests that labour market explanations, the fear of creating unemployment at a time of full employment economic policy and of the costs resulting from stoppages associated with larger units, largely account for the inability to integrate production and create large-scale plants.[92]

What then were the consequences of this failure? On one level, the results were in the structure of the industry, which was characterised by a multiplicity of unmodernised plants.[93] Official reports and academic analyses have concurred with the assessment of failure to integrate structure and production strategy as one of the crucial problems of the industry.[94] Ten years after the creation of British Leyland, the company had nine main assembly plants, seven of which were operating with an estimated maximum two shift capacity of less than 170,000 cars.[95] Even the major volume assembly plants of Longbridge and Cowley only had estimated maximum two shift capacities of 300,000–350,000 and 350,000–400,000 respectively.[96] Ford, by comparison had two plants in 1973, Halewood with a two shift car assembly capacity of 250,000 and Dagenham with 300,000.[97] The full implications of these failures however can only be fully understood in the context of technological change and the inability of the British industry to benefit from the potential offered by new technology.

4.5 Technology and scale economies

Technological change

The pattern of firms in the British motor vehicle industry concealed a less than ideal configuration of plants and models. An assessment of the technology available to the industry permits a view of what that ideal configuration was at various dates. In addition to plant and firm size in relation to the market, the dimensions include the extent of vertical disintegration, the variety of models and the independence of commercial vehicles. Plant size mattered because the technology of the industry placed an increasing premium on high volume production. Each process however operated at different minimum efficient sizes. The largest determined the least cost throughput of an assembler unless standardisation of parts or processes between assemblers allowed some sharing of overheads, as with body pressing in the 1930s.

Figure 4.1 shows the sequence of operations in motor vehicle manufacture. Two sets of operations fed into the final assembly plant. The first was the casting, forging and machining of the power train – the engine, transmission and axle. The second was the stamping, welding and painting of the body. Motor vehicle production in the postwar, as in the interwar period, was a highly complex process. By the beginning of the 1970s each car consisted of about 4,000 different items and, since many of them were duplicated, the total number of components could be over 20,000.[98] The bulk of the raw materials consisted of steel, sheet steel, cast iron and aluminium. These materials were cast, forged, pressed or otherwise processed by a vast quantity of machine tools. Motor vehicles employed more machine tools and more sheet steel that any other industry in the country.[99]

The various stages of the manufacturing process did not change in the postwar period, with the important exception of the switch to unitary construction. Before the war, complete bodies were added to a chassis, complete with sub-assemblies, at the final assembly stage. After the war, there was a move away from the separate chassis on which the body was placed; the body was built up and assembled so as to serve as a chassis as well. From the late 1940s, unitary construction became common practice among the European producers.[100] Although the practice of unitary construction altered the final process to some extent, the process was

Figure 4.1 Sequencing of operations in motor vehicle production

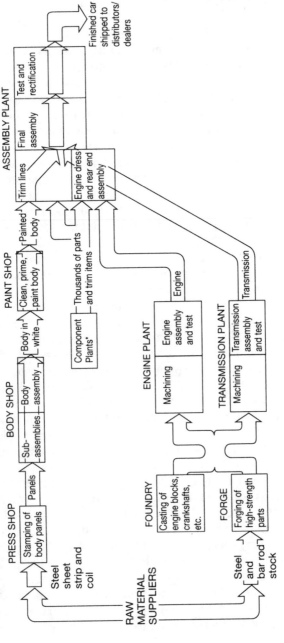

Source: Central Policy Review Staff, *The Future of the British Car Industry,* London: HMSO, 1975. Crown copyright. Reproduced with the permission of the Controller of Her Majesty's Stationery Office.

118

essentially the same.[101] Technology did not require these operations necessarily be carried out within the same company, but the four principal British companies in this period all pressed bodies, made engines and assembled cars and commercial vehicles.[102] On the other hand all operations were not typically conducted on the same site. Within Ford, Dagenham was the most integrated site, but after the decentralization of the 1960s, Halewood relied upon Dagenham for supply of various components. At the other end of the spectrum, by the mid 1970s, Vauxhall was mainly concerned with the assembly of kits.[103]

The motor vehicle industry passed through a number of changes in the manufacturing process some of which were linked to the product life cycle.[104] We saw in Chapter 1 the initial phase of flexible but low productivity production processes associated with a high level of product differentiation. Chapter 2 described the second phase when a dominant standard product design emerged. This 'new' product could be manufactured at high levels of output and efficiency because it sold well. Phase two continued into the 1950s and 1960s. The price however was inflexibility, for mass production capital equipment was extremely expensive; the costs of replacing such equipment made radical product innovation prohibitive. A third phase in which standardised production was shifted to low labour cost countries was largely prevented by political reactions, by technology changes and by the transformed economic environment of the 1970s. Instead, the impact of the oil price shocks, the growth of safety and emission control legislation, the emergence of micro-electronic technology and the rise of the Japanese motor vehicle industry in the 1970s inaugurated a phase of fuel-efficient 'world cars', exemplified by the Ford Fiesta, and later the Escort and General Motors' Cavalier, saleable and produced in a wide range of industrial country markets.[105]

Overall technological change in the 1950s and 1960s increased greatly the optimum level of production and placed a premium on mass producers achieving high outputs of standardised product. Introduction of micro-processor technology from the 1970s reduced the optimum level.[106] The first phase favoured mass producers while the second transformed the prospects for smaller scale manufacturers. During the 1950s and 1960s the continuation of the second phase of the product cycle allowed technological innovation to be concerned with more automatic and specially designed machines arranged in sequence. Automation further offered the potential of dealing with the main production bottleneck, the time loading and unloading parts. Costly machinery could be used much closer to optimum capacity as loading and unloading times declined and the operating speed was allowd to increase. Consequently automation not only offered large economies of scale in the long run, but also yielded quite considerable reductions in the average total unit costs of production, at a given volume of output.

An engineering estimate of the cost advantages of flow production in the 1950s was a reduction of approximately 25 per cent, a decline in work in progress of between 10 and 15 per cent, and a cut in operating labour which yielded a saving of 60 to 80 per cent of the labour required by previous processes.[107] The greatest benefit, however, was in machine utilisation; machine tool utilisation rose to 85 to 90 per cent (a gain of about 15 per cent) and general engineering shop utilisation rose from an average of about 40 per cent to about 60 per cent. The net effects were substantial: a gain of 50 per cent.[108] The disadvantage, which was to contribute to the growth of new technology in the 1970s, was the inflexibility, and consequent risk, of employing ever greater amounts of specialised equipment in an industry which was notoriously subject to fluctuations in market demand.

The first really large scale flow production developments occurred in the United States. Ford's engine plant at Cleveland in 1956 is generally considered to be the nearest to the automatic factory.[109] Automatic methods diffused slowly throughout Europe. The less rapid introduction is explicable by lower European output volumes. The huge, inflexible and costly machinery used by Ford was only justified in the American motor industry with its huge scale of production and even there, by as early as 1955, the Americans were beginning to question the viability of such machinery. From the mid 1950s the American producers began to steer away from high cost inflexible machines in favour of the automation of single machines and automatic lines which incorporated standard types of machines.[111]

The Europeans, who were operating in a different league of production volumes, never fully followed the American system and adopted variants rather than the full version of the American model. The European version focussed on building automatic transfer lines by adapting standard machines.[112] This variant offered the possibility of automatic lines, whilst avoiding the heavy capital costs and inflexibility of the American special purpose machinery. By 1960, the British and French system of adapting standard limited purpose machines was the basis for their transfer machines and automatic transfer lines.[113]

In Europe, Renault pioneered the adoption of standard unit machines to form an automatic transfer line.[114] In Britain, Austin is generally considered to have been in the vanguard, although Ford and Vauxhall were the first firms to adopt automatic transfer machines.[115] Vauxhall operated 12 transfer stations by 1948. In 1950, Ford had 24 such stations. Austin began installing transfer machines in 1948 and, by 1952, had 4 large transfer lines in operation.[116] Three years later, 120 rotary transfer machines had been added to their plant. Automatic machinery was introduced in Standard in the late 1940s.[117] By 1960, Austin's 23,000 employees were producing 6,755 vehicles in a 42.5 hour week and were citing direct labour cost savings of up to 85 per cent.[118]

The technology is important for understanding Britain's relative decline in the motor vehicle industry. First, it became crucial that large volumes of production at each stage in the production process were achieved in order to realise economies of scale. The British producers had problems achieving large output volumes. Second, access to large financial reserves was required in order to pay for the necessary capital expenditure. As Chapter 5 demonstrates, low and fluctuating profits which followed from the inability to produce large output volumes, constrained investment. Finally, the new technology made competition by annual model changes unviable given, for example, the high fixed costs of presses which had to be spread over several years. The tendency in this period was to keep the same basic body shell for several years (for anything from 5 to 20 years), and to amend existing, rather than introducing new, models by modifying body panels.[119] The prewar practice of annual model changes thus ceased in the postwar period to be a feature of the industry.

Implementation of postwar flow production came in three distinct investment phases in Britain. The first investment phase, which lasted from 1950 to 1953, was motivated by an attempt to meet rising demand and to replace and update prewar buildings and equipment.[120] As a result, productive capacity was raised to 1,300,000 cars and commercial vehicles (Table 4.8).

The next phase, between 1954 and 1958, was aimed at increasing the capacity of the industry. The major producers all carried out a programme of expansion and re-equipment: Ford at Dagenham, Vauxhall at Luton and Dunstable and BMC at Longbridge, as a result of which the industry's productive capacity was increased from 1.3 million to just under two million cars and commercial

Table 4.8: British vehicle producing capacity, 1955, 1960 and 1965 (estimate, '000s)

	1955	1960	1965
Cars	1,000	1,400	2,000
Commercial vehicles	300	475	600
Total	1,300	1,875	2,600

Source: Aubrey Silberston, *The Motor Industry, 1955–1964*, University of Cambridge, Department of Applied Economics, 1966, Reprint Series, No. 248, Table 5.2, p. 266.

vehicles.[121] The third phase from 1960 to 1965 was characterised by an expansion of operations on new sites (largely reflecting government directions and financial inducements). BMC's commercial vehicle operation was moved to a new plant at Slough, whilst Ford's truck production was transferred to Scotland. It was also in this period that Ford and Vauxhall's Merseyside plants came into full operation. By the end of the 1960s, BLMC's total capacity was around one and a quarter million cars and commercial vehicles; that of Ford 750,000, Vauxhall 400,000 and Rootes about 300,000.[122] The result of this third phase was to increase total productive capacity to about two and a half million vehicles a year.[123]

A new wave of technological change began to transform process technology from the mid 1970s; the application of robots and computer technology both to individual operations and to the whole manufacturing process. Robots were not model-specific and therefore the product-risk of investment was reduced. Robotic operations were applied to four stages in the manufacturing process: stamping, the engine, body and final assembly, while computerised numerical controls were introduced into engine and transmission machining. In the body construction stage robots were used in the welding operations, while the flexibility resulting from the introduction of automated stamping lines in the press shops allowed rapid die changes. Press runs therefore became shorter, with savings on inventory costs.[124] The one area of the manufacturing process which, in this period, was not subject to automation was the final assembly (save for welding bodies).[125] Assembly remained a comparatively labour-intensive area because of the number of different parts and complexity of the operations. As processes moved 'downstream' towards the finished product, they become less susceptible to automation, and less capital-intensive. They operated with progressively smaller production runs and, most importantly, they offered fewer opportunities for securing economies of scale.[126]

The next major investment phase thus began in the mid 1970s and was largely concerned with the introduction of automated production of the micro-processor 'revolution'. Ford retooled Dagenham and Halewood in 1982 and 1980 respectively; British Leyland also undertook a major retooling exercise at Longbridge (in 1979) and at Cowley (in 1982).[127] Investment in new technology was an important part of the Edwardes plans after 1977 for British Leyland; £106 million was, for example, spent on the automatic body line for the Metro at Longbridge by British Leyland.[128]

The new technology enhanced flexibility and reduced the minimum efficient scale for any particular model. Capital costs could be spread over several products. Automation enabled manufacturers to adjust the balance of different models produced in response to changes in demand and to achieve a higher level and consistent quality of output.[129] This in turn allowed manufacturers to maximise the utilisation of plant by varying the mix of models.

Poor relative international performance of the British industry might be traced in part to the delayed introduction of this new technology, although the delay itself may be a reflection of a more fundamental cause. Volkswagen, Fiat, Renault and Saab all introduced robot technology in the early 1970s. The first British company to do so was Ford in 1976 when automatic welding was used on the Ford Fiesta line. Dagenham and Cowley subsequently switched to robot technology in the welding operations. The first large-scale use of the new technology at British Leyland dates from the introduction of robotic and multiwelders in body assembly on the Metro line at Longbridge. The Metro was launched in 1980.

The overall effects of technological change in the 1950s and 1960s was to increase greatly the optimum level of production and flow production techniques of the period up to the 1970s and to place a premium on mass producers achieving high outputs of a standardised product. The net impact of the introduction of micro-electronic technology from the 1970s was to reduce the optimum level. Some have argued that this phase transformed the prospects for smaller scale manufacturers. Nonetheless, part of the explanation for Britain's problems in the earlier postwar decades lies in the inability of the industry as a whole, and firms in particular, to achieve output volumes sufficient to reap all scale economies.

The measurement of scale economies

Any estimate of economies of scale in the motor vehicle industry in the postwar period is complicated by two factors: first, they change over time with the introduction of new processes and new technology, second, they differ at each stage of the production process. Where the minimum efficient scale is different for different stages in the productive process, then the overall optimum for the plant complex is the lowest common denominator of each stage minimum efficient scale.[130]

The minimum efficient scale of firm production grew from 150,000 in 1947 to 600,000 in 1954 and 750,000 in 1960.[131] In the early 1970s, minimum efficient scale for an integrated car firm with a range of three basic models was one million units a year.[132] There was widespread agreement by the mid to late 1970s that individual models should be produced at levels exceeding 200,000 per annum.[133]

The most important area for the realisation of economies of scale derived from the press shop (Table 4.9). By the early 1970s only a yearly output volume of about two million would allow maximum utilisation of each body press. This was an area which had seen substantial technological change in the 1950s and 1960s, which doubled the minimum efficient scale.[134] Similar increases took place in the foundry. In the late 1950s, an annual output for castings of 100,000 cars a year was sufficient to avoid serious handicap. Technological change again substantially raised economies for output at this stage in the production process in the 1960s. By the early 1970s minimum efficient scales of one million were being cited and, by the mid 1970s, two million.

Proceeding through the production chain, the potential for realising economies of scale diminished. Minimum efficient scales in both engine and transmission, as well as final assembly were lower than those in the foundary and press shop. Pratten, writing in 1971 on engines and transmission equipment, believed that there were large economies of scale up to an output of 250,000 units per annum but that economies were exhausted at that level of output. His evidence suggests that at this stage in the production process, British producers were achieving volumes sufficient to derive

Table 4.9: Estimates of minimum efficient scale ('000 units per annum)

	Operations			
Date and source of estimates	Foundry and forge	Pressing	Engine and transmission	Final assembly
Pratten, 1971	1,000	500	250	300
Rhys, 1972	200	2,000	1,000	200
White, 1971	'small'	400	260	200
McGee, 1973	2,000			
Euro Economics, 1975	2,000	2,000	1,000	250

Notes: The estimates relate to a single, basic model type, but embracing two door and four door variants and options in respect of engine, transmission, colour and trim.
Sources: C. F. Pratten, Economies of Scale in Manufacturing Industry, University of Cambridge, Department of Applied Economics, 1976, Occasional Papers, No. 47; D. G. Rhys, The Motor Industry, London: Butterworths, 1972; John S. McGee, 'Economies of Size in Auto Body Manufacture', Journal of Law and Economics, 16, 2, Oct. 1973; L. J. White, The American Automobile Industry Since 1945, Cambridge, Mass.: Harvard University Press, 1971; Euro Economics, 'The European Car Industry – The Problem of Structure and Overcapacity', March 1975; Nicholas Owen, Economies of Scale, Competitiveness, and Trade Patterns within the European Community, Oxford, 1983, Table 4.12, p. 71.

economies of scale.[135] The A series engine was first introduced into BMC in the early 1950s. Together with engines made for stock, export and replacement, total output volumes of these engines could exceed 850,000.[136] Ford's basic engine, which powered the Escort, Cortina and Capri models was produced in numbers in excess of 700,000.[137] Output volumes were thus sufficient to justify investment in capital equipment and to use the technically most efficient equipment available, since the high initial capital cost could be spread over a large volume and the costs written off over a period of 10 to 15 years.[138]

Although the minimum efficient scale in final assembly, by comparison with other production proceses, was low, technological change in the 1960s, in particular the introduction of more auto-mated tools for assembly, more than doubled minimum efficient scales. In the late 1950s Maxcy and Silberston were quoting levels of about 60,000 cars per annum,[139] whereas Rhys estimated that 'between the early postwar period and the late 1950s . . . the optimum assembly output had doubled from 100,000 units to 200,000'.[140] The consensus would seem to be that by the early to mid 1970s, minimum efficient scales were between 200,000 and 300,000 units per annum. The relatively low figure (i.e. relative to other production processes) stemmed from the complexity of the product, the importance of direct labour and the non-specific nature of most of the equipment. The increase in the minimum efficient scale in this period derived from greater mechanisation and the emergence of electrophoretic paint plants.

The cost penalties of operating at lower than optimum volumes were considerable. Rhys estimated that unit costs fell by 23 per cent as total volumes rose from 100,000 to 500,000; each doubling of volume therefore would lead to a 10 per cent cost reduction.[141] Pratten derived similar conclusions over a volume range from 250,000 to 500,000,[142] whilst Owen estimated that compared to the 100,000 unit manufacturer, the 250,000 manufacturer had a unit cost advantage of 15 per cent; the 500,000, a cost advantage of 20 per cent and concluded that 'the manufacturing technology employed in manufacture implies that unit costs decline by 10 per cent with every doubling of volume right up to two million a year'.[143]

There were other, competitive, implications of not achieving economies of scale for individual companies. Pratten, for example, cited four non-technical forces which affected competition, namely distribution costs, marketing, labour relations and reasearch and development.[144] Both Maxcy and Silberston, writing in the late 1950s, and Rhys, writing in the early 1970s, underlined the importance of innovation, product improvement and improvements in production methods and noted that only the financially strong firm could afford to innovate and spend the necessary large sums on research and, even if they were not responsible for particular innovations, to have the resources which would enable them to introduce innovations more speedily than smaller firms.[145]

Engineering estimates of minimum efficient scale assume that manufacturers operate plant at designed levels of output. In practice, it is generally agreed that 70 to 80 per cent capacity utilisation is the norm.[146] Even accepting this rider, production volumes among British motor manufacturers were too low to fully realise economies of scale (Table 4.10). The combined output of cars and commercial vehicles for the industry as a whole in Britain first passed the one million mark in 1954 and the two million mark in 1963. Total car and commercial vehicle production exceeded two million units a year from 1964 until 1973 (with the exception of 1967 when production fell to 1,937,000 units). Total production for the rest of the 1970s steadily declined and never exceeded two million units in any year between 1974 and 1979; by 1979 combined car and commercial vehicle production stood at 1,478,000 units.[147]

Table 4.10: Minimum efficient scale of production and the largest British motor firm (selected years)

	Largest firm's production share (%)	Total production ('000)	Estimate of largest firm's production[a] ('000)	MES[b] ('000)	MES estimate
1947	21	287	60	150	0.4
1954	38	769	292	600	0.5
1960	36	1,352	486	750	0.6
1967	45	1,552	700	1,000	0.7
1974	48	1,543	740	1,250	0.6
1977	49	1,315	651	2,000	0.3

Notes: [a] The largest firm refers in 1947 to Nuffield: 1954 and 1960 to BMC; in 1967 to BMH and 1974 and 1977 to British Leyland. Dunnett's figures for the largest firm's production are estimates since actual production figures are not available. [b] Minimum efficient scale.
Source: P. J. S. Dunnett, *The Decline of the British Motor Industry: The Effects of Government Policy, 1945–1979*, 1980, London: Croom Helm, Table 2.4, p. 23.

Between 1968 and 1978 no British producer achieved overall output volumes of one million cars a year. The highest volume output year for BLMC was 1972 when it produced 917,000 cars.[148] Other European manufacturers, by comparison, did achieve output volumes in excess of one million units. Owen's estimates of production in Europe for 1977 placed British Leyland in seventh position, after Volkswagen, Peugeot-Citroën, Ford Europe, Renault, Fiat and General Motors Europe, all of whom had total volumes in excess of one million units (Table 4.11). The performance of Volkswagen (1.6 million units), Peugeot-Citroën (1.35 million) and Ford Europe (1.34 million) was outstanding. If one sets comparative performance in terms of international production, the position of British Leyland sinks to twelfth place, well below production volumes for General Motors (9.1 million), Ford (6.4 million), Chrysler (3.1 million) and Toyota (2.7 million).[149]

British Leyland's shortfall of production from actual capacity was not unusual; what was unusual was the extent of deviation. Capacity utilisation in the company in 1974 was only 62 per cent: the

Table 4.11: Major European Community motor manufacturers, 1977 ('000 units)

Firm	Germany	France	Britain	Italy	Belgium	Total volume
Volkswagen	1,600					1,600
Peugeot-Citröen		1,350				1,350
Ford Europe	540		510		290	1,340
Renault		1,260				1,260
Fiat				1,200		1,200
General Motors Europe	920		90			1,010
British Leyland			650	40	50	740
Chrysler Europe		480	170			650
Daimler-Benz	410					410
BMW	290					290
Alfa-Romeo				200		200

Source: Nicholas Owen, Economies of Scale, Competitiveness, and Trade Patterns within the European Community, Oxford: Clarendon Press, 1983, Table 4.3, p. 49.

second lowest among the major European producers. Volkswagen, Renault, Peugeot-Citroën and Chrysler were all operating within the empirically observed norms of 70 to 80 per cent utilisation (at 80 per cent, 78 per cent, 72 per cent and 72 per cent respectively). Only General Motors (Vauxhall/Opel), at 51 per cent, fell below the performance of British Leyland.[150] For the British producers, even the sum of the record years of each producer was only 80 per cent of total theoretical capacity (Table 4.12). The industry as a whole suffered from a chronic inability to operate at anything like its full capacity of 2.5 million cars a year. The best actual production was in 1972 – when the industry was operating at 76 per cent capacity.[151] The problem applied to all British producers. Even during years of record production, none of the major manufacturers operated at their full potential. Peak production at Ford was 553,000 (72 per cent capacity) in 1968, Chrysler 281,500 (77 per cent) in 1971, and Vauxhall 245,000 (67 per cent) in 1968. Peak production at Austin-Morris, 720,000 was in 1964 (85 per cent).

The upshot was first, that British producers, even when operating at full capacity, were not operating at optimum levels, second, that actual capacity utilisation fell far short of planned capacity utilisation. Fluctuations in production were expensive. The nature of production technology in these years was to raise the costs of operating below capacity. Because of the failure to rationalise and integrate production, the industry was unable to manufacture in a

Table 4.12: British motor firms: capacity and production, 1972

Firm	Maximum planned car capacity on a two shift basis	Record output volume	year	1972 Best global year
Austin-Morris	850,000	720,000	1964	697,684
Jaguar	45,000	31,500	1971	24,492
Triumph	190,000	144,000	1968	138,216
Rover	60,000	55,800	1972	55,848
BLMC	1,145,000			916,240
Ford	650,000	553,000	1968	546,728
Chrysler	365,000	281,500	1971	263,900
Vauxhall	365,000	245,000	1968	183,976
Total	2,525,000	2,030,800		1,910,844

Source: House of Commons, Fourteenth Report from the Expenditure Committee, Session 1974–5, The Motor Vehicle Industry, 6 August 1975, House of Commons Papers 617, PP 1974/5, Table 8, p. 22.

smaller number of larger plants. Instead all plants operated below minimum efficient scale.

Model variety and scale economies

The models introduced in the immediate postwar years remained unchanged, save for face lifts, until the end of 1955. It was in 1956–7, the early 1960s and the early 1970s that new rounds of major model changes took place.[152] In the 1950s and 1960s, BMC tended to maintain models longer than its major domestic competitors. In the 1960s, Ford tended to work to a four year life cycle, with the significant exception of the Anglia, whilst Vauxhall changed its basic body shells every three years. The life cycle of BMC models, by comparison, was extremely long. The Morris Minor was 23 years old when it was discontinued in 1971; the Mini, first launched in 1959, was still being produced in 1994.

Thus one explanation for the growing problems of the British motor vehicle industry by the 1970s lies in the model life cycle, for by 1973 all of the British car manufacturers had reached the point at which most of their model range was in need of renewal.[153] The problem was particularly acute in the case of British Leyland which, in the 1970s relied on three ageing models, namely the Mini, the Allegro and the Marina for its volume car market.[154]

An additional explanation for the problems of the motor vehicle industry lies in the fact that British producers were not making sufficient numbers of each model to avoid such obsolescence. Maxcy and Silbertson, writing in the late 1950s, estimated that a total production run of 400,000 to 500,000 units was required to spread the cost of special tools and equipment associated with a particular model. At prevailing annual output volumes, this implied a life of five years or more for a model. At the end of the 1940s it was estimated that the full advantages of volume production would only be secured when the annual output of a particular model (or two models in which similar engines and parts were used) was between 30,000 to 35,000 units a year.[155] Before the war the only models reaching this level of production were the Austin Seven and Ten and the Morris Eight and Ten.[156] By the early 1970s, mass producers needed a model run of at least one million body units to allow maximum spreading of special tooling and equipment costs. At 1970s annual output volumes, this resulted in a life cycle for each model of at least five years. By the 1960s even annual face lifts, where a minority of body dies were altered, became extremely rare.[157]

The standard models of BMC, namely the Mini and the Austin Morris 1100/1300 were produced in volumes in excess of 200,000. Between 1962 and 1977, over 200,000 Minis were produced every year; whilst between 1963–4 and 1970–1 over 200,000 1100s were produced every year save one.[158] Production totals for other models however, for example, the A55/60 and the Austin Maxi never achieved production totals in excess of 81,000 and 66,000 units.[159]

Utilisation of scale economies also required a marked reduction in the number of models produced.[160] Before 1939, over 30 makes of car were being produced in Britain, with 136 basic models and 299 body variations.[161] The three best-selling models in the United States, by comparison, were achieving production volumes of between 350,000 and 600,000 each in 1939.[162] Although most manufacturers trimmed down the number of models and engines, in 1947 when 19 American manufacturers produced over 4 million cars a year with 42 basic models (some of which had similar engines), 20 British manufacturers produced under 400,000 cars, with 51 basic models.[163] Subsequent years however witnessed a marked decline in the number of models. By the end of 1956, something like 16 fundamentally different models competed in the mass market, although this figure tends to exaggerate the variety given the considerable standardisation between models. In 1957, the two largest British firms made an average of 6 basic models; the 3 largest continental producers, by contrast, had an average of only 3.[164] The 1960s witnessed some movement to reduce this variety, but by 1965 the 'Big Five' still produced 6 basic engines and 20 different body styles.[165] By 1970, 18 completely different car engines and about 30 different body shells were made by British car manufacturers, but over 60 per cent of the car output covered just 3 basic engine types and 5 body shells. Four basic cars accounted for 41 per cent of car sales in Britain, British Leyland's 1100/1300, Ford's Escort, Vauxhall's Viva and Hillman's Avenger in 1970.

4.6 Conclusion

The failure to rationalise plant and product meant that the industry was saddled with many low volume models and low volume plants with excess capacity which, in turn, constrained productivity and, by increasing the unit costs of output, decreased profitability. In 1955 productivity in the British motor vehicle industry was second only to that of the United States. By 1965, productivity in the British had been exceeded by Germany, France, Italy and Japan.[166] Economies of scale mattered in the postwar motor vehicle industry.

British producers were clearly failing to utilise scale economies, but was this a symptom, rather than a cause, of the motor industry's problems? The question has fuelled much debate in the literature and forms the focus of the following chapters. The evidence suggests that under-capacity working was a serious problem and that this can be traced to two aspects of postwar years: first, the priority given to export earnings which precluded rationalisation after the war and second, discussed further in Chapter 6, the implicit social contract which placed a high premium on full employment and which in turn constrained rationalisation throughout most of the postwar period. Labour relations and management will emerge as

the two, related, key factors in this implicit social contract. The industry was locked into an institutional framework which would undermine its competitive advantage from the early 1950s and which ultimately was to precipitate its decline.

CHAPTER FIVE

COMPETITIVE BEHAVIOUR AND MARKET POSITIONING, 1945–1978

Which businesses survived and prospered not only depended upon their sizes, but also on their corporate strategies and styles. Motor business strategies included designing, building and pricing models aimed at particular market segments. Assemblers also tried to increase the demand for their products by advertising and by updating or restyling them. The success with which they pursued these objectives determined their profitability. That in turn determined their ability to invest in new model development and in plant improvements. Another form of investment was in research and development, including the continuing absorption of information fed back from salesmen and servicemen.

In this chapter we first discuss in Section 1 the multidimensional nature of competition in the motor industry – product innovation, model proliferation, pricing, advertising. Section 2 considers the competitive strategies adopted by the major firms to see what precisely triggered the decline of the British producers. Investment is a key to longer term competitive strategy. How investment was paid for and what constrained finance is considered in Section 3. In particular we ask whether there was some peculiarity of the British economy that led to 'short-termism', or an irrational unwillingness to invest. Yet another aspect of strategy is policy towards foreign markets. Foreign trade is assessed in Section 4. In the earlier postwar period the British industry was able to reap greater scale economies through substantial exports, than when confined to a

purely national market. By the 1970s import penetration curtailed this advantage, as the domestic industry lost competitiveness.

5.1 The nature of competition

Offering a better vehicle to the public is one way a manufacturer might compete. Product quality can be enhanced, or changed, in two ways. Either more of the same characteristics can be embodied, or the range of characteristics can be altered. Buyers might be offered 'more car', perhaps a more powerful engine, at the same price. Or, for instance, the Maxi's five speed gearbox and hatchback altered the characteristics usually included in a family saloon. What combinations could be embodied depended on the available technology. Apart from the transverse engine (and possibly hydrolastic suspension), vehicle development was remarkably gradualist. Power continued to be provided by the increasingly fuel efficient internal combustion engine. As in the interwar years, electrical power was handicapped by the failure to reduce battery weight sufficiently for general use. Dr Felix Wankel's rotary engine of 1951, with few moving parts, was smaller, lighter and ran more smoothly than the conventional internal combustion engine, but was less durable. Its use in cars was pioneered by NSU but even from the late 1960s, after being taken up by Toyo Kogyo of Japan, the Wankel did not clearly dominate conventional car engines, and did not appear in a British car. Fibreglass bodies were a lighter alternative to steel, adopted by Reliant for their small volume Scimitar and Kitten models. Like the Wankel, these bodies failed to affect mainstream industry technology, in this case because they were difficult to manufacture in large quantities. Product conservatism paid.

During the period 1957–68, motor car firms in the short run probably priced as monopolists, since changes in price could be disguised by the introduction of new models.[1] In the longer term, the responsiveness of market share to price changes was high because customers spent a good deal of time and money searching for information about alternative models, in view of the high value of the purchase.[2] Pure price competition was rare because of the high fixed costs of motor vehicle production. 'Model-price' competition, whereby quality was the competitive weapon for a given price, was the norm. Detection of 'quality-adjusted price' cutting was more difficult than identifying 'pure' price cuts and therefore was less likely to provoke a price war. Rivals would in any case be unable to react comparably in the short run because model modification takes considerable time. When firms raised prices they would want rivals to follow as quickly as possible. So quality-adjusted price *increases* were undertaken by price hikes; rather than reduce quality for given price, prices were increased for given quality. However quality changes were not linked to price decreases.[3]

Customers chose the products of particular firms not only because of better quality and prices, but because of the number of models of each manufacturer (or brand) available within a given price range, and the proximity of a sales outlet.[4] Barker's variety hypothesis supposes that economies of scale prevent domestic producers making all the combination of characteristics demanded by domestic consumers. As incomes rise, the taste for variety can be indulged, despite the higher transport costs of overseas products in the domestic market. According to this hypothesis a simple model of market share determination is that for each firm the two key explanatory variables are the number of models offered and the number of dealers. For the years 1975–80 this specification of a regression model under-predicted Ford's market share because that company was an efficiency leader.[5]

Manufacturers were obliged to choose whether to market a full range of models, or to restrict their attention to a few. They also needed to decide whether to market the full line under a single brand name, or go for 'badges' as symbols of quality. Customer loyalty clustered round images of marques; Ford acquired an image of mechanical reliability, Volvo of safety and so on. Once customer loyalty was acquired, there was a high probability that replacement purchases would be from the same marque, if a suitable product was available. Hence a bottom of the range car could attract a young customer who would trade up to more expensive models as income rose with age. That was a reason advanced for 'underpricing' the Mini.

Advertising, marketing, credit facilities and locational factors additionally influenced the demand for a firm's vehicles. In the early postwar decades, when motor manufacturers were operating in a sellers' market, they did not need to incur heavy advertising costs to secure market shares. Such advertising as there was, was designed to ensure future demand. Once supply constraints receded however, and as the market became more saturated, particularly from the mid 1960s, advertising assumed a more prominent role in achieving and maintaining market shares. The re-emergence of 'model-price' competition from the early 1950s, with its emphasis on product differentiation and style features, increased the requirement for manufacturers to publicise the particular advantages of their models.[6] By 1968, total advertising by car firms amounted to £4.4 million, the bulk of which was placed in the printed media. A decade later, expenditure had reached £18.2 million and had expanded to encompass television advertisements. The upsurge in advertising in the early 1970s was initiated by importers who spent heavily on advertising to break into the British market at a time when British producers could not meet demand.[7] By the mid 1970s, domestic producers had increased their outlays on advertising in an attempt to preserve and increase their market share.[8]

Over the period 1957–68 motor companies' advertising adopted a long run rule of thumb to spend a certain proportion of sales revenue on advertising. In the short run reductions in market share were met by greater advertising (although British Leyland's increased expenditure on advertising in 1974 and 1975 failed to rectify falling sales).[9] Car firms recognised increased advertising was likely to be at least partly matched by their rivals. That would partly offset any extra sales their advertising generated. They therefore held their expenditures below levels that would have been profitable for a monopolist.[10]

Advertising in the commercial vehicle market, by comparison, was negligible. In the late 1970s, advertising on commercial vehicles only amounted to 5 per cent of that on cars.[11] Commercial vehicle users were less impressed with generalised and often superficial information on product differentiation and styling features and more concerned with the basic economics of a particular vehicle. Such information was gleaned both by word of mouth and from detailed perusal of the numerous trade journals.

5.2 Corporate strategies and styles

Over the period 1945–78 the years immediately after the war were exceptional; motor manufacturers were operating in a sellers' market. Supply rather than demand factors were the main constraints in a world desperate for motor vehicles, in stark contrast to most of the interwar years.[12] Consequently less attention was paid to the market than to production.

With its massive, purpose-built, Dagenham plant, Ford was the most successful firm. Chapter 4 has shown how Ford increased market share at the expense of nearly all other producers.[13] BMC also increased output, but by less than Ford, and neglected modernisation of plant and equipment.[14] BMC's share of British vehicle production fell from 43.4 per cent in 1946 to 39.4 per cent by 1950 while the company's share of the market sliped from 40.1 per cent in 1947 to 38 per cent in 1954.[15]

Ford's achievement between 1946 and 1956 was based on building cars to the conventional price in each class. The infrequent and small price changes which were implemented were either associated with the introduction of new models or reflected changes in input prices.[16] Price cuts by Ford in 1948 and 1952 and by Austin and Hillman in 1953 and 1954 respectively went unchallenged.[17] These instances of short run price competition were intended to improve declining market shares and, in the case of Ford, to pass on new economies of scale. The £30 reduction of the Anglia price by Ford in 1964 reflected the savings from moving to the new Liverpool factory with a daily capacity of 600 units.[18]

Individual company policy and styles might diverge considerably from the industry norm, often as the unintended outcomes of company institutions and structures, or inheritance. The organisational location of designers and their skills could be crucial to the long run prospects of a business for example. Embodying new, or more, characteristics in a car was a problem of design. The more radical the changes, the greater the risk either that the product would not find favour or that there would be hitches in manufacturing. Equally a radical product could be immensely profitable, although that does not seem to have been true of the motor industry in this period. The extraordinary role of Sir Alec Issigonis in the British motor industry after 1945 is most instructive. Issigonis may have designed three of the five best-selling British made cars, the Morris Minor, the Mini and the 1100, but he was dismissive of styling which, according to Church, he associated with fashion and the unwholesome influence of women.[19] Yet even his formula of brilliant individualism ran out of steam with the Maxi.[20] In British motor businesses, it was rarely adequately supported either by testing, production engineering, market research, or costing.[21] Ford Europe's vice-president of supply later summarised a widespread opinion, that British motor businesses were technologically innovative but had no 'follow-through' so that reliability and servicing were poor.[22]

BMC/BLMC's reliability compared unfavourably with Ford, with dangerous implications for BMC's competitiveness. Market share depended not only on product style, features and value for money but on consumer confidence in the product. BMC cars often included innovative characteristics, particularly the revolutionary front wheel drive models. The front wheel drive afforded greater cabin space by the transverse location of the engine, without fore-going engine power. BMC adopted the front wheel drive in more of its models than any other manufacturer. Design innovation was not however backed up by sufficient product testing and appropriately timed launches. BMC tended to announce new cars before large numbers were ready for sale and before production teething problems had been resolved. Ford designs were more conventional but their reliability fostered goodwill at a time when BMC lost customer loyalty from both poor quality and long waiting lists.[23]

Two measures of innovative activity, research and development expenditure and patent activity are indicative of the loss of competitive behaviour on the part of the British manufacturers in general and British Leyland in particular. In the late 1960s and 1970s, expenditure on research and development in the British motor industry was minimal when compared with that of its major rivals (Table 5.1), whilst patent activity all but collapsed at British Leyland from the mid 1970s.[24]

Ford UK only produced two basic models for many years.[25] Ford supplied medium size cars for the fleet and business market and in so doing dominated a growth sector which was not seriously contested by other manufacturers.[26] Although during the 1960s the company extended its range, in 1970 it was still producing only five basic models. In contrast, by the mid 1970s, British Leyland made more main saloon models than any of its major competitors – nine, as against Toyota's seven and Renault's eight. Ford of Europe,

Volkswagen and Fiat, each only made five main saloon models.[27] Model proliferation may be an appropriate strategy in an increasingly affluent market, or it may be a reflection of the shortcomings of former market leaders. In the first case, the more successful models a manufacturer supplies, the larger the market share.

Table 5.1: *International research and development expenditure, 1967–1979 (in US dollars (millions) at 1975 prices and exchange rates)*

	United States	Japan	West Germany	France	Britain
1967	1,151	234	419	201	205
1969	1,621	325	626	244	210
1971	1,631	476	751	313	199
1973	2,209	674	621	373	193
1975	1,789	654	623	361	192
1977	2,173	812	751	443	193
1979	2,501	1,143	842	464	239

Source: Daniel T. Jones, 'Technology and the UK Automobile Industry, *Lloyds Bank Review*, No. 148, April 1983, Table 1, p. 22

Two explanations have been offered for BMC/BMH/British Leyland's reluctance to reduce the number of models offered – failure to integrate after the mergers and encouraging subsidiary companies to produce models in competition with each other. This competition or duplication might have deterred entry to the industry by multinationals, or improved performance by a form of 'yardstick' competition. But as Williams has argued, BMC's constituent companies were chasing a declining, minority market.[28] In contrast to Ford, BMC based its strategy on the mass production of small cars with low profit margins. BMC/BLMC failed to produce one car which took 20 per cent of the small car market on which it was increasingly dependent. Consequently the company had to introduce or keep in production a variety of models which sold in small quantities to defend its market share.[29] The Central Policy Review Staff in 1975 contended an *insufficient* range of inadequate models in the small car segment lost the British-owned industry market share. The product range provided less car for the money than foreign competitors. Performance, handling and road holding, dimensions, interior finish and comfort, additional refinements, fuel economy and seating were typically less than fully competitive.[30] The problem was not model proliferation but failure to introduce satisfactory new models.

A major difference between postwar and interwar competition was the tendency of manufacturers to maintain different shares within different segments of the market. According to Williams, the growing problems of the native British motor vehicle producer can be traced to the inability of first BMC and then BLMC to identify segments in national markets in which the company could achieve profitable sales in sufficient volume.[31] The company's 'failure' in these terms meant it was pinned down in particular sectors of the home market which did not have volume potential. The first such 'mistake' on the part of BMC was its decision after 1952 to base its strategy of output expansion on the mass production of small cars. This, though successful in the short run in expanding output, had negative long term repercussions in tems of the low profit margins on small cars. In the 1950s the two best selling small cars of the company were the Austin A30/A35 and the Morris Minor, both of which sold for below £400.[32] These were replaced by the Mini in 1959, and by the 1100/1300 in 1962. The Mini achieved high sales (between 1968 and 1974 it was produced at an average rate of 297,000 vehicles a year), but it was sold close to or below cost.[33]

The 1100/1300 models suffered from similar production cost problems. Issigonis's transverse front wheel drive applied to the 1100/1800 models, required high body weight and thus pushed up manufacturing costs. The 1100/1300 models moreover never achieved the success of the Mini, the highest annual production volume being 279,599 in 1965–6.[34]

Despite the high production volumes, BMC was never able, either in the Austin A30/A35 and the Morris Minor in the 1950s or the Mini and 1100/1300 in the 1960s, to produce one car which took 20 per cent of the small car market (Table 5.2). The Mini and the 1100/1300 *together* took 20 per cent of the market between 1965 and 1969.[35] This in turn meant that the company had to introduce or keep in production a variety of other models, such as the Farina A40 and the A55/A60 models, which sold in small quantities, to defend its market share.

Nor was BMC able to find a best-seller among its larger front wheel drive cars in the 1500–1800 cc class. The 1800 only twice topped annual volumes of 50,000 units per annum (in 1965–6 and in 1970–1); whilst the 1500/1750 cc Maxi only exceeded annual production runs of 50,000 units in 1971–2 and 1972–3.[36] BLMC was left concentrating on the small, private segment of the car market which, according to Williams, was to cost the company dear. Consumers traded up market, importers catered for the market's increased propensity for product differentiation and the business

Table 5.2: New registrations of the Mini and 1100/1300, 1965–1974 (per centage of all registrations)

	Mini	1100/1300
1965	9.5	14.4
1966	8.8	14.5
1967	7.4	11.8
1968	7.8	13.7
1969	7.0	13.8
1970	7.5	12.3
1971	8.1	10.4
1972	5.9	6.2
1973	9.8	3.6
1974	7.1	0.6

Source: SMMT, The Motor Industry of Great Britain, selected years.

market assumed greater importance. After the oil shock of 1973–4, consumer demand reverted to smaller vehicles. But this demand was soon met also by Ford and increasingly, by imports.[37] By 1975 the company was recording negative returns on sales (Table 5.3).

Table 5.3: Return on British Leyland sales, 1968–1975

1968	5.02
1969	4.71
1970	1.39
1971	3.97
1972	3.20
1973	3.72
1974	1.22
1975	−2.04

Note: Return on sales defined as trading profit before interest, tax and extraordinary items divided by the value of sales, expressed in percentage terms.
Source: British Leyland Motor Corporation Limited, Annual Report and Accounts, 1976, pp. 32–3.

In the 1960s and early 1970s Ford concentrated on medium sized cars for the fleet and business market and thus assumed dominance in a growth sector which was not seriously contested by other manufacturers. From 1965 to 1978 Ford achieved the largest market share in the medium car class, largely as a result of the success of the Cortina which not only outsold all other models in this class but outsold the combined share of BMC's models once the company entered this market from 1967 and 1971 with the launch of the Maxi and the Marina respectively (Table 5.4).

Table 5.4: British market shares in the medium car class, 1965–1978 (percentage)

	Ford Cortina	BL Maxi	BL Marina	Vauxhall Cavalier
1965	10.6			
1966	12.1			
1967	14.9	3.1		
1968	12.5	2.7		
1969	12.0	3.2		
1970	11.4	3.4		
1971	7.9	3.3	3.2	
1972	11.4	3.3	6.4	
1973	10.9	3.2	6.9	
1974	10.3	2.8	6.4	
1975	8.9	2.3	6.6	
1976	9.8	2.6	5.5	2.3
1977	9.1	2.0	5.0	3.1
1978	8.7	2.0	5.3	3.5

Note: Gaps in table indicate model not yet introduced.
Source: SMMT, The Motor Industry of Great Britain, selected years.

BMC and then BLMC thus concentrated on a market segment with low margins, which was shrinking and which, from the early 1970s was increasingly threatened by importers who sold to private buyers. By 1974, the private buyer segment accounted for 60 per cent of the market and half of these purchasers were buying imports. By the early 1970s, BLMC was trying to sell volume cars in a home market which only accounted for at most just under two-thirds of the market, but half of which was being served by imported cars (Table 5.5). Its problems in the small car segment were compounded when in 1977 Ford entered this market with the Fiesta, which in the early 1980s was to take 7 per cent of the small car market. Ford also continued to retain the loyalty of fleet purchasers and suffered no major inroads by importers into its profitable business market segment. In 1974, only 4 per cent of the fleet market was taken by imported cars. Williams summed up the situation: 'BLMC's problem was not the limited size and low growth of the British car market as a whole . . . (but) the contraction of the particular market sector which BMC had traditionally dominated'.[38]

By the early 1970s an obvious strategy for BLMC was to break into the fleet market with a more conventional model. To this end in 1971 the company launched the Marina, designed to compete

Table 5.5: British import share of new car registrations, 1965–1978 (percentage)

1965	5.2
1966	6.5
1967	8.3
1968	8.3
1969	10.4
1970	14.3
1971	19.3
1972	23.5
1973	27.4
1974	27.9
1975	33.2
1976	37.9
1977	45.4
1978	49.3

Source: Karel Williams, John Williams and Dennis Thomas, *Why are the British Bad at Manufacturing?*, London: Routledge Kegan Paul, 1983, Appendix, C, Table 5, p. 280.

against Ford's Cortina. The Marina failed to break Ford's dominance of the medium car class. Market penetration never exceeded 6.9 per cent of sales. New registrations reached a high point of 115,000 units in 1973, and declined thereafter.[39] Disappointing sales of the Marina and Allegro compounded the problems of BLMC, not least because there was a doubling of development and tooling costs per unit sold.[40] These models failed in part because far fewer resources were invested in their development than in other companies' new models. They were aimed at a national market rather than at the continent like Ford products but British Leyland's managerial shortcomings also played a part, as amply demonstrated by the later Rover SD1 project.[41]

The SD1 project was an attempt to make a high volume luxury car in a completely new plant. British Leyland's weak corporate design resources with few graduate engineers quickly showed up in the inability to manage computer aided design, which meant among other things that errors were repeated and time wasted. The design process did not sufficiently integrate the product and the production process. SD1 car clinics were only introduced after the product had been developed and the key features established, and so major alterations were too expensive. In a car clinic, a representative cross-section of potential customers owning either the company's or rival manfuacturer's products are shown the new car, unbadged and anonymous, along with competing models, and their reactions noted. Their responses are used to judge how well it will sell and at what price. The SD1's design and development lasted from 1968 to 1976, an unusually long time by industry standards, although it did win the 1977 European Car of the Year award. When launched, a six month waiting list quickly built up and a blackmarket emerged by July 1976. Unfortunately in November 1976 a spot check showed only 6 per cent of the newly made cars were fit for immediate sale. Problems persisted with quality, especially originating from the new paint plant. The model failed to expand the market share of the predecessor model. Overheads therefore remained crippling and in March 1982 the SD1 plant was closed and production switched to Cowley.

The Mini replacement story was similar. The ADO88 project absorbed £300 million of investment between 1974 and 1977. Then car clinics showed that only 3 per cent of customers would make the car their first choice compared with 39 per cent the Fiesta.[42] A new larger vehicle, the LC10, with unmatchable interior space but shorter than competing models, was therefore born from the ADO88 at the end of 1977. Virtually every exterior body panel was changed to give extra length and width, and more glass area. The penalty was one year delay in the launch date, until October 1980.

With a far more systematic management style and a simpler organisation, Ford went from strength to strength.[43] Until the early 1970s, Ford showed no interest in the small car market, preferring to concentrate on the light, medium and large car markets. Ford's model line up by the late 1960s comprised the Escort, the immensely successful Cortina, the Granada and the Capri. In the mid 1970s, however, the company ventured into the small car market with the launch of the Fiesta, in an attempt to establish a strong marketing base in the French, Spanish and Italian markets.[44] The Fiesta (Bobcat) project was confirmed in 1973 after higher oil prices enhanced the attractiveness of small fuel-efficient vehicles.[45] This first 'world car', with its $1 billion of investment, expanded Ford's market by switching demand away from other manufacturers. Second car Fiat owners were the principal 'switchers' on the continent. For 1976/7, 500,000 vehicles per annum were planned. Engines were made in Spain and transaxles in France. The cars were assembled in Spain, Saarlouis in West Germany and Dagenham. The Fiesta also exposed the difficulties faced by a world car, when national markets continued to be differentiated. 'Federalizing' the Fiesta for the American market, into which it was to be imported, required 559 unique parts, including a new 1600 cc engine and carburettor.[46] Such modifications reduced the cost advantages that had been anticipated from production for the whole world.

Competition in the finished vehicle market was intense, but less evident in component production. Restrictive practices in the electrical equipment sector were largely concerned with the replacement rather than the new market, and with the price differentiation between new and replacement goods. Champion and Lucas, in particular, priced to earn excessive profits, according to the Monopolies Commission.[47] In the tyre industry, the leading producers charged similar prices in the early 1960s for their products. But this was taken as evidence, not of cartels, but of a competitive market in equilibrium, of the bargaining power of the vehicle producers and of the price leadership of Dunlop.[48] Competition in this branch of the components industry, moreover, became more intense with the growth of Michelin, Goodyear and Firestone in the British market from the middle of the 1960s.

Distribution

Motor vehicle manufacturers emphasized the competitiveness of their product market, yet they felt co-operation to ensure 'fair play' was entirely consistent. Between 1945 and the mid 1950s, the industry was faced with excess demand at current prices. The industry's professional body, the British Motor Trades Association, introduced schemes to discourage dealers from selling at above list price and to discourage customers from reselling their vehicles, almost immediately after receiving delivery, on the second-hand market. Both retailers and retail purchasers easily circumvented such restrictions.[49]

Manufacturers were also concerned that their distributors should maintain sufficient resources to provide an efficient after sales service. They contended that distributor price cutting threatened that service and imperilled the reputation of their products. The 1956 Restrictive Practices Act made mutilateral price maintenance illegal, but strengthened individual retail price maintenance by making it easier for manfuacturers to take legal action against price cutters. At first, the Association tried to circumvent the Act by substituting a series of bilateral Agreements between the Association and the indivudual dealers for the general arrangements preveiously in force, but such devices were declared illegal.[50] The Act prevented motor manufacturers from forcing dealers to be members of the British Motor Trades Associatin by agreeing to supply only Association members with cars. It also prevented the British Motor Trades Association from issuing stop lists of firms failing to abide by the Association's rules on resale prices. The effect of the 1956 was, in Rhys's view, only to make explicit what had been conventionally accepted before, namely the imposition of individual resale price maintenance by single firms.[51] After 1956 collective control by the British Motor Trades Association was replaced by individual control by vehicle manufacturers. After the Resale Prices Act of 1964, the policy of enforcing resale prices was abandoned throughout the trade. Manufacturers merely recommended the prices to be charged by retailers.[52]

Ford's superior distribution network contributed substantially to corporate profitability. Throughout the postwar period Ford built up a distribution network to serve the important business sector, consisting of a few larger retailers geared up to making volume sales and in prarticular to making company fleet sales in lots of 20 or more cars.[53] The success of the Cortina range referred to above was helped by the distribution network of specialised dealers. By comparison, BLMC's distribution network of a multitude of small retailers reflected and compounded the company's dependence on the individual private buyer. When in the 1970s, the company tried to rectify this problem by rationalising its dealer network (between 1968 and 1977, British Leyland reduced its number of retail outlets form nearly 6,000 to 2,250),[54] it only intensified the fierce competition in its traditional markets, as importers took over an estimated one-third of BLMC's former dealers.[55] At the end of the 1970s, imports accounted for nearly 50 per cent (4,000) of all retail outlets.[56] In this one stroke BLMC removed an important barrier to foreign firms entering the British markets whilst failing to achieve its declared intention of increasing average sales per outlet by concentrating sales into a small number of relatively large dealerships.[57] In 1977, average BL car and light vans sales per outlet were 143, compared with Ford's 302 and General Motors' 221.[58]

Hire purchase

Hire purchase played a similar role to advertising and distribution as competitive weapons. In the postwar period consumer credit was instrumental in the emergence of the mass market for motor vehicles; at the same time control of consumer credit also became an instrument target of demand management in the 1950s and 1960s (Chapter 7).

Hire purchase facilities assumed increased importance from the mid 1950s and were to underpin the growth of sales of all categories of vehicles, but especially used cars for the private consumer. New cars sales on hire purchase terms were only about one-quarter of sales of used cars on hire purchase terms. In 1953, hire purchase contracts accounted for 9 per cent of new car sales and 13 per cent of new commercial vehicle sales. In that year there were 167,600 hire purchase sales of used cars and 26,200 hire purchase sales of used commercial vehicles.[59] Over the next ten years, an increasing number of motor vehicle sales were made on hire purchase terms. In 1963, 179,331 second-hand cars were sold, of which 48 per cent were sold by hire purchase. [60] In the mid 1960s it was estimated that 86 per cent of used cars for private use had been purchased on hire purchase terms.[61] Although less extensively used, hire purchase was also directly instrumental in stimulating the private new car and the business market. By the mid 1960s, 59 per cent of new cars acquired for private use had been purchased on hire purchase terms, whereas 14 per cent and 41 per cent of used and new cars acquired wholly or partly for business use respectively had been bought with hire purchase facilities.[62] Because of the link between the new and second-hand markets (Chapter 7), hire purchase sales of used cars also indirectly expanded new purchases.

5.3 Investment

Competitive new products needed new investment, and investment needed financing.[63] By the early 1970s, there was no question that there had been a lack of investment in the British-owned industry. Official inquiries of the 1970s into the fortunes of the British mnotor vehicle industry (and British Leyland in particular) drew attention to the relationship between technology and capital investment, and, especially, the industry's long term record of inadequate and under-investment, but failed to agree on the causal significance of investment. The Ryder Report saw under-investment as the key to British Leyland's problems; the Central Policy Review Staff believed under-investment paled into significance in comparison with the company's history of unsatisfactory work practices.[64] The House of Commons Expenditure Committee took a middle position, agreeing that the investment mattered: 'inadequate investment and the lower productivity of old plant have been the greatest contributors to the poor profitability of the mass production car side of the industry', but added that this 'had been exacerbated by capacity under-utilisation, whether caused by industrial disputes, poor production planning or the uncertainties resulting from Government policies'.[65]

The likelihood was that investment was low because more investment would not be profitable. The question then becomes why was investment unprofitable. The following paragraphs explore the evidence on capital investment, traces this back to the wider issues of the industry's financial performance and demonstrates that the key issue was less the level of capital investment than the efficiency with which capital was used.

Estimates of both capital expenditure and fixed assets per employee confirm the view that one symptom of the poor performance of the British motor vehicle industry and its inability to utilise the economies of scale afforded by the new technology of the period was low capital investment (Table 5.6). In 1974, fixed asets per man in British Leyland were only £920, compared with £2,657 in Ford, £1,356 at Vauxhall and £1,456 at Chrysler UK. By 1970–3, of the three least capitalised European firms, three were British, whilst of the five most capitalised, three were German. Between 1970 and 1973 capital expenditure at British Leyland (at 1973 exchange rates) amounted to £222 million (Table 5.7). Although not the lowest among the European companies, British Leyland's record was dwarfed by that of its major competitors.

Investment needed to be profitable if it was to be sustained. Poor profitability during the 1950s and 1960s suggests why assets were so low in British Leyland, and to a lesser extent in most of industry, by

Table 5.6: Value added per man and fixed assets per man, 1974 (£)

Firm	Value-added per man	Fixed assets per man
BL	2,129	920
Opel	5,875	3,612
Daimler-Benz	5,207	2,694
Volvo	4,886	4,662
Ford Germany	4,883	3,608
Saab	4,637	3,141
Renault	4,133	2,396
Ford UK	3,901	2,657
Chrysler UK	2,765	1,456
Vauxhall	2,560	1,356
Fiat	2,259	3,160

Source: House of Commons, Fourteenth Report of the Expenditure Committee; Session 1974–5, *The Motor Vehicle Industry*, 6 August 1975, House of Commons Paper 617, PP 1974/5, Table 14, p. 36.

Table 5.7: Capital expenditure of various international motor firms, 1970–1973 (at December 1973 exchange rates), £m

Volkswagen	1,041
Fiat	575
Daimler Benz	490
Nissan Datsun	414
Toyota	407
Opel	257
Volvo	239
British Leyland[a]	222
Ford-Werke	209
Ford UK	190
Citroën	165
Peugeot	162
British Leyland[a]	127
Simca	69
Vauxhall	61
Chrysler UK	30

Note: [a] The £222 million figure for British Leyland was taken from the *Annual Accounts*; the £127 million figure for British Leyland excludes tools, acquired companies and regional grants (Bhaskar, *Future of the UK Motor Industry*), p. 66.
Source: Krish Bhaskar, *The Future of the UK Motor Industry*, London: Kogan Page 1979, Table 3.13, p. 66

1969. The profit performance of the motor vehicle industry in the postwar decades falls into two distinct periods. Up to 1961, profits grew fairly steadily.[66] After 1961, the industry entered an era of marked fluctuations, with sharp declines in after-tax profit in 1961, 1962, 1964, 1966, 1970 and 1974. From 1961 fluctuations became noticeably more severe. This pattern was very different from, and much worse than, that of British industry as a whole, and suggests that explanations have to be sought within the industry itself rather than in the wide economic environment.[67] The vulnerability of the domestic producers to fluctuations in profitability was not limited to the 1960s. BMC from its inception recorded low and unstable profits relative to the American producers. Indeed, low and fluctuating profits were a characteristic of the major domestic producer from the date of the merger in 1952 and have been explained by both Rhys and the Expenditure Committee in terms of under-capacity working with its attendant increase in fixed costs.[68]

Although comparisons of firms must be treated with caution,[69] Table 5.8 indicates that the profit problem was most acute in BMC and Rootes. The most profitable firms in the 1960s were Ford, Vauxhall and Standard-Triumph; Rootes had the worst record, while BMC recorded the most wildly fluctuating performance. Only Ford generated a net cash flow sufficiently large to ensure the company's survival. Standard paralleled BMC, rather than the American-owned manufacturers.[70] In the first two postwar decades, Ford was achieving pre-tax profits which were, on the whole, far superior to that of BMC/BMH. In 1961, BMC was making £6.50 profit per vehicle; Ford £45.[71] Nor did the merger of 1968 improve the financial position; between 1970 and 1974, British Leyland made only small net pre-tax profits, which did not match the sum of the previous best years of its individual parts, even nominally, until 1976 and even then its profits for distribution and retention were higher than they should have been given the insufficient provision made for depreciation.[72] In 1975 Ryder was to report that 'profits were wholly inadequate and insufficient to maintain the business on a viable basis'.[73] In that same year, the company recorded a pre-tax loss of £112 million and five years later a pre-tax loss of £388 million.

The main sources of finance for investment are retained earnings, the capital markets and, in relevant cases, a parent company.[74] Of course profits must be earned before they can be retained or the capital market persuaded to contribute funds.[75] From 1956 to 1967, the average annual retained earnings in BMC were roughly double Vauxhall's, but then Vauxhall was a much smaller company. If investment were a function of retained earnings, the evidence suggests that, relative to Ford, but not Vauxhall, BMC would have

Table 5.8: Pre-tax profits of British manufacturers, 1945–1980 (£m)

	Rootes	Austin	Morris	BMC	Leyland	BLMC	Ford	Vauxhall
1945	1.5	0.9	1.9				1.4	2.1
1946	− 0.4	1.0	3.0				3.2	1.5
1947	0.6	1.8	2.6				3.9	2.0
1948	1.5	1.8	1.5				5.5	2.0
1949	1.1	1.6	2.6				5.5	2.7
1950	2.0	5.2	2.1				9.7	2.7
1951	9.8	7.2	8.7				9.8	2.7
1952	3.4			5.2			9.6	5.3
1953	2.2			12.3			15.7	9.9
1954	3.5			17.9			19.0	12.4
1955	3.3			20.3			18.1	10.8
1956	1.7			11.7			10.0	6.4
1957	− 0.8			11.2	6.1		18.4	0.6
1958	3.4			21.0	6.4		24.7	1.1
1959	3.9			15.7	5.3		32.2	13.5
1960	4.4			26.9	9.2		33.7	14.1
1961	2.9			10.1	6.9		22.2	14.5
1962	− 0.89			4.2	5.5		17.0	16.0
1963	− 0.25			15.4	10.98		35.0	16.3
1964	1.8			21.8	18.2		24.0	17.9
1965	− 0.2			23.3	20.45		8.9	17.7
1966	− 3.1			21.8	16.43		7.4	13.7
1967	− 10.5			− 3.28	18.0		25.4	12.0
1968	3.9					37.95	43.0	12.2
1969	0.61					40.0	38.1	1.6
1970	− 10.0					4.0	20.0	− 5.1
1971	0.4					32.0	− 30.7	1.8
1972	1.6					32.0	46.8	− 4.3
1973	3.7					51.0	65.4	− 4.1
1974	− 17.7					2.3	8.7	− 18.1
1975	− 35.5					− 23.6	40.8	− 2.5
1976	− 31.9					− 112.4	140.2	7.4
1977	− 8.2					72.5	263.1	5.2
1978						15.3	242.0	2.0
1979						− 112.2	386.0	− 31.7
1980						− 387.5	226.0	− 83.3

Note: Gaps in figures indicate mergers.
Sources: P. Dunnett, *The Decline of the British Motor Industry*, London: Croom Helm, 1980, Table 3.2, p. 39; D. Thoms and T. Donnelly, *The Motor Car Industry in Coventry Since the 1890s*, Beckenham, Kent: Croom Helm, 1989, Table 6.7, p. 163; D. G. Rhys, *The Motor Industry: An Economic Survey*, London: Butterworths, Table 10.3, p. 361.

invested little from the time of the Morris–Austin merger. From 1956 to 1967, the retained earnings in BMC averaged £5.4 million per annum and the cumulative retained earnings of the company amounted to £64.8 million.[76] This was impressive when compared with Vauxhall's cumulative figure of £31.2 million (average £2.8 million per annum), but not when compared with Ford's.[77] Ford's retained earnings over the same period were considerably greater even though her unit volume was below BMC/BMH's.[78] Ford's retained earnings over the same period averaged £8.5 million per annum and totalled £93.4 million over the period.[79] From 1968 to 1978, BLMC was operating at negative retained earnings, which averaged −£14.9 million per annum and led to a cumulative figure of −£164.2 million by 1978.[80] Ford, by comparison, achieved annual retained earnings of £43.9 million in the period and a cumulative figure of £482.5 million by 1978.[81] Again, low retained earnings appear to have been peculiar to motor vehicles; retentions in the vehicle industry were half those in manufacturing industry as a whole between 1949 and 1977.[82]

American ownership was not sufficient for profitability in the British industry, for other American multinationals did not repeat Ford's success. During this period, Vauxhall and Rootes/Chrysler also experienced troubled financial performances. From 1968 to 1977 Vauxhall also recorded negative cumulative retained earnings, but the extent of the deficit, at −£51.7 million, was only 41 per cent of that recorded by BLMC.[83] By the late 1970s government intervention was required to ensure the continuation of Chrysler and British Leyland (see Chapter 7).

The level of and fluctuations in profits, which in turn followed from under-capacity working, undermined a long run investment strategy. The problem was compounded by low retained profits. Between 1949 and 1977 the amount of post-tax profit retained in the motor vehicle industry was low; too low to provide a large enough surplus for reinvestment or to attract sufficient investment.[84] For each year in which the industry failed to achieve profits on a par with its competitors, the less it was able to re-invest in capital which, given the premium on mass production techniques using the latest up-to-date technology, was essential to its long term viability. The result was a vicious circle in which inadequate capital investment precluded investment in new technology which, in turn, increased costs of production and hence decreased profits which led back to insufficient funds for new model development. Low and erratic profits and retained earnings were both cause and effect of low levels of investment.

From the mid 1960s BMC/BLMC was earning insufficient profit to finance new production facilities on any scale at a time when the tooling and development costs of new models were inceasing. Thoms and Donnelly have estimated that at 1974 prices, the expenditure involved in a new car body was £75 million and £150 million for a new engine.[85] BLMC's total internal investment fund between 1968 and 1974 averaged only £44.57 million a year, which only permitted the introduction of new body shells using existing equipment and levels of technology. Capital expenditure was obviously insufficient to meet the costs of new car bodies or new engines. Between 1968 and 1974 the capital outlay of the company amounted to £264 million; average annual expenditure on plant over this period amounted to £30.3 million (Table 5.9).

Table 5.9: British Leyland's capital expenditure, 1968–1974 (£m)

Year to 30 September	Plant	Properties	Total
1968	27	4	31
1969	23	6	29
1970	34	6	40
1971	25	4	29
1972	20	2	22
1973	30	6	36
1974	53	24	77

Source: House of Commons, *British Leyland: The Next Decade* (Ryder Report), 23 April 1975, House of Commons Paper 342, PP 1974/5, Table 4.4, p. 20.

In the early part of the period the bulk of the investment was internally financed. Ford's expansion between 1954 and 1958 was self-financed. Internally generated funds were used to finance the general expansion in the industry in 1960 and between 1963 and 1965.[86] Increases in equity capital and bank loans added to investment funds throughout the period, but increasingly so from the 1960s. Vauxhall's expansion programme of the mid 1950s was largely financed by external sources (a £3 million loan from General Motors Corporation and £2 million of long term loans).[87] BMC, Rootes and Standard also used external funding at this time. From the 1960s, use of equity capital and external funding accelerated. British Leyland raised £49 million through a rights issue in 1972.[88]

There was an increase in debt finance throughout British manufacturing industry in the period, with all industries recording a steady increase in gearing ratios throughout the postwar decades. The tendency, however, appears to have been particularly marked in the vehicle sector.[89] In 1948, Austin raised long term capital amounting to £2.6 million; BMC raised £4.1 million in 1954. Between 1949 and 1954, Rootes raised £5.5 million.[90] Only Ford remained aloof.[91] From the late 1960s, bank loans became increasingly important for the motor vehicle industry.[92] In 1960, bank loans amounted to £3 million; in 1967 they amounted to £129.7 million.[93]

Bank loans, however, were used mainly to finance liquid assets and formed a small proportion of total assets employed.[94] Gilbert Hunt, Chairman of Crysler, maintained in the mid 1970s that there had been a much heavier emphasis on short term finance since his company regarded it as a banker's function rather than that of the company's shareholders to provide the firm with working capital.[95] In 1967, bank loans still accounted for only 11 per cent of assets employed. The implication is that from the late 1960s if retained earnings were deficient, the motor companies resorted to bank funding but only to finance liquid assets. This could reflect the industry's inability to raise finance and may have been an early signal as to the market's falling confidence in the industry. Movements in net earnings may explain the direction of changes in gross investment in the industry as a whole between 1959 and 1968; they do not, in Rhys's view, explain the magnitude.[96] The explanation would appear to be rooted in the financial decision to reduce dependence on outside sources of funds wherever possible. Thus according to Rhys, when internally generated funds increased, the industry took the opportunity to reduce its dependence on outside sources of funds whereas when internal funds fell then increased recourse was made to outside sources.[97] This implies that investment was given a lower priority than reducing dependence on outside sources and, as such, may reflect the financial decision to forgo short term investment.

Inadequate investment may reflect not only a low and erratic profit record, but also the decision to distribute as dividends a high percentage of after-tax profits. Traditionally, the literature has explained low retentions by dividend payments being afforded a higher priority than retained income. Between 1959 and 1968, dividends were the only financial element not subject to wild swings.[98] High and stable dividend policy, not surprisingly, has been identified as a factor in the low retained earnings record of BLMC between 1968 and 1974 and, by implication, as a factor in the investment record of the company. The practice was singled out by the Ryder Report as a particularly misconceived policy on the part of BLMC, for 'despite this low level of profits British Leyland has over the period (1968–1974) distributed nearly all of them as dividends. In our view this policy was clearly wrong'.[99] Ryder did not acknowledge that even if all earnings had been retained, there would still have been a massive shortfall of investment, and the failure to pay dividends would have excluded the possibility of raising future finance from outside the firm.

Inadequate capital expenditure left British Leyland operating with an unacceptably high proportion of old plant. In 1974, the company was using a large amount of plant which had been acquired in the 1950s and, indeed, even before 1952[100] and was only able to record slender profits because it was failing to set aside funds for plant replacement.[101] The problem was not just the failure to invest in new technology which could have raised efficiency, but old plant which was susceptible to technical failure, was less accurate, slower and more expensive to run than up to date machinery.[102] The implications, according to the Expenditure Committee, were that:

> this means that until investment substantially increases the capital stock, productivity in the British motor industry will not be able to equal productivity abroad . . . given roughly equivalent environments, the inefficient use of resources as a result of poor management, marketing, capacity utilisation or industrial disputes accounts for a very much lower proportion of productivity differences than might be imagined.[103]

Not surprisingly, the rate of return on capital for the industry compared unfavourably with that of European competitors. Between 1967 and 1971 the average rate of return on capital employed in the motor vehicle industry was 3.0 per cent. The rate of return on capital in Italy was 4.8 per cent, in France 6.8 per cent and in Germany 12.4 per cent.[104] But the biggest differences were to be found within Britain (Table 5.10). Between 1970 and 1978 the ratio of net profit before interest and tax to net capital employed averaged 21.7 pe cent in Ford, but only 8.0 per cent in British Leyland.

In view of the trends in profitability, the stock market and the banks do not seem to have been particularly astute, but their increased participation in the industry as profitability was declining is inconsistent with 'short-termism'. Eventually they saw the writing on the wall and left the field clear for the most remarked upon source of external funding; the £2,051 million British Leyland received from the government between 1975 and 1983.[105]

Table 5.10: Capital efficiency at Ford and British Leyland, 1970–1978

	Ratio of turnover to net capital employed		Ratio of net profit before interest and tax to net capital employed	
	Ford	BL	Ford	BL
1968	1.6	n.a.	3.2	n.a.
1969	2.3	2.8	18.0	16.0
1970	2.5	2.5	11.2	6.3
1971	2.2	2.7	n.a.	12.7
1972	2.7	3.0	19.2	12.0
1973	3.2	3.3	27.6	16.3
1974	2.7	3.1	7.0	8.2
1975	2.5	3.7	8.8	n.a.
1976	3.6	4.2	30.9	n.a.
1977	4.7	3.2	55.4	8.9
1978	3.2	3.1	35.2	7.7

Source: The Times 1000, 1977–78, pp. 16–17; 1980–1, pp. 20–1.

Writing in 1981, and posing the question as to why the market mechanism had not taken corrective action, Prais noted that the market had, in fact, pronounced its verdict: 'left to itself British Leyland, with all the subsidiaries it has absorbed over the years, would some years ago have been in liquidation. The government has saved it with palliatives: with grants and loans and with promises of loans.'[106]

5.4 Foreign trade

As Chapter 4 has shown, by the 1970s, individual motor firms in Britain needed to produce overall volumes of at least one million cars and about 200,000 of each model if unit costs were to be at a minimum. The home market was not sufficient to absorb such numbers. New registrations of the most popular medium size car of its day, the Ford Cortina, reached a high point of 165,000 in 1967.[107]

The most popular small car, the Mini, recorded 104,000 new registrations in 1965 – 47 per cent of total production for that model.[108] In order to produce at volumes which would enable manufacturers to realise economies of scale, it was essential to secure export markets.

The increased premium on securing export markets took place against the background of a massive increase in the international production of motor vehicles.[109] This large increase in production, facilitated by technological change, reflected increased output from established producers, the emergence of new producers and the heightened influence of the multinationals.[110] In the interwar years the international motor vehicle industry had been based on domestic markets. In the postwar years, although domestic markets remained crucial for long term viabiity, competition increasingly manifested itself in the drive to win export markets. For motor vehicle producers competition was based on the protection of home markets against foreign competition and increasingly on the extension of markets overseas. As international production and competition grew, as the need to realise economies of scale at large volumes of output came to dominate all global motor vehicle producers, the drive to win and secure export markets became increasingly important. The British producers had to win exports in an increasingly competitive global environment. Since 1941 the Board of Trade had been warning them to prepare for 'a much more bracing export climate'.[111]

In the early 1950s the industry seemed well on this course. In the immediate postwar years, the British motor vehicle industry was the key player in the global export industry and found it could sell everything it could make. Between 1949 and 1951 Britain was the world's leading exporter of cars and trucks.[112] During this period, however, British manufacturers focussed on increasing output and export volumes, other overseas manufacturers re-equipped.

1969 was the peak year for exports, with 771,634 complete new cars sold abroad (Table 5.11). Exports of commercial vehicles quadrupled between 1946 and 1969. By 1969 the industry was exporting over 180,000 commercial vehicles a year (Table 5.11). From 1971, however, exports began a steady decline, reaching just under 467,000 cars and just under 142,000 commercial vehicles by 1978 (Table 5.10).

In the 1950s BMC sent large numbers of vehicles to the

Commonwealth. Australia and New Zealand were by far the most important markets. In 1950, two-thirds of British car exports went to the Commonwealth.[113] This market was increasingly curtailed by the late 1950s as regulations were introduced or tightened requiring manufacture with substantial local content. Although BMC could manufacture in these markets, by the late 1950s it was unable to export to them. Attention was then switched to North America,

Table 5.11: Summary of British exports of motor vehicles, 1946–1978

Year end December	New cars Complete and chassis		New commercial vehicles Complete and chassis	
	No.	£000	No.	£000
1946	84,358	19,448	45,087	18,288
1947	140,691	37,347	48,783	23,163
1948	224,374	59,356	73,996	36,263
1949	257,250	72,505	92,737	42,032
1950	397,688	116,268	144,251	61,590
1951	368,101	118,802	136,880	69,080
1952	308,942	110,795	128,203	77,831
1953	307,368	106,045	104,696	60,417
1954	372,029	120,945	118,796	65,859
1955	388,564	127,816	104,048	80,498
1956	335,397	119,886	126,671	86,145
1957	424,320	157,053	122,957	86,932
1958	484,034	187,169	112,205	81,725
1959	568,971	222,532	128,055	88,968
1960	569,889	224,634	146,128	104,468
1961	370,744	147,874	167,931	121,932
1962	544,924	215,474	149,870	114,011
1963	615,827	237,205	159,007	121,393
1964	679,383	256,709	168,606	126,529
1965	627,567	250,859	166,189	137,124
1966	556,044	234,356	165,924	142,056
1967	502,596	211,413	135,188	116,769
1968	676,571	280,100	142,036	124,942
1969	711,634	340,939	181,152	168,526
1970	690,339	327,711	172,387	179,612
1971	721,094	368,843	194,747	225,892
1972	627,479	329,879	139,932	175,168
1973	598,816	372,818	163,148	214,104
1974	564,790	418,502	160,722	250,082
1975	516,219	483,260	179,633	428,634
1976	495,796	633,230	188,103	548,204
1977	474,826	751,926	191,887	652,680
1978	466,382	923,584	141,992	553,651

Source: SMTT, The Motor Industry of Great Britain, 1992, Table 83, p. 206.

with substantial short run success. In 1959–60 Canada and the United States took 39 per cent of BMC's vehicle exports.[114] Export sales to these markets declined however as American producers started to manufacture smaller cars in 1960. From then on BMC exports to the North American market were limited to specialist sports cars such as the MGB.[115]

Contributors to the relative decline of Britain in the global motor vehicle trade were the re-emergence of the European car industry, the gradual loss of preferential markets and the growth in American imports, as the dollar shortage eased. To some extent it was inevitable that Britain would be unable to retain the pre-eminence she enjoyed in world trade in 1949–50. But British manufacturers were increasingly handicapped by a lack of competitiveness which originated from domestic sources. According to Hennessy the problem stemmed from the postwar export drive during which the satisfactions of the rapid regaining of export levels masked the absence of investment in new equipment which would have provided the platform for a sustained production drive. The 'blame' he attributes not just to the manufacturers, but to the economic ministries in Whitehall.[116] But as Chapter 4 has already indicated, the work of Johnman and Tiratsoo indicates that the reformist plans of the Board of Trade had to take second place to the export drive and manufacturers were able to use this as a powerful bargaining tool to resist structural change. Adeney also condemns the manufacturers rather than government departments and has taken the argument one step further. He argues that the successes of this period put off difficult decisions – in particular easy profits were not turned into sufficient new investment and quality was sacrificed to the perceived greater need for increased production. As a result; 'the legacy of the 1940s and 1950s is one of defeat snatched from the jaws of victory; of the canker of decline concealed among the fruits of victory'.[117]

The problem, however, was not just related to investment and production shortcomings. Criticisms have also been levied against the sales and marketing tactics (or rather the absence of them) of British manufacturers. It is claimed, for example, that they rarely adopted the aggressive sales methods of their European competitors with their efficient sales and service organisations.[118] The British industry was accused of failing to pay sufficient attention to meeting delivery dates, to quality control or even to ensuring that distributors held sufficient stocks to satisfy demand.[119] The Standard Vanguard, for example, which had been rushed out to meet postwar demand without proper testing, quickly acquired a reputation for unreliability.[120] The Expenditure Committee, however, related the poor marketing and distribution performance back to the premium on boosting exports after the war, during which it claimed car makers paid more attention to maximising short term export sales than to the sales and service infrastructure, as a result of which British vehicles aquired a reputation for poor reliability, and the vital areas of marketing and after sales service were virtually ignored.[121]

In the early 1960s BMC turned to European markets which, again in the short run, proved rewarding.[122] By 1964 Western Europe took 41 per cent of BMC's world exports.[123] Western Europe was, however, an intensely competitive market, dominated in the 1960s and 1970s by six and (following the merger of Peugeot and Citroën in 1974) later five major volume producers, (Volkswagen, Peugeot-Citroën, Renault, Fiat and British Leyland), three American multinationals (Ford, General Motors and Chrysler) and three high performance specialists (Daimler-Benz, BMW and Alfa-Romeo).

Ten years later, the Western European car producing nations had overtaken North America as the largest car producing area in the world.[124] Intra-Community motor vehicle trade grew four times as fast as car production between 1965 and 1977.[125] Before the formation of the Community, interpenetration of European car markets was extremely limited and national markets were essentially isolated. Tariffs of 30 per cent or more in France, Britain and Italy were barriers to imports. But by 1962, reduced tariffs within the Community and trade between community members entered a period of substantial growth marked by increased import penetration by France, Germany and Italy into each others' markets.[126]

Owen's analysis of the pattern of European decades in these years has shown that until the middle of the 1960s, the pattern of European trade was essentially one of bilateral equilibrium with France, Italy, Germany and Britain all being roughly in balance with each other. By 1970, this situation had been reversed as clear winners and losers emerged; a pattern which was to continue through that decade (Table 5.12). By 1976 France was the clear leader in securing footholds in its neighbours' markets and in defending its own market against them. The clear loser was Britain which conceded one-third of its market to continental producers whilst gaining 'trifling' exports to France, Germany and Italy.

One explanation for the British loss of market share within the rapidly growing European trade area was Britain's 'exclusion' from the EC trading bloc until 1973.[127] In an industry with constant returns to scale, exclusion would make little difference. Some of the

Table 5.12: Penetration of European Community car markets, 1955–1976 (percentage shares in terms of unit sales)

German exports Market	France	Britain	Italy
1955	1.1	1.1	0.8
1960	2.9	2.2	3.4
1965	7.3	2.6	6.7
1970	6.6	3.4	13.3
1976	8.9	7.9	12.2
French exports Market	Germany	Britain	Italy
1955	1.0	0.8	0.3
1960	4.8	4.8	1.6
1965	5.8	1.1	3.7
1970	10.9	4.2	10.2
1976	9.5	10.4	19.4
Italian exports Market	Germany	Britain	France
1955	3.0	0.4	0.1
1960	7.4	0.5	1.3
1965	5.8	1.1	3.1
1970	8.2	2.7	6.8
1976		6.6	5.5
British exports Market	Germany	France	Italy
1955	1.0	0.7	0.3
1960	0.7	1.0	1.3
1965	0.4	2.6	1.0
1970	0.7	0.5	3.9
1976	0.6	0.7	0.5

Source: Nicholas Owen, Economies of Scale, Competitiveness, and Trade Patterns within the European Community, Oxford: Clarendon Press, 1983, Table 4.6, p. 55.

gains from international specialisation would be lost but the tariff and non-tariff barriers to trade would not have eliminated them. For an industry such as motor vehicles for which scale economies are vital, market size is of central importance. British consumers gained from cheaper EC cars, but not from cheaper British cars. British cars makers could not drive down their costs so far because they could not hope for similar production runs. There were ways of reducing this difficulty for a multinational company, but not for one that primarily supplied the British market.

The formation of the EC gave multinational motor businesses the chance to increase their scale of operations by rationalising and integrating their European activities.[128] Until 1966 Ford in Europe operated as two independent entities in Britain and Germany, each with their own distinct product ranges, components and suppliers. In 1967 Ford merged these two companies into a single Ford of Europe organisation. The Capri, launched in 1969, the Cortina/ Taunus (1970) and the Granada (1972) were designed jointly and assembled in both Germany and Britain.

Exclusion from EC membership is not however the only, or the principal, explanation for Britain's problems. Membership would have helped Continental manufacturers take advantage of the weaknesses of British motor vehicle industry; when Britain enterned the Community in 1973, import penetration by other EC producers grew. In the immediate postwar period, Britain bought very few vehicles abroad. The upturn in imports dates from 1957 (Table 5.13).

The rise in import penetration was not unique to motor vehicles among British industries in this period. But the problem was particularly acute in the motor vehicle industry and was the inevitable accompaniment to the inability of firms in Britain, whoever owned them, to make motor cars as well as other manufacturing economies.

5.5 Conclusion

By the mid 1960s it was clear that British Leyland could not compete profitably with Ford. A wide range of models, some probably underpriced, held up market share but at the expense of profits and investment. In due course that became apparent with new models. Inadequate sums and too little top management time were spent on new model development. The Maxi had a terrible gearbox, the Allegro suffered a marketing disaster when first launched because of its square steering wheel, the Rover SD1 was a good concept but poorly built, the Princess was never properly engineered. The Maestro, Montego and Ambassador were not successes, the Mini had become a niche product, the Marina was nothing special, only the Metro was successful. So the appreciation of the exchange rate was less to blame for the contraction of British Leyland than the range of models by 1980.

Although the model range suffered from under-investment, that

Table 5.13: Summary of British net imports of motor vehicles, 1946–1977

Year end December	Cars Complete and chassis		Commercial vehicles Complete and chassis	
	No.	*£*	*No.*	*£*
1946	63	27,688	31	43,288
1947	222	128,423	71	70,796
1949	1,868	579,848	880	316,665
1950	1,375	359,005	193	93,907
1951	3,723	1,134,014	237	90,446
1952	1,876	713,305	102	97,415
1953	2,067	759,633	49	52,346
1954	4,660	1,680,116	684	331,810
1955	11,131	4,052,703	989	622,130
1956	6,885	2,343,979	791	638,384
1957	8,828	3,055,490	1,129[a]	739,832
1958	10,940	3,926,415	1,205[a]	580,889
1959	26,998	8,99,610	1,248[a]	622,320
1960	57,309	19,100,948	2,919[a]	1,462,733
1961	22,759	8,510,001	3,649[a]	1,955,338
1962	28,610	10,679,891	4,488[a]	1,930,919
1963	48,163	18,768,336	2,924	2,157,184
1964	65,725	27,139,392	3,970	2,211,576
1965	55,558	22,986,412	2,392	1,830,089
1966	66,793	26,567,382	2,683	2,956,827
1967	92,731	39,143,855	3,827	5,141,316
1968	102,276	49,327,950	3,903	5,877,308
1969	101,914	53,494,576	5,517	7,451,869
1970	157,956	85,005,552	10,317	13,388,651
1971	281,037	171,464,613	18,575	20,855,186
1972	450,314	324,405,819	34,855	38,898,817
1973	504,619	436,900,000	36,870	53,729,000
1974	375,421	355,005,000	39,589	91,141,000
1975	448,749	514,047,000	25,563	90,099,000
1976	533,901	886,397,000	27,368	122,725,000
1977	698,464	1,323,878,000	36,874	211,161,000

Notes: [a] Includes a small number of car chassis which could not be separately identified. Value figures from 1973 are shown to the nearest thousand.
Data for 1948 not available.
Source: SMMT, *The Motor Industry of Great Britain*, 1978, Table 73, p. 258.

stemmed from a lack of profits. Despite declining profitability, increasing access to financial markets kept BMC/BMH/BL afloat longer than otherwise would have been possible. Failure to join the EC earlier cannot be assigned responsibility for poor performance, for a scenario in which Britain signed the Treaty of Rome in 1957 would quite likely show an early rise in import penetration as the lack of competitiveness of the British industry was exposed earlier.

In the following chapter, it is argued the poor model range was in part a reflection of poor industrial relations, from which management cannot be separated. Both management and industrial relations styles were ultimately an outgrowth of the British postwar 'settlement' or social relations and of limited ideas about the nature of the firm. Ultimately these threatened the world position of the most professionally managed British-based motor business, Ford UK. In this period however, Ford remained an exception in the British industry, when both General Motors and Chrysler were increasingly unprofitable and BMC/BL was in difficulties. Ford of course owned the most integrated facilities in Britain, and Ford of Britain was the Ford Europe flagship at least initially. By contrast General Motors made their principal European investment in Germany and for most of their history were somewhat ambivalent about their British subsidiary. Ford also first planned production and marketing on a European scale. Had BL been able to do so, the history of the industry in the 1970s may have been different. But for that alternative scenario to have been realised, BMC/BL would have been better managed, and financed, with better industrial relations in the later 1940s and 1950s.

CHAPTER SIX

INDUSTRIAL RELATIONS, 1945–1978

After 1945 Ford shop stewards quickly came to epitomise a new breed of unofficial trade union representatives, wielding unprecedented power. By the 1960s the motor industry had become a symbol of Britain's allegedly poor industrial relations[1] and British Leyland was a by-word for industrial anarchy in the early 1970s. It is therefore tempting to single out labour relations as the cause of the industry's decline. Yet a number of recent studies have maintained that would be a mistake. For much of the period, the costs of stoppages in forgone output were relatively slight, some contend.[2] Ford prospered while British Leyland declined in a similar labour relations environment. More important than trade union restrictions was the failure of British Leyland's management to develop and market suitable models.[3] Management initiatives in payment systems exacerbated rather than alleviated shopfloor tensions, it has been alleged; British Leyland's change from piece work to time rates without ensuring tight control over work organisation and the effort bargain, was ill-judged.[4] The market environment outside control of the car companies also soured labour relations, some have argued. Greater demand stability, untroubled by government 'stop–go' policies would perhaps have avoided the periodic layoffs that were at the root of poor relations between labour and management. Yet another frequent assertion is that the lack of worker autonomy and discretion made mass car manufacture an intensely alienating experience.[5]

This chapter assesses these views and examines the industrial relations legacy. We begin by describing the institutions governing industrial relations. This is followed by a review of working conditions and methods of payment, which have attracted so much controversy. We then analyse the causes of disputes. A discussion follows on the extent to which disputes or other pathologies of labour relations accounted for Britain's falling relative productivity. Management's contribution to industrial relations shortcomings concludes the analysis.

6.1 Institutions

The origins of both management and labour industrial relations institutions lay far in the past. The Engineering Employers Federation was established in 1896 as a means of challenging the control of skilled engineers on the shop floor.[6] Since the 1890s large multiplant enterprises, growing by acquisition, became the norm for much of British manufacturing industry, yet institutions designed to regulate relations between skilled artisans and small scale manufacturers remained at the heart of British industrial relations in the British car industry through much of the twentieth century. Decentralised or federal structures, which allowed individual plants a great deal of autonomy meant that for many purposes, concentration of control was more apparent than real. This was particularly true of industrial relations.[7] The Federation repeatedly refused to set up a permanent national forum for negotiation with the unions for fear of limiting management autonomy. Virtually all that was provided by industrial relations institutions was a grievance procedure designed to insulate the individual firm from national union campaigns and to maximise managerial prerogatives at the factory level. From 1898 until 1970, workplace disputes might be referred to a local Works Conference and then to a Local Conference away from the factory. Unresolved disputes were passed to national union and employer representatives' 'Central Conference', held monthly at York. At each stage the employers' representatives presided. There was no procedure for independent arbitration. The failure of the York Procedure, heavily weighted in the employers' favour, to act as an effective vehicle for settling employee grievances, served to enhance the power and authority of the shop steward. In 1964 over 4,000 EEF disputes were passed to Works Conferences. Of these, 80 per cent were 'disposed of' at that level in 1958–63 and 76 per cent in 1964. In addition there were occasional national meetings to discuss wage claims for the whole industry, but regional negotiations and agreements were ultimately of far greater significance. In 1970 all semblance of national negotiations were abandoned.

By the 1960s the Federation consisted of some 4,500 firms employing one and a half million workers. BMC itself was not affiliated but its subsidiaries participated in district employers associations. The American companies, Ford and Vauxhall, remained aloof from the EEF. Attempts to form a Motor Council foundered on the differences between the centrally organised American companies with substantive industrial relations strategies, on the one hand, and the British on the other. From its foundation in 1968, British Leyland gave the reform of industrial relations top priority. After ten years British Leyland achieved a centralised structure with uniform pay arrangements. But such developments came at least a decade too late to check the rise of shopfloor trade unionism.

Two separate forms of worker organisation coexisted in the postwar motor industry. From the 1940s union membership extended massively, mainly in the AEU and TGWU. In Table 6.1 the figure 100 per cent reflects the acceptance by federated car firms of the (post-entry) union shop for manual workers, subject to exceptions for principle or conscience. In theory federated car firms could be required to negotiate with any one of the Confederation of Shipbuilding and Engineering Union's 31 affiliated unions. Even Ford's agreement required equal representation of 21 unions on its central negotiating body.

The formal divorce of the union branch from the workplace gave rise to provision for direct representation of shop stewards' views within the union structure. But this was an *ad hoc* arrangement which was not sufficient to encourage the formation of a coherent union policy on the motor industry. The immense growth in workplace bargaining together with a strong demand for labour increased the shop stewards' status in bargaining. In Austin, Morris Commercial and Pressed Steel during the 1960s a works committee of seven management and seven stewards elected by other stewards played a part in dispute settlement. Most union rules required stewards to form a shop committee which could elect a convener. Six or seven conveners from different unions might then form a works committee for bargaining entirely outside the formal union structure. Nationally closed shops increased from one in six of the early 1960s to one in four by 1978. Shop stewards almost doubled in numbers between the mid 1960s and the late 1970s. In essence the uncoordinated pattern of collective bargaining through a dispersed shop steward system developed to fill the institutional vacuum in British manufacturing.

Table 6.1: Estimated trade union strengths in British car firms, 1965–1966

Firm	% members (manual)	% trade unionists by union				
		AEU	TGWU	NUVB	NUGMW	Other
BMC	100	37	28	20	3	12
Ford	99	24	41	10	15	10
Vauxhall	85	66	–	29	0	5
P Steel	100	21	47	27	0	5
Rootes	100	50	33	9	0	8
STI	100	36	43	15	0	6
Rover	100	27	15	48	5	5
Jaguar	100	32	32	25	0	11
Total	98	35	31	20	5	9

Source: H. A. Turner, G. Clack and G. Roberts, Labour Relations in the Motor Industry: A Study of Industrial Unrest and an International Comparison, London: Allen and Unwin, 1967.

The BMC merger was not accompanied, as it should have been, by any rationalisation of procedures for handling the labour problems created.[8] Austin, Morris and Rootes bargained every day over the rate for the job in the event of the slightest change.[9] Importantly, the fact of affiliation to the EEF may have inhibited firms from developing their own procedures to regulate collective bargaining. Senior management simply assumed that shopfloor matters were being dealt with effectively by operational management and that no fundamental changes were necessary.

In Ford, by contrast, Patrick Hennessy had agreed to negotiate wage rates with national union officials as a strategy to reduce the role of shop stewards as bargaining agents. When Ford acquired Briggs in 1953 it was absorbed into Ford system, but not without difficulty, for Briggs Motor Bodies had paid by the piece. There were 600 unofficial incidents in following four years. In 1955 a procedure agreement was signed by the company and representatives of 22 unions formalising centralised negotiations. Ford's distinctive style was one of imposing rather than seeking agreement. The strategy of excluding shop stewards from formal bargaining rebounded on the company. Rather than becoming marginalised, shop stewards gained even greater authority with the shopfloor as their authentic voice. Stewards confirmed their legitimacy in day to day confrontations with supervisors and by lobbying union executives during formal bargaining.

Despite winning a series of major confrontations over the shop stewards in the early 1960s, Ford did not succeed in stabilising its industrial relations.[10] Labour shortages and high turnover levels undermined the company's selective recruitment policy, while the young workforce posed immense disciplinary problems for supervisors. The opening of Halewood in 1963 provided a opportunity to recreate 'Fordism' with only two unions, but the rigour of the supervisory regime provoked disorganised shopfloor conflict. Bitter disputes between 1968 and 1972 finally undermined Ford's attempt to limit collective bargaining to senior union officials. Ford's strategy had delivered vandalism, poor quality and stoppages. Bob Ramsey's appointment as director of industrial relations in 1973 symbolised the company's final rejection of the mixture of paternalism and direct control characteristic of Ford's British operations since 1911. From the mid 1970s winning employee endorsement of collective agreements was regarded as essential to the long term stabilisation of labour relations and enhancing productivity. Company industrial relations nonetheless continued to be bedevilled through the 1970s by the tensions between Ford's national strategic initiatives and plant management's insistence on unilaterial control. Whatever the limitations, however, Ford's strategic approach to industrial relations conferred a significant competitive advantage over the merely reactive labour policies of the British-owned companies.

6.2 Conditions of work

For many of the general public, the tedium of working conditions in the motor industry was exemplified by the production line scenes from Charlie Chaplin's film *Modern Times*. Union representatives and workers often stressed the 'soul-destroying' nature and the physical strain of many jobs.[11] Repetitive track tasks typically took five to fifteen minutes each. The work was certainly less boring than textile spinning or machine minding though the effort involved could be much greater. Automation lightened the physical effort of work in the decades after the Second World War. Physical surroundings were on the whole clean and well-kept. Standards of lighting, heating and ventilation were generally adequate. There was dust in polishing shops, noise and welding sparks in some body shops but jobs were not dirty, so for example trackmen seldom wore protective clothing. But factory facilities even in the mid 1960s were not always calculated to enhance worker satisfaction. The availability of toilet paper, and the location of toilet roll holders on the outside of the doors at Cowley, cast some light on management attitudes towards the workforce.[12] Vauxhall's Dunstable plant, by contrast, provided extremely good employee facilities.

Labour turnover in the British motor industry was not only lower than in British manufacturing as a whole but also lower than in continental Europe.[13] Over the typical employees' time in the industry, a high probability of initial wastage gave way to a long duration of employment. Conceivably this reflected or caused a greater use of 'voice' than 'exit' as a response to dissatisfaction relative to continental Europe; workers were more likely to express their dissatisfaction with job conditions by stoppages or by 'working to rule' rather than by looking for other jobs. Alternatively, low labour turnover suggests that, given the wages, conditions were acceptable.

Shift working was among the less satisfactory aspects of the job for many employees. From the 1950s there was a growing demand from management that operatives accept a three shift system which was universally unpopular with car workers. About 60 per cent of males worked a pattern of hours other than the 'normal' day in the mid 1970s. Just over three-fifths of male shiftworkers worked on rotas with alternating day and night shifts. The use of alternate day and night shift system as the norm in the motor industry was unique to Britain. Normally operatives worked five day shifts of between eight and nine hours in one fortnight and four or five night shifts of eight to ten hours each in the next. Day and night shifts were separated by several hours, giving management flexibility over the length of the working day. Britain was the only major vehicle producing country where large scale assembly of cars was carried out on a regular night shift. Continental managers alleged that the quality of cars might be affected.

Shiftworking is intended to increase the utilisation of fixed capital; overtime provided operating flexibility. An advantage of the 'day and night' shift system was the facility for overtime which could extend the working week by about 20 per cent. Under the 'double day' system overtime is more difficult to operate, especially for assembly. The margin was closer to 10 per cent. Probably the British shift system was a response to the greater uncertainty of the British market and management's committment to 'incrementalism' (or an unwillingness to engage in forward planning). However, the workforce came to see regular overtime as a right and since hours did not vary much, management lost the flexibility it hoped to maintain with the system. Between the 1940s and 1960s average overtime work in British industry as a whole rose to a higher level than in other countries. Control over the extent and allocation of overtime working became a focus for shop stewards bargaining, highlighting weak managerial control and information systems.[14] Moreover, unlike the back to back double day system, the day-night system did not facilitate communication. The industry was left with a shift system that delivered the high wages of overtime combined with a source of friction on the shopfloor, intractable communication difficulties and little gain in operating flexibility. Workforce job control was not universal though, nor did it persist throughout the period. Ford, with its characteristically tougher policy, operated a 'labour pool' whereby workers were expected to move to whatever job was required, from the 1960s. The other British companies wanted to emulate Ford's greater control over labour deployment but found it difficult to match in practice. At Cowley from early 1970s there was, in principle, complete worker job flexibility on and off tracks. In reality Cowley management remained hemmed in by custom and practice which regulated supervision by internal precedents rather than by contemporary best practice in the industry as a whole.

Methods of payment

Despite increasing automation in the British motor industry, the method of payment in the 1940s and 1950s remained independent of the speed of the production line. Instead of being paced by the track, the worker, usually as a member of a group, was motivated by an incentive payment system. With piecework, each section of the assembly line worked as a gang and was paid by results. However, earnings were not wholly within the control of the individual or the work group by any means. Temporary line stoppages, for whatever reason – breakdowns, material shortages or small-scale industrial disputes – lost workers earnings. Such stoppages were flashpoints, raising questions of equity with, for example, office staff who were subject to no such arbitrary and unpredictable disruption of earnings. Stoppages also called into question the competence of first-line management.

Piecework, together with the adoption of automatic techniques, accentuated a tendency for direct labour earnings to outstrip those of ancilliary workers. Firms bought acceptance of change by the operatives affected, which introduced additional complexities and anomalies into the wage structure. Comparability disputes were inherent to the formal and informal wage bargaining in British car factories. Nor were such comparisons restricted to the individual plant; company mergers increased the possibilities for interplant comparisons.

The growth of ever more complex piecework systems and the rise of informal shopfloor bargaining led by shop stewards were linked. Piecework gradually ceased to be a substitute for management maintaining and increasing worker effort and production efficiency. Individual piece rates were daily points of dispute between shop stewards and production managers. By identifying the smallest change as constituting an entirely new job, stewards could demand a renegotiation of wage rate and bonus calculations.[15] Involvement in such bargaining absorbed a great deal of management time and energy. The formal industry-wide bargaining procedure was incapable of dealing with this incessant guerilla warfare and became an irrelevance to day to day life in British car factories.

Both sides of the industry had allowed the piecework system to be abused. When new models were launched unions would delay agreement on piecework rates, costs would then go up and the learning curve would allow workers markedly to increase their earnings. Wages drifted upwards and the ensuing different earnings on old and new cars gave rise to dissension. Even minor changes in existing models were difficult to make because bargaining over the new piece rates brought delay and dispute.[16] Indirect workers, supplying the assembly lines, could not be paid on piece rates and therefore lost out. At Cowley, a plant which averaged 2.5 strikes a day in 1970, managerial authority was always contested. Long term planning was impossible in a factory described by one former Cowley manager as characterised by 'management by stoppage'.

For the industry, the greatest advantage of piece rates was that they did enlist worker ingenuity in keeping the line running and the product quality acceptable. These were considerable benefits in under-capitalised British plants, such as Cowley, relying on anti-quated machinery. Such equipment was likely to produce ill-fitting components. In the case of windscreens, operatives found out that placing a piece of cane over the glass edge allowed them to compensate for inadequate tolerances and fit the screens snuggly. The piecework system meant that workers had a material interest in circumventing assembly problems caused by poorly machined components. Such *ad hoc* approaches to manufacturing were typical of the British engineering production tradition, and demonstrate both its strengths and weaknesses. With the introduction of measured day work, component fit and quality became exclusively a management problem. When piecework was abolished assembly workers did not employ their initiative to ensure Marina Traveller rear air vents fitted.[17]

Shop stewards played a key role in operating the piece rate system, often chasing up material so that earnings would not drop.[18] They controlled the work environment even down to deciding when shedding labour was neccessary. They could do so because of the strong demand for cars and management's willingness to barter best practice against maintaining production.

Because of their potential for disputes and their irrelevance for mechanised production, by the later 1960s no American car firms employed incentive payments: continuity and predictability were the key concerns of their highly integrated production systems. Vauxhall abandoned production bonuses in the mid 1960s for a simple time wage system, avoiding piece rate haggling and con-tributing to a peaceful record. Vauxhall was also institutionally and geographically isolated from British manufacturing. Not only was the company independent of the EEF but Luton was also distant from other factories and the British engineering craft traditions. But it was also fairly sophisticated in its labour relations. Vauxhall operated a profit sharing scheme which distributed £500,000 annually. It was also remarkably strike free by industry standards until the later 1960s. Senior management continuity ensured consistency in personnel policies. Sir Charles Bartlett was Luton's managing director from 1930 to 1953. Bartlett's strategy, according to one Vauxhall worker, was to create an environment of mutual co-operation, very much as in the later Japanese transplant companies.[19]

Introduction of 'lay-off pay' was one attempt to encourage such attitudes. But the potential for stoppages in such a highly complex and strife-torn industry was generally too great for such schemes to address adequately. Ford operated a centralised Lay-off Fund paying 80 per cent compensation for up to 15 days. In 1970 BLMC operated a scheme to compensate workers for up to 28 days' stoppage for a strike outside the company. Similarly a Cowley Body worker was compensated for a stoppage due to a dispute outside Cowley, if his entitlement was not exhausted. He did not receive compensation for the many stoppages within Cowley however. Some European countries approached the lay-off problem by allowing companies to augment state unemployment benefits. In Britain, motor company lay-off pay had to *replace* state benefits, imposing a great burden upon corporate financial resources.[20]

Measured day work at British Leyland

Later than Vauxhall or Chrysler, British Leyland adopted a strategy of abandoning piecework, so as to reduce steward control of production and abolish the over 400 bargaining units. British Leyland management was also convinced that replacing piece rate negotiation by a central joint negotiating committee on pay, similar to Ford's, would reduce the number of disputes. By the end of the 1960s piece rates at Cowley were becoming unmanageable and increasingly irrelevant to machine-paced work.[21]

The Cowley pay system was reformed after a long and bitter struggle. As with other initiatives pragmatism was the hallmark of BL management's approach. Management offered trade unions plant-level bargaining, or company-wide bargaining, a choice designed to eliminate the option of playing one plant off against another. The result was company bargaining. Without the tight supervisory regime of Ford, British Leyland's introduction of time rates at first cut productivity.[22] Even individual union branches could hamstring the management by determined resistance to new working methods.[23] Management at Cowley at the beginning of 1971 found they had little leverage to secure even the previous levels of efficiency under the new payment system. Even previously attained production levels were liable to be revised downwards. In the early 1960s 35.5 Cowley 1100s an hour were made for 16 hours a day from 2 lines; branch 5/55 achieved a line speed reduction from 35 Marinas to 30 an hour. Without effective supervision, output restriction followed from the absence of a bonus element and thus of any direct financial incentives to maintain work effort. The piece rate tradition had eroded any non-pecuniary workforce motivation and managerial attempts to recover line speed under measured day work gave rise to even more small-scale strikes. The production programme was never fulfilled so that the sales division did not know when they could expect car deliveries. Management time was diverted by industrial relations to the extent that the plant director's office at Cowley was like a war operations room. The cost of these battles was shown by British Leyland's loss of market share to Ford and Vauxhall, which were not handicapped by comparable pay arrangements.

British Leyland's attempt to emulate Ford's strategic approach to production and industrial relations extended as far as the wholesale recruitment of senior executives from the American multinational. These former Ford managers played a critical role in attempts to incorporate senior shopfloor union representatives into corporate planning. By committing plant convenors to binding agreements, British Leyland hoped to reduce workplace militancy and halt the company's downward slide. The most tangible indicator of this new management style was British Leyland's readiness to try to achieve steward endorsement of major change in work organisation.

Consider the case mustered by one former Ford manager, Derek Whittaker in negotiations with the unions in 1973. Whittaker pointed out that British Leyland unit sales in 1972 were virtually identical to those achieved as in 1965, despite £266 million investment in new plant and equipment. In the same period, Whittaker continued, British Leyland had fallen from fifth to tenth in the world league of aggregate share values, to well below BMW and to less than half of the market valuation of Volvo (which achieved a turnover lower than that of Oxford plants). Low profits, reflected in the stock market value, left little to invest in fixed assets and offered no encouragement for external funds. This vicious circle of decline guaranteed low labour productivity and ensured poor industrial relations. Employment rose while output fell at the Cowley body, and assembly, works. During the previous financial year there had been 266 disputes at the Cowley assembly plant and 146 disputes in the body plant. Such stoppages lost the company 68,652 units, valued at over £80 million.[24]

Whittaker's initiative, in an environment that had an accumulated lack of trust, without suitable institutional support, or strong managerial hierarchies, was unable to effect any radical change. In the bargaining tradition established by 1973, the lightening strike was likely to be a trade union first response rather than last resort.[25] An engineering union official, explained, 'if a small group of workers is in dispute we might as well all come out in support because we will be shut out anyway.'

After British Leyland's financial position had further deteriorated, in 1975, a delegation discovered its competitors in Japan had been able to cultivate a 'Confucian spirit' among the workforce that it envied. British Leyland noted there the common status that British trade unionists had been pressing for, as well as company uniforms and one union per company that would have then proved less acceptable. Moreover, quality circles at Toyota generated an average of eight suggestions per employee in 1974 from 19,000 workers who received a total of £450,000 in payment for them.[26] Japanese motor factories, unlike those in Britain were landscaped with trees, fountains and fishponds. Equipment was highly automated and all employees were paid monthly on the basis of measured day work plus a bonus based on company profits. Retirement took place at 60 when workers received a lumpsum pension. The visiting team noted that stock levels equivalent merely to production of 30 minutes and 2 hours were held for items such as 'body in white', sub-assemblies, engines and soft trim, even though producers were more than 30 km from the assembly site. Model lead times were considerably less than at British Leyland. But it was one thing to note that production could be arranged differently, and another to transform organisations with the legacy of Britain's motor industry.

The Ryder Report attempted precisely such a radical innovation. Workers and management were to be brought together for planning in participation committees to restore a sense of commitment by labour in the success of the enterprise that measured day work seemed to have eliminated.[27] However, there were no shopfloor elections; the unions were to decide themselves which union stewards were to take up seats on the various participation committees. The new structure left ultimate power to management but required serious attempts to achieve consensus be made through the committees. 'Participation' did not succeed in improving industrial relations and productivity despite a great deal of effort. Representatives became isolated from shopfloor union members, who believed stewards were supposed to bargain on their behalf, not to run the company. When Michael Edwardes was appointed British Leyland chief executive at the end of 1978, his abolition of 'participation' committees was not widely mourned.[28]

6.3 Causes of disputes

The most visible manifestation of poor industrial relations were strikes. Working days lost through strikes (Table 6.2) are likely to be greater the larger the industry, other things being equal. From 1955 to 1975 the trend in days lost per vehicle does not look so disastrous but that index does not allow for rising productivity. Measured in days lost per employee the deterioration is far more serious. Between 1960 and 1970 employment rose by about 14 per cent whereas strikes per employee increased by 114 per cent. The United States, Canada and Italy at first suffered more from strikes than Britain, but from the 1960s, Britain's relative position deteriorated. Unofficial strikes were increasing nationally from the late 1950s. Frangmented workplace bargaining and inappropriate bargaining institutions in all sectors proved sources of disputes, as did British employers invariable preference for market based arrangements, such as piece rates, rather than solutions internal to the firm.[29]

The marked increase in motor industry strike activity in the period can be traced to several predisposing causes, the first of which was the multiple unionism noted in the first section of this chapter. Whereas in the United States and Japan, one union represented all workers, in Britain numerous unions, each with differing policies, leadeship attitudes, internal structures and differing alliances of labour interests external to the motor industry, were represented in the motor vehicle industry. In the 1960s there were

36 unions in British Leyland and 22 unions in Ford. This fragmentation conferred local authority on shop stewards without providing the structure for a consistent union policy. Not only were

Table 6.2: Labour unrest in the British motor vehicle industry, 1949–1978

	No. of strikes	No. of workers involved ('000s)	Working days lost ('000)
1949	38	7.9	47
1950	53	24.3	132
1951	67	53.5	265
1952	44	38.1	457
1953	40	300.7	560
1954	46	33.4	98
1955	76	62.8	452
1956	48	87.3	361
1957	65	154.8	800
1958	84	72.8	160
1959	135	157.6	465
1960	129	186.3	515
1961	102	121.5	425
1962	116	508.3	747
1963	129	148.3	315
1964	165	150	429
1965	165	218.9	874
1966	170	134.2	344
1967	223	200.6	504
1968	233	402.5	898
1969	276	276	1,636
1970	336	271.4	1,105
1971	241	340.3	3,100
1972	217	247.3	1,355
1973	297	422.6	2,082
1974	223	296.6	1,255
1975	150	164.0	829
1976	191	206.0	785
1977	208	234.3	2,593
1978	194	366.6	3,495

Source: Ministry of Labour, Labour Gazette, various issues.

coherent management or union policies to deal with the issues on which the labour unrest focused missing until the end of the 1960s, but also there were rivalries over recruitment and demarcation. Demarcation barriers created by the craft union tradition hindered continuity of production; when a welding gun broke down the operative was unable to repair it. Disputes became particularly acute as inflationary expectations grew and unions fought to maintain and improve on historical parities.[30]

Multiple unionism led to rivalry in recruitment and increased the complexity of industrial relations but was not a direct cause of strikes. More important was the stimulus to general union militancy for recruitment purposes. In the early 1960s Bob Fryer and the TGWU stewards led the campaign for higher wages and the 100 per cent unionisation of the BMC Cowley plant. Fryer recalled 'During the 100 per cent drive in the paint shop . . . I called a meeting of all the paint shop on Phipps Road. "Look, you are now on £10 per week on piecework", I told them, "If you all join the union and make it a 100 per cent shop I can promise you that within nine months we all will be earning £20 per week." Nine months later . . . they all produced their pay slips – they were all over £20.'[31]

Wage demands were also driven by the labour force's insistence on wages parity. Unequal wages for equal work stemmed from the fragmentation of the industry. Parity could be sought at three levels: between companies (Ford and Vauxhall paid the same rates in all different plants, which led to demands for parity between companies), between workers within the same company (differentials between BLMC plants were particularly acute after the merger of the constituent companies to form British Leyland in 1968, and led to demands for parity between the different parts of the company), and between plants.

All workers wanted to earn the high pay given to Midlands operatives.[32] In 1969 the net rate per hour for an identical task was 15s 8d at BMC Longbridge, but 10s 6d at Ford, 9s 10d at Vauxhall and 17s 4d at Rootes in Ryton.[33] The demand for parity with the Midlands was, for example, a crucial issue in the severe strike at British Leyland in 1969.[34] Unrest related to the wage structure was most frequent in times of booms and thus considerably more disruptive to production. Differentials were not, however, the prime cause of unrest. Turner's analysis of the strke propensity in the 1950s and 1960s led him to conclude that the elimination of the differences in average hourly rates between firms and plants would not eliminate or even substantially reduce the potential for unrest.

Far more important for stoppages was the insecurity and fluctuations in earnings.[35] Some instability of earnings was inevitable in an industry subject to annual and seasonal fluctuations in output for those workers dependent on a weekly pay packet and payment by results. Wage instability was more acute in the motor vehicle industry than in engineering in general due to the variation in hours worked (particularly in relation to overtime earnings) and the method of payment by results. To a large extent wage instability was the inevitable outcome of the manning pattern adopted by management. The British strategy was to employ sufficient men to produce at maximum capacity throughout the year and to meet falls in production by short time working (with its consequent effects on wages). All operatives suffered and were likely to unite against management. By contrast, the American system geared manning to minimum yearly production, which offered greater security to those in employment. 'Insiders', those with relative job security, were likely to be in a majority, and unwilling to tolerate disruption by the minority of 'outsiders' who provided the buffer labour force.

Fluctuations in pay could also derive from technical hold-ups and breakdowns in the production process, changes in models or equipment and strikes in other departments or plants. The high pay enjoyed by motor vehicle industry workers enabled workers to afford a strike, and insecurity of earnings and employment creating a disposition to press any occasion to raise wages. Fear of redundancy was the source of many instances of labour unrest during times of slump. The combination of high with fluctuating wages was in the opinion of many observers a particularly explosive one.[36] Car workers in this period became used to seeing much of their earnings or even their jobs lost overnight. Ill-will was exacerbated by the uncertain operating environment. The industry's postwar history of disagreement and dispute between management and labour fostered an atmosphere of mutual distrust and suspicion.[37]

Variable demand and management policy were major contributions to official strikes. The principle of management's right to lay-off workers without consultation triggered a series of disputes, culminating in the industry-wide stoppage of 1956. The NUVB authorised the Austin strike of 1953 which originated from a shop steward's dismissal arising out of a threatened redundancy. The TGWU encouraged strike action against BMC's dismissal of 6,000 workers at Cowley in 1956. Unsold vehicles were building up as demand turned down, evoking fears of market saturation. Every man with less than three years' service was sacked with no more than 48 hours' notice, without any consultation. The ensuing strike and picketing ultimately gained full union recognition and a redundancy agreement. Thereafter there were no redundancies until 1966.[38] Management was eventually constrained by the Contracts of Employment Act 1963 which obliged employers to provide a written statement of terms and conditions of employment and entitlement to a minimum period of notice according to length of service. Otherwise management's reliance on their traditional prerogitives, and on *ad hoc* arrangements, remained strong.

From 1961 the Ministry of Labour's emphasis on due procedures perhaps inhibited official union support for strikes. But threat of an official strike at Ford in 1962 and the beginning of 1963 also over redundancy led to the 'Jack' Court of Inquiry. During 1964 and 1965 there were official stoppages at Standard, Rover, Austin and even Vauxhall.[39] These appeared serious because the number of workers who came out in any dispute was influenced by official union attitude. But the effective loss of the companies may have been attenuated by the low level of demand in 1965 (see below).

On the one hand, by the 1960s most of the workforce had known only conditions of full employment all their working lives. They therefore expected jobs would be available by right. On the other hand, they could expect to be dismissed at very short notice if there was an unexpected downturn in demand, as there often was. They were aware that white collar workers and management, who were given privileges they were not, were also not subject to the same hazard. An 'us and them' attitude was only a rational response to their work conditions. Industrial action was often merely a way of drawing attention to a grievance. At Ford, without a strike a problem might have taken up to a year to reach the National Joint Negotiating Committee, whereas a strike would ensure the grievance would be addressed fairly quickly.[40] The 1971 Industrial Relations Act was ineffective in remedying these burgeoning disputes.

6.4 The impact of disputes

Disputes cut output, but if there happened to be insufficient demand at the time of the dispute then output must anyway have been cut back; strikes were not in those circumstances the fundamental cause of reduced production. Turner, Clack and Roberts contend that when demand fell, a strike could be a convenient way for management to avoid paying wages without dismissing workers. In 1965 working days lost leapt to double the 1963–4 rate; perhaps 10 per cent of output was lost by disputes. If provoking strikes was a consistent and deliberate management policy during periods of falling demand, days lost through strikes might be expected to rise when output fell and fall when output picked up. Although that pattern fits 1964 and 1965, thereafter until the 1968 peak, days lost in strikes moved inversely with production (see Table 4.1 p. 94). Moreover Table 6.2 shows that *number* of strikes in 1965 and in 1964 were identical, the difference lay in the number of workers involved. In 1963 and in 1964 the number of workers involved were similar, but the number of strikes increased, with output.

Other evidence supports the view that although strikes genuinely did cut output, they were not primarily a management strategy. The Department of Employment concluded that at the end of the 1960s industrial disputes accounted for half of lost output.[41] The Ryder Report of 1975 accepted the same figure. Strikes during the 1970s by direct workers on new model lines, at the time of a new model launch, or during the build up for the August sales peak, were extremely damaging in vehicles lost relative to wages saved.[42] Moreover the threat of disruption when a new model was about to be introduced to the market or when new equipment was being introduced could become a severe deterrent to future investment.

The SMMT contended that although only 1.5–2.5 per cent of working days might be lost directly through strike action, there were much greater indirect effects on other companies.[43] Multinational companies concerned with the reliability of supplies of components would naturally try to source from countries whose industrial relations did not lead to disruptive strikes. Some intra-firm evidence of trade in engines during 1970 suggested that strikes were an important reason for differences between countries' exports. At the means of the variables, a 10 per cent difference in strike activity was associated with an inverse 4 per cent difference in (mainly) car engine exports, other things being equal including output.[44] The British industry, with a record of unpredictable disruptions, was therefore not a long term favourite for expansion in an increasingly international market. Since British-owned overseas subsidiaries were short-lived, effectively the immediate future lay with the American companies, which would not choose Britain for major production plants.

Poor labour relations were the proximate cause of the inability to operate large scale, low unit cost, plants.[45] And the industry's problem lay in large plants, for they produced the great bulk of output. Observers continually emphasised the inability of British motor vehicle manufacturers to concentrate production into bigger establishments so as to reduce cost.[46] Most of British Leyland's main assembly plants during the 1970s were far too small to achieve the economies attained abroad, although Ford's plants were closer to the minimum efficient scale.[47] There were, of course, good reasons why larger production units did not emerge in Britain. Strike proneness, working to rule and other forms of disruption were particularly acute in big factories. The probability of stoppage in any period was dependent on the number of people in the plant. Plants with over 5,000 employees in motor vehicle manufacturing showed an average of five strikes per plant per year – three times the rate in the rest of manufacturing industry for plants in the same size group.[48] Plants in the size range of 1,000 to 2,000 employees could expect two to three stoppages a year in the 1970s. Car plants among Britain's main competitors were in the 40,000 employees range. A British plant of that size would have had an enormous number of stoppages. Man days lost through strikes in Britain's motor industry was anyway ten times higher than in Germany, with its larger plants, between 1968 and 1974. Larger plants in Britain would merely have enhanced the disadvantage.[49] British car plants of a size common in Germany would have been even less competitive in Britain so long as traditional British labour relations persisted.[50] Small British plants were not, however, necessarily immune from poor industrial relations. Demarcation disputes at the tiny Aston Martin Lagonda Newport Pagnell works were common before June 1972. Thereafter new management radically improved relations by consultation and communication.[51]

An industry could support a certain type of strike without being made too uncompetitive. The set piece confrontations of the German engineering union I G Metall were widely perceived as relative undisruptive because employers could plan in advance for the dispute. That was not an option for British management because the real British strike problem was not the official strike but the multitude of unofficial stoppages, and even they were only the tip of the iceberg of restrictions on labour productivity.

The clearest evidence that it was not so much strikes as work practices that underlay poor productivity comes from comparing British and German plants producing the same models within the same company. In the study by Jürgens and others, there was a 100 per cent difference in labour productivity between plants during the years 1978 to 1984. Absences in the British plant were less than in Germany or in the United States and that remained true even after the greater number of British days lost through industrial conflict is taken into account.[52] In an attempt to close the productivity gap, at the British 'Hartmoor' plant in 1976 management unilaterially announced a change in labour relations, declaring war on restrictive practices such as dividing up the work so that individuals could take an informal break while others did their work for them.[53] Portable time clocks, replaced fixed time clocks repeatedly destroyed by operatives, so that foremen could resume checking in and out workers. Management locked out the workforce in retaliation for a few operatives walking out. Judging by the number of recorded disputes the battle continued without a break until 1985. Unlike in the United States plants, no joint employer–worker strategy emerged in the British subsidiary; no consensus was reached about acceptable ways to manage. Chapter 8 considers how the legacy of low trust industrial relations was addressed during the 1980s.

6.5 Management and industrial relations

A function of management must be to initiate institutional and other changes necessary to ensure that operations are not hampered or disrupted by poor industrial relations. In that sense they must bear responsibility for the rising number of disputes and falling productivity of the 1970s. The physical layout of the plant and the organisation of parts delivery, supervision of production maintenance, and repair and training programmes may well have contributed to productivity failures and, if so, they apparently reflect managerial shortcomings.[54] Controlling for product mix, capital equipment and the age of tools, British production was inefficient compared with that in other countries, even where machinery of similar type and vintage was used for the same models. Yet the industrial relations constraints under which management worked may have rendered their task impossible.

The centrality of industrial relations in the decline of the British car industry has been challenged by a number of recent studies. Both Streeck and Willman maintain shopfloor bargaining did not impose major constraints on the introduction of new technology.[55] Similarly, in an exhaustive study of the management of technical change in British Leyland during the 1970s, Willman and Winch concluded that such was management's obsession with the 'labour question' that work organisation was distorted and British Leyland's small car production break-even point was disastrously raised. To minimise the chances of disputes, direct labour was reduced to a minimum on the Metro production line, pushing up fixed costs and raising the break-even threshold to a commercially unsustainable level.[56] Much less effort was directed to improving supplier relations, training, quality control and marketing, where it was greatly needed. For the management, this 'obsession' with labour problems was not a boardroom neurosis but a reaction to the debilitating impact of industrial relations on company performance over two decades. In the late 1970s British Leyland lost an average of 5 per cent of working hours per year to strikes, compared with just 1.5 per cent a decade later. A far greater proportion of management time was absorbed by industrial relations during the 1970s than in continental motor plants. Much of the time-consuming 'walking the patch' and 'touching the problem' was an attempt to anticipate potential hold-ups. In turn these delays originated in workforce controls triggered by grievances, which caused chaos up and down the line. A great deal of the complexity faced by management stemmed from its acceptance of workplace restrictions, on manning levels, on promotions and on the interchangeability of tasks.[57]

In this environment, British management's 'incrementalist' approach to task design and manning levels, its minimal adaption to problems only as they arose, was a rational response to the uncertainties it faced and over which it exercised little control. Incrementalism was further encouraged by the influence of the accountant who not only imposed and monitored the targets of individual profit centres but also, by focusing on budgeting, induced a mixture of opportunism and pragmatism by top management, rather than long term planning. Incrementalism and opportunism explain management resistance to even considering restructuring work organisation in the way that Volvo did in its Kalmar plant, focused on small group assembly.[58]

Management training, which might have widened managerial perspectives, was only supported when some specific changes in operating procedures were required. Indeed for many departmental heads and plant managers, their subordinates' attendance at courses represented not only a temporary loss of resources but a potential threat to their future authority. Neglect of systematic management development was rationalised by the need to preserve local management autonomy. The veneration of the 'practical man', of empiricism over professionalism, was not peculiar to the motor industry but a common feature of British manufacturing as a whole. Managers in engineering as a whole usually began as ex-craft apprentices or as work-study trainees. Few production managers had experience beyond their plant, far less of more than one company. BMC was well known for its unwillingness to employ graduates. Again Ford gained a competitive advantage through its systematic approach to management recruitment and training. As late as 1981 British Leyland recruited only 100 graduates with a workforce of 50,000, an annual intake comparable with that of IBM, which employed less than one-third of the car company.

Turner and associates, Rhys and Bhaskar all identified mangement as one of the main factors influencing labour relations and the incidence of strikes. Equally the Central Policy Review Staff regarded poor lines of communication from management through trade unions and shop stewards to the workforce as conducive to misunderstanding and mistrust.[59] For the earlier postwar period labour relations were not judged a vital strategic issue but rather were regarded as the concern of operational management. Plant-level management was exposed to opposing pressures: to maintain production and to maintain shopfloor discipline. At British Leyland Donald Stokes would not support sustained resistance to strikes once three days' car production was lost.[60] But buying off trouble only served to store up problems for the future.[61] Bhaskar and Rhys see poor labour relations as the outcome, rather than the cause, of the industry's problems and thus bring the circle back to the failure to rationalise production. This failure they contend created financial vulnerability, impeded product development and led to the very conditions of instability which gave rise to strike proneness.[62] The personnel manager at British Leyland during the 1970s, Geoffrey Whalen, reached similar conclusions, but emphasised the historical legacy; management during the 1950s and

1960s were insufficiently far-sighted and courageous.

Ford's management of industrial relations was profoundly different from that of British Leyland. Ford prevented the development of independent shopfloor organisation for a long time, sharing that goal with national union organisations in the 1940s and 1950s. Unions only consolidated their position at Ford from the late 1960s. So successful was Ford's anti-union policy that it experienced problems with labour recruitment in the 1960s because wages had failed to rise adequately. A second drawback of Ford's policy was that trade unions could not enforce discipline because they were out of touch with their members. Ford's pursuit of control for its own sake was ultimately not particularly helpful. What was needed was workplace flexibility to cope with the variety of model specifications that the market demanded, but Ford's unwillingness to delegate authority created difficulties in this respect. Industrial relations were neglected, without the excuse of membership of EEF.[63]

Even so, Ford's refusal ever to adopt piece rates or affiliate to the EEF probably conferred an advantage over British Leyland and predecessor companies. An insistence on direct management control often contributed to a large number of disputes but enhanced Ford's competitiveness over other British producers into the 1980s. It apparently sufficed to equalise Ford UK's labour productivity with Ford Germany's in 1973 (Table 6.3). Ford UK did not improve its share of British production relative to British Leyland before 1978, but that does not imply the company was no more competitive than British Leyland until 1978. Ford UK possessed an advantage in being able to import vehicles from other Ford subsidiaries to maintain profitability. But Ford was making cars in Britain for profit, while British Leyland was receiving subsidies from the British taxpayer in order to continue producing.

Ford was never able to find a satisfactory solution to British industrial relations. Each Ford operation took on a different character, strongly influenced by national bargaining institutions. Ford US differed from Ford UK, which in turn could not be compared with the far more legalistic Ford Germany with its works councils. American management concepts did not always fit comfortably in the British industrial relations environment, but Ford UK was able to flourish for many decades because of its professionalism in product development and cost control.

British management were well aware of harmful attitudes in

motor industry labour relations but was unable to understand or grapple with the experience that gave rise to them. A key problem was how to persuade motor industry employees to identify with their firm, and work for the collective end rather than for short term

Table 6.3: Productivity of selected motor vehicle manufacturers, 1974 (Value added per employee at purchasing power parity, Britain = 100)

General Motors US	397
Ford US	368
Average United States	385
Opel (General Motors)	168
Daimler-Benz	149
Ford Germany	140
Volkswagen	136
Average Germany	145
Ford UK	141
Chrysler UK	100
Vauxhall (General Motors)	92
British Leyland	77
Average Britain	100
Renault	156
Fiat	127

Source: Daniel T. Jones, Maturity and Crisis in the European Car Industry: Structural Change and Public Policy, Sussex European Papers, No. 8, University of Sussex, Brighton, 1981, Table 16, p. 103.

apparent personal advantage. German firms achieved more identification with the goals of the enterprise by being more paternalistic. They gave holidays for family occasions such as marriage, supplementing public pensions, organising welfare services, all of which receded into the background in the post 1945 British motor industry. German companies also had Works Councils, an innovation only half-heartedly (without direct elections) tried in Britain after the Ryder Report. Lack of collective commitment in Britain lowered productivity relative to the potential, through disputes with management and other workers over rights and obligations of particular jobs. When the commitment was there, as in the Rover, Solihull, plant, management failed to cash in on it. Workers wanted to contribute their assembly experience to the design of the SD1 but were ignored. They were sufficiently concerned about the poor quality of the new models in 1976 to write to the managing director of British Leyland.[64]

Why could not management deal more effectively with industrial relations? In Nissan during the 1980s it did. Ian Gibson, the chief executive, and Peter Wickens, the personnel director, were former Ford UK men. But they did by then have a different conception of the firm and they started with a relatively clean slate. British Leyland's inability to achieve a rapid and efficient transition to the measured day work regime reflected a long tradition of industrial hostility that could not easily or quickly be dispelled.

6.6 Conclusion

Better industrial relations would have allowed management to improve productivity substantially, but there is no reason to stop the explanation at that point. Industrial relations were poor because managements immediately after the war and into the 1950s did not take the opportunity to create a new set of relations within their firms more appropriate to the changed conditions, full employment in particular. Industrial relations institutions no doubt contributed; the multiplicity of non-workplace unions, the two tiers of worker representation, the piece rate system and the decentralised procedures of the EEF all played a role. But ultimately the root of the problem was an inappropriate conception of the firm and relations within it. The American-owned companies showed that there were different ways of organising relations, although they were hardly ideal. Ford's professionalism and Vauxhall's relatively harmonious industrial relations and low wage drift until the mid 1960s demonstrated these could be profitable. British-owned companies maintained arms-length, incrementalist styles of management supervised by the accountant and generally ceased to be profitable once they became large. Immediately after the war was the opportunity for reform. As adversarial relations became more entrenched and profitability declined, constructive change became increasingly difficult.

The proximate causes of disputes were well known – redundancy, managerial authority in dismissing or disciplining individuals, wage relativities. Yet no fundamental solution was attempted until the 1970s or achieved, as it often was abroad. Management of some firms was not even able to distinguish between dismissals and voluntary quits of their firms in their internally generated data during the 1960s.

Erratic demand for the motor industry's product made management's task more difficut, but even without it the course of the industry would not have been greatly different. Industry unions may have given greater incentive to the workforce to consider the long term future of their jobs, and have provided a more coherent structure of representation than was available through shop stewards. Nissan's success starting on a green field site with a one union agreement in the 1980s is consistent with an adverse effect of traditional British unionisation. On the other hand increasing unionisation over the 1950s and early 1960s may have been as much effect as cause of the industry's conditions.

Only a major shock would in fact suffice to stir the British to radical institutional reform. For electoral reasons, governments devoted a good deal of money to saving Chrysler and British Leyland from the consequences of their performance. Even Ford was the beneficiary of Japanese 'voluntary export restraint' from the 1970s. In short, reform had to await the savaging of the industry in the 1980s.

CHAPTER SEVEN

DEMAND AND GOVERNMENT POLICY, 1945–1978

Unlike government policies towards the motor industry during the interwar years, those after 1945 increasingly operated on supply, as well as on demand. From the later 1960s policies were concerned with the industry as an end itself, as well as an instrument. On the side of demand, the replacement in 1947 of the horsepower tax by a flat rate annual charge,[1] invariant with the size of the vehicle, removed one incentive to make low horsepower models, but heavy petrol taxation ensured small cars would still be favoured in the British market. Tariff protection at 33.3 per cent, limiting import penetration, continued unchanged until 1960. Section 1 considers the nature of demand. The regulation of car hire purchase became even more controversial during the 1950s and 1960s than the horsepower tax had been between the world wars. The implications of 'stop–go' policies for the industry are assessed in Section 2. Like hire purchase regulation, regional policy used the motor industry to achieve other state objectives, primarily during the 1960s. Also like hire purchase regulation, the longer term consequences of shifting the industry's new plants, hundreds of miles from the parent factories, have been blamed for some of the industry's difficulties. Operating on supply, regional policy in that respect resembled government intervention to restructure and rescue the industry from 1968. The implications of regional policy for the industry are discussed in Section 3. The desirability of the state-sponsored creation of British Leyland, and its subsequent nationalisation, together with the bail-out of Chrysler UK, have all been questioned after the events. Section 4 addresses industrial policy in relation to British Leyland and Section 5 considers the Chrysler intervention of 1975.

7.1 Demand

As Chapter 4 showed, the motor vehicle industry after 1945 was one of the largest industries in the country, measured by contribution to gross domestic product and export earnings. The current and capital direct and indirect requirements of the industry accounted for 12 per cent of total industrial production in 1963, whilst 32 per cent of the growth in industrial production could be attributed to the motor vehicle industry.[2] Rhys estimated that if the value of the motor industry's output fell by 6 per cent, then total economic activity would decline by almost 2 per cent.[3] Since fluctuations in the industry could have such profound repercussions on economic activity in general, any attempt to influence the level of economic activity was almost inevitably bound to focus on the motor vehicle industry. As motor vehicle ownership grew, spending not only on purchasing but on running a car assumed growing importance in consumer expenditure. Controlling expenditure on motor vehicles thus became an obvious way of stimulating or dampening demand in the economy.[4]

The transport and location policies pursued by postwar governments of both parties created additional difficulties for the industry, most notably in the delayed construction of motorways and improvement in the major arteries in Britain. The London to Birmingham motorway was only opened in 1959, almost a generation after Germany's first autobahn. Some observers judged these policies deterred greater use of the private car and dampened demand for the industry's products.[5] Continued support for the railways with social service grants and subsidies may also have depressed private demand by creating a viable alternative form of transport.[6] The delay in motorway building, however, may have reduced exports since manufacturers could have been dissuaded from producing cars capable of sustained high speed cruising, highly saleable in Europe and North America.[7]

Freight vehicle demand was boosted by the changing pattern and location of industry, to which improvements in vehicles and roads contributed. Railways lost business and the network was cut back; the Beeching cuts of 1961 were particularly radical. Road accidents increased with vehicle use to the extent that by 1968 some 350,000 were injured and 7,000 were killed on the roads.

How the demand for cars was influenced by any particular measure depended on the way in which a number of markets interacted, especially the second-hand and business markets. The demand for cars is a demand for a set of transport services such as speed, convenience, capacity and comfort. Car ownership is necessary to acquire these services. The price or cost of ownership depends upon the sale price of the vehicle when finally it is disposed of, and the purchase price. Both of these may be determined in second-hand markets. The more buoyant the second-hand price the lower the cost of new car ownership, other things being equal. Policies which depressed second-hand prices were therefore also likely to depress the demand for new vehicles.

When car ownership extends through the population, the increase has often been dubbed 'new' demand for cars. The total demand for cars is greater than that because the existing car stock is continuously subject to wearing out and scrapping. The proportion of car stock that is demanded in each period and is not accounted for by increased registrations is often allocated to this 'replacement' demand. The relationship between 'replacement' and 'new' demand can be employed as an indicator of the maturity of the market. When ownership is at saturation levels, the demand for cars will be entirely 'replacement'. It is important to bear in mind, however, that, where private ownership is concerned, market-widening actually occurred mainly through the second-hand market in this period; the 'new' demand was a statistical classification rather than a behavioural concept.

Car ownership in 1938 had reached over 20 per cent of households.[8] In the immediate aftermath of the war, domestic demand far exceeded supply allocated to the home market. New cars were rationed and the trade devoted a great deal of effort to preventing buyers profiting from their purchases at less than free market prices. Many of the 1.6 million pre-war cars on the road in 1955 were bought and sold at prices far exceeding the prewar new list price.[9] Predictions of car ownership were almost as conservative as they had been in the early 1920s, bearing in mind the higher base from which they were starting. An early forecast of the saturation level of car ownership in 1948, of 12.5 vehicles per 100 implied with a population of 55 million a saturation car 'park' of 6.875 million, a figure that was exceeded in 1963.[10] By 1965 over half of all households in Britain owned a car; by 1970, 63 per cent of households were car owners.[11] Until the mid 1960s most growth was in 'new' demand. Between 1960 and 1964, 'replacement' demand constituted just over one-quarter (28 per cent) of total annual demand.[12] By the first half of the 1970s, two-thirds of the total was 'replacement' demand.[13] In 1970–1 around 4 million second-hand cars were traded, compared with new sales of 1.2 million and a car 'park' of 13 million. Mean age of scrapping fell from 13 in 1965 to almost 11 in the late 1970s. How vital car ownership was is underlined by the sums people regularly spent on motoring. The average car owning household spent 15.8 per cent of expenditure on the car, divided roughly equally between usage and acquisition costs. Over the postwar years to 1980, expenditure on cars trebled, cars were changed more frequently, and caravanning and touring became popular car-using holidays.

In the immediate postwar years, when priority was given to fleet users and business customers, some 80 per cent of new car sales were financed directly or indirectly by businesses.[14] The growth of private car use led to a decline in the proportion of sales financed by business. In the mid 1950s, business sales accounted for between 40 and 50 per cent of total new sales.[15] The business sector however continued to constitute a significant and important market for the motor manufacturers. In the 1970s, 40 per cent of demand was non-private, i.e. fleet sales to businesses and hire companies.[16] Sales to the business sector were sought not least because fleet users' demand could counterbalance fluctuations in the private market.[17]

7.2 Hire purchase regulation

There were two main instruments of direct regulatory policy which directly affected the motor vehicle industry after 1945: hire purchase and taxation.[18] Hire purchase restrictions covered both the minimum deposit required and the maximum period for repayment. Purchase Tax and later Value-Added-Tax were levied sometimes with a view to influencing spending on motor vehicles. Other fiscal instruments such as road fund licences, business allowances and petrol taxes were also employed.

In 1955 the business allowance on cars was abolished, while in 1956 in the midst of the Suez crisis, petrol taxes were raised and petrol rationing introduced.[19] During the balance of payments crisis in the third and fourth quarters of 1967, in addition to an increase in restrictions on hire purchase in the November, Road Fund licence payments were increased and were raised again in the 1968 budget.[20] For the industry, the significance of the tax increases lay in the uncertainty they created in the market, and in the periodic restrictions of home demand for vehicles. The tax burden carried by the British motor vehicle user continued to be higher than that of many other Europeans. In November 1962, when British purchase taxes were at an all time low, the British rate corresponded to a sales tax of 21 per cent; the equivalent rate in Germany was 13 per cent, in France 28 per cent and in Italy 12 per cent.[21]

The expansionary phases of 'stop–go' were short lived. When in 1955 the official reserves fell to £2,120 million and the deficit on the visible balance of trade reached £293 million, a 'stop' period, lasting until 1958, was inaugurated. For the motor industry this meant increases in purchase tax, the abolition of business allowance on cars and the re-introduction and increase of hire purchase restrictions. By the final quarter of 1957, new registrations of cars had fallen to 24,000 (the lowest quarterly figure from 1956 to 1959). The downturn in domestic sales was mitigated to some extent by the revival of exports to North America as a new market for Britain's small cars was tapped across the Atlantic. By 1958 official reserves had recovered (to £3,069 million in that year) and the deficit on visible trade had been transformed into a surplus of £29 million. A new phase of 'go' policy followed involving a relaxation in purchase tax in April 1959 and, in October 1958, the removal of hire purchase restrictions, which markedly increased domestic demand. In 1959, registrations of new vehicles were averaging 53,975 a quarter and new credit advanced soared from an average quarterly value of £121 million in 1957 to £197 million in 1959 and £221 million in 1960.[22]

The 1960s brought greater instability for the motor vehicle industry. In contrast to the 1950s, each phase of the 'stop–go' cycle in the 1960s was relatively short-lived and the industry had to react to frequent changes in taxation and hire purchase regulations. The decade began with balance of payments problems; by the third quarter of 1960 the current balance of trade had slipped to a deficit of £109 million. Yet again, the motor vehicle industry became the target for restrictive policies to counter the deficit. Hire purchase conditions were tightened in April 1960 and January 1961; in July 1961 Purchase Tax was raised. By the end of 1961, new registrations of cars, at 41,000, were at an all time quarterly low for the 1960s. At the end of 1961 production had fallen to half a million units a year. But from 1962 to 1964 the industry enjoyed a three year boom, the result of the revival of export markets in both Europe and the United States and the increase in consumer confidence at home following from Chancellor Reginald Maudling's 'Dash for Growth'.

By the end of 1963 the industry was operating at full capacity and new registrations of cars in 1962 and 1963 were at record quarterly average levels of 74,625. The boom ended in 1964 when the government attempted to resist devaluation by raising income tax and squeezing credit to improve the balance of payments. A series of measures, notably the 1965 and 1966 increases in hire purchase restrictions and purchase tax, restrained demand and ushered in five years of decline. In 1966 and 1967 the value of retail sales of motor vehicles fell to an average quarterly level of £21 million; and quarterly registrations of motor cars fell to an all-time seasonal low for the 1960s of 48,000 in the last quarter of 1966. In November 1967 the government was forced to devalue; for the motor industry this stimulated exports as export prices were set at more profitable levels. Continued wage growth required increases in November 1968 of both hire purchase restrictions and Purchase Tax. Post devaluation measures are estimated to have cut home car sales from 1.3 million to 1.1 million.[23]

It is not surprising then that many commentators have claimed that government policy had serious long term negative repercussions on the industry. Although few would argue that Britain's poor growth rate could be attributed to 'stop–go', there would appear to be some consensus that the policies did bear particularly hard on the consumer durables industries in general and on the motor vehicle industry in particular.[24] The extent to which such policies 'explain' the declining fortunes of the industry is, however, much debated.

At one extreme, the 'stop–go' cycles of the 1950s and 1960s are said to have had a deleterious effect on long term planning and to have destabilised the home market. Rhys, Adeney and Bhaskar have all cited the adverse effects of 'stop–go' policy in this period on production planning and market behaviour.[25] In Adeney's opinion: 'at its worst, the frequent changes made a nonsense of the industry's attempts to plan; at best it presented it with great difficulties';[26] whilst Bhaskar has claimed: 'it has been successive and consistent Government action which is primarily to blame for the poor state of

Table 7.1: Hire purchase restrictions on motor vehicles in Britain, 1952–1982

Types of vehicles affected	Date	Nature of changes	Minimum deposit (%)	Maximum period for repayment (months)
Cars and CVs	Feb. 1952	Restrictions introduced	33.3	18
	July 1954	Restrictions abolished	0	0
Cars	Feb. 1955	Restrictions reintroduced	15.0	24
	July 1955	Minimum deposit increased	33.3	24
Cars and CVs	Feb. 1956	Restrictions increased on cars and reintroduced on CVs	50.0	24
Cars and LCVs	Dec. 1956	Restrictions eased	20.0	24
Other CVs		Unchanged	50.0	24
Cars and CVs	May 1957	Restrictions unified	33.3	24
HCVs	Sept. 1957	Restrictions removed	0	0
Cars and LCVs		Unchanged	33.3	24
Cars and LCVs	Oct. 1958	Restrictions removed	0	0
	Apr. 1960	Restrictions reintroduced	20.0	24
	Jan 1961	Repayment period extended	20.0	36
	June 1965	Minimum deposit increased	25.0	36
	July 1965	Repayment period reduced	25.0	30
	Feb. 1966	Repayment period further reduced	25.0	27
	July 1966	Restrictions increased	40.0	24
	June 1967	Restrictions eased	30.0	30
	July 1967	Restrictions eased	25.0	36
	Nov. 1967	Restrictions increased	33.3	27
	Oct. 1968	LCVs definition changed		
Cars and LCVs	Nov. 1968	Restrictions increased	40.0	24
	July 1971	Restrictions abolished	0	0
Cars only	Dec. 1973	Restrictions reintroduced	33.3	24
	June 1977	Restrictions abolished on car purchases by companies (but retained on private purchases)		
	July 1982	Restrictions abolished		

Notes: CV: Commercial vehicle
LCVs: Light commercial vehicles below 30 cwt carrying capacity. In October 1968 definitions changed to cover goods vehicles below 40 cwt unladen weight and fitted, constructed or adapted to be fitted, with side windows to the rear of the driver.
HCV: Goods vehicles of 30 cwt carrying capacity and buses with 12 seats or more
Source: SMMT, The Motor Industry of Great Britain, 1991, Table 110, p. 283.

the industry as a whole'.[27] This is a view endorsed by Rhys: 'the effects of government activities on the state of the market was a major factor in the harm done to the industry's profitabiity in the 1950s and 1960s and hampered its ability to invest in new products and facilities.'[28] The most single-minded exponent of this hypothesis, Dunnett, has placed all of the industry's problems at the feet of governments of both political parties between 1945 and 1978.[29]

But how exactly is demand management supposed to have caused serious and long term damage to the industry? 'Stop–go' is seen by Adeney, Bhaskar and Rhys to have increased uncertainty, deterred long term planning and to have undermined the power of management to manage.[30] Between February 1952 and June 1977, there were 23 changes in hire purchase restrictions on motor vehicles in Britain (Table 7.1), the majority of which (twelve) occurred between October 1958 and November 1968. In some years, notably 1955, 1956, 1957, 1965, 1966, 1967, 1968 there were several changes within one year. Taxation policy was equally unstable. Between April 1950 and November 1968 the former was changed eleven times, with six of the changes occurring in the 1960s (Table 7.2).

Table 7.2: Purchase Tax and Value Added Tax on motor cars in Britain, 1940–1979

	Changed to rate (%)
October 1940	33.33
June 1947	66.66
April 1950	33.33
April 1951	66.66
April 1953	50.00
October 1955	60.00
April 1959	50.00
July 1961	55.00
April 1962	45.00
November 1962	25.00
July 1966	27.50
March 1968	33.33
November 1968	36.66
July 1971	30.00
March 1972	25.00
April 1973	25.00[a] (VAT = 17%)
May 1979	31.00[a] (VAT = 22%)

Note [a] = VAT introduced at 10% plus car tax.
Source: Peter J. S. Dunnett, The Decline of the British Motor Industry: The Effects of Government Policy, 1945–1979, London: Croom Helm, 1980, Table 5.2, p. 89.

Such changes do appear to have limited motor vehicle sales. The tightening of restrictions in 1965 and 1966, for example, had adverse effects on all segments of the motor vehicle industry, with hire purchase sales of new and used cars and commercial vehicles all recording substantial falls (Tables 7.3 and 7.4). All motor manufacturers experienced declining new and used hire purchase sales (Tables 7.5 and 7.6).

Table 7.3: Hire purchase sales of private cars in Britain, 1960–1970

	New motor cars	Used motor cars
1960	163,532	745,787
1961	172,218	725,363
1962	176,403	682,052
1963	263,127	823,437
1964	329,325	1,065,223
1965	318,816	1,078,986
1966	276,204	994,148
1967	301,467	1,158,581
1968	296,674	1,160,779
1969	234,482	1,033,844
1970	261,052	1,068,731

Source: HP Information, *Monthly Statistical Returns; Private Cars; Registration by Makes of Hire Purchase Agreements*, Finance Houses Association, London.

Table 7.4: Hire purchase sales of commercial vehicles in Britain, 1960–1970

	New vehicles			Used vehicles		
	Vans	Carriers	Coaches	Vans	Carriers	Coaches
1960	52,819	16,201	776	126,025	13,629	1,878
1961	68,485	13,224	758	114,057	10,970	1,579
1962	64,159	9,663	479	96,955	8,344	1,366
1963	48,463	11,651	584	109,905	9,242	1,546
1964	51,841	15,347	758	130,178	9,837	1,514
1965	50,275	13,832	652	110,798	8,332	1,639
1966	47,419	11,422	886	83,569	6,419	1,495
1967	37,103	15,603	657	79,297	8,730	1,717
1968	43,033	21,440	772	73,811	8,805	1,758
1969	73,811	25,795	709	62,597	8,539	1,717
1970	50,752	25,201	793	63,059	8,876	1,917

Source: HP Information, *Monthly Statistical Returns; Motor Vehicles: Registration of Hire Purchase Agreements*, Finance Houses Association, London.

What precisely were the costs of the policy? In the first place, demand restrictions impeded the realisation of scale economies. As Chapter 4 outlined, one of the key problems of the industry and of the firm was that even when utilising full capacity, the British producers were not operating at optimum outputs. If production fell below full capacity, then the industry would be even further below optimum volumes. Any shortfall in production would have then

Table 7.5: New cars bought on hire purchase in Britain, by make, 1956–1970

	Austin	Morris	Singer	Ford	Vauxhall
1956	8,774	8,774	418	35,924	5,322
1957	15,557	15,557	580	33,137	7,360
1958	20,672	20,672	1,287	40,500	11,219
1959	22,561	22,561	1,849	46,791	17,962
1960	25,296	16,288	1,575	47,481	19,357
1961	28,326	20,545	1,680	60,125	11,569
1962	31,713	23,820	3,222	52,776	19,101
1963	49,514	40,497	3,758	72,606	28,310
1964	57,987	44,698	5,828	90,016	41,144
1965	52,674	40,916	10,849	86,927	43,032
1966	41,369	35,876	8,345	75,250	34,882
1967	35,405	30,549	10,170	81,407	45,968
1968	35,270	32,953	6,571	85,500	45,658
1969	29,497	23,869	3,210	67,610	31,928
1970	33,380	24,684	1,026	75,234	28,924

Source: HP Information, *Monthly Statistical Returns; Private Cars: Registration by Makes of Hire Purchase Agreements*, Finance Houses Association, London.

Table 7.6: Used cars bought on hire purchase in Britain, by make, 1956–1970

	Austin	Morris	Singer	Ford	Vauxhall
1956	60,542	48,356	4,007	73,199	27,596
1957	106,602	79,087	5,787	124,424	45,662
1958	127,554	86,847	6,971	159,336	61,838
1959	145,060	90,416	6,938	200,072	74,835
1960	139,568	92,879	5,698	205,647	72,726
1961	129,277	86,490	5,556	218,129	69,423
1962	122,172	81,640	5,644	210,739	65,751
1963	147,666	99,560	7,359	257,664	78,759
1964	190,949	138,062	11,090	329,575	102,428
1965	189,232	140,691	14,470	325,025	110,741
1966	170,839	134,768	16,148	291,145	104,183
1967	190,042	152,407	23,037	338,069	132,934
1968	183,647	149,890	24,312	335,552	139,198
1969	152,141	126,566	23,372	295,307	133,623
1970	147,502	121,858	23,692	313,108	147,055

Source: HP Information, *Monthly Statistical Returns; Private Cars: Registration by Makes of Hire Purchase Agreements*, Finance Houses Association, London.

entailed two costs: the original penalty for failing to reach optimum levels of production and that entailed in not reaching full capacity output.

Most observers have failed to fully appreciate this link between the initial failures to reach optimum levels of production and the costs of 'stop–go'. Yet the two are intrinsically linked. At various stages during 'stop' phases of the 1950s and 1960s the industry was operating significantly below capacity. In the period prior to 1953, in 1961 and again in 1969, the industry was operating at less than half capacity. Unit production costs were therefore increased, with the consequent adverse effects on profitability. The 'stop' phase of the cycle in the 1950s, for example, delayed the utilisation of capacity created in the industry during the two investment phases of that decade. It was not until 1958 that the extra capacity created in the industry since 1954 was fully utilised for the first time.[31] But just three years later, as a result of the tightening of hire purchase conditions in April 1960 and January 1961 and the raising of Purchase Tax in July 1961, the industry was operating at 40 per cent capacity.[32] At the end of 1961, production had fallen to half a million unit a year, at the very time when capacity was being increased to three million units a year.[33]

Were the fluctuations in output in Britain any more serious than those experienced in competitor nations? Writing on the period 1955 to 1975, Prais claimed that German and American car industries showed the same relative variability about a trend as had the British car industry and that, as such, the instability of demand was not a major factor in the industry's problems.[34] Matthews however maintained that although Britain ranked low among countries in the magnitude of fluctuations in gross national product, it ranked nearly at the top in the magnitude of fluctuations in consumer durables.[35] The estimates of Bowden and Turner, which extend the coverage to other European nations as well as Japan and which use the period 1955 to 1970 (thereby eliminating the post 1973 oil crisis effects) indicate that movements in British production were markedly higher than those in comparative European manufacturing nations and that the average growth rate around which the fluctuations took place in Britain was around half that in France, Germany and Italy.[36]

Silberston maintained that during the 1950s hire purchase controls on used car sales had repercussions on used car prices.

Through trade-in controls on total new car sales, they permanently affected the volume of hire purchase business while they persisted.[37] Evidence from the 1960s shows that hire purchase changes in that decade also had a lasting effect on hire purchase business.[38] In the 1960s, the 'easiest' terms were in 1967, when the maximum period for repayment was extended to 36 months and the minimum deposit was reduced to 25 per cent (Table 7.1). Hire purchase sales do not indicate any substantial recovery from the tight conditions operating in 1966: with the exception of hire purchase sales of new cars, hire purchase sales of motor vehicles continued to fall. According to one econometric estimate, between 1970 and 1973 more than one-third of the increase in registrations of 629,000, was a consequence of reductions in the minimum hire purchase deposit.[39]

Fluctuations in demand as a result of direct regulatory policy appear to have adversely affected all British producers. Hire purchase facilities were important to all the motor manufacturers in this period. Ford however dominated the league table of hire purchase sales of new cars (Table 7.5). Hire purchase sales of Ford motor cars always exceeded the combined total for Morris and Austin. However, hire purchase facilities were proportionately more important to BMC and BLMC than they were to the Ford or Vauxhall. In 1970, hire purchase sales accounted for 17.7 per cent of new registrations of BLMC cars, agaisnt 15.5 per cent of new Ford cars. That 2 per cent difference indicates how much more serious demand management by hire purchase was for the British-owned producer.

Each of the major producers sold more used than new cars on hire purchase terms in the 1960s. Again, the evidence suggests that in volume terms, Ford dominated hire purchase sales of used cars (Table 7.6). The absence of data recording total used car sales by make precludes any estimation of the percentage of hire purchase financed used car sales for each firm.

Did fluctuations in demand for cars increase the uncertainty and risk surrounding investment planning? Uncertainly as to future levels of demand consequent upon government policies could have deterred long-run planning, particularly in relation to large scale investment expenditure. It may be that the industry was reluctant to invest in expanding capacity if there was a risk of the government instigating a stop to home demand or for the individual firm the effect of fluctuations was to depress the rate of return on capital. Matthews, whilst conceding that investment may have been constrained at best and depressed at worst and that the direct evidence is 'rather thin', did note that investment in machinery and equipment had been very stable by international standards – in contrast to consumer durables which were affected to a greater degree by stop–go policies.[40] Even the Treasury ultimately conceded the point, admitting in its evidence to the Expenditure Committee that fluctuations in demand during the 1960s had had a destabilising effect and had made comprehensive planning over a long time difficult.[41] 'Stop–go', however, is more likely to have contributed indirectly to poor profit performance, by raising costs as a result of under-capacity working, which had implications for investment rather than by acting directly as a deterrent to investment, although the Expenditure Committee did believe that in some cases it had 'deterred the will to invest'.[42]

Poor labour relations in the industry have also been traced by many observers to demand management policies.[43] One way in which the industry tried to contain variable costs at a time of government restrictions was by lay-offs and redundancies. Both fostered the climate of insecurity within the labour force which was a key element in the increased strike propensity of the industry in the 1960s. The industry itself had few doubts as to the cause of its problems. George Turnbull, managing director of the British Leyland car division, described the effects of government policy;

> In those days it was just a little fiscal regulator. If the economy was overheated, put some more purchase tax on motor cars. The Government was totally oblivious and if I was ever going to apportion blame for the parlous state of the British motor industry got into, you have got to put it at the door of the Government. I don't care which complexion or which colour . . . they treated it with derision. There's no other word for it.'[44]

The government's 'demand management' policy in the 1950s is said to have encouraged the motor industry to concentrate on the home market but to turn to export markets in times of difficulty. For example, in the 'go' period of the 'stop–go' cycle between 1953 and 1955, the industry was persuaded to concentrate on home market sales. Bowden and Turner found that there was a danger that exports were treated as a 'dumping ground' and that surplus production had the dominant role in explaining changes in exports between 1955 and 1970. But they stress that export performance cannot be explained solely by stop–go,[45] thus adding to the evidence that 'stop–go' cannot be held responsible for the manifold problems of the industry in these years.

By the 1970s, governments had come to appreciate the adverse effects of continual changes in hire purchase and tax levels on the motor vehicle industry. Sales taxes and hire purchase deposits and maximum repayment levels remained virtually unchanged from 1973 until the general increase in Value Added Tax in 1979.[46]

The evidence thus supports the view that 'stop–go' did lead to greater fluctuations in production than that experienced in other European competitor nations. It further suggests that 'stop–go' did contribute to the under-capacity problem in the British industry with its consequent implications for costs, profitability and investment. Ford may have been in a better position to withstand the policies, since hire purchase accounted for a smaller share of its sales than British Leyland and because of its dominance of the business fleet market, where increasingly leasing rather than hire purchase became the normal method of financing. Stop–go, however, cannot be singled out as the sole culprit. Ford became increasingly profitable in the later 1950s and BMC/BMH much less so, despite both companies being subject to similar demand fluctuations. Under-capacity cannot be blamed solely on stop–go. Under-capacity relates back to the postwar agenda which gave short run export performance a higher priority than long term rationalisation, to the postwar consensus which created labour relations problems, to the failure to produce vehicles which would sell in sufficient volumes. In the absence of 'stop–go' policies, such factors would still have undermined the industry's long run competitive position.

7.3 Regional policy

Like hire purchase regulation, regional policy in the 1950s and 1960s assumed the motor industry could be used to achieve other policy goals without any major harmful consequences. Between 1959 and 1971 government policy strongly decentralised the motor industry. In the first stage of the product cycle the industry had been widely scattered with companies in Glasgow, Cowes, Southport and Lowestoft, but even then the west Midlands dominated. During the interwar years the standardisation of the second stage placed a greater premium on input availability and market access, and so the centre of gravity of the industry shifted southwards.

After 1945, application of Industrial Development Certificate controls restricted expansion of car factories on existing sites and prohibited new plants in the south-east or west Midlands.[47] Instead motor businesses were obliged to open new factories in Merseyside, Clydeside, Swansea, and Edinburgh. Figures 7.1–7.3 show the regional employment patterns, and the extent to which Chrysler and British Leyland acquired greater transport costs because of this decentralisation. Chrysler's Linwood factory created 250-mile linkages. Bathgate put 3–4 per cent on the price of a British Leyland truck. Ford was running 30 liner trains a week in 1970s, ironically having become the biggest private user of British Rail.

On the other hand the Halewood plant reduced Ford distribution costs.[48] Chrysler received £1.1 million of grants in 1971 for establishing the Linwood plant. Later, the £163 million financial support for the bankrupt Chrysler helped placate Scottish nationalist sentiment (see Section 5). Moreover, the obligation to move away from traditional motor industry employment areas was an opportunity to construct new industrial relations and break free from the established patterns of conflict. Ford certainly tried this at Halewood but with a notable lack of success. In 1963 the new plant provided an opportunity to recreate Fordism with only two unions, but the rigour of the regime provoked disorganised shopfloor conflict. Halewood stewards acquired control over manning levels and the pace of work by end of 1960s, which they were unable to achieve at Dagenham.[49]

In fact almost all the new plants of 'outer Britain' suffered from poor if not poorer industrial relations than the original sites. Although theoretical qualitative arguments for regional policy can be advanced, based on locational congestion and utilisation of infrastructure, in practice the costs of job creation in development areas was socially, as well as financially, expensive. The regions from which the jobs were attracted became economically weaker over the period of active regional policy, suggesting that an additional cost of policy was that more jobs may have been lost in the more prosperous areas than were created elsewhere. In short, regional policy may have raised the natural rate, or non-accelerating inflation rate, of unemployment. That is certainly consistent with the motor industry's experience. Nissan's Sunderland plant from 1984 might be adduced as evidence that companies could

have pursued better policies in their new, dispered, plants so that regional policy was an advantage rather than a handicap. Against that position is the view that Nissan was able to utilise the flexibility

Figure 7.2 Employment in British Leyland's manufacturing plants, 1976

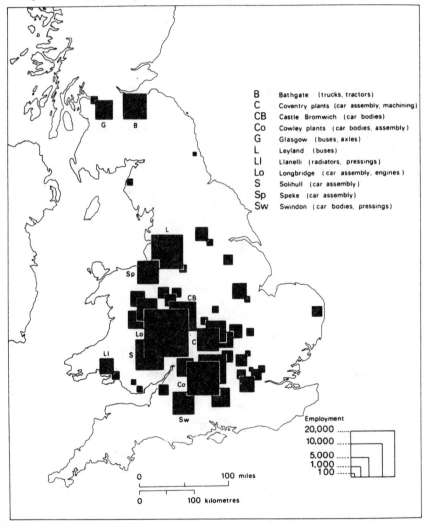

B	Bathgate (trucks, tractors)
C	Coventry plants (car assembly, machining)
CB	Castle Bromwich (car bodies)
Co	Cowley plants (car bodies, assembly)
G	Glasgow (buses, axles)
L	Leyland (buses)
Ll	Llanelli (radiators, pressings)
Lo	Longbridge (car assembly, engines)
S	Solihull (car assembly)
Sp	Speke (car assembly)
Sw	Swindon (car bodies, pressings)

Employment
20,000
10,000
5,000
1,000
100

0   100 miles

0   100 kilometres

Source: D. Keeble, *Industrial Location and Planning in the United Kingdom*, London: Methuen, 1976, Chapter 7.

beaten into British organisations and attitudes by a decade of industrial decline and heavy unemployment.[50] During the 1960s, among a generation that had only worked in conditions of full employment,

Figure 7.3 Chrysler UK: interplant linkages, 1975

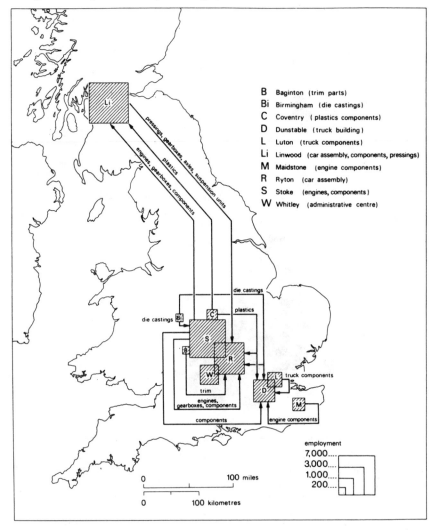

Source: D. Keeble, *Industrial Location and Planning in the United Kingdom*, London: Methuen, 1976, Chapter 7.

that may not have been possible.

Shortly after active regional policy was reduced, an active industrial policy was called into play to protect motor industry jobs in the industrial heartland of the West Midlands. But before then, premonition of the British-owned motor industry's shortcomings had already prompted some supportive government intervention.

7.4 Industrial policy; British Leyland

BMH was in financial difficulties, which had starved the company of investment, and stifled new model development. Leyland, on the other hand, was extremely profitable and Donald Stokes had acquired a very favourable public reputation. Merging the two businesses would allow the rationalisation of designs, greater utilisation of economies of scale, synergy from linking marketing and distribution networks, concentration of 'thinly spread' management skills and pooling research and development. Tony Benn, Minister of Technology, and the Prime Minister, Harold Wilson, favoured a merger between Leyland and BMH.[51] They offered the new Industrial Reorganisation Corporation (IRC) as an intermediary in exploratory talks at the end of 1966.[52]

Questions were raised about the desirability of putting the entire British-owned motor industry in one business, about the impact on labour relations and about the ability of management to cope with a larger company. Negotiations had already taken place between the two companies but a stumbling block continued to be BMH's unwillingness to concede Leyland control, despite BMH's poor financial position.

The IRC pushed through an agreement which otherwise may not have led to a merger, for Stokes had reservations about launching a contested takeover bid. An IRC loan of £25 million to British Leyland encouraged the IRC to monitor the merger, and they did manage to extract from Leyland quarterly sales and profit figures. The IRC were concerned about British Leyland's industrial relations problems and the need to shed jobs if labour productivity was to be raised. Rootes built car bodies with half the man-hours of British Leyland. Instead British Leyland was increasing its labour force and Stokes insisted that productivity would be raised by output expansion. British Leyland also resisted any positive role for the IRC. Stokes was unwilling to disturb the successful parts of the group to help the group as a whole.

With hindsight the merger brought little apparent benefit, for British Leyland's market share continued to fall. Management was swamped by the intractable problems of the Austin–Morris car division. In the final analysis, the new company had neither the financial nor the managerial resources to deal with the scale of the inherited problems of BMH – a problem which came as no surprise to the Expenditure Committee which reported in 1975 that 'British motor industry management has failed to complete the transition from enthusiast–entrepreneur to professional manager – in contrast with the Continental and American firms, where the process seems to have been completed by 1945.'[53]

Leyland was convinced its company was too small to survive independently, in particular the funding of new models was problematic. Charles Villiers at the IRC, formerly working for BMH's financial advisers, thought there was a strong possibiity of BMH going into liquidation. Yet, given that IRC was unable to intervene in the operation of the new company, the question remains as to whether BMH's earlier liquidation might have been better for the long term prospects of the industry. The profitable operations might have been saved, and the introduction of time rates may have been eased. In short, policy did not rely on market disciplines, perhaps for sound political reasons, but nor was any alternative provided. If Leyland was so profitable before the merger, arrangements should have been possible to raise the money for new model development. After the merger Leyland's bankers, financial advisers or suppliers should have been able to press for more radical policies.

By 1974 British Leyland had run out of money and asked the British government for £200 million. Wedgwood Benn offered a £50 million guarantee while the head of the proposed new National Enterprise Board (NEB), Sir Don Ryder, prepared his report. Among the recommendations of the Ryder team, appointed by Wedgwood Benn on 18 December 1974 and reporting 26 March 1975, was the formation of a Works Councils at British Leyland to address the industrial relations problem.[54] Workers and management were to be brought together for planning. The investment programme was to be staged on the condition that workforce and management were reducing industrial disputes and improving productivity.

The Central Policy Review Staff (CPRS, 'think tank') report of 1975 asserted that the country needed 'a viable, substantial, internationally competitive and unsubsidised car industry in the 1980s'. The government's White Paper of January 1976 broadly accepted the CPRS's arguments. Unfortunately assumptions as to the future market share of British Leyland failed to take into account the need for new models and the length of time needed for their development. But the key was that works councils failed to address the industrial relations issues. More investment funds from the NEB appeared only to be financing strikes, not production. The Chrysler bail-out encouraged a strike at Stoke over a large wage demand, apparent in the belief that British Leyland's bankruptcy would lead to nationalisation.[55] TGWU and AEU leaders, respectively Jack Jones and Hugh Scanlon, asked the employees to go back to work in September 1976 because of the importance of the British Leyland 'experiment'. Their efforts were not ultimately rewarded. The Ryder Report had placed great emphasis on the under-investment as a cause of the company's problems, rather than the lack of continuity of production. Yet the 1977 toolmakers' strike lost British Leyland £100 milion and 50,000 vehicles and this was not the most severe strike between 1975 and 1977.

By the time Lord Ryder resigned from the NEB in August 1978, British Leyland's management needed backing up. Management confidence and clarity had been undermined by the ability of trade union representatives on the NEB to represent management as inadequate, passing that message on to the Leyland Board and the government. Lord Ryder's resignation ushered in the era of Michael Edwardes, in which the threat of complete and permanent closure, and direct communication with the shopfloor, were used regularly to secure the compliance of the workforce. Confrontation over the 1981–2 pay claim in which car group shop stewards refused to even consider the 3.8 per cent offered was nonetheless regarded by some commentators as unnecessarily aggressive.[56] Edwardes' threat to close the business was linked with his demand for new loans from the Thatcher government, which he saw as necessary only because of the rise in the exchange rate.

Simulation of the effects of liquidating British Leyland in Table 7.7 supports the official view that it was cheaper to gamble on a rescue than living with the effects of closure. Between 1975 and 1984 British Leyland received £2.4 billion of state money, much of it under the regime of a prime minister dedicated to a free market policy. Dunnett maintained that if the funds pumped into British Leyland during the 1970s had instead been invested in Ford, the British taxpayer would have gained a better deal.[57] He asserted major decisions were made on non-commercial grounds. The Metro was built to keep down Britain's import bill, not because it would be profitable.[58]

7.5 Chrysler UK and Peugeot

Almost immediately after the government decided to support British Leyland it was engaged in rescuing Chrysler UK in 1975. Financing a second British based car maker precluded any consistency in government policy towards the motor industry.

Table 7.7: The cost of closing British Leyland, 1982–1983

	1982	1983
GDP	− 0.62 per cent	− 0.77 per cent
Unemployment	+ 204,000	+ 230,000
Balance of payments £ bill	− 0.7	− 0.5
PSBR £ bill	+ 0.2	+ 0.37
Fixed investment	− 0.5 per cent	− 1.0 per cent

Notes: GDP: Gross Domestic Product.
    PSBR: Public Sector Borrowing Requirement.
Source: Cambridge Econometrics, cited in S. Wilks, Industrial Policy and the Motor Industry, Manchester University Press, 1988, p. 221.

Chrysler entered European production much later than its fellow American multinationals, Ford and General Motors, and therefore was not well placed to acquire good plants. In 1964, Chrysler took a 30 per cent shareholding in Rootes, manufacturer of Hillman, Humber, and Singer medium size quality cars, and the poorly selling, small, Hillman Imp. Rootes Motors' serious financial difficulties was the first problem the new IRC was required to address. Chrysler was willing to provide the needed £20 million but only if it was allowed to extend its control to more than 50 per cent. The IRC was asked to work out an alternative solution and it was also obliged by the government to take up £3 million of Rootes preferred ordinary and loan stock in exchange for the right to appoint a director to the Rootes Board. Chrysler increased its stake to 66 per cent in 1967, and introduced the Hillman Avenger made at Ryton. However it switched the other two new models, the Chrysler 180 and the Alpine, to France, apparently because of poor industrial relations in Britain.

Between 1964 and 1975 the British company lost £69 million net. Losses in 1975 alone were £35 million. In that year the Americnan Chrysler chairman, John Riccardo, announced that he would not consider further cash investment and Chrysler was considering pulling out of Britain.[59] Chrysler presented three options to the government in November: liquidation by the end of 1976, giving the company to the government, or Chrysler was to transfer more than 80 per cent to the government. Chrysler was rescued despite Cabinet disagreements,[60] to prevent the resignation of the Scottish Office minister, which would have been a setback for the policy of devolution, and because of the employment and export implications of closure.[61] Prime Minister Harold Wilson apparently believed the company to be a lame, rather than a dead, duck.[62] According to Thoms and Donnelly, closure would have cost 55,000 jobs at a time when unemployment was already high, added some £150–£160 million to social security payments, opened the way for overseas producers to acquire Chrysler franchises and put in jeopardy export links with Iran.[63] The government therefore persuaded Chrysler to remain open on condition of a guaranteed payment of £162.5 million between 1976 and 1979, with no equity stake, and competing with the state-owned British Leyland.[64]

Michael Edwardes presents the decision to support Chrysler as exacerbating the difficulties of management at British Leyland.[65] It was harder to convince sections of the workforce that their jobs were at risk if the company did not make profits. They expected that they too would continue to be bailed out whatever happened, for fear of unemployment rising too high. Actually prospective unemployment was only an indirect motivation for this industrial support. The workforce was not enthusiastic about its rescue because the political objective was very clear from the pattern of redundancies. Ryton suffered 63 per cent job losses, whereas Linwood, with its poor performance record, lost only 21 per cent. It was apparent that the final deal was agreed by shop stewards sitting on the planning agreement working parties.[66]

Despite the loans and the planning agreement, in 1978 Chrysler sold its European interests to Peugeot-Citroën.[67] Chrysler received

$230 million from the sale and a 15 per cent stake in the French company, together with a seat on the supervisory Board. Peugeot-Citroën took over the Chrysler planning agreement. If the objective was to maintain motor manufacturing in Britain the sale made good sense. Chrysler's expertise had little to contribute to the Rootes group, although European designs, the Plymouth Horizon and the Dodge Omni, helped Chrysler gain market share in the United States. Peugeot wanted to become the largest European producer, on the grounds that only the biggest would survive. Peugeot renamed Chrysler UK, Talbot in 1978 and in 1980 Peugeot.

Multinationals like Chrysler and Peugeot need to demonstrate that they are good corporate citizens so that they can claim political protection and finance when necessary. They are not all-powerful manipulators of government to their own exclusive advantage, but they do need to make profits in order to survive. The British government achieved its objectives with the Chrysler–Peugeot planning agreement: the saving of jobs at Linwood and new models for Britain. By 1981 the closure of Linwood, dogged by poor indus-trial relations throughout its short history, was accepted as inevitable by most of the workforce. A gradual reduction of employment probably was less damaging socially than a quick shut-down. In any case the Redundancy Payments Act of 1966, which raised the costs of immediate closure and favoured down-sizing by natural wastage, encouraged a policy of gradualism.

What consequences flow from ownership of the motor industry in Britain by Peugeot, Ford, General Motors, Nissan and Honda, continues to be controversial. Ultimately employment, investment and new model development decisions are taken by foreign nationals, and these are not necessarily in British interests, critics contend. Geoffrey Whalen, managing director of Peugeot UK, conceded that local national pressures mattered and that French unions might be less internationalist than French management when job losses were needed. Sentiment may play a part as well, but by and large relative national costs and productivity determine the location and output of plants. When between 1980 and 1982 Peugeot sales in Britain fell, almost the entire decline was mirrored in British production; French imports hardly changed.[68] That was a reflection of relative national productivity which was subsequently reversed. By 1984 Peugeot UK's Ryton plant achieved an output of 37 cars per man without robots, almost certainly a higher productivity than the French factories. Geoffrey Whalen noted that the profitability of Peugeot subsidiary in Britain was influenced heavily by how many cars were made at Ryton compared with the volume of built-up imports from France. Growing production at Ryton, with cars being exported, as well as being sold in the British market, enhanced the profitability of Peugeot Talbot in the mid 1980s. Peugeot was able to increase market share so that Britain became the company's largest market outside France.[69] That owed nothing directly to government policy towards multinationals or the motor industry but a great deal to the efficiency of British Peugeot production and the strength of British demand for Peugeot's products.

The final state motor industry subsidy in pursuit of jobs during the 1970s was an attempt to draw new business to regions of high unemployment, rather as Nissan was attracted to Sunderland in 1984. But the story of the De Lorean Motor Company (DMC) was far more bizarre. In 1978 the British government agreed to subsidise John De Lorean's proposal for a sportscar plant in Belfast. New York, Miami and Dublin had already resisted the blandishments of the former vice-president of General Motors, and saved themselves a great deal of money. By February 1982, when De Lorean's business was in the hands of the receiver, the British government had paid out almost £80 million, with very little to show for it. The last act came when, in an attempt to raise money that was otherwise not forthcoming to keep DMC afloat, De Lorean was trapped by a five month FBI scam, and arrested in Los Angeles during October 1982 on charges of distributing cocaine.[70]

7.6 Conclusion

By the mid 1970s government policy towards the motor industry was concerned with what some saw as undoing the damage wrought by government policy in the 1950s and 1960s. If the government had been content to run the economy at a lower and more stable level of demand and a higher level of unemployment, in conditions more like those of the interwar years, the deficiencies of the British method of organising large scale production would perhaps have not been apparent so soon. Equally had those organisational deficiencies been remedied, stop–go would not have been so harmful. The evidence for these claims is that Ford UK prospered under the government policies that ruled when BMC/BL declined. A similar argument applies to regional dispersion.

By merging all British motor businesses into British Leyland in 1968, government laid a trap for itself. When BMH dragged Leyland into bankruptcy the organisation was so large that the government might reasonably fear the employment costs as well as the loss of the only possible 'national champion'. The very fact that the company was rescued by the state enhanced the difficulties of turning it around. The government was obliged to construct a new order with the agreement of a trade union hierarchy which could do little to influence industrial relations in the industry. That the impact of market forces had been averted by government intervention (only temporarily as it turned out) encouraged elements of the workforce to believe that scarcity could be abolished by the state. Hence securing compliance with restructuring and raising productivity continued to be problematic despite attempts at introducing a form of workforce participation. If British Leyland were smaller, there might have been some hope of inducing a private business to distinguish what parts of the group were worth salvaging. But a tradition of the omnicompetent state that could be manipulated by interest groups, ruled out that option. Experience with British Leyland shows that the temptation to blame scheming multinationals for the industry's problems is entirely misplaced. Chrysler, and other multinationals, merely faced a budget constraint that was harder than the 1970s British government's. They were and are therefore no more able than the state to contravert the logic of price and cost over the decades.

A less interventionist government policy would have left a more regionally concentrated industry but one at first more dispersed between businesses. The industry would have faced a less fluctuating demand for its products. Labour might have been less confident in the permanent ability of the industry to offer jobs also. But ultimately, although it would have cost the taxpayer, and therefore the economy less, the history of the industry would not have been radically different.

CHAPTER EIGHT

FROM FORDISM
TO LEAN
PRODUCTION?

From the late 1970s, both production technology and the car market have changed fundamentally. Through the preceding decade the principal multinationals sought the holy grail of mass production: a standard world car which could be manufactured in enormous volumes and raise economies of scale to new heights. But over the last fifteen years British and European car companies have come under pressure to manage a revolutionary transformation from mass production to 'lean production'.[1] The future of motor vehicle production as the keystone of British manufacturing seemed threatened during the early 1980s. General Motors and Peugeot radically reduced their making of complete cars in Britain, instead importing and assembling kits from Europe. By 1984 Ford had cut its exports from Britain to their lowest level since 1946. Rover, the sole British-owned volume producer, shrank to the size of the more profitable German specialist manufacturer, BMW. Holding this level of production was only achieved by co-operation with Honda. At the beginning of 1994 Rover ceased to be British-owned when British Aerospace (BAe) sold the company to BMW, and Honda announced it intention to terminate its links as quickly as possible.

Thanks to a remarkable competitive advantage, the Japanese presence in the British motor industry increased sharply and by demonstration, as well as directly, raised productivity and exports. The arrival of Nissan in 1984 was followed by Toyota and Honda in 1992. The Japanese competitive advantage is based on a unique combination of high productivity and rapid product innovation that has eluded their Western competitors. Mass production, exemplified by Henry Ford I's assembly line in 1911, achieved efficiency through product standardisation, a highly integrated division of labour and single-purpose machinery. Unskilled workforces with little scope to exercise initiative, intensive supervision, rigidity, extensive inventories and elaborate managerial control mechanisms, were all essential features of the 'Fordist' factory. By contrast, 'lean production', a form of management and work organisation pioneered by Japanese motor manufacturers after 1945, maximises flexibility, efficiency, quality, innovation and responsiveness. The determined efforts of British based car manufacturers to close the gap between themselves and their Japanese rivals is the central theme of this chapter.

We begin by reviewing changes in production, employment and productivity during the 1980s. Section 2 examines the dynamics of the British car market since 1979. This is followed by sections examining changes in industrial relations and the relationship between manufacturers and their component suppliers, both critical areas in the transition from mass production to lean production. We then (section 5) trace the fate of the only British-owned volume car producer, British Leyland, subsequently Rover. This includes a number of unusual events; privatisation, the company's deepening collaboration with Honda, and crucial changes in corporate strategy.

8.1 Production, employment and productivity

Between 1979–81 the British car industry was hit hard by the rise in the sterling exchange rate and by deep recession. Exports became far less profitable and competitive while imports rose rapidly. Production, which in 1977 was just under that achieved in 1960, dropped by one-third to the trough of the depression in 1982. A decade later the 1977 output had still not been recovered (Table 8.1)

The declining international competitiveness of the 1970s continued, with exports of cars and all vehicles reaching their nadir in 1986 at about one-quarter of 1971 totals (Table 8.2). By 1990 they had doubled, exceeding the levels of the beginning of the decade. About one-third of British car production was exported in 1990 and rather more of commercial vehicles. The only British-owned manufacturer, the Rover group, was the largest producer. Rover was also by far the biggest exporter even in 1990, lacking multinational plants from which to service foreign markets (Table 8.3).

Home market sales offer a different picture. Ford accounted for one-quarter of 1990 new registrations, almost twice Rover Group's proportion (Table 8.4). General Motors also exceeded Rover's British market share. Imports accounted for more than one-half of sales, helped by Ford's importing 40 per cent of British sales, General Motors' importing over one-third, while Nissan, Peugeot and Honda shipped in around three-quarters of their British sales (Table 8.5). For Nissan and Peugeot, however, this pattern reflected international specialisation of production, as, unlike Ford and Vauxhall, these companies exported similar proportions of their output.

Until the mid 1970s employment in the British car industry was on a long term upward trend. Car output peaked in 1972 and then fell much more sharply than employment until 1978. A steep decline in employment then continued until 1983 when, broadly speaking, something approaching the 1970 crude labour productivity was restored.[2] Almost one-fifth of all jobs in car manufacture disappeared in 1981 alone. The most concentrated phase of rationalisation occurred between 1980 and 1983 when a total of 165,800 jobs were shed in car manufacture. The most significant

Table 8.1: Total production of passenger cars in Britain, 1977–1992

1977	1,328,000
1978	1,223,000
1979	1,070,000
1980	923,000
1981	954,650
1982	887,679
1983	1,044,597
1984	908,906
1985	1,047,973
1986	1,018,962
1987	1,142,683
1988	1,226,835
1989	1,229,082
1990	1,295,610
1991	1,236,900
1992	1,291,880

Source: SMMT.

closures occurred within British Leyland and Peugeot, the owners of Chrysler Europe from 1979. The rationalisation of British Leyland's product line resulted in the closure of thirteen plants, including the Speke sports car plant and Coventry component factories where employment plummeted from 27,268 in 1975 to 8,221 just seven years later.[3] Within the three years 1977–80 British Leyland halved its capacity. Talbot, Peugeot's new name for Chrysler UK, was in severe crisis in 1979–80, losing market share, haemhorrhaging losses and without the finance necessary to modernise its dated product line. Peugeot centralised its British operations in Coventry at the expense of around 8,000 jobs in its Ryton and Stoke plants and 4,000 in the doomed Linwood factory

Table 8.2: British motor exports, 1971–1990

	All vehicles	Cars
1971	947,478	741,788
1979	535,996	374,673
1980	469,495	314,519
1981	417,871	300,623
1982	327,297	231,898
1983	298,022	233,658
1984	260,866	201,207
1985	296,279	226,471
1986	230,223	186,158
1987	275,188	219,940
1988	283,216	212,534
1989	377,538	280,863
1990	475,245	393,164

Source: SMMT.

Table 8.3: British production and exports of cars and commercial vehicles by firm, 1990

Firm	Cars		Commercial vehicles	
	Production	Exports	Production	Exports
Rover Group	464,612	168,928	35,920	13,699
Ford	329,597	32,336	131,844	46,621
Peugeot	116,548	83,591	94	
Nissan	76,190	59,739		
Vauxhall	256,293	25,358	19,673	
Jaguar	41,891	32,032		
Leyland Daf			35,181	12,528
Total	1,295,611	405,769	270,346	95,707

Source: SMMT.

outside Glasgow.[4] The car companies contained workforce resistance to closure and rationalisation by avoiding compulsory redundancy, preferring early retirements, natural wastage and voluntary redundancy.[5] Opposition to total closure was dampened by the threatened loss of redundancy payments.[6] The pace of

Table 8.4: New registrations by country of origin, 1990

Firm	No.	Country of origin
Citroën	60,899	
Fiat	54,945	
Ford	507,260	(Britain 301,233, Germany 107,710)
General Motors	323,054	(Britain 210,971, Germany 57,277, Spain 54,786)
Honda	31,750	(Britan 7,462)
Nissan	106,783	(Japan 81,869)
Peugeot	123,671	(France 93,604)
Renault	67,578	
Rover Group	281,385	
Volvo	66,017	
Total	2,008,934	
Imports	1,139,813	
Imports as % of registrations		
Ford	40.6	
General Motors	34.7	
Peugeot	75.7	
Nissan	76.7	
Honda	76.5	
Imports as % of total sales		
Imports	56.74	
Diesel	6.38	
Automatics	10.94	

Source: SMMT.

Table 8.5: British exports of cars as a percentage of production, by firm, 1990

Firm	%
Rover	36.3
Jaguar	76.5
Nissan	78.4
Peugeot	71.7
Vauxhall	9.9
Ford	9.8

Source: SMMT.

rationalisation slackened after 1982 and the severe downturn in demand since 1989 did not at first result in widespread redundancies because production more or less held up. In total, between 1979 and 1992 direct employment in the British car industry fell by over 50 per cent.

From 1979 the critical objectives of Britain's car companies have been to achieve major efficiency gains and to reduce significantly their break-even point. Despite the unreliability of official productivity statistics, the trend is clear. From 1980 the motor industry achieved annual gains of nearly 7 per cent, almost 50 per cent above that achieved by manufacturing as a whole.[7] Initial productivity gains derived from the closure and rationalisation of the least efficient and productive plants. Ford UK, for example, experienced a strong upward trend in productivity during 1980–5, a period of intense rationalisation. Factory sales per employee, a rough guide to productivity, suggests that this surge was approximately 45 per cent. For Ford, the competitive pressure to boost efficiency was intensified by a sharp increase in fixed costs resulting from heavy investment in flexible technologies, notably in the Dagenham assembly plant.[8] Ford of Europe estimated that its productivity improvement between 1980 and 1989 amounted to almost 60 per cent.[9] The sales recovery of the mid 1980s was met by increasing domestic output faster than employment, so enhancing productivity levels.

The closure of inefficient plants, the reduction of product ranges, and a massive shake-out of labour combined to produce a step-change in manufacturing productivity. Equally, the changing balance of power on the shopfloor encouraged management to confront well-established job controls and the culture of mutuality which respected custom and practice. The new working practices which accompanied major capital investments were designed unilaterally by management rather than through negotiation. From the mid 1980s, however, management adopted a two-pronged approach to productivity improvement: incremental gains were pursued both through firm supervision and employee involvement strategies. Nissan's Sunderland plant, with a capacity of around 300,000 motor vehicles in 1993, showed what could be achieved on a British green field site. Micra assembly and body building was far faster than that of any similar manufacturer in Europe, at 10.5 hours a car. The closest European plant was General Motors' Bochum, Germany, plant which could assemble an Astra in 18 hours.

8.2 Product market

Growth of the demand for cars in all industrial countries slowed under the impact of recession and the predominance of 'replacement' demand during the early 1980s. Even so, such was the strength of the upswing from the trough in 1981 to the 1989 peak, that British motor vehicle registrations grew by more than one-half, or at an annual average compound rate of 5.7 per cent (Table 8.6).

Table 8.6: British vehicle registrations, 1980–1993

1980	1,513,761
1981	1,484,622
1982	1,555,027
1983	1,791,698
1984	1,749,650
1985	1,832,408
1986	1,882,474
1987	2,013,693
1988	2,215,574
1989	2,300,944
1990	2,009,000
1991	1,592,000
1992	1,594,000
1993	1,778,426

Source: SMMT.

At the same time, the market became increasingly segmented. The demand for variety and individuality further discouraged manufacturers from committing very substantial capacity to one model.[10] Their general strategy was to offer a wide range of engine options and hatchback, saloon, coupé and estate versions of a limited number of basic models. Option, feature and price ranges around a given 'platform' size class expanded enormously, to create market segments based on differentiation by consumer groups. Competitive strategy moved from maximising volume and driving down costs to price realisation through satisfying niche markets. Each model was increasingly being stretched across a wider range of price points; different consumer segments were targeted by the same basic car with different finish and performance specifications.

Supply factors were also crucial in fragmenting the British car market. The effective end of restrained competition between British Leyland, Ford, Vauxhall, and Chrysler during the second half of the 1970s transformed the market. The collapse of British Leyland from 1977 allowed Ford to become market leader and provided new opportunities for importers (Table 8.7). British Leyland's market share, and an inefficient manufacturing regime based on an excessive number of body shells, was sustained only by what at best can be described as a revenue-maximising strategy.[11] By the close of the 1970s British Leyland's sprawling product range included nine basic models and four sports cars. British Leyland was hugely inefficient: it had twice as many models as General Motors but only one-fifth of its output.[12] By contrast, Ford UK pursued a strategy that emphasised profits over market share. In 1979 Ford UK made four basic models and one sports coupé. Ford's strategists were also determined not to precipitate British Leyland's collapse, a scenario which would certainly see further state subsidies to stave off crisis and jeopardise public perceptions of Ford as a 'British' company. For more than a decade Ford managers had been anticipating the crumbling of British Leyland's frail finances. From 1977 British Leyland's slow crisis accelerated into a headlong collapse which culminated in a 20 per cent slump in output and losses of £112 million in 1979. Between 1977 and 1980 British Leyland's market share fell from 24.3 per cent to 18.2 per cent. Its decline accelerated through 1980 with sales and output falling by over 20 per cent.

Table 8.7: Changes in market shares in the British car market, 1970–1990 (percentage points)

	1970–7	1977–81	1981–85	1985–90
BMC/BL/Rover	− 13.8	− 5.1	− 0.9	− 4.3
Ford	− 0.8	+ 5.2	− 4.4	− 1.2
General Motors	+ 0.2	− 1.8	+ 8.0	− 0.5
Other imports	+ 10.3	+ 3.1	− 0.6	− 0.7
Japanese imports	+ 10.2	+ 0.4	− 0.2	+ 4.4
Other British suppliers	− 5.9	− 1.8	− 2.1	+ 2.3

Source: Monopolies and Mergers Commission, *A Report on the Supply of New Motor Cars within the United Kingdom*, Vol. 1, London: HMSO, 1991.

During the first nine months of 1979 Chrysler UK's production fell by almost 50 per cent, and its domestic problems were compounded by the collapse of the company's important Iranian export market for ready to assemble kits.

British Leyland's and Chrysler's slide was paralleled by Vauxhall, the weak link in General Motors' global empire. In the same period Vauxhall's production fell by 23 per cent and, like Chrysler, an archaic and limited product range held out little prospect of short term recovery.[13] Between 1968 and 1980 Vauxhall's production fell by 77.5 per cent and market share dropped from 13.5 per cent to 6 per cent. The initial phase of Vauxhall's fall occurred between 1968 and 1974, a decline worsened by the corporation's decision to stay out of the mini-car segment, triggering a major shift in strategy. From 1976 General Motors began restructuring its European manufacturing base. General Motors' German subsidiary, Opel, was designated the strategic core of an increasingly internationalised production system in which Vauxhall was left with little control over product design and engineering. The rundown of the Viva line in 1979 effectively marked the end of Vauxhall as an integrated car manufacturer with the full range of design and engineering capabilities: Vauxhall was now effectively a subsidiary of Opel.

After suffering losses in eight of the preceding ten years Vauxhall's fortunes plummeted to new depths in 1979. Vauxhall's market share hit bottom in 1979 at 6.5 per cent but the losses of £31.3 million were surpassed in 1980 when losses soared to £83.3 million. Vauxhall's parlous financial position scarcely improved in 1981 with losses of £72.4 million. By 1984, a House of Lords Select Committee investigating the motor industry concluded that Vauxhall was no longer even a junior partner in the General Motors international production system:[14]

> The design of vehicles, the replacement of worn-out productive equipment, and the manufacture of major components all gradually ceased at Vauxhall. 1984 saw the end of car engine manufacture by General Motors in the United Kingdom. The result of all this was that little was made in the UK which could become part of a cross-flow of GM cars and components. Instead the flow was one-way – inwards. All the major investment by GM in the 1970s and 1980s was on the continent.

The simultaneous fall of British Leyland, Chrysler and Vauxhall coincided with a rising market, partly due to a delayed replacement cycle caused by the 1973–4 oil crisis, which peaked in 1979 with record sales of 1.7 million vehicles. There were two main beneficiaries of the simultaneous decline of British Leyland, Chrysler and Vauxhall in the late 1970s: Ford and non-Japanese imports. Ford UK increased its market share from 25.7 per cent in

1975 to 30.7 per cent in 1980, a level it sustained for two years. During these critical years, Ford's entire five car model range featured in the top ten British sellers. Ford maximised its advantage in the British market by fully exploiting its European production system. This represented a major shift in strategy by Ford. In 1975 Ford UK sales were 99.8 per cent domestic made but by 1982 this had fallen to 51 per cent.[15] The Thatcher government's retention of an over-valued exchange rate was critical in shaping the sourcing policies of the American multinationals. In 1980 Ford UK produced approximately one-third of the Fiestas imported from its sister plant in Spain, a 58.5 per cent increase in import volume over 1979.[16] In the first half of the 1980s foreign sourcing by Ford UK consistently exceeded 40 per cent.[17] Nor was this wholly offset by Ford UK's contribution to the corporation's pan-European production system. Ford UK's reduced role in the European company's complex pattern of multilateral manufacturing, marketing and investment became clear between 1977 and 1982. High margin vehicles were single sourced on the continent while products made in British plants were produced in at least one other location. The complex cross-trading pattern in Fiestas between Dagenham and Valencia, for example, involved the British plant sending components and sub-assemblies such as cylinder blocks and heads, crankshafts, radiators, and carburettors while the Spanish plant exported complete vehicles.

Between 1977 and 1981 Ford UK reaped the harvest of the anticipated collapse of British Leyland's market leadership. The extra volume and market share won in the late 1970s earned colossal windfall profits and made the British company the cornerstone of Ford of Europe's rapid rise in profitability. Higher levels of plant utilisation and a steep increase in tied imports inflated Ford UK's profits faster than the expansion in production volumes between 1979 and 1981. Net profits for Ford of Europe rose from $1045 million in 1977 to $1271 million in 1978 before dipping slightly to $1219 million in 1979. Rising profitability fuelled a rapid growth in Ford UK's cash reserves, spiralling from £115 million in 1977 to £512 million in 1981. Ford UK's cash rich position was carefully nurtured by tightly controlled dividends, retaining almost 75 per cent of its earnings per share between 1977 and 1981. Ford UK's record trading performance and powerful cash reserves coincided with net losses of $3.3 billion in the American parent corporation between 1980 and 1982, or an average net loss of $1.44 billion per annum. The revenue and profits posted by Ford of Europe were vital to the survival of its beleaguered parent. At a moment when Ford Werke also incurred losses Ford UK emerged as the mainstay not just of the European company but of Ford worldwide. In 1979 Ford UK's profits of £386 million accounted for around 70 per cent of the corporation's global profits.

The second major beneficiary of the falling market share of British Leyland, Chrysler and Vauxhall was non-Japanese imports. A critical factor in the rise in imports was rationalisation of dealer networks by established players in the British market which provided foreign companies with ready-made distribution outlets. In 1977–8 alone British Leyland jettisoned 23 per cent, Ford and Chrysler 10 per cent, and Vauxhall 21 per cent of their dealers. Approximately 35 per cent of dealers who lost their franchise from a British company or American multinational obtained import franchises.[18] Equally important, the importers' assault on the soft British market was backed by a powerful advertising campaign costing almost twice as much per car as that spent by their British rivals.

In just three years Ford had become the unchallenged market leader in Britain. But by 1981–2 Ford had hit the limits of its dominance: the very ubiquity of Ford vehicles meant that further increases in market share had become virtually impossible. As *Motor Business* put it in late 1981, 'when every other person is seemingly driving a Ford, further sales become almost self-defeating – a chance for Vauxhall perhaps to play a bigger role, especially with the new 'J' registration car – the Cavalier'.[19]

Both Vauxhall and British Leyland pursued product led recovery strategies. General Motors' 'world car' – the Cavalier/Ascona – was unveiled in 1982 at the same time as its first mini-car the Corsa/Nova. From 1982 there would be full-range competition between the two American companies in British and continental markets. Ford's uneasy transition from the ultra-conventional but highly successful Cortina to the futuristic design of the Sierra coincided with the launch of Vauxhall's Cavalier. Slow consumer acceptance of the Sierra, particularly in the vital fleet sales market, allowed Vauxhall to capture market share from Ford. By the end of 1983 the Cavalier had edged ahead of the Sierra with 8.2 per cent of the total market. Similarly, in the mini-car segment, Ford's Fiesta faced a strong challenge from the British Leyland's Metro. Both British Leyland's marginal improvement of 0.6 per cent in market share and Vauxhall's significant gain of 3 per cent were made at Ford's expense. The growing market position of British Leyland and Vauxhall provoked Ford to initiate a price war in defence of its market dominance.

General Motors' new products stimulated Vauxhall's renaissance in the British market. From 1981 General Motors gradually increased its market share to 16 per cent in 1985, displacing Rover from second place. The Cavalier was the cutting edge in General Motors' assault on Ford's position in the British market. Competition in the vital medium size market segment, dominated by fleet car sales, centred on the confrontation between the Ford Sierra and General Motors' Cavalier. The Sierra proved unable to hold onto the strong position it inherited from the Cortina. In 1982 the Sierra outsold the Cavalier by three to two, with 12 per cent and 8 per cent of the total market respectively. Within six months, however, the Cavalier had edged ahead of the Sierra with an 8.2 per cent share of total sales to the Sierra's 7.5 per cent. The success of General Motors' new products was not immediately reflected in a turnaround in financial performance. Between 1980 and 1986 General Motors incurred heavy losses as the result of corporate restructuring, product development, and the creation of a more complex international manufacturing and marketing organisation.[20]

The car industry in Britain enjoyed an unparalleled boom between 1985 and 1989. During this period Ford, the market leader, increased total sales but by less than the rate of market growth. In 1986–7 Peugeot achieved a sales growth of 25 per cent, Citroën expanded sales by 46 per cent and General Motors by 12 per cent. Ford, by contrast, achieved sales growth of just 1 per cent.[21] In addition, the success of Japanese and continental manufacturers contributed to the fragmentation of the British market. In 1977 Japan formally agreed to restrict her exports to Britain to 11 per cent of the market.[22] In 1990 Japanese suppliers accounted for 11.9 per cent of car sales, 86 per cent of which were imported. Nissan's 45 per cent of Japanese import sales dwarfed Toyota's 18 per cent, Honda's 13 per cent and Mazda's 10 per cent.[23] A key indicator of the fragmenting British market was the shrinking combined market share of the 'Big Three' – Ford, Vauxhall and Rover – from almost 62 per cent in 1984 to 55 per cent in 1989.[24]

The recession which hit the British car industry in 1989 affected Ford especially severely. Over-capacity and excess stocks, the comparative strength of rival products, heavy advertising and promotional expenditure, and falling market share plunged Ford UK into its first losses in twenty years. Ford UK recorded pre-tax losses of £274 million in 1990–1, exacerbated by the £1.6 billion purchase of Jaguar at the end of 1989. Product relaunches, notably the Escort in 1990, failed to boost sales. Ford's response was to start a ruinously expensive price war: marketing costs rocketed from 14 per cent of revenue in 1990 to 24 per cent in 1991. But this attempt to protect market share did not halt Ford UK's deteriorating performance: from 1989 Ford UK has under-performed in a falling market. In 1991 Ford UK sustained record losses of £920 million, around half incurred by the appalling performance of its Jaguar subsidiary. Not only had Ford bought the company at the peak of the boom and paid accordingly, but Ford's 'Transition Report' on the acquisition made shocking reading. The slow recovery of Ford's European finances in 1992 owed much to the transfer of Jaguar from Ford UK to the American parent company in 1991.

Movements in aggregate market share mask complex shifts in corporate competitiveness within a series of distinct market segments. In all segments, however, the tendency is towards broad based competition challenging Ford's dominance. The erosion of Ford's dominace of the fragmenting British market is most graphically illustrated in fleet car sales. Fleet sales of 25 or more vehicles comprised approximately 30 per cent of the total British market in 1980, growing at twice the rate of the total market from 1986 onwards to account for 52 per cent of all new car sales in 1990.[25] Quite apart from its importance in terms of sales volume, fleet sales play a vital role as the conduit through which high value-added product innovations are introduced into the retail market. In 1980 Ford enjoyed a stranglehold in this market segment. Ford's 76 per cent share of the fleet sales segment owed much to the long popularity of the Cortina. Despite design difficulties and consumer resistance, the Cortina's replacement, the Sierra, still held around 44 per cent of this market segment in the mid 1980s. In the mid 1980s more than two-thirds of Sierra sales were to fleet buyers. Vauxhall and Rover staged product led recoveries to gain market share at Ford's expense from 1986. By the early 1990s Ford remained market leader but its 28 per cent gave it a slender 5 per cent advantage over Vauxhall, with Rover a strong third on 18 per cent. The entry of all major car makers into the fleet sales segment from 1985 increased competition in this sector. The three market leaders now face aggressive campaigning by Peugeot and Renault with around 4 per cent market share, while VW-Audi and the three big Japanese manufacturers each hold 2 per cent respectively. These rapid changes in the nature of the fleet sales market signal an intensification of competitive pressures in terms of price, product innovation, product renewal cycles and marketing.

The final striking characteristic of the British car market is the sharp increase in import penetration. In 1979 imports exceeded British produced sales for the first time since the early 1920s, accounting for 56 per cent of British sales. This chronic imbalance in Britain's international motor trade was driven by the decline of Rover and the increased reliance of Ford, General Motors and Peugeot on tied imports. The post-1986 sales boom sucked in yet more imports. Citroën and Peugeot in particular made spectacular gains. In the three years after 1986 Citroën and Peugeot achieved an average rate of sales growth of 46 per cent and 25 per cent respectively. Peugeot clawed back its losses of the early 1980s to double its market share to 9 per cent. Other imported marques –Volvo, Fiat and Nissan – have experienced sharp losses of market share since 1989. But while Volvo and Fiat's steady losses of sales indicate a deep consumer disaffection, Nissan's loss of almost one-third of its market share between 1989 and 1992 reflected disruption caused by a dispute with its former importer. The minor importers, including Toyota, BMW and Mazda, all made marginal gains in market share between 1988 and 1993. Excluding the tied imports of the American and French multinationals, imports accounted for approximately 40 per cent of all British car sales in 1992.

The British car market experienced two major transformations after 1979. The first change centred on the decline of British Leyland which opened up sales opportunities exploited by Ford UK. The second unfolding of the contours of the product market occurred from the mid 1980s. Again Ford UK was a central player. Unlike the previous period, however, Ford UK experienced a decline in its dominance and a fall in market share. In 1987 Ford UK's market share was approximately double that of General Motors and Rover. However, by 1992 Ford UK's leadership was reduced to just 5 per cent over General Motors and 10 per cent over

Rover. Equally significant has been the emergence of a strong second tier of competitors – Peugeot, Volkswagen and Renault – competing on all fronts in the British market. The main players now confront each other in all market segments.

8.3 Technology, work organisation and industrial relations.

Between 1970 and 1981 the Japanese cut the total hours needed to build a car from 250 to 140, compared with about 200 hours in the United States and Germany. These reductions were achieved before the microelectronic revolution in production. Continuous production was fine tuned, eliminating much expensive work in progress, cutting maintenance and improving quality control. By 1984 the volume of Japanese car production was double that of Germany and only 10 per cent less than that of the United States. Japanese unit costs were less than one-third of those in the United States (as they had been in 1970). Some of this difference was due to lower input prices but Japanese technical efficiency was also 13 per cent above that of the United States. Slower Japanese car output growth in the 1980s heralded a narrowing of the gap.[26] Since then, computer aided design, engineering and manufacturing reduced the time and money necessary to introduce a new model. Flexible automation technology facilitated the making of prototypes. In production, robotic welding, painting and handling, machining and stamping have lowered model economies of scale, offering small scale producers such as Rover the prospect of competing with the major players – Ford and General Motors – in their domestic market.

Despite the new technology, a critical feature of lean production is its dependence upon management actively engaging the employee in achieving continuous improvement in efficiency and quality. As a former Ford UK director of industrial relations explained, in the mass production factory, by contrast, 'you are not looking for initiative' but strict adherence to a predetermined work schedule for each individual assembly worker.[27] From 1979 every major European volume car company attempted to transform its industrial relations and work regime from Fordism to lean production.[28] Major national differences nonetheless persisted between plants in Britain, the United States and in Germany of even the same company during the 1980s and there were significant divergences in the trajectory of change between the British car companies. In Britain it was impossible to obtain a consensus between unions and management at the top. Employee participation or group work were blocked by the unions. Among British car makers, Ford UK pursued a cautious approach to innovations in the management of human resources in which a traditional productivity agenda remained central to mainstream collective bargaining. Unlike Ford, Rover collapsed collective bargaining and human resource innovations into a single change process. Such contrasting patterns of change reflect the competitive position of the companies and their industrial relations legacy.[29] The fullest development of new forms of management and work organisation were in Nissan's Washington plant established in 1984. But the most dramatic *transformation* of industrial relations in the British car industry occurred in Rover, formerly British Leyland.

A critical element at British Leyland was the shift in government policy towards the beleaguered company. During his five year tenure at British Leyland, Michael Edwardes enjoyed the unambiguous support of the Thatcher administration for the restructuring of the company's industrial relations.[30] A central element in the Edwardes recovery plan was the forceful reassertion of managerial prerogative in work organisation. Wielding the threat of closure, Edwardes confronted the institutions and practices of shopfloor trade unionism between 1980 and 1983. Working practices were no longer negotiable but solely a managerial function: mutuality gave way to 'management's right to manage'. Edwardes appealed directly to the workforce over the heads of the shop stewards to secure endorsement for the company's survival package. In October 1979 management bypassed shop stewards and won 87 per cent support for its corporate plan. Six months later in April 1980, Edwardes performed an even greater act of brinkmanship by sacking the Longbridge convener, Derek Robinson. Again, the workforce decided against industrial action. Such set-piece confrontations with the shop stewards were the prelude to rationalisation and a rapid erosion of the institutions of workplace trade unionism. Shop steward organisation survived but in a much circumscribed and chastened form.[31] At plant level, management opportunism was as important as corporate strategy, particularly in the reorganisation of the vital maintenance crafts.[32]

Plant bargaining displaced the national level as the main locus of bargaining in the 1970s, and the 1980s witnessed the shift from the plant to company level. From 1980 British Leyland moved to a form of company bargaining long established at Ford and Vauxhall.[33]

Some commentators have been sceptical of Edwardes' claim that the reform of working practices was the basis of a 'productivity miracle' in British Leyland. From 1977 to 1982 plant closures and capital investment were the principal factors accounting for improved output per employee.[34] However, from the mid 1980s Rover achieved gains in efficiency through innovations in labour useage. In 1979 Rover was producing six cars per employee per year. In 1993 it manufactured 35 per employee, compared with a European average of 30 and a Japanese average of 45.[35]

During Edwardes' tenure at British Leyland teamworking initiatives sat uneasily with his aggressive reassertion of management's 'right to manage' and dismantling of the 'mutuality' principle. By the mid 1980s, however, Rover's senior managers were forced to acknowledge that the centralisation of collective bargaining and the diminution of the shop stewards' role had created a communications vacuum on the shopfloor. In Longbridge particularly, surveys of employee opinion revealed deep insecurity and disaffection. In 1986 Rover launched its 'Working with Pride' initiative, a communications programme based on supervisors briefing around 25 operatives on company plans and its implications for their work area. This innovation was introduced with minimal consultation with the trade unions.[36] Rover's 'Zone Briefings' bore many similarities to Quality Circles. Importantly, management's intention was to improve the existing pattern of work organisation and to strengthen supervisory authority by enhancing its communiations role. Rover's experience of trying to blend Japanese techniques into established management structures proved an unhappy one. Less than eighteen months from their inception, supervisor unease and steward opposition combined to stifle this initiative.[37] Shopfloor trade unionism in Rover has suffered considerable losses from 1977 but has remained the focal point for workforce opposition to unpopular management initiatives.

Rover's decision to treat the R200 production line established in 1989 as a *de facto* green field site was the clearest expression of the company's new manufacturing policy. The R200 line was based on a series of 'mini-factories', each directed by young managers with no traditional supervisory experience. Continuing efforts to fully implement Just-in-Time production (JIT) and Total Quality programmes more generally, however, have been bedevilled by familiar problems. But, despite the continued hostility of some line managers and the wary endorsement of union conveners, Rovers' labour relations strategy represented a clear departure from the Fordist aspirations of the Edwardes regime towards flexibility and employee involvement.[38]

Rover's move towards a lean production regime in work organisation and industrial relations was signalled by the company's 'New Deal' in 1992. Building on the negotiated introduction of teamworking and total quality management in 1987, the core of the New Deal was workforce acceptance of total flexibiity, continuous improvement and single-table bargaining arrangements for blue and white collar employees. In return, Rover offered benefits including a commitment that there would be no compulsory redundancies and a single status sick-pay scheme. They also offered workers £100 per annum to spend on any educational course they chose to encourage learning. That was intended to increase the number of suggestions from the shopfloor as to how the organisation and management of work could be improved, from an average of one suggestion per worker per year in 1993. These changed attitudes might be expected to cut absenteeism, traditionally high in the 'Fordist' factory – from 10 per cent in Vauxhall in 1979 lean production reduced rates to 5 per cent by 1993. Toyota's green field site recorded absenteeism of less than 1 per cent in 1993.[39]

The TGWU, which organised around 75 per cent of Rover's hourly paid employees, prefered pragmatic cooperation with the New Deal to the total opposition it would have offered as recently as the mid 1980s. The central reason for the TGWU's change of heart was a recognition that Rover's future competitiveness hinged on the adoption of lean production. There was one other reason underlying the TGWU's agreement to become 'partners' in the introduction of lean production: union bargaining power had been whittled away by more than a decade of rationalisation and by the piecemeal erosion of custom and practice on the shopfloor. For the unions, as Jack Adams, the TGWU's chief negotiator explained, Rover's New Deal ws not so much collective bargaining as 'concession bargaining'.[40] Only by going with the grain of corporate strategy could the TGWU hope to exert any influence over the development of lean production. In particular, the union was concerned to protect those employees unable to become 'all-singing, all-dancing' team members or cope with the added stress of the new working methods. The TGWU executive was at pains to reassure its 450 Rover shop stewards that the New Deal remained some distance from the agreements in force in Nissan and Toyota's British plants: the shop steward's constituency was still the workgroup; that no 'neutral' forum such as a Company Council had been introduced alongside conventional collective bargaining procedures; management had no automatic right to hire temporary labour; and that redundancy and transfer arrangements were still based on a policy of 'last in, first out'. But, despite the union's denial that the 1992 New Deal constituted a sharp break with past industrial relations practices, the cumulative impact of developments during the 1980s was colossal. By 1992 Rover's union negotiators accepted the inevitability of lean production. The agenda was characterised by accommodation, grudging perhaps, rather than total opposition.

The trigger for the reform of Rover's industrial relations structures and processes was the company's competitive weakness. Strategic choice has proved equally vital in Ford UK's industrial relations experience since 1979.[41] Ford's new emphasis on increasing product innovation and quality and accelerating the model replacement cycle raised major questions about an industrial relations strategy which had consistently pursued tight control and structural containment as its main objectives. In part, Ford's new industrial relations strategy was also a reaction to the failings of its own legacy. Historically, Ford had vigorously upheld the principle of managerial prerogative. But, as Tolliday demonstrates, the company's efforts to translate this principle into effective controls on the shopfloor were constantly frustrated by the informal resistance of unions and workforce.[42] The result was a downward spiral of efficiency and product quality checked – but not reversed – by repeated managerial efforts to tighten control.

Ford differed from British Leyland in a number of crucial respects. Not only was Ford UK consistently profitable until the late 1980s, it also has had a unique form of employment contract. Historically, Ford (and Vauxhall) remained aloof from industry-wide bargaining, preferring comprehensive contracts in which work organisation was exclusively determined by management rather than negotiation. Managerial prerogative and comprehensive employment contracts combined to provide Ford with a comparative advantage over its British rivals in terms of superior labour productivity, lower strike records and fewer disputes over workloads and job content.[43] Since 1979 Ford UK could also draw on the experience of its American parent in framing its labour relations strategy. Two major change initiatives have dominated the Ford UK experience since 1979. The first, 'After Japan' (AJ), was the outcome of an innocuous study trip in 1978 by Bill Hayden, vice-president of manufacturing for Ford of Europe. Before AJ, Ford measured its relative European efficiency against its German company, Ford Werke. After AJ, however, the efficiency benchmark was that set by emerging Japanese competitors. The AJ studies conducted after Hayden's shocked return from Japan revealed that Japanese manufacturers enjoyed a significant efficiency advantage at all stages of the production process. AJ challenged Ford management's preconceptions about the company's competitive position in the global car industry.

But the new managerial agenda set by AJ remained confused and owed much to the company's Fordist past. In part, this reflected short term expediency rather than strategic confusion. At a moment in which Ford UK was making a vital contribution to maintaining the solvency of the global corporation, there was enormous pressure to avoid any moves which could destabilise labour relations. At this moment, the relatively weak operational control exercised by Detroit over the European company permitted hardline Ford UK Manufacturing executives to unilaterally introduce a severe new disciplinary code. The resulting running battles with the Halewood workforce – and the condemnation of Detroit – were crucial in convincing Ford UK of the futility of trying to bludgeon through change.[44] Against this background, Ford's intitial attempt to introduce Quality Circles in 1980–1 without negotiation was a dismal failure. For Ford management, this episode reinforced lessons drawn from the company's American experience: the endorsement of national union leaders was an essential precondition for radical change in work organisation. 'It used to be easy to hate (Ford) managers', reflected Jimmy Airlie one of the AEEU's national negotiators, 'because they were so awful. It is a bit more difficult these days because the company have become a bit cleverer. The company seems to have realised that you can catch more flies with honey than with vinegar'.[45]

Ford UK had little success in introducing Human Resource Management techniques directly onto the shopfloor. Significant reforms were achieved through conventional collective bargaining. In 1985 Ford UK negotiated major reforms of the highly complex, rigid system of job classifications. With the agreement of union leaderships, archaic demarcation lines were eliminated and broader job roles were established with the intention of creating a more flexible workforce, intensifying capital usage, and ensuring greater continuity of production. The 1985 contract negotiations included the novel departure of increasing wage rates for the acquistion of supplementary skills rather than greater output.[46] Workforce resistance to the imposition of new work practices was central to the national Ford strike of 1988, the first for a decade. The resulting settlement tempered the 1985 enabling agreement, ratified by national union officials, by adding that reforms of work practices had also to be endorsed through local negotiations.[47] In effect, shop stewards reasserted a degree of mutuality over changes in work organisation. Together the 1985 and 1988 Agreements embody both change and continuity in Ford's approach to industrial relations. If the 1980s marked a pause in the long term deskilling of work then Ford management continued to insist on the centrality of managerial prerogative in reshaping work organisation.

For all British car makers the discovery of the Japanese efficiency advantage stimulated a reappraisal of their assumptions about scale economies and production organisation. The shared point of departure for innovations in employment and management was the rejection of past practice and the aspiration to move towards Japanese forms of work organisation. Peter Wickens describes the basis of Nissan's operating philosophy in its Washington plant as a 'tripod' consisting of flexibility, quality and teamwork.[48] It is the totality of the production system, including its company culture, which distinguishes Nissan from its British competitors. Supervisor-led Quality Circles are the cornerstone of a culture in which ensuring continuous improvement in efficiency and quality is considered the responsibility of every employee rather than that of management alone. The structure of industrial relations is equally distinctive. In contrast to the multi-unionism characteristic of British manufacturing, Nissan recognises only one union, the AEEU. Initially, only one in four of Nissan employees joined the union, a percentage which has gradually fallen. The final stage of collective bargaining is the introduction of the Advisory, Conciliation, and Arbitration Service (ACAS) as an external arbitrator. After this process is exhausted, a strike is legitimate but would, according to Wickens, be regarded by both union and company as an admission of their failure to resolve their differences in-house.[49] Salary progression is not, however, established by collective bargaining but by the appraisal of individuals' behaviour – teamworking, job knowledge, flexibility and work quality.[50]

Garrahan and Stewarts' *The Nissan Enigma* offers the first critical study of the arrival of Nissan and the transplantation of Japanese methods. They counter the plant's image of consensual employment relations. 'Control, exploitation and surveillance', they argue, are 'the other side of quality, flexibility, and teamwork.'[51] Far from empowering workers and increasing their discretion over working practices Garrahan and Stewart maintain Nissan's combination of JIT and Quality Circles 'strips out' worker knowledge more systematically than traditional Fordism. Teamworking constitutes a radical new politics of production in which surveillance and discipline is not exclusively top down but inscribed in the very constitution of the workgroup. Surveillance is no longer the prerogative of the supervisor but the responsibility of every team member: the individual becomes tightly enmeshed in a dense latticework of control.[52] The combination of teamworking and JIT creates a powerful form of 'management by stress'.[53] Equally, despite the rhetoric of multi-skilling, the 'Nissan Way' remains based on routine assembly work which closely resembles that found in other British car plants. Skills are essentially plant-specific and job enlargement entails the intensification of work through task accretion. Nissan's response to the persistent recession of the early 1990s shows how shopfloor involvement strategies can be mobilised by management even in the most difficult of circumstances. Nissan management concluded by 1993 they employed too many workers for the level of demand over the next two years or so. But redundancies could threaten the mutual trust that had been nurtured since 1984. They therefore put the problem out to consultation with the workforce. The resulting proposal was that any redundancies should be voluntary, they should be quick and they should be paid. In essence this was agreed by management, subject to the dispensability of the volunteers, and their being paid six months' wages, regardless of length of service. For Nissan management this consultative approach to redundancy enhanced rather than eroded workforce identification with corporate objectives.

All British car companies have traced a similar trajectory in industrial relations and work organisation, albeit with varying degrees of success. Moving from Fordism to lean production is central to the competitive strategies of all the major players in the British market. On the shopfloor, this strategic choice has underlain the introduction of more flexible capital equipment, new participative styles of supervision, and the widening of job definitions. Winning the active support of union leaderships and shop stewards has emerged as a universal managerial concern. On the other hand, continuing redundancies, chronic insecurity of employment, weakened shopfloor unionism and an increasing intensity of work have combined to produce an unfavourable environment in which to increase employee involvement.[54]

The secular trend towards flexibility has been both difficult and uneven. The greatest distance has been travelled by Rover, while Ford UK's progress has been more halting, reflecting a management strategy of negotiating change through conventional collective bargaining and the greater resilience of shopfloor trade unionism. In turn, this reflects the contrasting outcomes of the confrontations between management and unions in the early 1980s: Michael Edwardes' devastation of shop steward organisation in British Leyland had no equivalent in Ford where shopfloor trade unionism remained intact. Equally, important differences remain in the power and influence exercised by the unions within the car companies. In Ford, Vauxhall and, to a lesser extent, Rover the unions continue to play a critical mediating role in the process of change. By contrast, in Nissan and Toyota the unions have only a nominal existence and have no bargaining role for shop stewards comparable to their counterparts in rival firms. Whereas in 1979 the British car industry was converging on Fordism and formalised collective bargaining as the route to stable, controlled production, in the 1980s this was displaced by a hesitant movement towards a lean prodution working regime.

8.4 Flexibility and the supply chain

Like the vehicle manufacturers, the automotive component sector has experienced profound structural change since 1979. The component sector was devastated during the first half of the 1980s. The decline of Rover was particularly painful because the company bought such a high proportion of components locally. Employment plummeted by around one-third and British companies' market share fell from over 60 per cent in 1979 to under 40 per cent of a much reduced market in 1987.[55] The prime stimulus for this process was the altered production priorities and increased internationalisation of the sourcing policies of the car industry's corporate giants. The components sector comprised producers of a host of intermediate products, from simple commodities such as nuts, bolts and sheet metal, through to high value-added mechanical and electronic sub-systems. The sector was highly concentrated, with the top ten firms accounting for over 80 per cent of output and surrounded by a penumbra of some 2,000 financially vulnerable and technically unsophisticated small firms.[56] Nor are the ties between vehicle assemblers and their supplier networks important solely in terms of production logistics and product quality. For European motor manufacturers, externally sourced components comprise between 50 and 60 per cent of total costs.[57] Component purchases are, therefore, a major element of the vehicle assemblers financial profile: Ford of Europe annually buys more than $7,000 million of materials and components from external suppliers, more than one-half from Germany and almost one-fifth from Britain.

The critical importance of the supplier network for Japanese car makers was exemplified by Toyota's implementation of its 'partnership' philosophy for its new British plant in 1989. Toyota surveyed 2,000 companies from fourteen European countries. In-depth examinations reduced this initial total to around 230 companies which were asked for quotations. Of these, 167 supplied prototypes which allowed Toyota to instruct 68 companies to commence production tooling. Toyota excluded temporary price differences from its deliberations and based its selection criteria on its evaluation of innovative capability and management stability of its potential suppliers. The objective was to establish the basis for a deep knowledge of Toyota's development plans and a high degree of organisational interpenetration. For Toyota, such long term relationships were not a consequence of striking long term contracts but rather a recognition of mutual self-interest. Toyota's director of corporate affairs and human resources explained,[58]

A long-term relationship is not a consequence of being given an order, but the result of mutual effort over many years in the search for continuous improvement of quality, cost and technical performance. Understanding and anticipation of each others' needs is essential for this to succeed and, therefore, the relationship between people both on the suppliers' side, and on Toyota's side is essential.

Nissan aims for open-book costing from its suppliers to ensure that there is a full understanding of cost structures and pricing and to provide a base from which future savings can be determined. In return it works with its suppliers to help them improve their quality, design, delivery, production and managerial capabilities. Subsequent cost reductions are shared between Nissan and its suppliers, but the suppliers, as a result, have also been able to win new customers, such as VW. Linking computer control systems between component suppliers and Nissan allowed direct delivery from supplier of the exact mix of products as needed by the model mix coming through to the required point on the production line, with only fifteen minutes to spare. The degree of co-ordination and integration attained between firms was higher than within most large British businesses a decade earlier.[59]

For European vehicle assemblers, restructuring their contractual and organisational relationships with their supplier base has become a vital factor in building or sustaining competitive advantage in the emerging era of lean production. A key indicator of the move to lean production is the ruthless pruning by manufacturers of their component suppliers and a dramatic change in the nature of their contractual relationship. Rover, for example, gradually reduced its supplier network from over 1,200 to between 150 and 200 supplier firms. But while Rover has maintained a largely British supplier base Ford has not only reduced its suppliers from 2,550 to 900 firms but also shifted to European rather than national sourcing. Previously manufacturers aggressively used their buying power to drive regular spot bargains with suppliers. Now manufacturers aim to develop a long-term relationship with a narrow base of supplier companies which are vetted for their use of a range of management techniques, particularly quality assurance and innovative design capabilities.

During the 1970s Britain's component and tyre manufacturers committed themselves to a mass production strategy based on rationalised product ranges, volume production and price based competition. Investment and acquisition decisions were geared to maximising scale economies. The moves towards lean production by car manufacturers fragmented the component market and imposed new pressures on their suppliers.[60] Fragmenting demand, accelerated change and greater variety in product specification undermined supplier strategies based on stable patterns of demand satisfied by mass production. In an environment in which the car manufacturers demanded small batch deliveries, volume orientated production systems were heavily penalised. Through the 1980s the key competitive factor was production flexibility. This shift led companies such as Lucas and GKN to abandon dedicated equipment and even to close plants laid down less than a decade after they were commissioned. The efficiencies of rigid volume production were sacrificed in order to regain some of the flexibility of more traditional, modular processes. At Lucas, work passed between cells of fifteen to twenty people who carried out their own scheduling, planning, quality control, set-up and maintenance activities under the guidance of a team leader. Effectively they acted as internal sub-contractors. Inputs arrived in panniers that were colour coded complete with the 'kanban' or demand note raised by the factory on receipt of the order and translated into appropriate amounts of materials available to each cell. Stock reductions worth millions of pounds were claimed for the new system.

What prompted the move was Lucas' trauma of 1981 when it recorded its first loss on annual operations. Cellular manufacturing was introduced to the company by John Parnaby, a former professor of production engineering. Profit levels were restored by what was one of the most thoroughgoing 'Japanisation' of any British company. Measured solely by the number of patents taken out in the United States, Lucas had become one of the most innovatory companies in Britain by the mid 1980s. But the company was still consistently outperformed by foreign competitors in motor vehicle components, such as Bosch and Seiko. Although the largest British component maker, Lucas ranked eighth among European automotive component manufacturers, measured by automotive sales of about $2 billion in 1987, far behind the leaders Michelin and Bosch (with automotive sales of $8 billion and $7.6 billion respectively). Sales, and to a lesser extent profit, remained in motor vehicle components, but most were created by Lucas Girling brake manufacturers and Lucas CAV fuel injection systems. Thse subsidiaries derived their reputations from inhouse prouct innovations over twenty years and from a design 'family' with an even longer pedigree.

The sharp break with the volume manufacturing philosophy of the 1970s had a significant impact on industrial relations in the components industry. Quality and flexibility displaced productivity as the central themes of industrial relations. As in the car plants, work organisation became more malleable by management and unrestrained either by craft traditions or the need to maintain 'mutuality' as a central organising principle during the reorganisation of work processes.[61] In Lucas' Birmingham factory, JIT and job flexibility resulted in 300 redundancies, a 25 per cent increase in productivity, the reduction of lead times from a fortnight to just one day, while inventory levels were reduced by £1.5 million.[62]

British car makers' move towards lean production forced parallel changes through their industry's supply chain. The internationalisation of the components sector was accompanied by increased concentration and even greater vulnerability for the small sub-contracting firms which form the industry's penumbra. The restructuring of the spatial, financial and organisational links between the car and component companies remained unfinished. Unlike the Japanese system with its high degree of financial, organisational and technological interdependence the British system retained important elements of the traditional buyer–suplier relationship. In particular, some British component suppliers regarded the new system as simply an additional layer of exploitation by manufacturers abusing their market power to pass on inventory costs. Among established firms the contractual and logistical characteristics of the Japanese system developed painfully in Britain through the 1980s. So also the collaboration and cooperation which is its functional core remained somewhat elusive.[63]

8.5 The paradox of Rover

The only surviving British owned volume producer shared all the characteristics of the industry discussed above. But there were also unique features. Although British owned Rover became dependent upon Japanese design expertise. For much of the 1980s the company aspired to be a mass producer and a luxury/niche player simultaneously. From 1978, after a decade of decline, what was to become the Rover company reduced the number of plants, retooled the survivors, introduced new manning levels and moved to a new model range. The principal surviving plants were Longbridge (Austin) and Cowley (Morris). Longbridge made the Metro, launched in 1980, and Cowley manufactured the Maestro and Montego, launched respectively in 1983 and 1984. Given Rover's limited development resources, only one model could be developed at one time, and development of the small car was so advanced that it could not have been halted in 1978. Rover was therefore faced with a gap in the crucial medium car range. That was the root of Rover's liaison with Honda.

On his arrival in 1978 Michael Edwardes sought a collaborator to fill this crucial gap in British Leyland's product range quickly. Renault, his first choice, was rejected because the French terms were too stringent and would have restricted British Leyland to satellite production solely for the British market. Edwardes preferred alternative was collaboration with Vauxhall. But this was rejected by General Motors' corporate management in Detroit.[64] Edwardes then turned to Honda.[65] He conceived the link with Honda purely as a temporary measure and not as the prelude to an enduring joint venture. However, many of the initial concessions made by British Leyland in striking this unequal bargain had long term consequences.

Rover was licensed to manufacture Honda designs. The first product of this liaison was the Rover 200, closely based on the Honda Ballade. The joint venture deepened with the joint design of the Rover 800/Honda Legend. Honda, however, retained the right of veto on all decisions concerning performance standards and vehicle engineering. By 1986 the joint venture had assumed a central role in Rover's strategy of profit-centred contraction initiated in 1982. Rover, in other words, had come to terms with the fact that it was no longer a volume car maker. Now it was operating on a similar scale to BMW and Mercedes but without their financial or product strength. The strategic legacy of the Edwardes era was a company which uncomfortably straddled the gap between volume and specialist car manufacture.

Michael Edwards' autobiographical account of his years with

Rover together with his successful public relations ensure him a prominent place in any recent history of the British motor industry. But identifying his unique contribution is not so easy. By 1978 British Leyland faced bankruptcy or severe contraction, irrespective of the political complexion of the government. Some variant of the Edwardes' strategy was inevitable. Equally, Edwardes' confrontational approach to industrial relations was paralleled by a no less aggressive clear-out of management. Edwardes launched an enormous management reshuffle, driven by psychological tests of questionable relevance, which inevitably placed a great strain on the operating capacities of the company. Moreover, Edwardes' decision to separate production and design facilities of the various marques was clearly an expensive mistake which he eventually reversed. The business could not afford multiple facilities at the volumes that were then being produced. A less radical approach may have required a les extreme contraction of manufacturing. Michael Edwardes resigned in 1982. Thereafter eighteen subsidiaries including Unipart, the replacement component makers, were sold off. Istel the management information systems developed by British Leyland was bought by AT & T, Jaguar was privatised in 1984, eventually to be acquired by Ford in 1989 and Leyland was sold to DAF.

From 1986 Rover determinedly moved upmarket, away from direct competition with the mass producers: profit was given priority over market share. In 1991 George Simpson, managing director of the Rover Group reflected on the development of the company's strategy and implicitly acknowledged the important strategic legacy of Michael Edwardes'[66]

> The process of change has been going on for four or five yeas now but I think the most important change took place quite some time ago when we realised that we were no longer a volume car manufacturer and we should not behave as if we were. If we were to be successful with our output of 500,000–600,000 cars per annum we acknowleged then that we had to become a manufacturer of specialist vehicles for particular niches in the market. We are now more tuned into financial viability and profitability.

In 1988 Rover and Honda reached a reciprocal manufacturing agreement with the Honda Concerto manufactured at Rover's Longbridge plant.[67] The 'Synchro' replacement for the Montego was to be built at Honda's Swindon plant for both Rover and

Honda. Three years later Honda decided to make the Concerto at Swindon instead of at Rover's Longbridge plant because it was dissatisfied with the quality of Longbridge's products. That left Rover to make its own Synchro's from 1993 at Cowley. Honda's rejection of Longbridge Ballades on quality grounds and withdrawal from an agreement to produce Legends at Cowley was a severe setback for the joint venture. This incident exemplified the unequal relationship between the two companies: Rover management was powerless to reverse a decision which it regarded as a reflection more of a build-up of Honda's inventory than of Rover's poor quality. If Rover conceived itself as an equal with Honda in the original Edwardes plan then the 1980s had demonstrated that, in reality, this was a highly unbalanced partnership. For Rover, the long term strategic advantage to be gained from its liaison with Honda was improving the company's product development process, an area in which the British company acknowledged a traditional weakness.[68] However, the importance of Honda's design capability to Rover increased over time, making the British company ever more dependent on maintaining and deepening the joint venture. Limited resources hindered Rover's ability to accelerate significantly its design process and confirmed the company's reliance on Honda expertise.

In March 1988 Lord Young announced that BAe was to buy Rover. BAe was concerned primarily with defence contracting, manufacturing in small volumes, customised products for a small number of buyers in an industry notorious for its inefficiency. The synergy from the acquisition was not obvious. Only Land Rover, which brought in a high proportion of Rover's export earnings, was attractive to BAe. Although Land Rovers were used by BAe for missile launchers for the Ministry of Defence and were sold to a number of foreign governments, what mattered to BAe was the short term financial gain from the deal. The government was by now anxious to get rid of its responsibilities to British Leyland. Political constraints precluded the company's sale to a foreign buyer and Land Rover and substantial property holdings were the profitable carrots used to persuade a British company to acquire British Leyland as a whole.

BAe offered £150 million and asked for £800 million to write off debt. The EC cut the write off to £549 million to which Young responded by adding 'sweeteners' of £44 million in the form of tax concessions. BAe declined to come up with the £1.5 billion needed for Rover's corporate plan, reducing the investment commitment by over two-thirds. Would a debt write-off have made Rover viable? It is unlikely that Rover's profit stream even then would have warranted the investment it believed it needed. BAe was entitled by the agreement to sell the car business after five years. It closed Cowley's South Works and the pressings plant at Llanelli. Diversification might have smoothed BAe's earnings, but defence demand collapsed with the fall of the Soviet bloc, swiftly followed by world recession.

In January 1989 British Leyland/Rover was privatised into BAe, the fourth change of leadership in seven years. Privatisation marked yet another shift in government policy towards the only British owned volume car producer. The state's relationship with British Leyland moved from passive investment in 1975 to the active stewardship of corporate plans after 1979. The privatisation of British Leyland was orchestrated by the Thatcher government to remove its financial obligation to the company whilst assuring its survival as a wholly British-owned concern. In 1988 British Leyland's capital debts amounted to around £3 billion. The selling price, excluding deferred payments which remain under review, was £148 million. In addition to a significant land-bank, including sites in central London and the Midlands, Rover held vehicle stocks worth approximately £440 million when the sale was concluded. BAe's net cash gain from the state, including regional aid and tax advantages, was £397 million, plus Rover. Intervention by the EC did little to change the substance of the transaction and effectively changed only the timing of the cash benefit received by BAe and of tax deferment against future Rover losses.[69]

Government policy was to subsidise competition. Nissan was given £115 million to establish production in Britain. Toyota was also subsidised, but Honda was not. A large proportion of the state funds committed to British Leyland was for redundancy payments. By comparison with British government policy towards Leyland, Renault lost £2.98 billion between 1982 and 1986, also receiving £500 million of state aid. In 1986 £1.26 billion of debt was written off, of which £370 million had to be repaid to the EC. Profitabilty was restored in 1992 and privatisation was proposed for 1994.

In July 1989 Rover and Honda strengthened their relationship still further through cross-shareholding. Honda acquired a 20 per cent shareholding in Rover which, in turn, gained a 20 per cent equity stake in the Japanese company's British operation. Honda's new manufacturing plant at Swindon was designed to produce both Rover and Honda versions of its new car ranges. Rover was to supply body panels for both companies. These latest moves appeared to signal that the relationship between the two companies had entered a new phase, in which Rover was dependent on Honda in both design and manufacturing capability. As Rover progressively became a more junior partner in the joint venture, Honda received considerable strategic benefits. Above all, Honda gained invaluable experience of British labour markets and supplier networks in preparation for beginning independent production in its new Swindon plant. On the other hand Rover was able to claim spectacular productivity increases. At Cowley where the manufacturing workforce was slimmed down to 3,000 by the end of 1993, about 30 cars per employee per annum were being made, compared with 11 in 1991. Rover manufactured five separate models and increased market share. With sales up by 5 per cent in 1993 to 442,000 units, Rover exceeded the reduced break-even point of 400,000.

8.6 Conclusion

The British car industry experienced a series of profound transformations after 1979. Ford first of all gained as BL/Austin-Rover/Rover declined. Then effective new products introduced by General Motors' subsidiary Vauxhall, by Rover and by Peugeot whittled away the dominance of Ford. Market fragmentation was accelerated not only by the increased number of companies seeking to build market share but also by their determination to contest all segments of the product market. With the onset of recession in 1989 Ford no longer set the pace of competition for the other companies to follow. Ford's initial determination to hold market share at the expense of margins slowly gave way to the type of profit-maximising strategy it pursued throughout the 1970s as the corporation shrewdly shadowed the pricing policy of the grossly inefficient British Leyland. The deep and lasting recession which hit the European car industry compounded the competitive pressures in an industry with approximately 20 per cent surplus capacity. The depth of crisis in the European market and the globalisation of competition will make tactical liaisons and more durable alliances between the major players increasingly attractive over the coming decade.

The employment prospects in the car industry based in Britain are equally uncertain. For the multinational manufacturers, the recession triggered shfts of output schedules away from British plants. Ford UK lost production of the Sierra and Mondeo to Genk, Belgium. Dagenham, a plant which failed fully to realise the potential flexibility of capital equipment installed in the early 1980s, is now solely dependent upon Fiesta production. Similarly, Ford cancelled massive investment of around £725 million intended for its Bridgend engine plant. Overall, Ford UK appears likely to play a much diminished role in Ford's European operations.[70] Nor are the medium term employment prospects for Rover encouraging. The end of Maestro and Montego production will result in the loss of assembly jobs. BMW is unlikely to provide compensation in the short term. In the medium term, the rapid expansion of Japanese-owned capacity will not offset the jobs lost in British car manufacturing since 1979.

Since the late 1970s the car manufacturers have converged on similar strategies aimed at managing the transition from mass production to lean production. All have sought to improve and accelerate their design capability, while also lowering their break-even point. The supply chain from component manufacturers to vehicle assemblers experienced massive restructuring. With the exception of the Japanese companies, who pursue a local sourcing policy, the multinational manufacturers shifted towards building transnational supply chains. This devastated the British component industry which was historically based on a handful of major players surrounded by innumerable small firms. Few of these small and medium sized enterprises had the financial, technical or managerial capabilities necessary to become privileged suppliers to the major car manufacturers.

In industrial relations the adoption of a 'lean' strategy hinged upon the forceful reassertion of managerial prerogative on the shopfloor. No longer were the unions and the shop steward necessarily a crucial intermediary in the negotiation of the reorganisation of work processes. With the exception of Nissan, starting on a green field site, and recruiting a new labour force, initial attempts to introduce problem-solving fora outside the control of collective

1995

Rover's improvement in productivity cleared the way for BAe to sell the company. BAe could no longer afford the required investment in an era of defence cuts and depressed air travel. When in 1992 BAe reached the decision, they favoured a management buy-out, retaining Honda's involvement. There were no difficulties in finding potential equity stakeholders, but the commercial banks were not prepared to advance the larger sum needed for loan capital. Their reticence was encouraged by BAe's sudden record loss in 1992. They added further fuel to the controversy over alleged short-termism of British financial institutions and the adverse impact on industry, although they may have been correct about the long term viability of a stand-alone Rover. Honda believed its own position was satisfactory without the commitment of taking a majority shareholding in Rover. Honda was prepared only to increase its holding from 20 to 47.5 per cent, and to value the company at 40 per cent less than their competitor's eventual bid, which was no remedy for BAe's problem.

In January 1994, to the surprise of Rover employees, Honda and the British government, BAe announced they had found a buyer. Honda's European strategy was shattered. BMW was willing to pay £800 milion for an 80 per cent shareholding and to take on some £900 million of Rover's debts in exchange for the Land Rover/ Range Rover prize, small car front wheel drive technological know-how and a production base in a low labour cost region which had learned some of the lessons of Japanese production. The takeover at last offered a remedy for the inability of the British industry to build up a competitive presence outside Britain. Four wheel drive, off the road, vehicles sold extremely well in the United States and BMW's dealer network was well placed to distribute the Land Rover range. With a profitable output of almost one million vehicles a year, the larger BMW could take advantage of scale economies and was better placed to create employment than larger, less profitable European companies, such as Volkswagen and Fiat. In a depressed European industry with excess capacity of 2–3.5 million cars, national champions were certain to become an endangered species. The largest car exporter from Britain was Japanese-owned Nissan, not British-owned Rover, at the time of the acquisition.

Bernd Pischetsrieder, BMW's chairman insisted Rover would retain its own indentity and that Honda's agreement to continue collaborating with the company secured the future of the Rover 600 and the replacement for the Rover 200. He expected to see a 50 per cent increase in Rover annual new model development expenditure. Rover's independent design capability seemed set for expansion. Design, research, development and engineering facilities in 1994 were concentrated at Canley near Coventry, and at a 900 acre site that included 26 miles of test track at Gaydon in Warwickshire. The 900 engineers at Gaydon could develop engines from scratch and did so with Rover's K-series multi-valve engine. At Canley 1000 designers and engineers styled vehicles from start to finish.

Should the logic of British motor industry decline have been clear from the later 1960s? Or could Rover have flourished on a continued and strengthened association with Honda? Suppose BAe had accepted Honda's offer to increase its stake in Rover to 47 per cent and the remaining shares were sold to the public. That would have been more consistent with the government's earlier acceptance of a political constraint on selling out entirely to an overseas business. It would also have required the banks placed more confidence in Rover's Japanisation, but the profit prospects relative to the debts and investment needs were not sufficiently favourably. Rover made pre-tax losses in each of the years 1991–3 (although the trend was improving despite depressed markets). An alternative scenario, which BAe wanted to accelerate, takes longer to work through but equally leads to the disappearance of British-owned car mass production; Honda, instead of BMW, eventually buys up Rover entirely.

Car market prospects are insufficiently buoyant to support many independent manufacturers. Future demand for the motor industry's products in Britain and in Western Europe will be largely for replacement. About 85 per cent of British households regularly used a car by the beginning of the 1990s and more than 20 per cent owned two or more cars. The scope for market widening must be small, as concern rises about the congestion and pollution by the existing stock of vehicles. Perhaps two-thirds of the effect of greater fuel efficiency since the first oil crisis has been dissipated in increased traffic congestion. Traffic flows during the 1980s rose more than 80 per cent on motorways and more than 50 per cent on minor roads. Further restrictions on car use, including perhaps road pricing and tighter emission controls, may be expected, with diminishing public tolerance of new road building and vehicular dominance of urban life. After acceptance of compulsory seatbelts, the general 70 mph limit and the breathalyser, in pursuit of road safety, the 1963 Buchanan Report's recommendation of separation of people and traffic in town centre pedestrian precincts, where people could walk and shop in safety and quiet, looks increasingly appealing. But shopping habits changed after 1963, so that the motor car determined town periphery hypermarkets captured much of the rising consumers' expenditure in the following 30 years. The car is therefore likely to remain an essential component of expenditure for a majority of households.

Britain faced this prospect in 1994 without a single British owned mass producer of road vehicles, yet she was unlikely to be unique among larger industrial countries by the end of the decade. Design capability has become critical. European and American manu-facturers take almost twice as many person hours to design a car as their Japanese rivals. New consumer priorities increase the pressure on design capabilities and favour the Japanese. Medium term pro-duct strategies emphasize economy, minimum environmental damage, safety and security. Reconciling all these characteristics in one vehicle is aided by computerised design technologies. But a new world car remains colossally expensive, at over £1 billion. Among the vital lessons Rover learned form Honda was the approach to development, costs and quality which allowed Rover to bring the four wheel Discovery into production in a mere 21 months. The need to accelerate product renewal will stimulate further interfirm alliances and mergers. Equally significant overcapacity and financial pressure will also encourage rationalisation in the European car industry. During the 1980s, Alfa-Romeo, Seat, Jaguar and Saab lost their independence. The 1990s will see the same trend among the bigger companies. Not only must the two parties be willing and able to decide terms, but if a new grouping is to be successful their assets, tangible and intangible, must be complementary. Renault and Volvo pulled out of a merger at the last moment in 1993. Fiat, which lost $1 billion in 1993, has already come close to merging with Ford and is a likely member of the first major reconfiguration of the decade.

Integration of the European market will influence policy of both European motor companies and importers. The Europeans will aim to reduce their dependence on any single market. Ford, General Motors, and to a lesser extent Volkswagen have truly European production and marketing. PSA, Renault and Fiat are vulnerable through their reliance on their home markets. For the French and German companies, domestic markets account for the bulk of their western European sales, and for Fiat, the figure is 67 per cent. Depending on EC policy towards the Japanese, it is the continental majors who will be most severely affected by Japanese competition. European business regulation thus will assume greater prominence. From 1992, all investment greater than $13.5 million which includes some element of subsidy, required clearance from Brussels.

Not only will British industrial policy be largely determined in Brussels, but British motor production will depend upon a small number of multinationals, headquartered in other countries. Even so, what sort of competitive advantages and disadvantages will accrue from locating production in Britain still depends on national economic characteristics. The Rover experience suggests it is increasingly possible that a new, ultimately more profitable, conception of the firm might take root in Britain. Large organisations share with giant oil tankers enormous momentum carrying them in directions established in the past. Great countervailing forces over a considerable time are necessary to change. In any period, most decision-takers are considerably restricted by tradition. Bearing that in mind, the turnaround of Rover was a considerable achievement. But in an industry where the number of businesses must shrink, it could not be enough to sustain independence.

NOTES

Notes to Chapter One

1 K. Richardson, *The British Motor Industry 1896–1939: A Social and Economic History*, London: Macmillan, 1977 on coal; D. Noble and G. Mackenzie Junner, *Vital to the Life of the Nation: A Historical Survey of the Progress of the British Motor Industry from 1869 to 1946*, London: SMMT, 1946, pp. 2–3 on repressive legislation; and J.-P. Bardou, J.-J. Chanaron, P. Fridenson and J. M. Laux, *The Automobile Revolution: The Impact of an Industry*, Chapel Hill: University of North Carolina Press, 1982 on the patent monopoly.

2 W. W. Rostow, *The Stages of Economic Growth: A Non-Communist Manifesto*, Cambridge University Press, 1960, pp. 84–5.

3 S. B. Saul, 'The British Motor Industry to 1914', *Business History*, Vol. 5, 1962, pp. 22–44. The present chapter draws heavily on this important article.

4 W. Lewchuk, *American Technology and the British Vehicle Industry*, Cambridge University Press, 1987.

5 W. B. Arthur, 'Competing Technologies, Increasing Returns and Lock-in by Historical Events', *Economic Journal*, Vol. 99, 1989, pp. 116–31.

6 United States Special Consular Report, *Vehicle Industry in Europe*, Bureau of Foreign Commerce, Department of State, GPO, 1900, pp. 400–1.

7 W. A. Lewis, *Growth and Fluctuation 1870–1913*, London: Allen and Unwin, 1978, p. 129.

8 J. S. Foreman-Peck, 'Diversification and the Growth of the Firm: The Rover Company to 1914', *Business History*, 25, 2, July 1983, pp. 179–92; A. E. Harrison, 'The Competitiveness of the British Cycle Industry 1890–1914', *Economic History Review*, 2nd series, Vol. 22, 1969, pp. 291–301; A. E. Harrison, 'Origin and Growth of the UK Cycle Industry to 1900', *Journal of Transport History*, 3rd series, Vol. 6, 1985, pp. 41–70; R. J. Irving, 'New Industries for Old? Armstrong Whitworth', *Business History*, Vol. 17, 1975, pp. 150–75.

9 Noble and Mackenzie Junner, *Vital to the Life of the Nation*, p. 8.

10 In this respect the experience of the late Victorian motor industry was not unique. Vested interests and safety concerns inhibited innovation in a number of other vital new British industries. Similar contemporary hindrances to the development of electricity and the telephone were placed at about the same time, by parliamentary legislation in 1881 and the Post Office telecommunications monopoly respectively.

11 T. R. Nicholson, *The Birth of the British Motor Car 1769–1897*, London: Macmillan, 1982, Vol. 1, p. 153, Vol. 2, pp. 288–315, Vol. 3, pp. 479–84; J. J. Flink, *The Automobile Age*, MIT Press, 1988, pp. 6–10; J. Mokyr, *The Lever of Riches: Technological Creativity and Technical Progress*, Oxford University Press, 1990, p. 131, n. 9.

12 If so it may be an example of the contribution of errors to economic evolution. The British road system has been hailed as a major reason for the superiority of eighteenth century British industry over French business (R. Szostak, *The Role of*

Transportation in the Industrial Revolution, Montreal and London: McGill-Queen University Press, 1990). French roads were constructed and maintained for military not commercial reasons. British and German nineteenth century roads, by then lacking much economic justification, were poor in comparison.

13 T. C. Barker, 'Introduction', in T. C. Barker (ed.), *The Economic and Social Effects of the Spread of Motor Vehicles*, London: Macmillan, 1987, pp. 18–20; J. M. Laux, *In First Gear: The French Automobile Industry to 1914*, Liverpool University Press, 1976, Chapter 1; G. Maxcy, 'The Motor Industry', in P. L. Cook and R. Cohen (eds.), *The Effects of Mergers*, London: Allen and Unwin, 1958, p. 356; C. St C. B. Davison, *History of Steam Road Vehicles*, London: Science Museum, HMSO, 1953, pp. 49–54.

14 C. F. Caunter, *The Light Car*, London: Science Museum, HMSO, 1970, pp. 8–9.

15 Flink, *Automobile Age*, pp. 51–5.

16 St J. C. Nixon, *Wolseley: A Saga from the Motor Industry*, London: G. T. Foulis, 1949, p. 24.

17 *Royal Commission on Motor Cars*, 1906, British Parliamentary Papers.

18 P. W. S. Andrews and E. Brunner, *The Life of Lord Nuffield*, Oxford: Blackwell 1954, pp. 87–8.

19 J. Wood, *Wheels of Misfortune; The Rise and Fall of the British Motor Industry*, London: Sidgwick and Jackson, 1988, pp. 25–6; Caunter, *The Light Car*; United States Special Consular Report, *Vehicle Industry in Europe*, 1913.

20 D. Thoms and T. Donnelly, *The Motor Car Industry in Coventry since the 1890s*, Beckenham, Kent: Croom Helm, 1985, pp. 60–1.

21 Second generation owners of French motor firms such as Peugeot went to an École Superiéure. The theoretical work of Lanchester in Britain was ignored by his countrymen, although his two volumes on aerodynamics became the basis for German research in the First World War and after. Communication from R. Loveridge.

22 Simms helped Robert Bosch invent the high voltage magneto.

23 J. S. Foreman-Peck, 'Diversification and the Growth of the Firm: The Rover Company to 1914', *Business History*, Vol. 25 No. 2, July 1983, pp. 179–92.

24 United States Special Consular Report, *Vehicle Industry in Europe*, 1907.

25 United States Special Consular Report, *Vehicle Industry in Europe*, 1912; *Vehicle Industry in Europe*, 1908.

26 The category 'not for sale' included tourists' vehicles and probably cars bought abroad and being driven to their new owners. With perhaps an average life of, say, five years, even granted the very rapid growth in the vehicle stock from 12,000 in 1904 to 46,000 in 1907, the estimated 300 vehicles scrapped in the equation is too low. However, when an extra one or two thousand balance of imports 'not for sale' over exports 'not for sale' is thrown into the equation, the scrapping and laying-up figure looks more plausible. It may well be also that the effectiveness of registration was still increasing; that is, new registration overstated the expansion of the vehicle stock. This conjecture might be borne out by the increase in registration during the depression year of 1908 exceeding that for prosperous 1907, at least for commercial vehicles. But the strength of home demand was apparently such that total home sales continued to rise in 1908, even though British production, focused on the volatile luxury market, apparently fell.

27 W. Lewchuk, 'The Return to Capital in the British Motor Vehicle Industry 1896–1939', *Business History*, Vol. 27, March 1985, pp. 3–25; A. E. Harrison, 'Joint Stock Company Flotation in the Cycle, Motor Vehicle and Related Industries', *Business History*, Vol. 23, 1981.

28 The proposition presupposes some separation of the British equity market from the American or other country share markets so that returns were not equalised at the

margin.

29 A. E. Harrison, 'F. Hopper and Co.: Problems of Capital Supply in the Cycle Manufacturing Industry 1891–1914', *Business History*, Vol. 24, 1982, pp. 3–23. Pollard concedes this point but still maintains the evidence could be interpreted as consistent with capital starvation: Sidney Pollard, *Britain's Prime and Britain's Decline: The British Economy 1870–1914*, London; Edward Arnold, 1989, pp. 97, 99.

30 R. A. Church, 'The Marketing of Automobiles in Britain and the United States before 1939', in A. Okochi and K. Shimokawa (eds.), *The Development of Mass Marketing: Automobiles and Retailing*, University of Tokyo Press, 1981; R. A. Church, 'Markets and Marketing in the British Motor Industry before 1914, with some French Comparisons', *Journal of Transport History*, 3rd series, Vol. 3, Spring 1982, pp. 1–20.

31 Lewchuck, *American Technology*.

32 Thoms and Donnelly, *The Motor Car Industry*, pp. 61–2.

33 S. Tolliday, 'Management and Labour in Britain 1896–1939', in S. Tolliday and J. Zeitlin, *The Automobile Industry and its Workers*, Cambridge: Polity Press, 1986.

34 Local Government Board, *Annual Report of the Local Government Board, 1908–9; Royal Commission on Motor Cars, 1906; Road Improvement Fund, Tenth Annual Report of the Road Improvement Fund*, 1921.

35 J. S. Foreman-Peck, 'Tariff Protection and Economies of Scale', *Oxford Economic Papers*, Vol. 31, No. 2, July 1979, pp. 237–57; J. S. Foreman-Peck, 'The Effects of Market Failure on the British Motor Industry before 1939', *Explorations in Economic History*, Vol. 18, 1981, pp. 257–89.

36 R. Vernon, 'International Investment and International Trade in the Product Cycle', *Quarterly Journal of Economics*, Vol. 80, 1966, pp. 190–207; R. Vernon, 'The Product Cycle Hypothesis in a New International Environment', *Oxford Bulletin of Economics and Statistics*, Vol. 41, 1979, pp. 255–67.

Notes to Chapter Two

1 R. A. Church, *Herbert Austin: The British Motor Industry to 1941*, London: Europe, 1979; P. W. S. Andrews and E. Brunner, The Life of Lord Nuffield, Oxford: Basil Blackwell, 1954, pp. 77–80; D. Noble and G. Mackenzie Junner, *Vital to the Life of the Nation: A Historical Survey of the Progress of the British Motor Industry from 1896 to 1946*, London, SMMT, 1946; H. R. Ricardo, *Memories and Machines: The Pattern of My Life*, Shoreham Sussex: Ricardo Consulting Engineers, 1990, Chapter 11.

2 *The Motor Trader*, 14 January 1920, 31 March 1920. Commercial vehicle manufacturers faced additional reductions of demand for their products as the government sold off army surplus lorries. G. C. Allen, 'The British Motor Industry' *London and Cambridge Economic Service*, No. 18, 1926.

3 C. Wilson and W. Reader, *Men and Machines: A History of D Napier & Sons, Engineers*, London: Weidenfeld and Nicolson, 1958, p. 111.

4 Andrews and Brunner, *Lord Nuffield*, pp. 98–103; K. Richardson, *The British Motor Industry 1896–1939 A Social and Economic History*, London: Macmillan, 1977, pp. 96–7; 'History of the Nuffield Group', *The Motor*, 2 May 1939.

5 Austin Motor Company, *Our First Fifty Years: Longbridge 1905–1955*, Longbridge, 1955; R. J. Wyatt, *The Motor for the Million: The Austin Seven 1922–39*, London: MacDonald, 1968.

6 J. Foreman-Peck, 'The American Challenge of the Twenties: Multinationals and the European Motor Industry', *Journal of Economic History*, Vol. 42, 1982, pp. 865–81.

7 G. Maxcy and A. Silberston, *The Motor Industry*, London: Allen and Unwin, 1959;

M. Wilkins and F. F. Hill, *American Business Abroad: Ford on Six Continents*, Detroit: Wayne State University Press 1964.

8 J. Foreman-Peck, 'Exit, Voice and Loyalty as Responses to Decline: The Rover Company in the Interwar Years', *Business History*, Vol. 23, July 1981, pp. 191–207.

9 *Ibid.*

10 M. Sedgwick, *Cars of the 1930s*, London: Batsford, 1970.

11 G. Turner *The Leyland Papers*, Birkenhead: Eyre and Spottiswoode, 1971, pp. 4–9; A. Holmes, 'Some Aspects of the British Motor Manufacturing Industry During the Years 1919–1930', unpublished Sheffield MA thesis, 1964.

12 W. Lewchuk, *American Technology and the British Vehicle Industry*, Cambridge University Press, 1987.

13 Turner, *Leyland Papers*, Chapter 6; R. J. Overy, *William Morris, Viscount Nuffield*, London: Europa, 1976, pp. 48–9.

14 R. Church, 'Family Firms and Managerial Capitalism: The Case of the International Motor Industry', *Business History*, Vol. 2–8, No. 2, April 1986, pp. 165–80.

15 Lewchuck *American Technology*, pp. 164–7; A. D. Chandler, *Scale and Scope: The Dynamics of Industrial Capitalism*, Cambridge, Mass., Belknap of Harvard University Press, 1990, pp. 345–8; *Dictionary of Business Biography*, ed. D. Jeremy; D. G. Rhys, 'Concentration in the Interwar Motor Industry', *Journal of Transport History*, ns 3, 1976.

16 C. F. Caunter, *The Light Car*, London: Science Museum, HMSO; Political and Economic Planning, *Motor Vehicles: A Report on the Industry*, London, 1950; SMMT, *The Motor Industry of Great Britain*, 1947; Ricardo Group, *Ricardo, the First 75 Years*, Shoreham, 1990.

17 A. Perry-Keene, 'The Incidence of On-Costs', *Journal of Production Engineers*, Vol. 40, 1931; J. P. Farrant, *Scout Motors of Salisbury 1909–21*, Salisbury and S. Wiltshire Group for Industrial Archaeology, n.d.

18 Public Record Office, Board of Trade 64/3187, Treasury 171/249; W. Morris, 'Policies that have Built the Morris Motor', *Business System*, Vol. 45, 1924, reprinted in *Journal of Industrial Economics*, Vol. 1, 1954; F. G. Woollard, 'Some Notes on British Methods of Continuous Production', *Proceedings of the Institution of Automobile Engineers*, Vol. 19, 1924–5.

19 *Engineering Production*, August 1924, p. 225; *The Automobile Engineer*, January 1924, p. 15; *The Automobile Engineer*, June 1935; J. B. Jefferys, *The Story of the Engineers*, London: Lawrence and Wishart for AEU, 1945.

20 W. M. Park, *The Automotive Industry and Trade of Great Britain and Ireland*, Washington DC: US Bureau of Domestic and Foreign Commerce, 1928; Overy, *Viscount Nuffield*, pp. 86–7.

21 *Motor Trader*, 7 January 1920; Public Record Office, Department of Scientific and Industrial Research 16/32, 16/93, 16/94. Total receipts of the organisation for the year 1921–2 amounted to a little under £10,000, and research was devoted to improvements in vehicle suspension, gearboxes, radiators and carburation.

22 Ricardo, *Memories and Machines*, Chapter 15, p. 116; 'History of the Nuffield Group', *The Motor*, 2 May 1939; Overy, *Viscount Nuffield*, pp. 81–2. On Morris's graduate recruitment, letter from E. H. Blake to R. Truslove, 8 January 1925. On Pressed Steel, J. Winlock, Metallurgist, to the Secretary, Oxford University Appointments Committee, 30 May 1927, concerning an organic chemist and to Professor C. F. Jenkins 9 March 1928, for an engineer at a starting salary of around £300 per annum. These are in Oxford University Careers Service records.

23 L. Rostas, *Comparative Productivity in British and American Industry*, Cambridge University Press, 1948.

24 Monopolies and Restrictive Practices Commission, *Report on the Supply of Elec-*

trical Equipment for Mechanically Propelled Land Vehicles, London: HMSO, 1963; R. A. Church, 'Innovation, Monopoly and the Supply of Vehicle Components in Britain 1880–1930: The Growth of Joseph Lucas Ltd', *Business History Review*, Vol. 52, 1978, pp. 226–49; H. Nockolds, *Lucas: The First Hundred Years*, Newton Abbott: David and Charles, 1976.

25 R. Storrs, *Dunlop in War and Peace*, London: Hutchinson, 1946; M. Adeney, *The Motor Makers: The Turbulent History of Britain's Car Makers*, London: Fontana/ Collins, 1989, p. 146.

26 Monopolies and Mergers Commission, *BMC and Pressed Steel Co: Report on the Merger*, London: HMSO, 1966. A similar problem emerged earlier in the American industry, between Fisher Body and General Motors, when a ten year contract of 1919 proved unsatisfactory to General Motors in changed market conditions. General Motors bought Fisher in 1926, the opposite solution to that in Britain, because General Motors was so much larger than Morris. B. Klein, 'Vertical Integration as Organisational Ownership: The Fisher Body-General Motors Relationship Revisited', in O. E. Williamson and S. G. Winter (eds.), *The Nature of the Firm: Origins, Evolution and Development*, Oxford University Press, 1991. On the other hand A. O. Smith the largest manufacturer of motor car frames in the world maintained an independent existence and a harmonious and close relation with General Motors for more than half a century. R. H. Coase, 'The Nature of the Firm: Influence', in Williamson and Winter, *The Nature of the Firm*.

27 G. S. Davison, *At the Wheel*, London: Industrial Transport Publications Ltd, 1931.

28 Public Record Office, Board of Trade 64/3187. Morris's complaint about high steel prices in 1939 no doubt helped to precipitate the official investigation. *New York Times*, 21 August 1939, in Nuffield Papers 16/23, Nuffield College, Oxford.

29 *Motor Trader*, 7 January 1920, 15 March 1922, p. 317; R. A. Church, 'The Marketing of Automobiles in Britain and the United States before 1939', in A. Okochi and K. Shimokawa (eds.), *The Development of Mass Marketing: Automobiles and Retailing*, University of Tokyo Press, 1981; 'The Secondhand Car', *Economist*, 17 September 1938, pp. 531–2.

30 W. Lewchuk, 'The Return of Capital in the British Motor Vehicle Industry 1896–1939', *Business History*, Vol. 27 March 1985, pp. 3–25; Maxcy and Silberston, *Motor Industry*; P. E. Hart, *Studies in Business Savings, Profits and Investment*, London: Allen and Unwin, 1965.

31 H. Wardley, 'Another Oxford: My Life Remembered', March 1992, St Antony's College, Oxford (privately circulated); G. Lanning, C. Peaker, C. Webb and R. White, *Making Cars: A History of Car Making at Cowley by the People Who Make Cars*, London: Routledge Kegan Paul, 1985; Ford Motor Company UK, *The Ford Motor Co. Ltd and Its Work People*, Dagenham, May 1937; Adeney, *Motor Makers*, pp. 167–8.

32 W. Greenwood, *How the Other Man Lives*, Labour Book Service, n.d.; G. H. Daniel, 'Some Factors Affecting the Mobility of Labour', *Oxford Economic Papers*, February 1940; S. Tolliday, 'Management and Labour in Britain 1896–1939', in S. Tolliday and J. Zeitlin, *The Automobile Industry and Its Workers*, Cambridge: Polity Press, 1986, pp. 144–79; T. Claydon, 'Trade Unions, Employers and Industrial Relations in the British Motor Industry c1919–1945', *Business History*, Vol. 29, 1987, p. 304–24; H. A. Turner, G. Clack and G. Roberts, *Labour Relations in the Motor Industry*, London: Allen and Unwin, 1967, pp. 241–271.

33 R. C. Whiting, *The View from Cowley: The Impact of Industrialisation Upon Oxford 1918–1939*, Oxford Clarendon Press, 1983.

Notes to Chapter Three

1 *Economist*, 7 December 1935; Political and Economic Planning, *Motor Vehicles: A*

Report on the Industry, 1950.

2 *Motor Trader*, 2 April 1919; Ford Motor Company *Statistics*.

3 H. G. Castle, *Britain's Motor Industry*, London: Clerke and Cocheran, 1950; *Motor Trader*, 4 February 1920, 24 March 1920, 13 June 1920.

4 J. R. N. Stone and D. A. Rowe, *Consumers' Expenditure in the United Kingdom 1920–38*, Vol. 2, Cambridge University Press, 1966; *Motor Trader*, 11 January 1922.

5 Public Record Office, Treasury 172/1513.

6 A. Holmes, 'Some Aspects of the British Motor Manufacturing Industry During the Years 1919–1930', unpublished Sheffield MA thesis, 1964.

7 G. C. Allen, 'The British Motor Industry', *London and Cambridge Economic Service*, No. 18, 1926.

8 L. F. Duval, 'The Motor Industry', in British Association for the Advancement of Science, *Britain in Recovery*, London, 1939; Stone and Rowe, *Consumers' Expenditure*; 'The Light Car and the Motor Cycle and Sidecar Compared', *Proceedings of the Institution of Automobile Engineers*, 1922–3; S. Bowden and P. Turner, 'Some Cross-Section Evidence on the Determinants of the Diffusion of Car Ownership in the Interwar UK Economy', *Business History*, Vol. 35, No. 1, 1993, pp. 55–69.

9 *Report of the Committee on Industry and Trade*, Cmnd 3282, 1929; W. M. Park, *The Automotive Industry and Trade of Great Britain and Ireland*, 1928; Public Record Office, Board of Trade 64/76, BT64/23; M. Olney, *Buy Now Pay Later: Advertising Credit and Consumer Durables in the 1920s*, Chapel Hill: University of North Carolina Press, 1991, pp. 95, 99, 113; S. Bowden, 'Demand and Supply Constraints in the Interwar UK Car Industry: Did the Manufacturers Get it Right?', *Business History*, Vol. 33, No. 2 April 1991, pp. 241–67; S. Bowden and P. Turner, 'The Demand for Consumer Durables in the United Kingdom in the Interwar Period', *Journal of Economic History*, Vol. 53, 1993, pp. 244–58.

10 United Kingdom Imperial Economic Committee, *A Survey of Trade in Motor Vehicles*, London: HMSO, 1936. Not all reports were so favourable. Officials of the Department of Overseas Trade were consistently derogatory about the competitiveness of the industry's products abroad; Public Record Office BT 59/24, BT 52/23, BT 59/1.

11 The RAC drew up the formula $D^2N/2.5$, where D is the cylinder diameter and N the number of cylinders, in 1906 as an approximate guide to an engine's power output. The formula was adopted officially for the tax introduced in 1909. Because of the formula, of two cars with engines of a given cylinder capacity, the one with the longer stroke and smaller bore was likely to pay less tax: *The Motor*, 31 August 1926; Bowden, 'Demand and Supply Constraints'.

12 H. Wyatt, *The Motor Industry*, London: Pitman, 1917, p. 126; Public Record Office T171/249; *Times*, 23 September 1919.

13 W. Beveridge, *Tariffs: The Case Examined*, London: Longhams Green, 1931, pp. 96–7, 104; *Report of the Committee on Industry and Trade*, pp. 267–7, 289. Morris was certainly convinced that tariff protection in the 1920s had allowed lower prices, while being aware that in less competitive industries, protection could encourage higher prices. 'Tariffs not a Justification for Higher Prices', *Sunday Pictorial*, 22 November 1931.

14 D. G. Rhys, 'Concentration in the Interwar Motor Industry', *Journal of Transport History*, ns 3, No. 4, 1976, pp. 241–64.

15 Public Record Office BT56/22.

16 G. N. von Tunzelman, 'Structural Change and Leading Sectors in British Manufacturing 1907–1968', in C. P. Kindleberger and G. di Tella (eds.), *Economics in the Long View: Essays in Honour of W. W. Rostow*, London: Macmillan, 1982, Vol. 3;

SMMT, *The Motor Industry of Great Britain*, 1937.

17 On railway social savings calculations see T. R. Gourvish, *Railways and the British Economy*, London: Macmillan, 1980. Railway rates from Table 7.4 in J. Foreman-Peck and R. Millward, *Public and Private Ownership of British Industry 1820–1990*, Oxford: Clarendon Press, 1994.

18 W. Plowden, *The Motor Car and Politics*, London, Bodley Head, 1972; *10th Annual Report of the Road Improvement Fund*, 1921; Royal Commission on Transport 1931.

19 Plowden, *Motor Car*; J. Foreman-Peck 'Death on the Roads: Changing National Responses to Motor Accidents', in T. C. Barker (ed.) *The Economic and Social Effects of the Spread of Motor Vehicles*, London: Macmillan, 1987; J. Foreman-Peck, 'The Effects of Market Failure on The British Motor Industry, *Explorations in Economic History*, Vol. 18, 1981, pp. 257–89.

20 J. H. Jones, *Road Accidents: Report*, London: HMSO, 1946.

21 So it was that the Rover Company became the first commercial developer of Frank Whittle's jet engine and ultimately in 1953 tested the first jet turbine car. Reputedly, the project originated when Whittle's wife raised the subject with the Rover managing directors wife over afternooon tea. But even in collaboration with Lucas, Rover lacked the capacity for aero engine development and the project was transferred to Rolls-Royce in 1943.

22 Numbers of shop stewards grew faster than the workforce in Coventry. T. Claydon, 'Trade Unions, Employers and Industrial Relations in the British Motor Industry c1919–1945', *Business History*, 1987, pp. 304–24; H. A. Turner, G. Clack and G. Roberts, *Labour Relations in the Motor Industry: A Study of Industrial Unrest and an International Comparison*, London: George Allen and Unwin, 1967, p. 194.

23 S. Tolliday, 'Ford and Fordism in Post War Britain: Enterprise Management and the Control of Labour 1937–1987', in S. Tolliday and J. Zeitlin (eds.), *The Power to Manage? Employers and Industrial Relations in Comparative Historical Perspective*, London and New York: Routledge, 1991.

24 C. Barnett, *The Audit of War: The Reality and Illusion of Britain as a Great Power*, London: Macmillan, 1986, p. 161. The Indian Army complained in 1930 that Morris six wheeled lorries were too slow for mountain roads and compared unfavourably with the Cheverolet four wheeler. Morris countered that the army had asked for a cross-country vehicle not a hill-climber. Public Record Office BT 56/23. Confused or varied specifications continued to plague British military vehicles until and during the Second World War. Morris identified lack of centralised control of aircraft shadow factories as a key problem in 1936. 'Nuffield Differs with Air Ministry', *Daily Telegraph*, 24 October 1936. See also R. J. Overy, *William Morris, Viscount Nuffield*, London, Europa, 1976, pp. 118–21.

25 J. D. Scott, *Vickers: A History*, London: Weidenfeld and Nicolson, 1962, p. 229, passim pp. 285–7; M. M. Postan, D. Hay and J. D. Scott, *Design and Development of Weapons: Studies in Government and Industrial Organisation*, London; HMSO, 1964, pp. 304–70; P. W. S. Andrews and E. Brunner, *The Life of Lord Nuffield*, Oxford: Basil Blackwell, 1954, p. 223.

Notes to Chapter Four

1 Nick Tiratsoo, 'The Motor Car Industry', in Helen Mercer, Neil Rollings and Jim Tomlinson (eds.), *Labour Governments and Private Industry: The Experiences of 1945–1951*, Edinburgh University Press, 1992, p. 167.

2 Martin Adeney, *The Motor Makers: The Turbulent History of Britain's Car Industry*, London: Fontana/Collins, 1988, p. 209; David Thoms and Tom Donnelly, *The Motor Car Industry in Coventry since the 1890s*, Beckenham, Kent: 1985, p. 155.

3 Labour Party, Research Department, 'Report on the British Motor Industry: Possibilities of Future Development with Special Reference to the Advantages and Disadvantages of Public Ownership, May 1948, Labour Pary Archive, National Museum of Labour History, Manchester, para. 219 (1), p. 62.

4 Board of Trade, *Census of Production*, value basis, current values.

5 Board of Trade, *Census of Production*, value basis, current values.

6 SMMT, *The Motor Industry of Great Britain*, 1978, Table 43, p. 96.

7 *Ibid.*

8 *Ibid.*, 1970, Table 105, p. 325 and Table 109, p. 331; *ibid.*, 1991, Table 79, p. 205.

9 *Ibid.*, 1991, Table 79, p. 205.

10 Board of Trade, *Census of Production*.

11 SMMT, *Motor Industry of Great Britain*, annual.

12 J. P. Bardou, J. J. Chanaron, P. Fridenson and J. M. Laux, *The Automobile Revolution: The Impact of an Industry*, Chapel Hill: University of North Carolina Press, 1982, p. 171.

13 *Ibid.*, p. 180.

14 *UN Statistics Yearbook*, annual.

15 SMMT, *Motor Industry of Great Britain*, 1970, Table 15, p. 26.

16 Krish Bhaskar, *The Future of the UK Motor Industry: An Economic and Financial Analysis of the UK Motor Industry Against a Rapidly Changing Background for European and Worldwide Motor Manufacturers*, London: Kogan Page, 1979, Table 2.2, p. 29.

17 Central Statistical Office, *Annual Abstract of Statistics*, London: HMSO, 1985, Table 12.2 p. 229.

18 Labour Party, 'Report on British Motor Industry', para. 83, p. 26.

19 *Ibid.*, para. 86, p. 27.

20 Peter J. S. Dunnett, *The Decline of the British Motor Industry: The Effects of Government Policy, 1945–1979*, London: Croom Helm, 1980, Table 2.3, p. 22; George Maxcy and Aubrey Silberston, *The Motor Industry*, London: Allen and Unwin 1959, pp. 77 and 79.

21 Dunnett, *Decline*, Table 2.3, p. 22.

22 Labour Party, 'Report on British Motor Industry', para. 81, p. 25.

23 Political and Economic Planning, *Motor Vehicles: A Report on the Industry*, 1950, Table 11, pp. 21 and 22.

24 *Ibid.*, Table 12, p. 22.

25 Labour Party, 'Report on British Motor Industry', para. 90, p. 27.

26 In 1924, when Austin was in the midst of financial difficulties, Dudley Docker of Vickers initiated merger proposals between Austin, Morris and Wolseley. The idea was blocked by Morris who resisted any attempt to diminish his personal control and independence. In 1931–2 Austin approached Henry Ford with a view to discussing a potential merger. This proposal proved equally abortive, for Ford never responded. Adeney, *Motor Makers*, p. 104. Compare the ineffective government attempts to promote rationalisation among commercial producers at the beginning of the 1930s in Chapter 3.

27 Labour Party, 'Report on British Motor Industry'.

28 Labour Party, Sub-Committee on Industries for Nationalisation, Minutes, 13 October 1948, Labour Party Archive, National Museum of Labour History, Manchester, No. 5, p. 2.

29 See S. Bowden, 'The Motor Vehicle Industry', in B. Millward and J. Singleton (eds.), *Industrial Organisation and the Road to Nationalisation in Britain, 1920–1950*, Cambridge University Press, 1994, for a full discussion of the arguments for and against full and partial ownership of the industry.

30 Labour Party, 'Report on British Motor Industry', para. 224 (11) p. 66; Ministry of

Supply, *National Advisory Council for the Motor Manufacturing Industry: Report on Proceedings*, London: HMSO, 1947, p. 10, para. 12.

31 Labour Party, 'Report on British Motor Industry', para. 224 (12), p. 66.

32 Tiratsoo, 'Motor Car Industry', p. 167. Bristol, however, was taken into state ownership with the nationalisation of the Tilling Group of bus companies in 1948 whilst Tiratsoo has shown how the Labour government became involved in Standard.

33 Lewis Johnman, 'The Labour Party and Industrial Policy', in Nich Tiratsoo (ed.), *The Atlee Years*, London: Frances Pinter, 1991, p. 45.

34 Tiratsoo, 'Motor Car Industry', p. 165.

35 Bowden, 'Motor Vehicle Industry'.

36 Johnman, 'Labour Party and Industrial Policy', p. 45.

37 Labour Party, 'Report on British Motor Industry', para. 230, p. 70.

38 Bowden, 'Motor Vehicle Industry'.

39 Tiratsoo, 'Motor Car Industry', p. 170; Peter Hennessy, *Never Again: Britain 1945–1951*, London: Jonathon Cape, 1992, p. 104.

40 Political and Economic Planning, *Motor Vehicles*, 1950, p. 20.

41 Ministry of Supply, *National Advisory Council*, para. 37, p. 16.

42 SMMT, *Motor Industry of Great Britain*, 1948.

43 Maxcy and Silberston, *Motor Industry*, p. 112.

44 Tiratsoo, 'Motor Car Industry', pp. 170–81.

45 S. J. Prais, *The Evolution of Giant Firms in Britain*, Cambridge University Press, 1976, Table 1.2, p. 8; P. E. Hart and R. Clarke, *Concentration in British Industry, 1935–1975*, Cambridge University Press, 1980, pp. 121, 122, 124 and 127; P. E. Hart, 'Recent Trends in Concentration in British Industry', *National Institute of Economic and Social Research*, 1985, Discussion Paper 82.

46 D. G. Rhys, *The Motor Industry: An Economic Survey*, London: Butterworths, 1972, Table 9.2, p. 312.

47 Gerald Bloomfield, *The World Automotive Industry*, Newton Abbott: David and Charles, 1978, pp. 197, 191, 159, 230 and 224.

48 George Maxcy, *The Multinational Motor Industry*, 1981, p. 220.

49 Three years later Chrysler took full control of Rootes with a 70 per cent shareholding. The remaining interests of Rootes were acquired by Chrysler in 1973. D. T. Jones, *Maturity and Crisis in the European Car Industry: Structural Change and Public Policy*, Sussex European Papers No. 8, University of Sussex, Brighton, 1981, p. 108.

50 Bardou et al., *Automobile Revolution*, pp. 174–5.

51 Bloomfield, *World Automotive Industry*, p. 183.

52 Jones, Maturity and Crisis, p. 42.

53 Registrations by make were 28,334 (Toyota), 19,480 (Honda), 10,612 (Colt) and 101,735 (Datsun). SMMT, *The Motor Industry of Great Britain*, 1979, Table 23, pp. 55–6.

54 By 1978 the French companies, Renault, Citroën and Peugeot between them accounted for 8.4 per cent of new car registrations in the UK *Ibid.*, Table 23, pp. 55–6.

55 In 1978 Fiat's 72,192 cars accounted for 4.5 per cent of new car registrations. *Ibid.*

56 Other German makes were BMW (0.7 per cent of new car registrations), Mercedes-Benz (0.4 per cent) and Opel (1.4 per cent). *Ibid.*

57 SMMT, *The Motor Industry of Great Britain*, 1979, Table 23, pp. 55–56.

58 Jones, Maturity and Crisis, 1981, p. 25; Rhys, 'Motor Vehicles', p. 194.

59 A. Silberston, 'The Motor Industry', in Duncan Burn (ed.), *The Structure of British Industry: A Symposium*, Cambridge University Press, 1958, Vol. 2, p. 9.

60 Bhaskar, *Future of the UK Motor Industry*, p. 240.

61 *Ibid.*, p. 240; G. Gulvin, 'Donald Gresham Stokes: Motor Vehicle Manufacturer and Salesman', *Dictionary of Business Biography*, London School of Economics, 1986, Vol. 5, p. 349.
62 BMC had previously extended its commercial vehicle interests when it merged with Jaguar in 1966 to form BMH. In 1960 Jaguar had acquired Daimler cars and commercial vehicles and, in 1961, had purchased Guy Motors, a truck producer. Bhaskar, *Future of the UK Motor Industry*, p. 240.
63 Rhys, 'Motor Vehicles', p. 181.
64 Silberston, 'The Motor Industry', p. 9.
65 Ford had formerly taken the whole of the production of Briggs. *Ibid.*
66 Rhys, *Motor Industry*, p. 60.
67 Maxcy and Silberston, *Motor Industry*, p. 27.
68 Rhys, *Motor Industry*, p. 60.
69 *Ibid.*, p. 61.
70 *Ibid.*, pp. 62–3; Silberston, 'The Motor Industry', p. 10.
71 Bhaskar, *Future of the UK Motor Industry*, p. 303; Rhys, *Motor Industry*, p. 60.
72 Stephen Davies, 'Concentration', in Stephen Davies, Bruce Lyons, Hugh Dixon and Paul Geroski (eds.), *Economics of Industrial Orgainsation*, Harlow, Essex: Longman, 1988, Chapter 3, pp. 73–126. J. G. Walshe, 'Industrial Organisation and Competition Policy', in N. F. R. Crafts and Nicholas Woodward (eds.), *The British Economy since 1945*, Oxford: Clarendon Press, 1991, pp. 345–8.
73 Adeney, *Motor Makers*, p. 200.
74 Moodies' Prospectus, 1968.
75 G. C. Allen, *British Industries and Their Organisation*, London: Longman, p. 165.
76 Rhys, *Motor Industry*, p. 25.
77 Adeney, *Motor Makers*, p. 201.
78 Daniel T. Jones, *The Import Threat to the UK Car Industry*, Science Policy Research Unit, University of Sussex, Brighton: 1985, p. 12.
79 Graham Turner, *The Leyland Papers*, London: Eyre and Spottiswoode, 1971, Chapter 6, pp. 88–100.
80 Rhys, *Motor Industry*, p. 379.
81 Dunnett, *Decline*, pp. 106–7.
82 Rhys, *Motor Industry*, pp. 447–52.
83 Central Policy Review Staff, *The Future of the British Car Industry*, London: HMSO, 1975, para. 97, p. 39.
84 Johnman, 'The Labour Party and Industrial Policy', p. 35.
85 Labour Party, 'Report on British Motor Industry', para. 224 (8), p. 65.
86 Justin Davis Smith, *The Atlee and Churchill Administrations and Industrial Unrest 1945–1955: A Study in Consensus*, London: Frances Pinter, 1990. See also Jim Tomlinson, 'The Labour Government and the Trade Unions 1945–51', and Bill Schwarz, 'The Tide of History: The Reconstruction of Conservatism, 1945–51', both in Nick Tiratsoo (ed.), *The Atlee Years*, London: Frances Pinter, 1991.
87 British Leyland Motor Corporation, *Annual Report and Accounts*, 1968, p. 21.
88 See in this respect, S. N. Broadberry and N. F. R. Crafts, 'British Economic Policy in the Early Postwar Period', University of Warwick, mimeo, May 1993.
89 S. J. Prais, *Productivity and Industrial Structure: A Statistical Study of Manufacturing Industry in Britain, Germany and the United States*, Cambridge University Press, 1981, pp. 150 and 155.
90 *Ibid.*, p. 162.
91 *Ibid.*, p. 163.
92 The wider implications of product market explanations, namely competitive behaviour, market positioning and export performance form the focus of Chapter 5.
93 Jones, *Import Threat*, p. 13.

94 K Bhaskar, *The Future of the World Motor Industry*, London: Kagan Paul, 1980, p. 147.

95 Bhaskar, *Future of the UK Motor Industry*, Table 7.1, p. 165.

96 *Ibid.*, Table 7.1, p. 165.

97 *Ibid.*, Table 6.2, p. 140.

98 Rhys, *Motor Industry*, p. 260.

99 Maxcy and Silberston, *Motor Industry*, p. 53.

100 Rhys, *Motor Industry*, p. 261; Maxcy and Silberston, *Motor Industry*, p. 54.

101 Rhys, *Motor Industry*, p. 261.

102 C. F. Pratten, *Economies of Scale in Manufacturing Industry*, University of Cambridge, Department of Applied Economics, 1971, Occasional Papers, No. 2–8, p. 132.

103 David Marsden, Timothy Morris, Paul Willman and Stephen Wood, *The Car Industry: Labour Relations and Industrial Adjustment*, London: Tavistock, 1985, p. 40.

104 R. Vernon 'International Investment and International Trade in the Product Cycle', *Quarterly Journal of Economics*, Vol. 80, 1966, pp. 190–207.

105 William J. Abernathy, *The Productivity Dilemma: Roadblock to Innovation in the Automobile Industry*, Baltimore: John Hopkins University Press, 1978; James P. Womack, Daniel T. Jones and Daniel Roos, *The Machine that Changed the World*, New York: 1990, pp. 21–69. See also Jones, *Maturity and Crisis*; Daniel T. Jones, 'Technology and the UK Automobile Industry', *Lloyds Bank Review*, No. 148, April 1983, pp. 23–5; Jones, *Import Threat*, pp. 14–16.

106 The optimum scale is defined as 'that point at which further mass production ceases to give substantial economies in cost', Maxcy and Silberston, *Motor Industry*, p. 75, quoting the definition of the Ministry of Supply, *National Advisory Council*, para. 16, p. 11.

107 Maxcy and Silberston, *Motor Industry*, p. 57.

108 *Ibid.*

109 *Ibid.*, p. 58.

110 *Ibid.*

111 *Ibid.*, Rhys, *Motor Industry*, p. 265.

112 Rhys, *Motor Industry*, p. 265.

113 Maxcy and Silberston, *Motor Industry*, p. 58; Rhys, *Motor Industry*, p. 265.

114 Rhys, *Motor Industry*, p. 265.

115 Maxcy and Silberston, *Motor Industry*, p. 59; Rhys, *Motor Industry*, p. 265.

116 Wayne Lewchuk, *American Technology and the British Vehicle Industry*, Cambridge University Press, 1987, p. 193.

117 *Ibid.*

118 Rhys, *Motor Industry*, p. 266.

119 *Ibid.*, p. 262.

120 *Ibid.*, p. 368; Thoms and Donnelly, *The Motor Car Industry*, p. 169.

121 Rhys, *Motor Industry*, pp. 368–9; Thoms and Donnely, *The Motor Car Industry*, p. 169.

122 Rhys, *Motor Industry*, p. 53.

123 *Ibid.*, p. 369.

124 Jones, 'Technology', p. 24; Jones, *Import Threat*, pp. 15–16.

125 *Ibid.*

126 Nicholas Owen, *Economies of Scale, Competitiveness, and Trade Patterns within the European Community*, Oxford: Clarendon Press, 1983, p. 69.

127 Jones, 'Technology', p. 24.

128 *Ibid.*; K Williams J. Williams and C. Haslam, *The Breakdown of Austin Rover: A Case Study in the Failure of Business Strategy and Industrial Policy*, Leamington

Spa: Berg, 1987, pp. 36–7.
129 Jones, *Maturity and Crisis*, p. 14.
130 Rhys, *Motor Industry*, p. 280.
131 Dunnett, *Decline*, Table 2.4, p. 23.
132 Bhaskar, *Future of the UK Motor Industry*, p. 25; Pratten, *Economies of Scale*, Table 14.5, p. 149.
133 Bhaskar, *Future of the UK Motor Industry*, p. 25.
134 Maxcy and Silberston, *Motor Industry*, p. 82.
135 Pratten, *Economies of Scale*, p. 138.
136 Rhys, *Motor Industry*, p. 287.
137 *Ibid.*
138 *Ibid.*
139 Maxcy and Silberston, *Motor Industry*, p. 79.
140 Rhys, *Motor Industry*, p. 282.
141 D. G. Rhys, 'European Mass-Producing Car Makers and Minimum Efficient Scale: A Note', *Journal of Industrial Economics*, Vol. 25, June 1977, pp. 313–32.
142 Pratten, *Economies of Scale*, p. 142.
143 Owen, *Economies of Scale*, p. 75.
144 Pratten, *Economies of Scale*, pp. 145–7.
145 Maxcy and Silberston, *Motor Industry*, p. 97; Rhys, *Motor Industry*, p. 296.
146 Rhys, *Motor Industry*, p. 268.
147 Tables 4.1 and 4.2.
148 Marsden et al., *The Car Industry*, Table 32, p. 258.
149 Gerald T. Bloomfield, 'The World Automotive Industry in Transition', in Christopher M. Law (ed.), *Restructuring the Global Automobile Industry: National and Regional Impacts*, London: Routledge, 1991, Table 2.4, p. 37.
150 Bhaskar, *Future of the UK Motor Industry*, Table 3.5, p. 55. Bhaskar based his data on the Central Policy Review Staff Report on *The Future of the British Car Industry*, p. 52, with modifications.
151 House of Commons Expenditure Committee, *The Motor Vehicle Industry*, para. 57, p. 22.
152 Maxcy and Silbeston, *Motor Industry*, p. 120.
153 Bhaskar, *Future of the UK Motor Industry*, p. 155.
154 Williams et al., *Breakdown of Austin Rover*, p. 69.
155 Labour Party, 'Report on British Motor Industry', para. 166, p. 50.
156 *Ibid.*
157 Rhys, *Motor Industry*, p. 315.
158 Karel Williams, John Williams and Dennis Thomas, *Why are the British Bad at Manufacturing?*, London: Routledge Kegan Paul, 1983, Appendix B, Table 2, p. 270 and Table 3, p. 271.
159 *Ibid.*, Appendix B, Table 1, p. 270 and Table 5, p. 271.
160 Political and Economic Planning, *Motor Vehicles*, pp. 129 and 131.
161 *Ibid.*.
162 L. Rostas, *Comparative Productivity in British and American Industry*, Cambridge University Press, 1948, p. 63.
163 Labour Party, Report on British Motor Industry, para. 163, p. 49.
164 Allen, 'The British Motor Industry', p. 164.
165 *Ibid.*, p. 162.
166 Bhaskar, *Future of the UK Motor Industry*, Table 3.19, p. 63.

Notes to Chapter Five

1 The short run price elasticity facing the firm was around − 2.
2 Keith Cowling and John Cubbin, 'Price, Quality, and Advertising Competition: An

Econometric Investigation of the United Kingdom Car Market', *Economica*, Vol. 38, 1971, pp. 378–94.

3 J. Cubbin, 'Quality Change and Price behaviour in the UK Car Industry, 1956–1968', *Economica*, Vol. 42, May 1975, pp. 43–58.

4 SMMT, *The Motor Industry of Great Britain*, 1981, Tables 24 and 25, p. 56; A. Murfin, 'Market Shares in the UK Passenger Market: Marketing, Expenditure and Price Effects, 1975–1980', *Applied Economics*, Vol. 16, 1984, pp. 611–32.

5 T. S. Barker, 'International Trade and Economic Growth: An Alternative to Neo-Classical Theories', *Cambridge Journal of Economics*, Vol. 1, 1977, pp. 153–72; D. Leech and J. Cubbin, 'Import Penetration in the UK Passenger Market: A Cross Section Study', *Applied Economics*, Vol. 10, 1978, pp. 289–303.

6 D. G. Rhys, *The Motor Industry: An Economic Survey*, London: Butterworths, 1972, pp. 332–3.

7 Krish Bhaskar, *The Future of the UK Motor Industry*, London: Kogan Page, 1979, p. 340.

8 D. G. Rhys, 1980, 'Motor Vehicles', in P. S. Johnson (ed.), *The Structure of British Industry*, London: Granada, 1980, p. 197.

9 Bhaskar, *Future of the UK Motor Industry*, p. 340.

10 Keith Cowling and John Cubbin, 'Hedonic Price Indexes for Cars in the UK', *Economic Journal*, September 1972.

11 Rhys, 'Motor Vehicles', p. 197.

12 Sue Bowden, 'Demand and Supply Constraints in the Interwar UK Car Industry: Did the Manufacturers Get It Right?', *Business History*, Vol. 33, No. 2, April 1991, pp. 241–67; Sue Bowden and Paul M. Turner, 'Some Cross Section Evidence on the Determinants of the Diffusion of Car Ownership in the Interwar UK Economy', *Business History*, Vol. 35, No. 1, Jaunary 1993, pp. 55–69.

13 George Maxcy and Aubrey Silberston, *The Motor Industry*, London: Allen and Unwin, 1959, p. 118; Rhys, *Motor Industry*, p. 313.

14 Bhaskar, *Future of the UK Motor Industry*, p. 18; Rhys, *Motor Industry*, pp. 314–15.

15 David Thoms and Tom Donnelly, *The Motor Car Industry in Coventry since the 1890s*, Beckenham, Kent: Croom Helm, 1985, Table 6.5, p. 161 and Table 6.6, p. 162.

16 R. W. Shaw and C. J. Sutton, *Industry and Competition: Industrial Case Studies*, London: Macmillan, 1976, p. 131; Rhys, *Motor Industry*, p. 313.

17 Maxcy and Silberston, *Motor Industry*, p. 115.

18 Rhys, *Motor Industry*, p. 110: Shaw and Sutton, *Industry and Competition*, p. 134.

19 Roy Church, 'Mass Marketing Motor Cars in Britain before 1950: The Missing Dimension', in Richard S. Tedlow and Geoffrey Jones (eds.), *The Rise and Fall of Mass Marketing*, London: Routledge, 1993, p. 53.

20 Martin Adeney, *The Motor Makers: The Turbulent History of Britain's Car Industry*, London: Fontana/Collins, 1988, pp. 196–8, and pp. 217–19.

21 Church, 'Mass Marketing Motor Cars', p. 53.

22 C. Carr, *Britain's Competitiveness: The Management of the Vehicle Components Industry*, London and New York: Routledge, 1990, p. 48.

23 Rhys, *Motor Industry*, pp. 313–14.

24 Daniel T. Jones, 'Technology and the UK Automobile Industry', *Lloyds Bank Review*, No. 148, April 1983, p. 23. Jones notes that by the early 1980s 'Nissan out patents all comers in the UK'.

25 Rhys, *Motor Industry*, p. 313.

26 Karel Williams, John Williams and Dennis Thomas, *Why are the British Bad at Manufacturing?*, London: Routledge Kegan Paul, 1983, pp. 232 and 233.

27 Bhaskar, *Future of the UK Motor Industry*, Table 3.14, p. 69.

28 Williams et al., *Why are the British Bad at Manufacturing?*.
29 *Ibid.* p. 231.
30 Central Policy Review Staff, *The Future of the British Car Industry*, London: HMSO, 1975.
31 Williams, et al., *Why are the British Bad at Manufacturing?*.
32 Maxcy and Silberston, *Motor Industry*, p. 112.
33 Williams et al., *Why are the British Bad at Manufacturing?*, p.223.
34 *Ibid.*, Appendix B, Table 3, p. 271.
35 With the exception of 1967. Together they failed to take 20 per cent of the market after 1970. *Ibid.*, Appendix B, Table 3, p. 271.
36 *Ibid.*, p. 223 and Appendix B, Tables 4 and 5, p. 271.
37 *Ibid.*, p. 234.
38 *Ibid.*, p. 232.
39 *Ibid.*, Appendix C, Table 3, p. 277.
40 *Ibid.*, pp. 242–3.
41 R. Whipp and P. Clark, *Innovation and the Auto Industry: Product Process and Work Organisation*, London: Frances Pinter, 1986.
42 M. Edwardes *Back from the Brink: An Apocalyptic Experience*, London: Collins, 1983, pp. 175–7; G. Robson, *The Metro*, Cambridge: Patrick Stephens, 1982.
43 Williams et al., *Why are the British Bad at Manufacturing?*, Appendix C, Table 3, p. 277.
44 Bhaskar, *Future of the UK Motor Industry*, p. 137; Williams et al. *Why are the British Bad at Manufacturing?*, p. 76.
45 E. Seidler, *Let's Call it Fiesta: The Autobiography of Ford's Project Bobcat*, Bar Hill, Cambridge: Patrick Stephens, 1976.
46 Emmission requirements had to be satisfied and an air conditioning option added. A different battery was necessary because the European model was not readily available in the United States for replacement.
47 Monopolies and restrictive Practices Commission, *Report on the Supply of Electrical Equipment for Mechanically Propelled Land Vehicles*, London: HMSO, 1963.
48 Monopolies and Restrictive Practices Commission, *Report on the Supply and Export of Pneumatic Tyres*, London: HMSO, 1955.
49 K. C. Johnson-Davies, *The Practice of Retail Price Maintenance: With Particular Reference to the Motor Industry*, London: Iliffe and Sons, 1955; Rhys, *Motor Industry*, p. 335.
50 G. C. Allen, *British Industries and Their Organisation*, London: Longman, 1970 edition, p. 174; Rhys, *Motor Industry*, pp. 335–8.
51 Rhys, *Motor Industry*, p. 335.
52 Allen, *British Industries*, p. 174; Rhys, *Motor Industry*, pp. 335–6.
53 Williams et al., *Why are the British Bad at Manufacturing?*, pp. 233–4.
54 Bhaskar, *Future of the UK Motor Industry*, p. 349 and Table 14.5, p. 353.
55 Central Policy Review Staff, quoted in Bhaskar, *Future of the UK Motor Industry*, p. 351.
56 Bhaskar, *Future of the UK Motor Industry*, p. 351; Rhys, *Motor Industry*, p. 197.
57 Bhaskar, *Future of the UK Motor Industry*, p. 355.
58 *Ibid.*, Table 14.5, p. 353.
59 Rhys, *Motor Industry*, Table 7.2, p. 229. The absence of data recording total sales of used commercial vehicles and cars precludes the estimation of percentage figures.
60 Consumer Credit, *Report of the Committee*, (Crowther Committee), Cmnd 4596, London: HMSO: Vol, 1, *Report*; Vol. 2, *Appendices*, Table A34, p. 456.
61 *Ibid.*, p. 463.
62 *Ibid.*
63 We are grateful to Andrew Coutts and Peter Moizier for their help and advice in

relation to the evaluation of the financial performance of the motor industry.

64 Central Policy Review Staff, *Future of the British Car Industry*, p. 87; House of Commons, *British Leyland: The Next Decade*, (Ryder Report), 23 April 1975, House of Commons Paper 342, pp. 1974/5, Summary, para. 28, p. 6; Chapter 8, para. 8.11, p. 29; Chapter 13, para. 14.4, p. 61 and para. 14.7, pp. 61–2.

65 House of Commons, Expenditure Committee Report, *The Motor Vehicle Industry*, Chapter 6, para. 90, p. 36 and para. 96, p. 39.

66 With the exception of a small fallback in 1957.

67 A. W. Goudie and G. Meeks, *Company Finance and Performance: Aggregated Financial Accounts for Individual British Industries*, University of Cambridge, Department of Applied Economics, 1986.

68 Rhys, *Motor Industry*, p. 367.

69 There are problems in comparing one firm with another and one particular firm over a period of time due to factors such as product mix changes, mergers and acquisitions.

70 Rhys, *Motor Industry*, p. 361.

71 House of Commons Expenditure Committee Report, *The Motor Vehicle Industry*, para. 31, p. 11.

72 *Ibid.* See also Williams et al., *Why are the British Bad at Manufacturing?*, pp. 246–8. Williams also maintains that profit was inflated by taking closure costs as special extraordinary items after profit had been declared and that this practice allowed BL to record small pre-tax profits rather than small pre-tax losses in 1970 and 1974. *Ibid.*, p. 248.

73 House of Commons, *British Leyland: The Next Decade*, para. 17, p. 4.

74 House of Commons Expenditure Committee Report, *The Motor Vehicle Industry*, Chapter 8, para. 132, p. 52.

75 *Ibid.*, p. 56.

76 BMC and BMH, *Annual Reports and Accounts*.

77 Vauxhall, *Annual Report and Accounts*.

78 *Annual Report and Accounts*, 1956–79 inclusive: Ford, BMC, BMH, BLMC and Vauxhall.

79 Ford, *Annual Reports and Accounts*.

80 BLMC, *Annual Reports and Accounts*.

81 Ford, *Annual Reports and Accounts*.

82 Goudie and Meeks, Company Finance and Performance.

83 Vauxhall, *Annual Reports and Accounts*, 1956–79.

84 House of Commons Expenditure Committee Report, *The Motor Vehicle Industry*, para. 141, p. 56.

85 Thoms and Donnelly, *The Motor Car Industry*, p. 204.

86 Rhys, *Motor Industry*, pp. 368 and 369.

87 Maxcy and Silberston, *Motor Industry*, p. 177.

88 House of Commons, *British Leyland: The Next Decade*, Annex 4.1, p. 22.

89 Goudie and Meeks, *Company Finance and Performance*.

90 Maxcy and Silberston, *Motor Industry*, Table 18, p. 177.

91 *Ibid.*, pp. 176–7.

92 Rhys, *Motor Industry*, p. 367.

93 *Ibid.*, Table 10.8, p. 367.

94 *Ibid.*, pp. 367–8.

95 House of Commons Expenditure Committee Report, *The Motor Vehicle Industry*, para. 139, p. 55.

96 Rhys, *Motor Industry*, p. 366.

97 *Ibid.*

98 *Ibid.*

99 House of Commons, *British Leyland: The Next Decade*, Chapter 4, p. 19.
100 Bhaskar, *Future of the UK Motor Industry*, Table 3.12, p. 67; House of Commons, *British Leyland: The Next Decade*, Chapter 4, Table 4.3, p. 20.
101 House of Commons, *British Leyland: The Next Decade*, p. 20.
102 Bhaskar, *Future of the UK Motor Industry*, p. 66.
103 House of Commons Expenditure Committee Report, *The Motor Vehicle Industry*, para. 90, p. 36.
104 *Ibid.*, Chapter 8, para. 133, p. 52.
105 Keith Boyfield, *BL: Changing Gear*, London: Centre for Policy Studies, 1983, p. 5.
106 S. J. Prais, *Productivity and Industrial Structure: A Statistical Study of Manufacturing Industry in Britain, Germany and the United States*, Cambridge University Press, 1981, p. 164.
107 Williams et al., *Why are the British Bad at Manfuacturing?*, Appendix C, Table 3, p. 277. In the 1970s, the Cortina achieved new registrations of 187,000 in 1972, 182,000 in 1973 and 194,000 in 1978.
108 Estimated from *ibid.*, Appendix B, Table 2, p. 270 and Appendix C, Table 3, p. 277.
109 In 1946 world production of cars amounted to 3 million; but 1973 it had reached just under 30 million. Production of commercial vehicles grew from 5 million in 1946 to 30 milion in 1970. J. P. Bardou, J. J. Chanaron, P. Fridenson and J. M. Laux, *The Automobile Revolution: The Impact of an Industry*, Chapel Hill: University of North Carolina Press, 1982, p. 171.
110 The number of countries with manufacturing and assembly plants grew from 50 in 1962 to 71 in 1972. G. T. Bloomfield, *The World Automotive Industry*, Newton Abbott 1978, p. 326.
111 Peter Hennessy, *Never Again, Britain 1945–1951*, London: Jonathon Cape, 1992, p. 106.
112 Hennessy, *Never Again*, p. 429.
113 Williams et al. *Why are the British Bad at Manufacturing?*, p. 236. In 1949 exports were valued at £64,314 million: Rhys, *Motor Industry*, Table 11.4, p. 418.
114 Williams et al., *Why are the British Bad at Manufacturing?*, p. 236.
115 *Ibid.*, p. 236–7.
116 Hennessy, *Never Again*, p. 429.
117 M. Adeney, *The Motor Makers: The Turbulent History of Britain's Car Industry*, London: Fontana/Collins, p. 195.
118 Rhys, *Motor Industry*, p. 40; Bardou et al., *Automobile Revolution*, p. 173.
119 Rhys, *Motor Industry*, p. 40; Thoms and Donnelly, *The Motor Car Industry*, p. 157.
120 Adeney, *Motor Makers*, p. 206.
121 House of Commons Expenditure Committee Report, *The Motor Vehicle Industry*, para. 26, p. 9.
122 Williams et al., *Why are the British Bad at Manufacturing?*, p. 237.
123 *Ibid.*
124 Daniel T. Jones, *Maturity and Crisis in the European Car Industry: Structural Change and Public Policy*, Sussex European Papers No. 8, University of Sussex, Brighton, 1981, Table 3, p. 89.
125 Nicholas Owen, *Economies of Scale, Competitiveness, and Trade Patterns within the European Community*, Oxford: Clarendon Press, 1983, p. 52.
126 *Ibid.*, Table 4.6, p. 55.
127 Rhys, 'Motor Vehicles' p. 187.
128 *Ibid.*, p. 194.

Notes to Chapter Six

1 For example, *Report of the Royal Commission on Trade Unions and Employers'*

Associations 1965–1968, (Donavon Report) Cmnd 3623, London: HMSO, 1968.

2 H. A. Turner, G. Clack and G. Roberts, *Labour Relations in the Motor Industry: A Study of Industrial Unrest and an International Comparison*, London: Allen and Unwin, 1967.

3 K. J. Williams, J. Williams and C. Haslam, *The Breakdown of Austin Rover: A Case Study in the Failure of Business Strategy and Industrial Policy*, Leamington Spa: Berg, 1987.

4 For example, W. Lewchuk, *American Technology and the British Motor Industry*, Cambridge University Press, 1987, pp. 214–15.

5 For example, J. P. Bardou, J. J. Chanaron, P. Friedenson and J. M. Laux, *The Automobile Revolution: The Impact of an Industry*, Chapel Hill: University of North Carolina Press, 1982, p. 119.

6 E. Wigham, *The Power to Manage: History of the Engineering Employers Federation*, London: Macmillan, 1973.

7 R. Loveridge, 'Business Strategy and Community Culture', in D. Dunkerly and G. Salaman (eds.), *The International Yearbook of Organizational Studies*, London: Routledge Kegan Paul, 1982.

8 H. A. Turner and J. Bescoby, 'An analysis of Post War Labour Disputes in the British Car Manufacturing Firms', *Manchester School*, Vol. 29, May 1961, pp. 133–60.

9 H. A Turner, G. Clack and G. Roberts, *Labour Relations in the Motor Industry: A Study of Industrial Unrest and an International Comparison*, London: George Allen and Unwin, 1967, p. 215; H. Beynon, *Working for Ford*, Harmondsworth; Penguin, 1973, Chapter 2.

10 S. Tolliday, 'Ford and Fordism in Post War Britain: Enterprise Management and the Control of Labour 1937–1987', in S. Tolliday and J. Zeitlin (eds.), *The Power to Manage? Employers and Industrial Relations in Comparative Historical Perspective*, London and New York: Routledge, 1991.

11 For example, Beynon, *Working for Ford*, pp. 75–6, 117–19. Writing in the mid 1960s Turner and associates maintained the tracks were not significant flash points for disputes, as might be expected if track tasks were oppressively tedious. They contend 'tedium' was a counter in bargaining. Turner et al., *Labour Relations*, pp. 168–9; House of Commons Expenditure Committee Report, *The Motor Vehicle Industry*, p. 86.

12 G. Lanning, C. Peaker, C. Webb and R. White, *Making Cars: A History of Car Making at Cowley by the People Who Make Cars*, London: Routledge Kegan Paul, 1985, p. 73.

13 Motor Manufacturing Economic Development Council, *Shiftworking in the Motor Industry*, London: NEDO, 1976.

14 E.g. H. F. Gospel, *Markets, Firms and the Management of Labour in Modern Britain*, Cambridge University Press, 1992, pp. 131–3.

15 David Simpson made his first visit to York as a manager for Chrysler in the late 1960s. The dispute concerned whether a new piece rate should be negotiated because the angle of welding of the accelerator pedal on to the stalk had been changed.

16 G. Whalen, interview.

17 Lanning et al., *Making Cars*,, pp. 84–5.

18 E.g. Beynon, *Working for Ford*, p. 149.

19 W. Lewchuk, *American Technology and the British Vehicle Industry*, Cambridge Univesity Press, 1987, p. 166.

20 House of Commons Expenditure Committee Report, *The Motor Vehicle Industry*, pp. 82–3.

21 However, Eric Lord, a former Cowley manager, disagreed that abolition of

piecework was necessary. Lanning et al., *Making Cars*.

22 At the MG plant at Abingdon measured day work still was unnecessary at the beginning of the 1970s because of the lower output volumes. A. Thompson, interview with J. F.-P. 1993; Lewchuk, *American Technology*. Supervision in BLMC was increased from one foreman to 50–60 hourly rated workers under piecework to one to every 20–25 by the mid 1970s. House of Commons Expenditure Committee Report, *The Motor Vehicle Industry*, p. 78.

23 Stephen Johns, *Victimization at Cowley*, London: Workers Revolutionary Party, Pocket Book No. 11, n.d., 1975? p. 37.

24 British Leyland, BL Body and Assembly Division Oxford Area, *Management Presentation to Trade Unions 7 November 1973*, Cowley: Nuffield Press. Over the previous four years there had been substantial investment in the Allegro production facilities, there had been consultation over redevelopment of Assembly Plant North Works, and job enrichment was being studied by a BL team sent to Volvo and SAAB.

25 A BL internal management letter was intercepted and copied to shop stewards who arranged a walkout on the basis of what they had read before any announcement or discussion, or even before the memo had reached its intended destination. Lanning et al., *Making Cars*, p. 82.

26 British Leyland, *The Japanese Motor Vehicle Industry: Report of British Leyland Study Tour June–July 1975*, Cowley: Nuffield Press, 1975.

27 House of Commons, *British Leyland: The Next Decade*, pp. 31–8. The formula for this experiment in industrial democracy was sketched out by Harry Urwin, deputy chairman of the NEB, and deputy general secretary of the TGWU.

28 G. Whalen, interview; A. Thornett, 'History of the Trade Unions in Cowley', in T. Hayter and D. Harvey (eds.), *The Factory and the City: The Story of the Cowley Automobile Workers in Oxford*, London: Mansell, 1993, pp. 107–11.

29 H. F. Gospel, *Markets, Firms and the Management of Labour in Modern Britain*, Cambridge University Press, 1992.

30 K. Bhaskar, *Future of the UK Motor Industry*, London: Kogan Page, 1979, p. 74; P. J. S. Dunnett, *The Decline of the British Motor Industry: The Effects of Government Policy, 1945–1979*, London: Croom Helm, 1980, p. 142; D. G. Rhys, *The Motor Industry: An Economic Survey*, London: Butterworths, 1972, p. 446; Turner et al., *Labour Relations*, p. 204.

31 Thornett, 'Trade Unions in Cowley'.

32 Beynon, *Working for Ford*, Chapter 11.

33 Rhys, *Motor Industry*, Table 12.7, p. 448.

34 *Ibid.*, p. 451.

35 Turner et al., *Labour Relations*, p. 145.

36 E.g. *ibid.*, p. 164.

37 Bhaskar, *Future of the UK Motor Industry*, p. 73; Rhys, *Motor Industry*, p. 453.

38 Lanning et al., *Making Cars*.

39 Turner et al., *Labour Relations*, p. 117.

40 House of Commons Expenditure Committee Report, *The Motor Vehicle Industry*, pp. 80–1.

41 *Ibid.*, p. 74.

42 D. Marsden, T. Morris, P. Willman and S. Wood, *The Car Industry: Labour Relations and Industrial Adjustment*, London and New York: Tavistock, 1985, pp. 134–5.

43 House of Commons Expenditure Committee Report, *The Motor Vehicle Industry*, p. 74.

44 J. Foreman-Peck, 'The Motor Industry', in M. Casson (ed.), *Multinationals and World Trade: Vertical Integration and the Division of Labour in World Industries*,

London: Allen and Unwin, 1986, pp. 141–73.
45 See also the discussion in chapter 4, pp. 115–16.
46 K. Bhaskar, *The Future of the World Motor Industry*, London: Kogan Page, 1980, p. 147.
47 Bhaskar, *Future of the UK Motor Industry*, Table 7.1, p. 165.
48 S. J. Prais, *Productivity and Industrial Structure*, Cambridge University Press, 1981, p. 161.
49 S. J. Prais and D. T. Jones, 'Plant Size and Productivity in the Motor Industry', *Oxford Bulletin of Economics and Statistics*, 1986.
50 Prais, *Productivity and Industrial Structure*, p. 163.
51 House of Commons Expenditure Committee Report, *The Motor Vehicle Industry*, p. 85.
52 U. Jürgens, T. Malsche and K. Dohse, *Breaking from Taylorism: Changing Forms of Work in the Automobile Industry*, Cambridge University Press, 1993, chapter 8.
53 Bill Hayden told Ford managers in the mid 1970s to get back control over the shopfloor at any cost.
54 T. Nichols, *The British Worker Question*, London: Routledge Kegan Paul, 1986, Chapters 4, 5, 8.
55 P. Willman, *Technological Change, Collective Bargaining and Industrial efficiency*, Oxford: Clarendon Press, 1986, Chapters 7 and 8; W. Streeck (ed.), *Industrial Relations and Technical Change in the British, Italian and German Automobile Industries: Three Case Studies*, Berlin: Science Centre of Berlin for Social Research, 1985.
56 P. Willman and G. Winch, *Innovation and Management Control: Labour Relations at BL Cars*, Cambridge University Press, 1987.
57 Loveridge, 'Business Strategy', p. 46.
58 R. Whipp and P. Clark, *Innovation and the Auto Industry: Product, Process and Work Organization*, London: Frances Pinter, 1986.
59 Bhaskar, *Future of the UK Motor Industry*, p. 172; Central Policy Review Staff, *The Future of the British Car Industry*, London: HMSO, 1975; Rhys, *Motor Industry*, pp. 456–9; Turner et al., *Labour Relations*, p. 184.
60 D. Simpson interview, with J. F. P.
61 Rhys, *Motor Industry*, p. 459.
62 Central Policy Review Staff, *Future of the British Car Industry*, p. 39; Bhaskar, *Future of the UK Motor Industry*; Prais, *Productivity and Industrial Structure*; Rhys, *Motor Industry*.
63 Tolliday, 'Ford and Fordism'.
64 Whipp and Clark, *Innovation*, p. 130.

Notes to Chapter Seven

1 D. G. Rhys, *The Motor Industry: An Economic Survey*, London: Butterworths, 1972, p. 247.
2 A. G. Armstrong and J. C. Odling-Smee, 'The Demand for New Cars: II, An Empirical Model for the UK', *Bulletin of the Oxford University Institute of Statistics and Economics*, Vol. 41, 1979, pp. 193–214.
3 Rhys, *Motor Industry*, p. 373.
4 Sue Bowden and Paul Turner, 'Stop–Go, Hire Purchase and the British Motor Vehicle Industry', Paper presented at the 1993 meeting of the Quantitative Economic History Study Group, Universtity of York, 9 September 1993.
5 See, for example, Peter Dunnett, *The Decline of the British Motor Industry: The Effects of Government Policy, 1945–1979*, London: Croom Helm, 1980, pp. 50, 81 and 115–16.
6 *Ibid.*, p. 81.

7 *Ibid.*, p. 116.
8 Sue Bowden and Paul Turner, 'The Demand for Consumer Durables in the United Kingdom in the Interwar Period', *Journal of Economic History*, Vol. 53, No. 2, June 1993, p. 245.
9 K. C. Johnson-Davies, *The Practice of Retail Price Maintenance: With Particular Reference to the Motor Industry*, London: Iliffe and Son, 1955, p. 30.
10 M. J. H. Mogridge, *The Car Market; A Study of the Statics and Dynamics of Supply–Demand Equilibrium*, London: Pion, 1983, p. iv.
11 Sue Bowden and Avner Offer, 'Household Appliances and the Use of Time: The United States and Britain since the 1920s', *Economic History Review*, Vol. 47, No. 4, November 1994.
12 K. Bhaskar, *The Future of the UK Motor Industry*, London, Kogan Page, 1979, p. 105.
13 *Ibid.*, p. 106.
14 G. Maxcy and A. Silberston, *The Motor Industry*, London: Allen and Unwin, 1959, p. 46; A. Silberston, 'Hire Purchase Controls and the Demand for Cars', *Economic Journal*, Vol. 43, No. 289, March 1963, p. 35.
15 Maxcy and Silberston, *Motor Industry*, p. 47, n. 1.
16 Bhaskar, *Future of the UK Motor Industry*, p. 106.
17 D. G. Rhys, 'Motor Vehicles', in P. S. Johnson (ed.), *The Structure of British Industry*, London: Granada, 1980, p. 189.
18 This section draws heavily on Bowden and Turner, 'Stop–Go'. We are grateful to Paul Turner for allowing us to draw on this paper and for his comments and advice in relation to demand management policies in this period.
19 Petrol rationing ended in the first quarter of 1957. Dunnett, *Decline*, p. 62.
20 *Ibid.*, p. 92.
21 Rhys, *Motor Industry*, p. 244, quoting estimates given in the *Sunday Times*, 11 November 1960.
22 Balance of payments and car registration data for the 1950s and 1960s taken from Central Statistical Office, *Economic Trends, Annual Supplement*, 1991, Tables 29 and 8 respectively.
23 Dunnett, *Decline*, p. 92, quoting estimates given in *The Times*, 4 December 1967.
24 R. C. O. Matthews, 'The Role of Demand Management', in Sir Alec Cairncross (ed.), *Britain's Economic Prospects Reconsidered*, London: George Allen and Unwin, 1971, p. 29; Jim Tomlinson, *Public Policy and the Economy since 1900*, Oxford: Clarendon Press, p. 259.
25 Martin Adeney, *The Motor Makers: The Turbulent History of Britain's Car Industry*, London: Fontana/Collins, 1988, pp. 210–11; Rhys, 'Motor Vehicles' p. 204; Bhaskar, *Future of the UK Motor Industry*, p. 15.
26 Adeney, *Motor Makers*, p. 211.
27 Bhaskar, *Future of the UK Motor Industry*, p. 15.
28 Rhys, 'Motor Vehicles', p. 204.
29 Dunnett, *Decline*.
30 Adeney, *Motor Makers*, pp. 210–11; Bhaskar, *Future of the UK Motor Industry*, p. 15; Rhys, *Motor Industry*, p. 204.
31 Dunnett, *Decline*, p. 62.
32 *Ibid.*, p. 91.
33 *Ibid.*, Rhys, *Motor Industry*, p. 369.
34 S. J. Prais, *Productivity and Industrial Structure*, Cambridge University Press, 1981, p. 160 and n. 33, p. 356.
35 Matthews, 'The Role of Demand Management', p. 29.
36 Bowden and Turner, 'Stop–Go', p. 2 and Table 1, p. 3.
37 Silberston, 'Hire Purchase Controls', p. 46.

38 HP Information, *Monthly Statistical Returns*, Private Cars: Registration by Makes of Hire Purchase Agreements, Finance Houses Association, London.

39 Calculated from Table 5 of Armstrong and Odling-Smee, 'Demand for New Cars'.

40 Matthews, 'The Role of Demand Management', p. 28 and 29.

41 Evidence of Sir Douglas Wass, Permanent Secretary at the Treasury. Reported in House of Commons Expenditure Committee Report, *The Motor Vehicle Industry*, para. 85, p. 34.

42 *Ibid.*

43 E.g. Adeney, *Motor Makers*, and Rhys, *Motor Industry*.

44 Quoted in Adeney, *Motor Makers*, p. 210.

45 Bowden and Turner, 'Stop–Go', pp. 20–1.

46 Rhys, 'Motor Vehicles', p. 204.

47 Adeney, *Motor Makers*, p. 229; Rhys, 'Motor Vehicles', p. 77.

48 D. Keeble, *Industrial Location and Planning in the United Kingdom*, London: Methuen, 1976; B. Moore and J. Rhodes, *The Effects of Government Regional Economic Policy*, London: HMSO, Department of Trade and Industry, 1986.

49 S. Tolliday, 'Ford and Fordism in Post War Britain: Enterprise Management and the Control of Labour 1937–1987', in S. Tolliday and J. Zeitlin (eds.), *The Power to Manage? Employers and Industrial Relations in Comparative Historical Perspective*, London and New York: Routledge, 1991.

50 Philip Garrahan and Paul Stewart, *The Nissan Enigma: Flexibility at Work in a Local Economy*, London: Mansell, 1992.

51 D. Hague and G. Wilkinson, *The IRC: An Experiment in Industrial Intervention: A History of the Industrial Reorganisation Corporation*, London: George Allen and Unwin, 1983; Graham Turner, *The Leyland Papers*, London: Eyre and Spottiswoode, 1971, Chapter 8, pp. 120–50.

52 Established by the Labour government in 1966, and abolished by the Conservatives in 1971, the IRC in a short period greatly influenced the evolution of the motor industry.

53 House of Commons Expenditure Committee Report, *The Motor Vehicle Industry*, para. 37, p. 13.

54 House of Commons, *British Leyland: The Next Decade*, London: HMSO, HC342, 1975.

55 S. Wilks, *Industrial Policy and the Motor Industry*, Manchester University Press (1984), 1988 edition.

56 E.g. Wilks.

57 Dunnett, *Decline*, p. 183.

58 *Ibid.*, pp. 159.

59 Ben Pimlott, *Harold Wilson*, London: Harper Collins, 1992, p. 672.

60 Reg Varley, the Industry Minister, was convinced that the company should not be rescued. Tony Benn is said to have been the only Cabinet Minister to have favoured nationalisation. Harold Wilson and Dennis Healey were ultimately won round to the case for a rescue package. D. Thoms and T. Donnelly, *The Motor Car Industry in Coventry since the 1890s*, Beckenham, Kent: Croom Helm, 1985, pp. 218–19.

61 Wilks, *Industrial Policy*, p. 285; Thoms and Donnelly, *The Motor Car Industry*, p. 219.

62 Pimlott, *Harold Wilson*, p. 672.

63 Thoms and Donnelly, *The Motor Car Industry*, p. 219.

64 *Ibid.*, pp. 219–20.

65 M. Edwardes, *Back from the Brink: An Apocalyptic Experience*, London: Collins, 1983.

66 Wilks, *Industrial Policy*, p. 199.

67 Cf. S. Young and N. Hood, *Chrysler UK: A Corporation in Transition*, New York:

Praeger, 1977; M. Casson, 'Foreign Divestment and International Rationalisation: The Sale of Chrysler UK to Peugeot', in J. Coyne and M. Wright (eds.), *Divestment and Strategic Change*, London: Philip Allan, 1986.

68 Casson, 'Foreign Divestment'.

69 Geoffrey Whalen, interview with J. Foreman-Peck.

70 'The Fixing of John Zachary De Lorean', *The Economist*, 23 October 1982, pp. 23–4.

Notes to Chapter Eight

1 The term 'lean production' was coined by Womack, Jones and Roos in their seminal investigation of the changing nature of competitiveness in the global automobile industry. J. Womack, D. Jones and D. Roos, *The Machine that Changed the World*, London: Macmillan, 1990.

2 U. Jürgen, T. Malsch and K. Dohse, *Breaking from Taylorism: Changing Forms of Work in the Automobile Industry*, Cambridge University Press, 1993, pp. 31–3; A. Campbell, 'The Battleground Approach to Workforce Adjustment: United Kingdom', in P. Auer (ed.), *Workforce Adjustment Patterns in the Steel and Automobile Industry*, Brussels: Commission of the European Communities, 1991, pp. 262–5.

3 D. Thoms and T. Donnelly, *The Motor Car Industry in Coventry since the 1890s*, London: Croom Helm, 1985, pp. 209–10.

4 *Ibid.*, pp. 220–3.

5 D. Marsden, T. Morris, P. Willman and S. Wood, *The Car Industry: Labour Relations and Industrial Adjustment*, London: Tavistock, 1985, p. 81.

6 D. Sims and M. Wood, 'Car Manufacture at Linwood: The Regional Policy Issues', unpublished paper, Paisley College, 1984, pp. 64–6.

7 A. Rajan and M. Thompson, *Economic Significance of the UK Motor Vehicle Manufacturing Industry*, London: Institute of Manpower Studies, 1989, pp. 31–3.

8 E. Silva, 'Labour and Technology in the Car Industry: Ford Strategies in Britain and Brazil', unpublished PhD thesis, Imperial College, London, 1988, p. 150.

9 *European Motor Business*, August 1990, p. 12.

10 D. T. Jones, *The Import Threat to the UK Car Industry*, Science Policy Research Unit, University of Sussex, Brighton, 1985.

11 K. Williams, J. Williams and C. Haslam, *The Breakdown of Austin Rover: A Case-Study in the Failure of Business Strategy and Industrial Policy*, Leamington Spa: Berg, 1987, p. 2.

12 P. Dunnett, *The Decline of the British Motor Industry: The Effects of Government Policy 1945–1979*, London: Croom Helm, pp. 159–60.

13 *Motor Business*, 1979, No. 97.

14 House of Lords Select Committee on the European Community, *The Distribution, Servicing and Pricing of Motor Vehicles*, London: HMSO, p. xliii.

15 Commission of the European Community, *Concentration, Competition and Competitiveness in the Automobile Industries*, Luxembourg, 1983, p. 98.

16 *Motor Business*, 1980, No. 104.

17 P. Geroski and A. Murfin, 'Advertising and the Dynamics of Market Structure: The UK Car Industry', *British Journal of Management*, Vol. 1, No. 2, 1990, pp. 82–3; S. Young, N. Hood and J. Hamill, *Foreign Multinationals and the British Economy: Impact and Policy*, London: Croom Helm, 1988, pp. 87, 225.

18 Central Policy Review Staff, *The Future of the British Car Industry*, London: HMSO, 1975, pp. 71–2.

19 *Motor Business*, 1981, No. 108, p. 12.

20 G. Bloomfield, 'The World Automotive Industry in Transition', in C. Law (ed.), *Restructuring the Global Automobile Industry: National and Regional Impacts*,

London: Routledge, 1991, pp. 52–7.

21 I. Robertson, *The UK Passenger Car Market*, London: Economist Intelligence Unit, 1989, p. 29.

22 D. Noble, 'Industry Dynamics in Europe: The Motor Industry', in S. Young and J. Hamill (eds.), *Europe and the Multinationals: Issues and Responses for the 1990s*, Aldershot, Edward Elgar, 1992, pp. 108–9.

23 Monopolies and Mergers Commission, *A Report on the Supply of New Motor Cars within the United Kingdom*, London: HMSO, 1992, Vol. 1, p. 29.

24 *Ibid.*, p. 34.

25 Monopolies and Mergers Commission, *Report on the Supply of new Motor Cars*, Vol. 1, p. 26.

26 A. Altschuler, M. Anderson, D. Jones, D. Roos and J. Womack, *The Future of the Automobile: The Report of MIT's International Programme*, London: Allen and Unwin, 1984; M. A. Fuss and L. Waverman, *Costs and Productivity in Automobile Production: The Challenge of Japanese Efficiency*, Cambridge University Press, 1992.

27 P. Roots, 'Do Companies Get the Trade Unions they Deserve?', Trent Business School Open Lectures on Industrial Relations, Trent Polytechnic, 6 November 1984.

28 F. Mueller, 'Flexible Working Practices in Engine Plants: Evidence from the European Automobile Industry', *Industrial Relations Journal*, Vol. 23, No. 3, autumn 1992, pp. 191–204; Jürgens, Malsch and Dohse, *Breaking from Taylorism*, 190–4, 381–2, for example.

29 For an overview see J. Storey, *Developments in the Management of Human Resources: An Analytical Review*, Oxford: Basil Blackwell, 1992.

30 S. Wilks, *Industrial Policy and the Motor Industry*, Manchester University Press, 1988, pp. 205–9. Although Michael Edwardes wrote that BL's relations with Labour were more workable than with the following Conservatives because with the Callaghan government BL knew where it stood. M. Edwardes, *Back from the Brink: An Apocalyptic Experience*, London: Collins, 1983, pp. 210–11.

31 P. Willman, 'Labour-Relations Strategy at BL Cars', in S. Tolliday and J. Zeitlin (eds.), *The Automobile Industry and its Workers: Between Fordism and Flexibility*, Oxford: Polity Press, 1986.

32 H. Scarbrough, 'Maintenance Workers and New Technology: The Case of Longbridge', *Industrial Relations Journal*, Vol. 15, No. 4, 1984, p. 12.

33 R. Martin, *Bargaining Power*, Oxford: Clarendon Press, pp. 148–9.

34 Williams et al., *Breakdown of Austin Rover*, pp. 14–34.

35 N. MacErlean, 'Carmakers' Fortunes', *Accountancy*, No. 111, June 1993, pp. 30–3.

36 D. Smith, 'Industrial Restructuring and the Labour Force: The Case of Austin Rover in Longbridge, Birmingham', in C. M. Law (ed.), *Restructuring*, p. 235.

37 D. Smith, 'The Japanese Example in South West Birmingham', *Industrial Relations Journal*, Vol. 19, No. 1, spring 1988, pp. 41–50.

38 E. Rose and T. Wooley, 'Shifting Sands? Trade Unions and Productivity at Rover Cars', *Industrial Relations Journal*, Vol. 23, No. 4, winter 1992, p. 257–67.

39 MacErlean, 'Carmakers' Fortunes'.

40 Proceedings at an Extraordinary Meeting of the Rover Group Joint Negotiating Committee, 28 October 1991–2 March 1992.

41 See K. Starkey and A. McKinlay, *Strategy and the Human Resource: Ford and the Search for Competitive Advantage*, Oxford: Blackwell, 1993, chapter 3.

42 S. Tolliday, 'Ford and Fordism in Post War Britain: Enterprise Management and the Control of Labour 1937–1987', in S. Tolliday and J. Zeitlin (eds.), *The Power to Manage? Employers and Industrial Relations in Comparative-Historical Perspective*, London and New York: Routledge, 1991, p. 101.

43 P. Willman, *Technological Change, Collective Bargaining and Industrial Efficiency*, Oxford: Clarendon Press, pp. 160–1, 210–11.
44 Tolliday, 'Ford and Fordism', pp. 102–3.
45 *Financial Times*, 10 November 1987.
46 R. Kaplinsky, 'Restructuring the Capitalist Labour Process: Some Lessons from the Car Industry', *Cambridge Journal of Economics*, Vol. 12, No. 4, 1988, pp. 451–70.
47 N. Oliver and B. Wilkinson, *The Japanization of British Industry: New Developments in the 1990s*, Oxford: Basil Blackwell, 1990, pp. 110–13.
48 P. Wickens, *The Road to Nissan: Flexibility, Quality, Teamwork*, London: Macmillan, 1987.
49 *Ibid.*, pp. 148–52.
50 *Ibid.*, 124–5.
51 P. Garrahan and P. Stewart, *The Nissan Enigma: Flexibility at Work in a Local Economy*, London: Mansell, 1992, p. 59.
52 G. Sewell and B. Wilkinson, ' "Someone to watch over me": Surveillance, Discipline and the Just-in-Time Labour Process', *Sociology*, Vol. 26, 1992, pp. 271–89.
53 Garrahan and Stewart, *The Nissan Enigma*, p. 73.
54 F. Devine, *Affluent Workers Revisited: Privatism and the Working Class*, Edinburgh University Press, 1992, pp. 101, 157–8, 184, for Vauxhall.
55 A. Amin and I. Smith, 'Vertical Integration or Disintegration? The Case of the UK Car Parts Industry', in C. Laws (ed.), *Restructuring*, pp. 169–70; A. Amin and I. Smith, 'Decline and Restructuring in the UK Motor Vehicle Components Industry', *Scottish Journal of Political Economy*, Vol. 37, 1990, pp. 209–40; C. Carr, *Britain's Competitiveness: The Management of the Vehicle Components Industry*, London and New York: Routledge, 1990, p. 83.
56 P. Sleigh, *The UK Automotive Components Industry*, London: Economist Intelligence Unit, Automotive Special Report 10, 1988.
57 P. Turnbull, N. Oliver and B. Wilkinson. 'Buyer–Supplier Relations in the UK Automotive Industry: Strategic Implication of the Japanese Manufacturing Model', *Strategic Management Journal*, Vol. 13, 1992, p. 162.
58 B. Jackson, 'How a Vehicle Manufacturer Selects its Suppliers', *The London Motor Conference*, 17 February 1992.
59 Peter Wickens, interview with J. F.-P., December 1993.
60 See Carr, *Britain's Competitiveness*, pp. 106–19, 133–4, 144–5, 175–6.
61 P. Turnbull, 'The "Japanisation" of British Industrial Relations at Lucas', *Industrial Relations Journal*, Vol. 17, No. 3, autumn 1986, pp. 196–8.
62 P. Turnbull, 'The Limits to "Japanisation": Just-in-Time, Labour Relations and the UK Automotive Industry', *New Technology, Work and Employment*, Vol. 3, No. 2, 1988, pp. 12–13; R. Loveridge, 'Lucas Industries: A Study in Strategic Domain and Discourse', Aston University, Work Organization Research Centre, Working Paper No. 32, January 1988; R. Loveridge, 'Crisis and Continuity: Renewing the Past to Preview the Future', in S. Srivasta, R. E. Fry and Associates, *Executive and Organizational Continuity: Managing the Paradoxes of Stability and Change*, 1992; P. A. C. Sleigh, *The European Automotive Components Industry*, London, Economist Intelligence Unit, Automotive Special Report 1186, 1989.
63 Turnbull et al., 'Buyer–Supplier Relations', pp. 166–7.
64 Edwardes, *Back from the Brink*, pp. 189–91.
65 *European Motor Business*, February 1990, p. 37.
66 *European Motor Business*, February 1991, p. 25.
67 Womack, Jones and Roos, *The Machine that Changed the World*, p. 168.
68 *Financial Times*, 18 August 1989: C. Greenhalgh and A. Kilmister, 'The British

Economy, the State and the Motor Industry', in T. Hayter and D. Harvey (eds.), *The Factory and the City: The Story of the Cowley Automotive Workers in Oxford*, London: Mansell, 1993.

69 *Motor Industry Review*, December 1988. J. Lovering and T. Hayter, 'British Aerospace: The Ugly Duckling That Never Turned into a Swan' in T. Hayter and D. Harvey (eds.), *Ibid.*

70 M. McDermott, 'Ford of Britain: A Diminishing Role in Ford of Europe', *European Management Journal*, No. 11, 1993, pp. 455–65.

Aaronovitch, S. and Sawyer, M. *Big Business: Theoretical and Empirical Aspects of Concentration and Mergers in the UK*, London: Macmillan, 1975

Abernathy, William J., *The Productivity Dilemma: Roadblock to Innovation in the Automobile Industry*, Baltimore: John Hopkins University Press, 1978

Adeney, M., *The Motor Makers: The Turbulent History of Britain's Car Industry*, London: Fontana/Collins, 1988.

—— *Nuffield: A Biography*, London: Robert Hale, 1993.

Ali, M. A., 'Hire Purchase Controls and the Post-War Demand for Cars in the UK', *Journal of Economic Studies*, Vol. 1, No. 1, 1965.

Allen, G. C., 'The British Motor Industry', *London and Cambridge Economic Service*, No. 18, 1926.

—— *British Industries and Their Organisation*, London: Longman, 1970.

Altshuler, A., Anderson, M., Jones, D., Roos, D. and Womack, J., *The Future of the Automobile: The Report of MIT's International Programme*, London: Allen and Unwin, 1984.

Amin, A. and Smith, I., 'Decline and Restructuring in the UK Motor Vehicle Components Industry', *Scottish Journal of Political Economy*, Vol. 37, 1990, pp. 209–40

—— 'Vertical Integration or Disintegration? The Case of the UK Car Parts Industry', in Christopher M. Law (ed.), *Restructuring the Global Automobile Industry: National and Regional Impacts*, London: Routledge, 1991.

Andrews, P. W. S. and Brunner, E., *The Life of Lord Nuffield*, Oxford: Basil Blackwell, 1954.

Armstrong, A. G. and Odling-Smee, J. C., 'The Demand for New Cars: II, An Empirical Model for the UK', *Bulletin of the Oxford University Institute of Statistics and Economics*, Vol. 41, 1979, pp. 193–214.

Arthur, W. B., 'Competing Technologies, Increasing Returns and Lock-in by Historical Events', *Economic Journal*, Vol. 99, 1989, pp. 116–31.

Austin Motor Company, *Our First Fifty Years: Longbridge 1905–1955*, Longbridge, 1955, *The Automobile Engineer*.

Bardou, J. P., Chanaron, J. J., Fridenson, P. and Laux, J. M., *The Automobile Revolution: The Impact of an Industry*, Chapel Hill, University of North Carolina Press, 1982.

Barker, T. C., Introduction, in T. C. Barker (ed.), *The Economic and Social Effects of the Spread of Motor Vehicles*, London: Macmillan, 1987.

Barker, T. S., 'International Trade and Economic Growth: An Alternative to Neo-classical Theories', *Cambridge Journal of Economics*, Vol. 1, 1977, pp. 153–72.

Barnett, C., *The Audit of War: The Reality and Illusion of Britain as a Great Power*, London: Macmillan, 1986.

Beveridge, W., *Tariffs: The Case Examined*, London: Longmans Green, 1931.

Beynon, H., *Working for Ford*, Harmondsworth: Penguin, 1973.

Bhaskar, K., *The Future of the UK Motor Industry: An Economic and Financial Analysis of the UK Motor Industry Against a Rapidly Changing Background for European and Worldwide Motor Manufacturers*, London: Kogan Page, 1979.

—— *The Future of the World Motor Industry*, London: Kogan Page, 1980.

Bloomfield, G. T., *The World Automotive Industry*, Newton Abbott: David and Charles, 1978.

—— 'The World Automotive Industry in Transition', in Christopher M. Law (ed.), *Restructuring the Global Automobile Industry: National and Regional Impacts*, London: Routledge, 1991.

Board of Trade: 64/3187, 64/76, 64/23, 59/24, 52/23, 56/22, 59/1, Public Record Office.

—— *Census of Production*, selected years.

Bowden, Sue, 'Demand and Supply Constraints in the Interwar UK Car Industry: Did the Manufacturers Get It Right?', *Business History*, Vol. 33, No. 2, April 1991, pp. 241–67.

—— 'The Motor Vehicle Industry', in B. Millward and J. Singleton (eds.), *Industrial Organisation and the Road to Nationalisation in Britain, 1920–1950*, Cambridge University Press, 1995, chapter 5.

Bowden, Sue and Offer, Avner, 'Household Appliances and the Use of Time: The United States and Britain since the 1920s', *Economic History Review*, 1994, November, No. 4.

Bowden, Sue and Turner, Paul M., 'Some Cross Section Evidence on the Determinants of the Diffusion of Car Ownership in the Interwar UK Economy', *Business History*, Vol. 35, No. 1, January 1993, pp. 55–69.

—— 'The Demand for Consumer Durables in the United Kingdom in the Interwar Period', *Journal of Economic History*, Vol. 53, No. 2, June 1993, pp. 244–58.

—— 'Stop–Go, Hire Purchase and the British Motor Vehicle Industry', Paper presented at the 1993 meeting of the Quantitative Economic History Study Group, University of York, 9 September 1993.

Boyfield, Keith, *BL: Changing Gear*, London: Centre for Policy Studies, 1983.

British Leyland, BL Body and Assembly Division Oxford Area, *Management Presentation to Trade Unions*, Cowley: Nuffield Press, 7 November 1973.

—— *The Japanese Motor Vehicle Industry: Report of British Leyland Study Tour, June*, Cowley: Nuffield Press, July 1975.

British Leyland Motor Corporation, *Annual Reports and Accounts*, 1968–78.

British Motor Corporation, *Annual Report and Accounts*, 1952–66.

British Motor Holdings, *Annual Report and Accounts*, 1967.

Broadberry, S. N. and Crafts, N. F. R., British Economic Policy in the Early Postwar Period', University of Warwick, mimeo, May 1993.

Campbell, A., 'The Battleground Approach to Workforce Adjustment: United Kingdom', in P. Auer (ed.), *Workforce Adjustment Patterns in the Steel and Automobile Industry*, Brussels: Commission of the European Communities, 1991.

Carr, C., *Britain's Competitiveness: The Management of the Vehicle Components Industry*, London and New York: Routledge, 1990.

Casson, Mark, 'Foreign Divestment and International Rationalisation: The Sale of Chrysler UK to Peugeot', in J. Coyne and M. Wright (eds.), *Divestment and Strategic Change*, London: Philip Allan, 1986.

Castle, H. G., *Britain's Motor Industry*, London: Clerke and Cocheran, 1950.

Caunter, C. F., *The Light Car*, Science Museum, London: HMSO, 1970.

Central Policy Review Staff, *The Future of the British Car Industry*, London: HMSO, 1975.

Central Statistical Office, *Annual Abstract of Statistics*, London: HMSO, 1985, *Economic Trends, Annual Supplement*, London: HMSO, 1991 edition.

Centre for Policy Studies, *BL: Changing Gear*, London: London Policy Studies Institute, 1983.

Chandler, A. D., *Scale and Scope: The Dynamics of Industrial Capitalism*, Cambridge, Mass: Belknap, of Harvard University Press, 1990.

Church, R., 'Innovation, Monopoly and the Supply of Vehicle Components in Britain, 1880–1930: The Growth of Joseph Lucas Ltd., *Business History Review*, Vol. 52, 1978, pp. 226–49.

—— *Herbert Austin: The British Motor Car Industry to 1941*, London: Europa, 1979.

—— 'The Marketing of Automobiles in Britain and the United States before 1939', in A. Okochi and K. Shimokawa (eds.), *The Development of Mass Marketing: The Automobile and Retailing Industries, Proceedings of the Fuji Conference in Business History*, University of Tokyo Press, 1981.

—— 'Markets and Marketing in the British Motor Industry before 1914: Some French Comparisons', *Journal of Transport History*, 3rd series, Vol. 3, spring 1982, pp. 1–20.

—— 'Family Firms and Managerial Capitalism: The Case of the International Motor Industry', *Business History*, Vol. 28, No. 2, April 1986, pp. 165–80.

Church, R., 'Mass Marketing Motor Cars in Britain before 1950: The

Missing Dimension', in Richard S. Tedlow and Geoffrey Jones (eds.), *The Rise and Fall of Mass Marketing*, London: Routledge, 1993, pp. 36–57.

Church, Roy and Miller, Michael, 'The British Motor Industry, 1922–1939', in Barry Supple (ed.), *Essays in British Business History*, Oxford: Clarendon Press, 1977, pp. 163–86.

Clarke, R. and Hart, P. E., 'Recent Trends in Concentration in British Industry', *National Institute of Economic and Social Research*, 1985, Discussion Paper, 82.

Claydon, T., 'Trade Unions, Employers and Industrial Relations in the British Motor Industry c1919–1945', *Business History*, Vol. 29, 1987, pp. 304–24.

Coase, R. H., 'The Nature of the Firm: Influence', in O. E. Williamson and S. G. Winter (eds.), *The Nature of the Firm: Origins, Evolution and Development*, Oxford University Press, 1991.

Commission of the European Community, *Concentration, Competition and Competitiveness in the Automobile Industries*, Luxembourg, 1983.

Consumer Credit, *Report of the Committee*, Cmnd 4596 (Crowther Committee), London: HMSO, March 1971, Vol. 1, *Report*; Vol. 2, *Appendices*.

Cowling, Keith and Cubbin, John, 'Price, Quality and Advertising Competition: An Econometric Investigation of the United Kingdom Car Market', *Economica*, Vol. 38, 1971, pp. 378–94.

—— 'Hedonic Price Indexes for Cars in the UK', *Economic Journal*, September 1972.

Cowling, Keith and Rayner, A. J., 'Price, Quality and Market Share', *Journal of Political Economy*, Vol. 78, No. 6, 1970, pp. 1292–309.

Cubbin, John, 'Quality Change and Pricing Behaviour in the United Kingdom Car Industry, 1956–1968', *Economica*, Vol. 42, 1975, pp. 43–58.

Cuthbertson, J. R., 'Hire Purchase Controls and Fluctuations in the Car Market', *Economica*, May 1961, pp. 125–36.

Cuthbertson, J. R. and Motley, B., 'Hire Purchase Fluctuations in the Vehicle Market', *Credit*, March 1962, pp. 17–22.

Daniel, G. H., 'Some Factors Affecting the Mobility of Labour', *Oxford Economic Papers*, February 1940, pp. 144–79.

Davies, Stephen, 'Concentration', in Stephen Davies, Bruce Lyons, Hugh Dixon and Paul Geroski, *Economics of Industrial Organisation*, Harlow, Essex: Longman, 1988.

Davison, C. St C. B., *History of Steam Road Vehicles*, London: Science Museum by HMSO, 1953.

Davison, G. S., *At the Wheel*, London: Industrial Transport Publications Ltd, 1931.

Department of Industry, *The British Motor Vehicle Industry*, Cmnd 6377, 1976.

Department of Scientific and Industrial Research: 16/32, 16/93, 16/94,

Public Record Office.

Department of Trade, *Census of Production*, selected years.

Devine, F., *Affluent Workers Revisted: Privatism and the Working Class*, Edinburgh University Press, 1992.

Dunnett, P. J. S., *The Decline of the British Motor Industry: The Effects of Government Policy, 1945–1979*, London: Croom Helm, 1980.

Duval, L. F., 'The Motor Industry', in British Association for the Advancement of Science', *Britain in Recovery*, London, 1939.

Edwardes, Michael, *Back from the Brink: An Apocalyptic Experience*, London: Collins, 1983.

Engineering Production

Euro-Economics, 'The European Car Industry – The Problem of Structure and Overcapacity', March, 1975.

European Motor Business, February 1990 and February 1991.

Farrant, J. P., *Scout Motors of Salisbury, 1909–1921*, Salisbury and South Wiltshire Group for Industrial Archaeology, n.d.

Flink, J. J., *The Automobile Age*, MIT Press, 1982.

Ford Motor Company UK, *Annual Reports and Accounts*, selected years.

—— *The Ford Motor Co. Ltd and its Work People*, Dagenham, May 1937.

Foreman-Peck, J., 'Tariff Protection and Economies of Scale; The British Motor Industry Before 1939', *Oxford Economic Papers*, Vol. 31, No. 2, July 1979, pp. 237–57.

—— 'The Effects of Market Failure on the British Motor Industry before 1939', *Explorations in Economic History*, Vol. 18, 1981, pp. 257–89.

—— 'Exit, Voice and Loyalty as Responses to Decline: The Rover Company in the Inter-War Years, *Business History*, Vol. 23, No. 2, July 1981, pp. 191–207.

—— 'The American Challenge of the Twenties: Multinationals and the European Motor Industry', *Journal of Economic History*, Vol. 43, 1982, pp. 865–81.

—— 'Diversification and the Growth of the Firm: The Rover Company to 1914', *Business History*, Vol. 25, No. 2, July 1983, pp. 179–92.

—— 'The Motor Industry', in M. Casson (ed.), *Multinationals and World Trade: Vertical Integration and the Division of Labour in World Industries*, London: Allen and Unwin, 1986, pp. 141–73..

—— 'Death on the Roads: Changing National Responses to Motor Accidents', in T. C. Barker (ed.), *The Economic and Social Effects of the Spread of Motor Vehicles*, London: Macmillan, 1987, pp. 264–90.

Foreman-Peck, J. and Millward, R., *Public and Private Ownership of British Industry 1820–1990*, Oxford: Clarendon Press, 1994.

Fuss, Melvyn A. and Waverman, Leonard, *Costs and Productivity in Automobile Production: The Challenge of Japanese Efficiency*, Cambridge University Press, 1992.

Garrahan, P. and Stewart P., *The Nissan Enigma: Flexibility at Work in a Local Economy*, London: Mansell, 1992.

Geroski, P. and Murfin, A. 'Advertising and the Dynamics of Market

Structure: The UK Car Industry', *British Journal of Management*, Vol 1, No. 2, 1990, pp. 82–3.

Gospel, H. F., *Markets, Firms and the Management of Labour in Modern Britain*, Cambridge University Press, 1992.

Goudie, A. W. and Meeks, G., *Company Finance and Performance; Aggregated Financial Accounts for Individual British Industries, 1948–1982*, University of Cambridge, Department of Applied Economics, 1986.

Gourvish, T. R., *Railways and the British Economy*, London: Macmillan, 1980.

Greenhalgh, C. and Kilmister, A., 'The British Economy, the State and the Motor Industry', in T. Hayter and D. Harvey (eds.), *The Factory and the City: The Story of the Cowley Automobile Workers in Oxford*, London: Mansell, 1993.

Greenwood, W., *How the Other Man Lives*, Labour Book Service, n.d.

Gulvin, Guy, 'Donald Gresham Stokes: Motor Vehicle Manufacturer and Salesman', in *Dictionary of Business Biography*, London School of Economics, 1986, Vol. 5, pp. 347–55.

HP Information, *Monthly Statistical Returns*, Private Cars; Registration by Makes of Hire Purchase Agreements, Finance Association, London.

Hague, D. and G. Wilkinson, *The IRC: An Experiment in Industrial Intervention: A History of the Industrial Reorganisation Corporation*, London: George Allen and Unwin, 1983.

Hannah, Leslie, *The Rise of the Corporate Economy*, London: Methuen, 1976.

Hannah, L. and Kay, J. A., *Concentration in Modern Industry*, London: Macmillan, 1977.

Harrison, A. E., 'The Competitiveness of the British Cycle Industry 1890–1914', *Economic History Review*, 2nd series, Vol. 22, 1969.

—— 'Joint Stock Company Flotation in the Cycle, Motor Vehicle and Related Industries', *Business History*, Vol. 23, 1981.

—— 'F. Hopper and Co.: Problems of Capital Supply in the Cycle Manufacturing Industry, 1891–1914', *Busines History*, Vol. 24, 1982, pp. 3–23.

—— 'Origin and Growth of the UK Cycle Industry to 1900', *Journal of Transport History*, 3rd series, Vol. 6, 1985, pp. 41–70.

Hart, P. E., *Studies in Business Savings, Profits and Investment*, London: Allen and Unwin, 1965.

—— 'Recent Trends in Concentration in British Industry', *National Institute of Economic and Social Research*, 1985, Discussion Paper, No. 82.

Hart, P. E., and Clarke, R., *Concentration in British Industry, 1935–1975*, Cambridge University Press, 1980.

Hennessy, Peter, *Never Again, Britain, 1945–1951*, London: Jonathon Cape, 1992.

Holmes, A., 'Some Aspects of the British Motor Manufacturing Industry during the Years 1919–1930', unpublished Sheffield MA thesis, 1964.

House of Commons, *British Leyland: The Next Decade: An Abridged*

Version of a Report Presented to the Secretary of State for Industry by a Team of Inquiry led by Sir Don Ryder (The Ryder Report), 23 April 1975, House of Commons Paper 342, PP 1974/5.

—— Eighth Report from the Expenditure Committee, Trade and Industry Sub-Committee, *Public Expenditure on Chrysler UK*, 1975–6.

—— Fourteenth Report from the Expenditure Committee, Session 1974–5, *The Motor Vehicle Industry*, 6 August 1975, House of Commons Paper 617, PP 1974/5; *Volumes of Evidence*, House of Commons Paper 617–11, 1975.

—— Minutes of Evidence taken before the Expenditure Committee, House of Commons Paper 396, 1976–7.

House of Lords Select Committee on the European Community, *The Distribution, Servicing and Pricing of Motor Vehicles*, London: HMSO, 1984.

Irving, R. J., 'New Industries for Old? Armstrong Whitworth', *Business History*, Vol. 17, 1975, pp. 150–75.

Jackson, B. 'How a Vehicle Manufacturer Selects its Suppliers', *The London Motor Conference*, 17 February 1992.

Jefferys, J. B., *The Story of the Engineers*, London: Lawrence and Wishart for AEU, 1945.

Johnman, Lewis, 'The Labour Party and Industrial Policy', in Nick Tiratsoo (ed.), *The Atlee Years*, London: Frances Pinter, 1991, chapter 3, pp. 29–53.

Johns, Stephen, *Victimization at Cowley*, London: Workers Revolutionary Party, Pocket Book No. 11, n.d.

Johnson-Davies, K. C., *The Practice of Retail Price Maintenance: With Particular Reference to the Motor Industry*, London: Iliffe and Son, 1955.

Jones, D. T., 'Output, Employment and Labour Productivity in Europe since 1955', *National Institute Economic Review*, No. 77, August 1976, pp. 72–85.

—— *Maturity and Crisis in the European Car Industry: Structural Change and Public Policy*, Sussex European Papers, No. 8, University of Sussex, Brighton, 1981.

—— 'Technology and the UK Automobile Industry', *Lloyds Bank Review*, No. 148, April 1983, pp. 14–27.

—— *The Import Threat to the UK Car Industry*, Science Policy Research Unit, University of Sussex, Brighton, 1985.

Jones, D. T. and Prais, S. J., 'Plant Size and Productivity In the Motor Industry: Some International Comparisons', *Oxford Bulletin of Economics and Statistics*, Vol. 40, No. 2, 1978, pp. 131–51.

Jones, J. H., *Road Accidents: Report*, London: HMSO, 1946.

Jürgens, U., Malshe, T. and Dohse, K., *Breaking from Taylorism: Changing Forms of Work in the Automobile Industry*, Cambridge University Press, 1993.

Kaplinsky, R., 'Restructuring the Capitalist Labour Process: Some Lessons from the Car Industry', *Cambridge Journal of Economics*, Vol. 12,

No. 4, 1988, pp. 451–70.

Keeble, D., *Industrial Location and Planning in the United Kingdom*, London: Methuen, 1976.

Klein, B., 'Vertical Integration as Organizational Ownership: The Fisher Body–General Motors Relationship Revisted', in O. E. Williamson and S. G. Winter (eds.), *The Nature of the Firm: Origins, Evolution and Development*, Oxford University Press, 1991.

Labour Party, Research Department, 'Report on the British Motor Industry: Possibilities of Future Development with Special Reference to the Advantages and Disadvantages of Public Ownership', May, 1948, Labour Party Archive, National Museum of Labour History, Manchester.

—— Sub-Committee on Industries for Nationalisation, Minutes, 13 October, 1948, Labour Party Archive, National Museum of Labour History, Manchester.

Lanning, G., Peaker, C., Webb, C. and White, R., *Making Cars: A History of Car Making at Cowley by the People who Make Cars*, London: Routledge and Kegan Paul: 1985.

Laux, J. M., *In First Gear: The French Automobile Industry to 1914*, Liverpool University Press, 1976.

Law, C. M. (ed.), *Restructuring the Global Automobile Industry: National and Regional Impacts*, 1991.

Leech, D. and Cubbin, J., 'Import Penetration in the UK Passenger Market: A Cross-Section Study', *Applied Economics*, Vol. 10, 1978, pp. 289–303.

Lewchuck, Wayne, 'The Return to Capital in the British Motor Vehicle Industry, 1896–1939', *Business History*, Vol. 27, March 1985, pp. 3–25.

—— *American Technology and the British Vehicle Industry*, Cambridge University Press, 1987.

Lewis, W. A., *Growth and Fluctuation, 1870–1913*, London: Allen and Unwin, 1978.

Loveridge, R., 'Business Strategy and Community Culture', in D. Dunkerley and G. Salaman (eds.), *The International Yearbook of Organizational Studies*, London: Routledge Kegan Paul, 1982.

—— 'Lucas Industries: A Study in Strategic Domain and Discourse', Aston University Work Organisation Research Centre, Working Paper No. 32, January 1988.

—— 'Crisis and Continuity: Renewing the Past to Preview the Future', in S. Srivasta, R. E. Fry and Associates, *Executive and Organizational Continuity: Managing the Paradoxes of Stability and Change*, 1992.

Lovering, J. and Hayter, T., 'British Aerospace: The Ugly Duckling That Never Turned Into a Swan', in T. Hayter and D. Harvey (eds.), *The Factory and the City: The Story of the Cowley Automobile Workers in Oxford*, London: Mansell, 1993.

Lowry, A. T., *A Financial Assessment of the West European Motor Industry*, Economist Intelligence Unit, 1985, Automotive Special

Report, No. 4.

MacErlean, N., 'Carmakers' Fortunes', *Accountancy*, No. 111, June 1993, pp. 30–3.

McDermott, M., 'Ford of Britain: A Diminishing Role in Ford of Europe', *European Management Journal*, No. 11, 1993, pp. 455–65.

McGee, John S., 'Economies of Size in Auto Body Manufacture', *Journal of Law and Economics*, 16, 2, October 1973.

Mair, Andrew, 'Parts Sourcing at Japanese Automobile Transplants: Controversy in the United States; The Case of Honda in North America and Implications for Transplants in Europe', *Change in the Automobile Industry: An International Comparison*, Discussion Paper No. 2, March 1991, Universities of Durham, Department of Geography and Manchester, Department of Sociology..

—— 'The Just-in-Time Strategy for Local Economic Development', *Change in the Automobile Industry: An International Comparison*, Discussion Paper No. 3, June 1991, Universities of Durham, Department of Geography and Manchester, Department of Sociology.

—— 'Just-in-Time Manufacturing and the Spatial Structure of the Automobile Industry: In Theory in Japan, in North America and in Western Europe', *Change in the Automobile Industry: An International Comparison*, Discussion Paper No. 4, March 1991, Universities of Durham, Department of Geography and Manchester, Department of Sociology.

Marsden, David, Morris, Timothy, Willman, Paul and Wood, Stephen, *The Car Industry: Labour Relations and Industrial Adjustment*, London: Tavistock, 1985.

Martin, R., *Bargaining Power*, Oxford: Clarendon Press, 1992.

Matthews, R. C. O. 'The Role of Demand Management', in Sir Alec Cairncross (ed.), *Britain's Economic Prospects Reconsidered*, London: George Allen and Unwin, 1971, chapter 1, pp. 13–55.

Matthews, R. C. O., Feinstein, C. H. and Odling-Smee, J. C., *British Economic Growth, 1856–1973*, Oxford University Press, 1982.

Maxcy, G., 'The Motor Industry', in P. L. Cook and R. Cohen (eds.), *The Effect of Mergers*, London: Allen and Unwin, 1958.

—— *The Multinational Motor Industry*, 1981.

Maxcy, G. and Silberston, A., *The Motor Industry*, London: Allen and Unwin, 1959.

Miller, M. and Church, R. A., 'Motor Manufacturing', in Neil K. Buxton and Derek H. Aldcroft (eds.), *British Industry Between the Wars: Instability and Industrial Development, 1919–1939*, London: Scolar Press, 1979, pp. 179–215.

Ministry of Labour, *Labour Gazette*, selected years.

Ministry of Supply, *National Advisory Council for the Motor Manufacturing Industry: Report on Proceedings*, London: HMSO, 1947.

Mogridge, M. J. H., *The Car Market: A Study of Statics and Dynamics of Supply–Demand Equilibrium*, London: Pion, 1983.

Mokyr, Joel, *The Lever of Riches: Technological Creativity and Technical Progress*, Oxford University Press, 1990.

Monopolies and Mergers Commission, *A Report on the Supply of New Motor Cars within the United Kingdom*, London: HMSO, 1992.

Monopolies and Restrictive Practices Commission, *Report on the Supply and Export of Pneumatic Tyres*, London: HMSO, 1955.

—— *Report on the Supply of Electrical Equipment for Mechanically Propelled Land Vehicles*, London: HMSO, 1963.

—— *BMC and Pressed Steel Co.: Report on the Merger*, London: HMSO, 1966.

Moore, B. and Rhodes, J., *The Effects of Government Regional Economic Policy*, London: HMSO, Department of Trade and Industry, 1986.

Morris, W., 'Policies that have Built the Morris Motor', *Business System*, Vol. 45, 1924, reprinted in *The Journal of Industrial Economics*, Vol. 1, 1954; *The Motor*, 31 August 1926.

Motor Business

Motor Industry Review, December 1988.

The Motor Trader, various issues.

Moyle, J., 'The Pattern of Ordinary Share Ownership, 1957–1970', University of Cambridge, Department of Economics, Occasional Paper, 31, 1971.

Mueller, F. 'Flexible Working Practices in Engine Plants: Evidence from the European Automobile Industry', *Industrial Relations Journal*, Vol. 23, No. 3, 1992, pp. 191–204.

Murfin, A. 'Market Shares in the UK Passenger Car Market: Marketing, Expenditure and Price Effects 1975–1980, *Applied Economics*, Vol. 16, 1984, pp. 611–32.

Nichols, T., *The British Worker Question*, London: Routledge Kegan Paul, 1986.

Nicholson, T. R., *The Birth of the British Motor Car 1769–1897*, London: Macmillan, 1982, Vols. 1 and 2.

Nixon, St J. C., *Wolseley: A Saga from the Motor Industry*, London: G. T. Foulis, 1949.

Noble, D., 'Industry Dynamics in Europe: The Motor Industry', in S. Young and J. Hamill (eds.), *Europe and the Multinationals: Issues and Responses for the 1990s*, Aldershot: Edward Elgar, 1992.

Noble, D. and Mackenzie Junner, G., *Vital to the Life of the Nation: A Historical Survey of the Progress of the British Motor Industry from 1896 to 1946*, London: Society of Motor Manufacturers and Traders, 1946.

Nockolds, H., *Lucas: The First Hundred Years*, Newton Abbott; David and Charles, 1976.

Nuffield Papers, 16/23, Nuffield Papers, Nuffield College, Oxford.

Oliver, N. and Wilkinson, B., *The Japanization of British Industry: New Developments in the 1990s*, Oxford: Basil Blackwell, 1990.

Olney, Martha, *Buy Now Pay Later: Advertising Credit and Consumer Durables in the 1920s*, Chapel Hill: University of North Carolina Press,

1991.

Overy, R. J. *William Morris, Viscount Nuffield*, London: Europa, 1976.

Owen, Nicholas, *Economies of Scale, Competitiveness, and Trade Patterns within the European Community*, Oxford: Clarendon Press, 1983.

Park, W. M., *The Automotive Industry and Trade of Great Britain and Ireland*, Washington DC: US Bureau of Domestic and Foreign Commerce, 1928.

Perry-Keene, A., 'The Incidence of On-Costs', *Journal of Production Engineers*, Vol. 40, 1931.

Pimlott, Ben, *Harold Wilson*, London: Harper Collins, 1992.

Plowden, W., *The Motor Car and Politics*, London: Bodley Head, 1972.

Political and Economic Planning, *Motor Vehicles: A Report on the Industry*, London, 1950.

Pollard, Sidney, *Britain's Prime and Britain's Decline: The British Economy, 1870–1914*, London: Edward Arnold, 1989.

Postan, M. M., Hay, D. and Scott, J. D. *Design and Development of Weapons: Studies in Government and Industrial Organisation*, London: HMSO, 1964.

Prais, S. J., *The Evolution of Giant Firms in Britain*, Cambridge University Press, 1976.

—— *Productivity and Industrial Structure: A Statistical Study of Manufacturing Industry in Britian, Germany and the United States*, Cambridge University Press, 1981.

Prais, S. J. and Jones, D. T., 'Plant Size and Productivity in the Motor Industry', *Oxford Bulletin of Economics and Statistics*, 1986.

Pratten, C. F., *Economies of Scale in Manufacturing Industry*, University of Cambridge, Department of Applied Economics, 1971, Occasional Papers, No. 28.

—— *A Comparison of the Performance of Swedish and U.K. Companies*, University of Cambridge, Department of Applied Economics, 1976, Occasional Papers, No. 47.

Rajan, A. and Thompson, M., *Economic Significance of the UK Motor Vehicle Manufacturing Industry*, London: Institute of Manpower Studies, 1989.

Report of the Royal Commission on Trade Unions and Employers' Associations, 1965–1968, (Donavon Report), Cmnd 1623, London: HMSO, 1968.

Report of the Committee on Industry and Trade, Cmnd 3282, 1929.

Rhys, D. G., *The Motor Industry: An Economic Survey*, London: Butterworths, 1972.

—— 'Employment, Efficiency and Labour Relations in the British Motor Industry', *Industrial Relations Journal*, Vol. 5, No. 2, summer 1974, pp. 4–24.

—— 'Concentration in the Interwar Motor Industry', *Journal of Transport History*, ns 3, No. 4, 1976, pp. 241–64.

—— 'European Mass-Producing Car Makers and Minimum Efficient

Scale; A Note', *Journal of Industrial Economics*, Vol. 25, June 1977, pp. 313–32.

—— 'Motor Vehicles', in P. S. Johnson (ed.), *The Structure of British Industry*, London: Granada, 1980, pp. 179–206.

Ricardo Group, *Ricardo; The First 75 Years*, Shoreham, 1990.

Ricardo, H. R., *Memories and Machines: The Pattern of My Life*, Shoreham, Sussex, Ricardo Consulting Engineers, 1990.

Richardson, K., *The British Motor Industry, 1896–1939: A Social and Economic History*, London: Macmillan, 1977.

Road Improvement Fund, *Tenth Annual Report of the Road Improvement Fund*, 1921.

Robertson, I., *The UK Passenger Car Market*, London: Economist Intelligence Unit, 1989.

Robson, G. *The Metro: The Book of the Car*, Cambridge: Patrick Stephens, 1982.

Roots, P., 'Do Companies get the Trade Unions They Deserve?', Trent Business School Open Lectures on Industrial Relations, Trent Polytechnic, 6 November 1984.

Rose, E. and Wooley, T., 'Shifting Sands?' Trade Unions and Productivity at Rover Cars', *Industrial Relations Journal*, Vol. 23, No. 4, winter 1992, pp. 257–67.

Rostas, L., *Comparative Productivity in British and American Industry*, Cambridge University Press, 1948.

Rostow, W. W., *The Stages of Economic Growth: A Non-Communist Manifesto*, Cambridge University Press, 1960.

Royal Commission on Motor Cars, British Parliamentary Papers, 1906.

Sadler, David, 'The International Automobile Industry: A Review of Recent Trends and Their Implications for the UK', *Change in the Automobile Industry: An International Comparison*, Discussion Paper No. 1, March 1991, Universities of Durham, Department of Geography and Manchester, Department of Sociology.

—— 'European Community Industrial Policy and Regional Development: Missing Link or Non-Existent Chain?' *Change in the Automobile Industry: An International Comparison*, Discussion Paper No. 6, July 1991, Universities of Durham, Department of Geography and Manchester, Department of Sociology.

—— 'Beyond 1992: The Evolution of European Community Policies Towards the Automobile Industry', *Change in the Automobile Industry: An International Comparison*, Discussion Paper No. 7, August 1991, Universities of Durham, Department of Geography and Manchester, Department of Sociology.

Saul, S. B., 'The British Motor Industry to 1914?', *Business History*, December 1962, pp. 22–44.

Scarbrough, H., 'Maintenance Workers and New Technology: The Case of Longbridge', *Industrial Relations Journal*, Vol. 15, No. 4, 1984, pp. 9–17.

Schwarz, Bill, 'The Tide of History: The Reconstruction of Conservatism, 1945–1951', in Nick Tiratsoo (ed.), *The Atlee Years*, London: Frances Pinter, 1991, chapter 9, pp. 147–66.

Scott, J. D., *Vickers: A History*, London: Weidenfeld and Nicolson, 1962.

Sedgwick, M., *Cars of the 1930s*, Batsford, 1970.

Seidler, E., *Let's Call It Fiesta: The Autobiography of Ford's Project Bobcat*, Bar Hill, Cambridge: Patrick Stephens, 1976.

Sewell, G. and Wilkinson, B., ' "Someone to watch over me": Surveillance, Discipline and the Just-in-Time Labour Process', *Sociology*, Vol. 26, 1992, pp. 271–89.

Shaw, R. W. and Sutton, C. J., *Industry and Competition: Industrial Case Studies*, London: Macmillan, 1976.

Silberston, Aubrey, 'The Motor Industry', in Duncan Burn (ed.), *The Structure of British Industry: A Symposium*, Vol. 2, Cambridge University Press, 1958, chapter 10, pp. 1–44.

―― 'Hire Purchase Controls and the Demand for Cars', *Economic Journal*, Vol. 73, No. 289, March 1963, pp. 32–53.

―― 'Hire Purchase Controls and the Demand for Cars', *Economic Journal*, Vol. 73, No. 291, September 1963, pp. 556–8.

―― *The Motor Industry, 1955–1964*, University of Cambridge, Department of Applied Economics, 1966, Reprint Series, No. 248.

―― 'The Relationship between Size and Efficiency', in Society of Business Economists, 'Changes in the Industrial Structure of the UK', Papers read at the Society of Business Economists Conference, Cambridge: April 1970.

Silberston, Aubrey and Pratten, C. F., *International Comparisons of Labour Productivity in the Automobile Industry, 1950–1965*, Department of Applied Economics, University of Cambridge, 1969, Reprint Series, No. 288.

Silva, E., 'Labour and Technology in the Car Industry: Ford Strategies in Britain and Brazil', unpublished PhD thesis, Imperial College, London, 1988.

Sims, D. and Wood, M., 'Car Manufacture at Linwood: The Regional Policy Issues', Paisley College, 1984.

Sleigh, P., *The UK Automotive Components Industry*, London: Economist Intelligence Unit, Automotive Special Report, No. 10, 1988.

―― *The European Automotive Components Industry*, London; Economist Intelligence Unit, Automotive Special Report, Special Report, No. 1186, 1989.

Smith, D., 'The Japanese Example in South West Birmingham', *Industrial Relations Journal*, Vol. 19, No. 1, spring, 1988, p. 41–50.

―― 'Industrial Restructuring and the Labour Force: The Case of Austin Rover in Longbridge, Birmingham', in Christopher M. Law (ed.), *Restructuring the Global Automobile Industry: National and Regional Impacts*, London: Routledge, 1991.

Smith, Justin Davis, *The Atlee and Churchill Administrations and Indus-*

trial Unrest, 1945–1955: A Study in Consensus, London: Frances Pinter, 1990.

Smith, R. P., *Consumer Demand for Cars in the USA*, University of Cambridge, Department of Applied Economics, 1975, Occasional Paper, No. 44.

Society of Motor Manufacturers and Traders, *The Motor Industry of Great Britain*, annual.

Starkey, K. and McKinlay, A. 'Beyond Fordism? Strategic Choice and Labour Relations in Ford UK', *Industrial Relations Journal*, Vol. 20, pp. 93–100.

—— *Strategy and the Human Resource: Ford and the Search for Competitive Advantage*, Oxford: Blackwell, 1993.

Stone, J. R. N. and Rowe, D. A., *Consumers' Expenditure in the United Kingdom, 1920–1938*, Vol. II, Cambridge University Press, 1966.

Storey, J., *Developments in the Management of Human Resources, An Analytical Review*, Oxford: Basil Blackwell, 1992.

Storrs, R., *Dunlop in War and Peace*, London: Hutchinson, 1946.

Streeck, W. (ed.), *Industrial Relations and Technical Change in the British, Italian and German Automobile Industries: Three Case Studies*, Berlin, 1985.

Szostak, R., *The Role of Transportation in the Industrial Revolution*, Montreal and London: McGill-Queens University Press, 1990.

Tanner, J. C., 'Car Ownership Trends and Forecasts', Transport and Road Research Laboratory, Department of the Environment, Department of Transport, TRRL Laboratory Report, No. 799, Crowthorne, Berkshire, 1977.

Thoms, David and Donnelly, Tom, *The Motor Car Industry in Coventry since the 1890s*, Beckenham, Kent: Croom Helm, 1985.

Thornett, A., 'History of the Trade Unions in Cowley', in T. Hayter and D. Harvey (eds.), *The Factory and the City: The Story of the Cowley Automobile Workers in Oxford*, London: Mansell, 1993.

Tiratsoo, Nick, 'The Motor Car Industry', in Helen Mercer, Neil Rollings and Jim Tomlinson (eds.), *Labour Governments and Private Industry: The Experience of 1945–1951*, Edinburgh University Press, 1992, pp. 162–85.

Tolliday, S., 'Government, Employers and Shop Floor Organisation in the British Motor Industry, 1939–1969'; in Steven Tolliday and Jonathon Zeitlin (eds.), *Shop Floor Bargaining and the State: Historical and Comparative Perspectives*, Cambridge University Press, 1985, pp. 108–47.

—— 'Management and Labour in Britain 1896–1939', in S. Tolliday and J. Zeitlin, *The Automobile Industry and its Workers*, Cambridge: Polity Press, 1986.

—— 'The Failure of Mass Production Unionism in the Motor Industry, 1914–1939', in C. Wrigley (ed.), *A History of British Industrial Relations*, Brighton: The Harvester Press, Vol. 2, 1987, pp. 298–322.

—— 'Rethinking the German Miracle: Volkswagen in Prosperity and

Crisis 1939–1992', Harvard University, The Business History Seminar; Competition and Industrial Structure, 4 November 1991.

—— 'Ford and Fordism in Post War Britain: Enterprise Management and the Control of Labour 1937–1987', in Steven Tolliday and Jonathon Zeitlin (eds.), *The Power to Manage? Employers and Industrial Relations in Comparative Historical Perspective*, London and New York: Routledge, 1991.

—— 'Transferring Fordism: The First Phase of the Overseas Diffusion and Adaptation of Ford Methods, 1911–1939', mimeo, University of Leeds, 1993.

Tolliday, Steven and Zeitlin, Jonathon, 'Shop Floor Bargaining, Contract Unionism and Job Control: An Anglo American Comparison', in Steven Tolliday and Jonathon Zeitlin (eds.), *The Automobile Industry and Its Workers: Between Fordism and Flexibility*, Oxford: Polity Press, 1986, pp. 99–120.

Tomlinson, Jim, *Public Policy and the Economy since 1900*, Oxford: Clarendon Press, 1990.

—— 'The Labour Government and the Trade Unions', in Nick Tiratsoo (ed.), *The Atlee Years*, London: Frances Pinter, 1991, chapter 6, pp. 90–105.

Treasury: 171/249, 172/1513, Public Record Office.

Tunzelmann, G. N. von, 'Structural Change and Leading Sectors in British Manufacturing 1907–1968', in C. P. Kindleberger and G. di Tella (eds.), *Economics in the Long View: Essays in Honour of W. W. Rostow*, London: Macmillan, 1982, Vol. 3.

Turnbull, P., 'The "Japanisation" of British Industrial Relations at Lucas', *Industrial Relations Journal*, Vol. 17, No. 3, autumn 1986, pp. 196–8.

—— 'The Limits of "Japanisation": Just-in-Time, Labour Relations and the UK Automotive Industry', *New Technology, Work and Employment*, Vol. 3, No. 2, 1988, pp. 7–20.

Turnbull, P., Oliver, N. and Wilkinson, B., 'Buyer–Supplier Relations in the UK Automotive Industry: Strategic Implication of the Japanese Manufacturing Model', *Strategic Management Journal*, Vol. 13: 1992.

Turner, Graham, *The Car Makers*, London: Eyre and Spottiswoode, 1963.

—— *The Leyland Papers*, London: Eyre and Spottiswoode, 1971.

Turner, H. A. and Bescoby, J., 'An Analysis of Post War Labour Disputes in the British Car Manufacturing Firms', *Manchester School*, Vol. 29, May 1961, pp. 133–60.

Turner, H. A., Clack, Garfield and Roberts, Geoffrey, *Labour Relations in the Motor Industry: A Study of Industrial Unrest and an International Comparison*, London: Allen and Unwin, 1967.

United Kingdom Imperial Economic Committee, *A Survey of Trade in Motor Vehicles*, London: HMSO, 1936.

UN Statistics Yearbook, annual.

United States, Bureau of Foreign and Domestic Commerce, *Motor Vehicle Installment Selling in Europe*, Trade Information Bulletin No. 550,

Washington, DC, May 1928.

—— Special Consular Reports, *Vehicle Industry in Europe*, Bureau of Foreign Commerce, Department of State, GPO, 1900, 1907, 1908, 1912, 1913.

Vauxhall, *Annual Reports and Accounts*, 1952–78 inclusive.

Vernon, R. 'International Investment and International trade in the Product Cycle', *Quarterly Journal of Economics*, Vol. 80, 1966, pp. 190–207.

—— 'The Product Cycle Hypothesis in a New International Environment', *Oxford Bulletin of Economics and Statistics*, Vol. 41, 1979, pp. 255–67.

Walshe, J. G., 'Industrial Organisation and Competition Policy', in N. F. R. Crafts and N. Woodward (eds.), *The British Economy since 1945*, Oxford: Clarendon Press, 1991.

Wansbrough, George, 'Automobiles: The Mass Market', *Lloyds Bank Review*, October 1955, pp. 31–44.

Wardley, H., 'Another Oxford: My Life Remembered', March 1992, St Anthony's College, Oxford (privately circulated).

Whipp, R. and Clark, P., *Innovation and the Auto Industry: Product, Process and Work Organisation*, London: Frances Pinter, 1986.

White, L. J., *The Automobile Industry Since 1945*, Cambridge, Mass., 1971.

Whiting, R., *The View from Cowley: The Impact of Industrialisation upon Oxford, 1918–1939*, Oxford: Clarendon Press, 1983.

Wickens, P., *The Road to Nissan: Flexibility, Quality, Teamwork*, London: Macmillan, 1987.

Wigham, E., *The Power to Manage: History of the Engineering Employers Federation*, London: Macmillan, 1973.

Wilkins, M. and Hill, F. F., *American Busines Abroad: Ford on Six Continents*, Detroit: Wayne State University Press, 1964.

Wilks, S., *Industrial Policy and the Motor Industry*, Manchester University Press (1984), 1988.

William, Paul, 'Labour Relations Strategy at BL Cars', in Steven Tolliday and Jonathon Zeitlin (eds.), *The Automobile Industry and Its Workers: Between Fordism and Flexibility*, Cambridge University Press, 1986, pp. 305–27.

William, Paul and Winch, Graham, *Innovation and Management Control: Labour Relations at BL Cars*, Cambridge University Press, 1985.

Williams, Karel, Williams, John and Thomas, Dennis, *Why are the British Bad at Manufacturing?*, London: Routledge Kegan Paul, 1983.

Williams, Karel, Williams, John and Haslam, Colin, *The Breakdown of Austin Rover: A Case Study in the Failure of Business Strategy and Industrial Policy*, Leamington Spa: Berg, 1987.

Willman, P., 'The Reform of Collective Bargaining and Strike Activity at BL Cars', *Industrial Relations Journal*, Vol. 15, No. 3, 1984, pp. 1–12.

—— 'Labour Relations Strategy at BL Cars', in S. Tolliday and J. Zeitlin (eds.), *The Automobile Industry and Its Workers: Between Fordism and Flexibility*, Oxford: Polity Press, 1986.

—— *Technological Change, Collective Bargaining and Industrial Efficiency*, Oxford: Clarendon Press, 1986.

Willman, P. and Winch, G., *Innovation and Management Control: Labour Relations at BL Cars*, Cambridge University Press, 1987.

Wilson, C. and Reader, W., *Men and Machines: A History of D. Napier and Sons, Engineers*, London: Weidenfeld and Nicolson, 1958.

Womack, James P., Jones, Daniel T. and Roos, Daniel, *The Machine that Changed the World*, London, 1990.

Wood, J., *Wheels of Misfortune; The Rise and Fall of the British Motor Industry*, London: Sidgwick and Jackson, 1988.

Woollard, F. G., 'Some Notes on British Methods of Continuous Production', *Proceedings of the Institution of Automobile Engineers*, Vol. 19, 1924–5.

—— 'Plant Depreciation and Replacement Problems', *Proceedings of the Institution of Automobile Engineers*, February 1925.

Wyatt, H., *The Motor Industry*, London: Pitman, 1921.

Wyatt, R. J., *The Motor for the Million: The Austin Seven, 1922–1939*, London: MacDonald, 1968.

Young. S. and Hood, N., *Chrysler UK: A Corporation in Transition*, New York: Praeger, 1977.

Young, S., Hood, N. and Hamill, J., *Foreign Multinationals and the British Economy: Impact and Policy*, London: Croom Helm, 1988.

INDEX

absenteeism 234
ACAS *see* Advisory Conciliation and
   Arbitration Service
accidents, road 83–4, 88, 193
accountants 185
ACV (AEC) *44, 99, 111*
Adams, Jack 234
Adeney, M. 159, 196–7, 198
Adler 10
advertising
   by assemblers 133
   importers' powerful campaign 227
   need for extensive 29, 135–6
   publicity stunts 28
Advisory, Conciliation and Arbitration
   Service (ACAS) 237–8
AEC *see* Associated Equipment
   Company
AEEU *see* Amalgamated Engineering
   and Electrical Union
AEU *see* Amalgamated Engineering
   Union
'After Japan' (AJ) 236
after sales service 29, 36, 59, 97, 160
agents
   dealing with cars of a number of
   companies 28
   Ford dismisses 60
   price-cutting 29
air-cooling 16, 20, 40, 47
aircraft manufacture, and motor industry
   84, 85
Airlie, Jimmy 236
AJ *see* After Japan
Albion Motors *14, 44*, 54, *99*, 106, 107,
   111
Alfa-Romeo 104, *128*, 160, 253
Alpine 212
aluminium 47
Alvis *44, 99, 111*
Amalgamated Engineering and Electrical

Union (AEEU) 236
Amalgamated Engineering Union (AEU)
   62–3, 84, 167, 211
Amalgamated Society of Engineers
   (ASE) 30
amphibious transport 87
apprenticeships 63
Argentina
   American products appropriate in 31
   motor exports to 78
Argyll Motor Company *14*, 19, 26
Argyll, near Glasgow 30
armoured cars 36
Armstrong-Siddeley *44*, 78, *99*
Armstrong-Whitworth 11, *14*
Arrol Johnston *14*
ASE *see* Amalgamated Society of
   Engineers
Ashfield, Lord 45, 78, 79
assembly 8, 19, 39, *118*, 122, 123, 125, 133,
   173, 222, 238
Associated Commercial Vehicles (ACV)
   107
Associated Equipment Company, and
   armoured/scout car development 86
Associated Equipment Company (AEC)
   44, 44–5, 49, 78, 79, *99*, 106, 107
Aston Martin 104
Aston Martin Lagonda Newport Pagnell
   works 183
AT & T 245
Atkinson 107
Audit of War, The (Barnett) 85
Austin 54, 61, 78, 104
   and automatic transfer lines 121
   and automatic transfer machines 121
   bargaining in 168
   and commercial vehicles 106
   construction method (pre-1914) 20
   cost control 49–50
   and dispute settlement 167